Time, Science, and Society in
China and the West

The instrument shown as our frontispiece combines a sundial to tell the time of day, a calendar that lists the climactic periods of the year, and a compass, which is a tool for geomancy, an intricate lore of ritual, geography, and numerology used in selecting sites for such things as buildings or graveyards. The device was made at the turn of the nineteenth century in Beijing.

The hour plate, hinged across the base plate, is supported by a bracket that allows it to be positioned according to latitude.

The gnomon is close to the center of a number of circular bands. They show an arrangement of the twelve terrestrial branches—names of parts that divide anything into twelve—here used to designate the twelve Chinese double-hours. The outermost band is divided into ninety-six quarter-hour segments, corresponding to European hours.

The notches on the back of the base plate are marked with the twenty-four climactic periods of the year, rain water, waking of insects, . . . forming of grain, grain in ear, . . . frost's descent, . . . slight cold, great cold.

The front half of the base plate has a geomagnetic compass inset.

The first band around the compass shows the eight trigrams, the ancient divinatory symbols from the *Book of Changes*. The second band has the names of the four cardinal directions of the map. The third band identifies twenty-four directions, using the numerological devices of the twelve terrestrial branches and the ten celestial stems—names of parts that divide anything into ten.

The outermost circle records the astrological correspondences of pre-Han classical Chinese geographical divisions from before 300 B.C.

Reproduction, courtesy of M. Alain Brieux, Paris, and Dr. Silvio A. Bedini, Washington, D.C. Photo by Kim Nielsen, Smithsonian Institution.

Time, Science, and Society in China and the West

The Study of Time V

Edited by J. T. Fraser, N. Lawrence, *and* F. C. Haber

The University of Massachusetts Press

Amherst, 1986

Copyright © 1986 by J. T. Fraser
Printed in the United States of America
LC 79-640956
ISBN 0-87023-495-1
Set in Monotype Plantin by Asco Trade Typesetting Ltd, Hong Kong

The Library of Congress has cataloged this serial
publication as follows:

The Study of time. v. 1–

   Berlin, New York, Springer-Verlag, 1972–

     v. ill. 26 cm.

   Vols. for 1972–   are the proceedings of the 1st–   conference of the
International Society for the Study of Time.

   Vol. for 1972 unnumbered but constitutes v. 1.

   Vols. 1–2 in English or German.

   ISSN 0170-9704 = The study of time.

    1. Time—Congresses—Collected works.   I. International Society for the
Study of Time.

   [DNLM: W1 ST952s]

QB209.S85   529   79-640956

                      MARC-S

Library of Congress   79[8502]
Acknowledgment is made to the following publishers for the use of material under copyright.

Macmillan Publishing Company, from *The Collected Poems of William Butler Yeats*, lines
from "Lapis Lazuli." Copyright 1940 by Georgia Yeats, renewed 1968 by Bertha Georgia
Yeats, Michael Butler Yeats, and Anne Yeats. Reprinted with permission of Macmillian
Publishing Company, Michael Butler Yeats, and Macmillan London, Ltd.

Research Centre for Translation, for material from *A Golden Treasury of Chinese Poetry*,
trans. John A. Turner, A *Renditions* book, published by The Chinese University Press, 1976,
and distributed by The University of Washington Press, Seattle and London.

European American Music for Alban Berg, *Kammerkonzert*, copyright 1925 by Universal
Edition, copyright renewed.

Sheila Lalwani Payne for material from *The White Pony*, ed. Robert Payne. Copyright 1947
by the John Day Company; renewed 1975 by Sheila Lalwani Payne. Reprinted by permission
of Sheila Lalwani Payne.

Harcourt, Brace and Company for a selection from "The Dry Salvages" from *Four Quartets*
by T. S. Eliot, © 1943 by T. S. Eliot; renewed 1971 by Esme Valerie Eliot. Reprinted by permission
of Harcourt Brace Jovanovich, Inc., and Faber and Faber Ltd.

For Joseph Needham

Contents

Acknowledgments

The editors wish to express their appreciation to those who helped them, over and above the call of their duty, in the labor of preparing the manuscript: Hans Ågren, M.D., Jacob A. Arlow, M.D., Prof. Margaret Mary Barela, Prof. Richard A. Block, Prof. Kenneth E. Folsom, Prof. George H. Ford, Prof. Eugene D. Genovese, Dr. Christine King, Dr. Liang Luen-chu, Dr. Richard Martin, Dr. Joseph Needham, FRS, FBA, Prof. Lewis E. Rowell, Prof. Helwig Schmidt-Glintzer, Prof. Kristofer M. Schipper, Prof. Albert J. Schmidt, Prof. Barry Schwartz, Prof. Mark Selden, Prof. Nathan Sivin, Prof. Eviatar Zerubavel, and Howard D. Zucker, M.D.

The senior editor would like to add his personal note of thanks to the Burndy Library for its ever ready welcome.

Opening Remarks by the President

Ladies and gentlemen,

For the past four years, since 1979 when our last conference was held in Austria, I have been serving as your President, and in that role it is my privilege to officiate at the opening of this conference.

In many countries, opening ceremonies are festive occasions such as when a president breaks a bottle of champagne over the bow of a newly constructed ship. In my country, the United States, there is a special kind of opening ceremony every spring in which our president inaugurates the baseball season by pitching the first ball. In our organization we have no symbolic rituals such as champagne bottles or baseball pitching; instead it is all accomplished by a simple and prosaic declaration, and I therefore hereby declare that the Fifth Conference of the International Society for the Study of Time is now officially open.

In 1976, one of my predecessors as president, David Park, noted in his opening remarks that the effect of presenting a scattered assortment of papers, during the first three conferences of our Society, had been "kaleidoscopic," and he advised us that the Society had decided its future meetings were to be less kaleidoscopic and more unified. This decision was implemented. Our Fourth Conference focused on the "single though many-headed" theme of "beginnings and endings" (see Foreword to *The Study of Time III*, ed. J. T. Fraser, N. Lawrence, D. Park [New York: Springer-Verlag, 1978]). Our Fifth Conference likewise has a unifying theme; it is of time in its relation to society and science in China and the West. The setting of our present conference in this ancient hilltop Castello di Gargonza, with its surrounding Tuscan landscape, is surely evocative of the medieval heritage of Western society, and it will be interesting here to reconsider that heritage in juxtaposition with the great intellectual heritage of China.

Surely all of us must rejoice to be meeting in these glorious surroundings, and we can express our thanks to Dr. and Mrs. Fraser who for many years have demonstrated an extraordinary skill in discovering beautiful locations for our conferences, as they did at Oberwolfach in the Black Forest, and at Lake Yamanaka in Japan, and twice at the lovely setting of Alpbach in Austria. And now they have done it again. For the arrangements for our present conference, we are also indebted to the strenuous efforts of the members of the Conference Committee: Professors Hans Ågren, Brian Goodwin, F. C. Haber, S. Kamefuchi, Nathaniel Lawrence, and Nathan Sivin. We are also indebted to Albert Mayr who has been serving as our one-man Italian local committee; he has been extraordinarily helpful in taking care of the innumerable preparatory details. And, most especially, we are indebted to our treasurer, Professor Rowell, who is ending his term of office with a dazzling display of ways to make sure that this meeting at Gargonza will achieve its desired objectives.

Above all, of course, we give thanks for the outstanding organizational skills of our Society's Founder—the only true begetter we might say—for his tireless efforts to make our Time Society fulfil its aims, and, more immediately, to make our present conference a success.

GEORGE H. FORD

A Message from Dr. Joseph Needham, FRS, FBA, to the Gargonza Symposium on "Time, Science, and Society in China and the West"

It is a source of much distress to me that I cannot be with you all for the symposium that Dr. J. T. Fraser has been planning for so long. This is partly because of the economic constraints of the times in which we live, but even more due to the infirmities of my wife, now in her eighty-seventh year, whom I cannot easily leave. I can assure you, if such an assurance were necessary, that I have a sustained interest in the theme of the meeting, and would like to wish it every success.

I suppose that in a sense I am one of the ancestors of the theme that you will be discussing, for it is now nearly twenty years since my monograph "Time and Knowledge in China and the West" was published in *The Voices of Time*.

In that monograph I attempted to show that Western Society had no monopoly of the sense of linear continuous time, in which there was room for both social evolution and scientific progress. I examined the claims that had been made for Europe as the only culture with any real sense of history, and rebutted them, revealing in Chinese culture the home of one of the very greatest of historiographical traditions. The Chinese knew of the cyclical time conceptions common to Greece and to India, but in general the *philosophia perennis* of Chinese thought accepted a single continuous time series, quite parallel to that of Christendom and the Peoples of the Book. Chinese attitudes to time and change could not, therefore, have been one of the leading factors in the inhibition of the development of modern science in that culture. Social and economic factors, I concluded, were much more likely to have been effective in preventing the Scientific Revolution in China.

In the first section of the monograph I sketched the role of time in ancient Chinese philosophy, especially among the Confucians, Mohists, Taoists, and Legalists. A good deal of elucidation of some of these doctrines has taken place during the past twenty years, and I should welcome an up-to-date discussion of these matters, especially as the Mohists understood them. I also discussed in this section the relation between linear continuous time and the "nesting" cycles of the astronomers and the alchemists (on this topic, see *Science and Civilisation in China*, vol. 5, pt. 4, pp. 222 ff., 230 ff., 286 ff., 378 ff.). Many new insights arose when my collaborators and I recognized elixirs as essentially "time-controlling substances."

In the second section I discussed the role of chronology and historiography within the bosom of continuous time. Perhaps the greatest tradition of history writing in the whole world was Chinese, and I tried to show how the original cadre of the dynastic histories gave way, as the centuries passed, to the writing of more continuous historical surveys. In China, history was always the queen of the sciences, *regina scientiarum*, not theology, or mathematics, nor philosophy, and following Stange and Vernant, I tried to show how it was that this came about. In any case, it is evident that no historian could think of history as anything other than real change in a time that was part of reality.

The third section took up the time of mechanical and hydro-mechanical time-measurement. The clock has been without question one of the most fundamental instruments of modern science, and yet the escapement, which has been called the soul of the mechanical clock, that device which splits time into small equal intervals, and slows down a set of wheels so that they keep pace with the diurnal revolution of the heavens, our primary clock—was not a European invention. In China there were six centuries of mechanical time-keeping before the Europeans achieved the same thing. It is hard to believe that this could have happened in a civilization for which time was not real and not continuous. Whatever culture the tag of the "timeless Orient" could have been reasonably applied to, it was certainly not China. The names of I-Hsing and Liang Ling-Tsan will live for ever in the history of horology.

Biological changes in time were taken up in the fourth section of the monograph. I spoke first about the conception of Laws of Nature, and pointed out how naive that would have seemed to all Chinese, and especially Taoist thinkers; after which I went on to show how the Neo-Confucian school, building its thinking about the universe entirely in terms of *ch'i* (matter-energy) and *li* (the patterning principles acting at all levels), worked out, six centuries before Erasmus Darwin, a theory of biological evolution in time. It was also shown that T'ang calculations of the age of the universe, amounting to millions of years, were immeasurably more spacious than those of the European sixteenth and seventeenth centuries, even the eighteenth, a full thousand years later.

Section five then took up the concepts of *Ta T'ung* (the Great Togetherness) and *Thai P'ing* (the Great Peace and Equality), showing how they inspired Chinese social thinkers through the ages, envisioning a kind of human social evolution, not excluding particular periods of rapid change or revolution. The Chinese, I said, did not live in a timeless dream, fixed in meditation on the noumenal world. On the contrary, history was for them perhaps more real and vital than for any other comparably ancient people; and whether they conceived time to contain perennial falls from initial perfection, or to pass on in cycles of glory or catastrophe, or to testify a slow but inevitable evolution and progress, time for them brought real and fundamental change. They were far from being a people who "took no account of time."

In the following section (six) I drew attention to the Chinese practice of the deification of discoverers as culture-heroes, giving a number of instances of this. More unexpected, perhaps, was the recognition by the Chinese of ancient technological stages in time. It was possible to show that the succession of stone, bronze, and iron in ancient societies was appreciated by them many centuries before the Danish archaeologists first formulated this in the Western world. Perhaps it was because the tempo of development in their ancient civilization had made them historians rather than prehistorians.

Next, in section seven, I took up the question of science and knowledge as co-operative enterprises cumulative in time. Although modern science did not originate in China, it was possible to show that there was a steady development of knowledge there, whether of numbers of plants, or drug-plants, or number of varieties of ornamental plants; or again of mineral and chemical substances. There was no Chinese century, I ventured to say, from which one could not find quotations to illustrate the conception of science as cumulative disinterested co-operative enterprise. If the emergence of modern science was ultimately inhibited largely by the institution of bureaucratic feudalism, that very system had in earlier times powerfully assisted scientific investigations.

In the last section, I took up again the parallelism between the Chinese ideology of linear continuous time on the one hand, and the Judaeo-Christian-Muslim conviction of a single "plan of salvation" working itself out in one continuous time. However much we may know today about space-time and its curvature, this continuous time is the same as that which the geologists and biologists have used to describe the changes our earth has undergone in the development of our solar system from the moment of the Big Bang onward. I argued that the Chinese were thinking in terms of this same time. And I ended by saying that if Chinese civilization did not spontaneously develop modern natural science, as western Europe did, it was nothing to do with attitudes to time and change. Other ideological factors remain for scrutiny, of course, though the concrete geographical, social, and economic conditions may yet suffice to bear the main burden of the explanation.

All new contributions which your symposium may bring forward will be of the greatest interest to me. We intend to publish a revised version of "Time and Knowledge in China and the West" in volume 7 of *Science and Civilisation in China*, and the process of my revision will be immensely helped by the thoughts that will assuredly arise during the symposium. May I once again wish it every success.

A Communication from the Chinese Academy of Social Sciences

Dear Dr. Fraser:

My responsibilities demand that at the time of your conference I should be in one of the distant regions of our land. Therefore, much as I regret it, I will be unable to attend your meeting in Castello di Gargonza. I have asked my colleagues, however, to convey to you my very best wishes.

The selection by your Society of the theme "Time, Science, and Society in China and the West" demonstrates a sense of history. For historical developments have advanced modern China into a prominent position in the contemporary world.

To the small number of Western scholars who have been traditionally interested in China, a rapidly growing number of others are being added, especially from the scientific disciplines. There is an increasing awareness among them of the privileged position that scientific work holds in the People's Republic. The expanding exchange between China and the West in matters of common interest will surely lead to an increasingly enlightened understanding of our achievements by the world community.

Once again, my very best wishes to you and your colleagues for an excellent meeting.

Yours sincerely,

YU GUANYUAN
Vice Chairman of the State Scientific
and Technological Commission of
the People's Republic of China and
Vice President of the Chinese
Academy of Social Sciences

Time, Science, and Society in
China and the West

The Problems of Exporting Faust*

J. T. Fraser

Summary   For more than a millennium before the Renaissance, the Chinese were ahead of Europe in applying their knowledge of nature to useful purposes. Yet the most powerful methods of such applications, those of modern science, were not born in China. Reasons for this inversion in the rate and direction of development of scientific knowledge have been sought in different social conditions, cultural values, philosophical stances, languages, and attitudes toward history.

This paper approaches the question of why modern science was born in the West by focusing on the functional basis of natural science: its demands for the mathematization of hypotheses about nature and the validation of those hypotheses by experiment. It suggests that the demands for number and measure originated in certain closely allied teachings about time that were native to the West.

The modern concept of scientific law grew out of the metaphysical conviction that processes may be divided into those that are timeless (lawful, quantifiable, eternal, divine) and temporal (contingent, qualitative, passing, earthly). This time-timeless dichotomy, with roots in Pythagorean number mysticism, Platonic idealism, and Christian theology, has become a part of the unquestioned metaphysical assumptions of science.

An identically stark division may be found in Christian moral philosophy. It is between the timeless, divine rules set for human conduct and the temporal demands of human instincts. The conflict between the rules and the needs suffuses the character of the industrial West: tenseness, restlessness, a mechanical-analytic turn of mind, admiration of inorganic naturalism, and the love of number and measure.

What we know as the scientific method is a pragmatic synthesis of the intellectual heritage of the West with Christian morality, in the spirit of the Reformation and in the service of early mercantile capitalism.

The absence of indigenous natural science in China might therefore be partly attributed to the traditional Chinese preferences for organic naturalism and to the Chinese regard of history as the most exalted form of knowledge, in contrast to the West's regard for mathematics as the queen of the sciences and its high esteem for inorganic naturalism.

The figure of Faust is used as a symbol for that cultural, social, and philosophical ambience that gave rise to the favored identification of truth with the numerical and the experimental. This paper examines some of the problems caused by transferring Faust from his native habitat to the heterogeneous cultural world of our age. The difficulty is in the taming and subordinating of modern science and technology to the needs of people.

In the People's Republic of China, the task is that of integrating modern science and industrial productivity into a non-Faustian civilization. In the West, it is the integration of the powers of the scientific industrial state into Western humanistic tradition.

It is argued that the necessary integration cannot be based on a natural philosophy that divides the world into time and the timeless, because such a bifurcation does not allow for a continuity in nature

---

* Founder's Lecture

between the atemporal, physical basis of the world at one end, and, at the other end, the demands of the human mind for free creativity, associated with noetic and social time.

As a replacement for the time-timeless dichotomy, this paper examines the hierarchical theory of time. Within the principles of natural philosophy appropriate to the hierarchical theory of time, a continuity among physical, organic, mental, and social processes may be traced in a manner resembling the ideas of evolution by punctuated equilibria.

The Platonic-Christian perception of time and the timeless corresponds to a conservative universe in static harmony. The hierarchical view of time corresponds to the contemporary perception of dynamic reality, organized along a hierarchy of increasingly complex structures and processes that remain, from the point of view of evolution, open-ended.

The ecumenical science of a contemporary Faust, it is concluded, must acknowledge at the basis of the universe the evolution of time itself.

Our epoch is characterized by a single, overwhelming economic fact: the needs of people for food, goods, services, and housing, judged in terms of immediate shortages and rising expectations, outrun what the productivity of nations can supply and the existing economic and political systems distribute. And if the productivity and means of distribution were available, it is not at all certain that the earth could keep on offering the necessary raw material and energy, in a sustainable manner. In spite of the phenomenal increase in the rates of production, the socioeconomic conditions at the end of the century demonstrate the continued validity of the principle of Thomas Malthus concerning population growth and the supply of goods.

The population explosion, together with increased expectations, has offset the increased rate of productivity. The ideas of Malthus, that nineteenth-century prophet of doom, are unpopular today because they do not conform to what has been called criminal optimism. The phrase stands for a slap-happy attitude popular with planners around the world, one that mistakes half-baked science fiction for social reality or else—or in addition—assigns magic powers to one or another ideology.[1]

The most frequently proposed remedy for catching up with the Malthusian lag and even for solving practically all other problems, from poverty and illness to war and pollution calls for more science and technology. The business concerns of the capitalist world build their promotion of more technology on the erroneous identification of the ascent of man with the history of science. As far as I can tell, the socialist countries do the same. It is only quite recently that these omnibus stances came to be challenged by calls for appropriate technology.

Assuming that increased scientific understanding of man and the world, without an accompanying humanistic-political control imposed by a major catastrophe, could in itself heal the ailments of our age, the question would still remain: What kind of science ought that healing knowledge be? How are we to select its principles and methods?

Joseph Needham has maintained a hope for the coming about of a single, ecumenical science as an accompaniment to the growth of organization and integration of human societies. He compared Chinese and Western mathematics, astronomy, physics, botany, chemistry, and medicine. He then constructed a graph, depicting the achievements of these sciences in a quasi-quantitative form, against a scale of centuries. The plot suggests the existence of "fusion points" in the development of the sciences into world-wide, ecumenical bodies of knowledge. He then remarks that "the more organic the subject-matter of a science, the higher the integrative level of the phenomena with which it deals, the longer will be the interval elapsing between the transcurrent point [of roughly equal sophistication] and the fusion point. . . .[2] However, he goes on, given enough time, all knowledge will be subsumed "into the same oecumenical natural philosophy . . . until the coming of the world cooperative commonwealth which will include all people as the waters cover the sea."

What kind of natural philosophy, what kind of conceptual scaffolding could correspond to the ecumenical science of this beautiful vision? Could we look to science, as science is understood today, to provide the necessary multidisciplinary and intercultural system of thought?

I do not believe so, at least not until after epistemology ceases to be patterned upon those theories of knowledge that have their roots in the Platonic idealism of time and the timeless.

1. The Eternal and the Temporal

The separation of the changing from the permanent, the unpredictable from the predictable, distinguishing a perspective of becoming from a perspective of being in the human experience of time, has been a favorite game of philosophers ever since the pre-Socratics held their own time-society meetings along the shores of Magna Graecia and on the islands of the Aegean Sea.

Little did they anticipate that by the time of Newton a particular way of separating the lawful from the unpredictable would have become the formal basis of a new natural philosophy that, through its offspring, the Industrial Revolution, would change the patterns of Western life. Neither could they have guessed that the Pythagorean duality of sky-geometry on the one hand and earth-existence on the other would have become, through the labors of Plato, the paradigm of scientific thought concerning the nature of time.

The cutting of the pie of human time experience into no more and no less than two slices—the eternal and the temporal—proved to have been necessary for the formulation of the Galilean laws of motion and for all subsequent laws of physical science.

The success of the natural sciences, which all employ this dichotomy, appears to have demonstrated that the division of the world into time and the timeless was an undebatable fact of nature. The duality entered the metaphysical foundations of physics, and through it became a dogma of contemporary knowledge in general.

The thesis of this essay is twofold. First, I will argue that the sharp division of the world into what is temporal and what is timeless, sometimes identified with a division between what is judged physical and what is regarded as mental, has outlived its usefulness as a scientifically supportable natural philosophy of time. Second, I will maintain that only by replacing the antiquated dichotomy by a model of time appropriate to our understanding of the universe, to wit, by the hierarchical theory of time, can we hope to create an ecumenical system of knowledge.

Dividing the world into time and the timeless is an inadequate matrix for social history and elucidating social fact; it is too restricted a scheme to aid in understanding psychology; it is not a rich enough temporal background to evolutionary biology, and it cannot even accommodate the temporal behavior of inorganic matter, as revealed by contemporary physics.

Furthermore, the rigidity of defining time by its contrast to the timeless (to eternity) has prevented the development of a theory of knowledge that could subsume, in a systematic whole, the many ways in which we have learned to explore the relationships between man and the universe, among different forms of life, and among human beings.

Since the different sciences must ask their questions in different forms and set different criteria for the testing of truth, it is futile to search for a single, prescribed method of inquiry and a single kind of test for legitimating fact or theory. Because of these varying demands, the plurality of principles and modes of understanding, current in physics, biology, psychology, and social science, appear to be chaotic and without any evident, overarching pattern. The absence of an obvious, common perspective and mode of inquiry has come to be regarded as an unavoidable corollary of the scientific method and, therefore, a necessary hallmark of our culture. But a fragmented, inchoate view of the world is intellectually moribund because it fails to account for the striking unity that, in our experience, holds together all natural structures and processes.

What is needed is a new theory of knowledge that can identify a continuity among the many ways of understanding the world, one that could somehow join those phenomena that have been regarded as timeless with those that have been judged as temporal. Such an epistemology must be able to subsume in itself the hierarchy of causations, identities, beginnings and endings, and different regions of undeterminacy that the sciences of matter, life, man, and society have identified.

The evidence of these hierarchies suggests a new natural philosophy, one based on the unorthodox assumption that time itself is of a hierarchical character. As do causations and identities, so would time itself appear as a corollary of the complexities of processes and structures, revealed by contemporary knowledge along the different, stable integrative levels of nature. Since the dynamics of the universe is one of the evolutionary development of complexifying structures and processes, it would then also follow that time itself has evolved with the increasing complexification of matter. Should such an unusual postulate about time be made plausible by detailed argument, we would then have a conceptual scaffolding for an epistemology, appropriate for a truly ecumenical science.

It is easy to demonstrate that the concept of time has undergone many historical changes; but this is *not* my claim. My proposition is that time had its genesis in the early universe, has been evolving in a manner that resembles the dynamics of punctuated equilibria, and remains developmentally open-ended. I have dealt elsewhere with the conceptual difficulties and pragmatic consequences of such a theory.[3] Here we are concerned only with those aspects of the hierarchical theory of time that are significant for the theme of our conference: time, science, and society.

Together with his ideas of time and eternity, Plato's legacy to us includes the significance of quantitative thought. I would like to take advantage of this heritage and approach an understanding of the three-cornered relationship among time, science, and society through a critique of quantitative thought, because thinking in terms of numbers was necessary for the birth and growth of Western science and industrial civilization. Specifically, I will examine the origins, justification, and limitations of the peculiarly Western preoccupation with number.

In my reasoning I will appeal to the collective judgment and social ambience of the industrialized West because it is social values that guide—even when they repel and thereby guide—individuals in their search for knowledge. I agree with Ludwig Feuerbach that "the single man for himself possesses the essence of man neither in himself as a moral being nor in himself as a thinking being. The essence of man is contained only in the community and unity of man with man; it is a unity, however, which rests only on the distinction between I and thou."[4]

2. *The Dominion of Number and Measure*

Even a cursory examination of the history of Chinese science and technology will reveal the presence of great refinement in observation, ingenuity in classification, and a remarkable diligence in collecting systematized knowledge about nature. However, as Joseph Needham remarked some time ago, "what the Chinese did not develop indigenously was the method of testing by systematic experiment of mathematical hypotheses about natural phenomena."[5] Chinese science became eclipsed in the seventeenth century by the mathematization of physics in Europe. Nathan Sivin thus summed up that fateful change in the Western perception of nature: "The Scientific Revolution was a transformation of our knowledge of the external world.... It established for the first time the dominion of number and measure over every physical phenomena."[6]

The doctrine that all things and forms are number, that *harmonia*, a balance and order according to number, is the law of the universe, is associated with the name of Pythagoras and with the Pythagoreans. The chief task of the philosopher, in the Pythagorean spirit, was to discover the rules of number. Numbers performed a divine dance and exhibited through it the ultimate principles of the universe. Having found in the rules of number the key to absolute truth in a cosmic context, members of the Pythagorean brotherhood appealed to those rules for the salvation of their souls.

Benjamin Farrington, in his work on Greek science, has considered the Pythagorean use of number in its relation to knowledge and society. Mathematics, he wrote, not only provided a better explanation about the nature of things than was theretofore available, but it also kept

> the souls of the brethren pure from contact with the earthly, the material, and suited the changing temper of a world in which contempt for manual labour kept pace with the growth of slavery. In a society in which contact with the technical processes of production became ever more shameful, as being fit only for slaves, it was found extraordinarily fortunate that the secret constitution of things should be revealed not to those who manipulated them, not to those who worked with fire, but to those who drew patterns on the sand.[7]

The quasi-religious and mystical principles of the Pythagoreans came to maturity in Plato's theory of knowledge, a philosophy of great beauty and power. It is a way of looking at the world, and probably the most significant single contribution of Greek antiquity to the birth and development of natural science. But the Platonic and Aristotelian notions of time as a countable image of eternity could not have achieved their privileged status in the history of Western thought—they are unlikely to have been incorporated in the ways that the laws of nature came to be written—had these notions not been reinforced through certain beliefs and practices in the daily lives of the people of Christendom.

Reflecting upon the rise of Christianity, Needham wrote in his Herbert Spencer lecture that, "for the ancient Mediterranean thinkers, the world, which had neither beginning nor ending, was growing neither better nor worse. It has been powerfully argued ... that the major contribution of Christianity and one of the principal reasons why it vanquished its competitors among the religions of the Roman Empire was precisely that it introduced change and hope into the stagnating sameness of the ancient world."[8]

After the downfall of the Roman Empire, the message of revolution taught by Christ and his immediate followers metamorphosed into the theological edifice of medieval Christianity. The intellectual and spiritual labors of the Church Fathers and of most of the Schoolmen form a majestic mire that tends to alienate the modern reader. Yet, it was a working synthesis between whatever they saw as the eternal, unchanging laws of God and the temporal, unpredictable fate of man.

As part of that religious-philosophical synthesis, the respect for number and quantity makes its explicit appearance very early. Thus, St. Augustine, writing at the turn of the fourth century about the rules of number and the rules of wisdom maintained that "although it is not clear to us whether number is a part of or separate from wisdom, or whether wisdom is a part of or separate from number, or whether they are the same, it is clear that both are true, and immutably true."[9]

Johannes Kepler, in the preface to the reader in his *Mysterium Cosmographicum,* composed twelve centuries after the days of St. Augustine, asserted that "Nay, the idea of quantities have been in God from eternity. Quantities are identical with God; therefore they are present in all minds created in the image of God. . . . In this matter both the ancient philosophers and the Doctors of the Church agree." And again, in his *De Harmonice Mundi,* he maintained that "geometry is coeternal with the mind of God, it is identical with God himself; it served as a model for the Creation of the world and together with the image of God it was transplanted into man, and not simply received [by man] through the eyes."[10]

Yet another 350 years pass and we read in Einstein's autobiography that "in a man of my type . . . the major interest disengages itself to a far-reaching degree from the momentary and merely personal, and turns toward the striving for the mental grasp of things."[11] For Einstein the mental grasp of things meant the Pythagorean geometrization of time into space-time. It is only a small step from here to C. W. Misner, K. P. Thorne, and J. A. Wheeler who go even further when they maintain that "the proper arena for the Einstein dynamics of geometry is not spacetime, but superspace."[12] A cut through superspace is "a leaf of history," which "describes the deterministic, dynamical development of space with time."[13]

By withdrawing into increasingly sophisticated mathematical abstractions, the contemporary scientific view of time—by which people invariably understand the views of time in physics—negates the significance of all events and processes that cannot be included in the numerical order. Parmenides and Plato would be proud of this brave denial of all that is generated, but we are stuck with a growing chaos of ideas concerning the nature of time. Each step of further abstraction offered as an elucidation of the temporal aspect of reality only moves the notion of time further away from experience and hence from the concerns and predicaments of life, man, and society.

Based on what and how St. Augustine, Kepler, and Einstein wrote on number and reality, there is little doubt that these men firmly believed that eternal, mathematical relationships constitute facts of nature entirely independent of man.

A metaphysical stance of such impressive continuity—from Plato to Einstein—could not have maintained itself if it had been detached from and independent of socially reinforced values implicit in the daily behavior of people. On the contrary. The identification of the eternal and timeless with number, and the simultaneous distrust of the free, the formless, and the unpredictable, maintained their hold upon the minds of those who created Western science, precisely because such opinions were organic parts of socially approved thought. In such matters, collective guidance works by embodying praiseworthy ideas among the teachings of praiseworthy conduct.

What among Christian practices and beliefs could have reinforced the high regard for number and geometry? What kind of behavior, expected of good Christians, has helped reinforce and perpetuate the dominion of number and measure in the Western understanding of nature?

Christianity in general and Protestantism in particular advocated that people control their most powerful drives, those associated with the preservation of the self and the perpetuation of the species, by means of sublimation rather than through satisfaction. With such teachings in the mind, the enterprise of life became a struggle between what people felt they really wanted to do and what they believed they ought to be doing.

In the ensuing call for self-control, the abstractness of geometry recommended itself for empolyment because geometrical forms and mathematical formulas are void of the temptations of "wine" and "women," though not totally of "song." The conspicuous absence of all human and animal figures from Islamic religious art and the ubiquity of geometrical forms in their stead is noteworthy. They demonstrate the intuitive realization that pure geometry does not tempt the flesh and seldom excites disturbing fantasies.[14]

In postulating laws of nature, deviation from geometrical perfection has been a taboo throughout the history of the exact sciences up to and including our own days.

The deep hold upon scientists by an aesthetic and even moralistic commitment to timeless forms has been described by G. J. Whitrow, following a term of Emile Meyerson's, as a trend for "the elimination of time." He saw it exemplified already in Archimedes' *On the Equilibrium of Planes*, a treatise that "attained the ideal, so earnestly sought in our days by Einstein and others, of reducing a branch of physics to a branch of geometry...."[15]

Around the turn of the sixteenth century, Johannes Kepler challenged the Greek ideal that the orbits of the planets must be circular or at least curves generated by the relative rotation of circles. He asserted, instead, that the planetary orbits were elliptical, but he remained unhappy about his "ovals." Early in 1605, in a letter to the Danish astronomer Christian Longomontanus, he would only insist that they are less reprehensible than the ideas of the Ancients.

"You accused me," he wrote to Longomontanus, "of having sinned with my 'ovals,' yet you hold the ancients faultless for their 'spirals' [epicycles and helices]. If my ovals are but a cartful of dung, the spiral of the ancients are whole stables full of dung." He insisted that his is a very great improvement over the received views—but *unum carrum fimeti*, just the same.[16] The power of geometrical idealism, the intellectual ancestor of Francis Haber's "technological idealism" was and remained great, disturbing as this idealism has been against collectively held rules.

Early in the twentieth century the German sociologist Max Weber remarked that the origins of natural science ought to be sought in the decided propensity of Protestant asceticism for empiricism that was rationalized on a mathematical basis. He observed that the favorite science of all Puritan, Baptist and Pietist Christianity was ... physics, and next to it all those natural sciences that used similar methods, especially mathematics.... The [mathematical] empiricism of the seventeenth century was the means for asceticism to seek God in nature. It seemed to lead to God, philosophical speculation away from him.[17]

The skillful use of number also brought the merchant increased prosperity, supporting his conviction that his belief in the immutable laws of nature and God were obviously correct. For the commercial and industrial capitalistic states, no less than for Plato, God was a mathematician.

Sir William Petty, the seventeenth-century founder of demographic statistics, wrote an essay called "Of Lands and Hands." In it he put forth the uses of number in the well-being of a nation.

> From the number of freeholders in each Country....
> From the number of other Electors....
> The numbers of people that are of every yeare old from one to 100....
> From the premises & the yearley interest of mony per cent....
> From the knowledge of the numbers of professors of all religionaryes who are distinguished by sensible marks....
> By knowing the number of working hands....
> By the knowledge of Naturall & Incurable Impotents....
> By the proportion between Maryd & Unmaryd teeming women....
> The number of persons living by seafishings....
> By the number of people & provisions of Cattle & Corne....
> By the number of ships yearly cast away & seamen drowned....
> By the number of Decrees, Verdicts & Judgements in all Courts...
> [may we judge the quality of our lives.][18]

The essay reads like a divine service, a litany, with the celebrant reciting the verses in praise of the efficacy of number, the faithful repeating the responsory. Indeed, in the history of the West, stemming from Greek antiquity and favored by Christianity, the absolute and ultimate principles of the universe had to be numerical and timeless. Time itself remained "but a walking shadow, a poor player/That struts and frets his hour upon the stage," and, after the teleological goal of Creation is reached in the Final Judgment, "is heard no more."

But the timeless cosmos, that Republic of Numbers, has not been without its troubles, which we will discuss, after a brief detour to the time of the first unification of the Middle Kingdom.

The Chinese have been very much interested in number but not in the quantitative. A notable exception was the ideology of the Legalists, a school of thought that rose to significance some time during the fourth century B.C. Theirs was a strict view of law and order, based on what may be called quantitative measures of justice.[19] They drew up a list of "Six Parasitic Functions" of people that sap the power of the authoritarian state. They included care for old age, beauty, love, and living without employment. They also had a list of Five Gnawing Worms, ruinous to the state, such as discussing benevolence and right-ousness. The early meaning of their Chinese name signified "standard," or law fixed beforehand (that is, without reference to custom). The only emperor who attained power with the help of the Legalists, in 221 B.C., standardized not only orthography but also weights, lengths, the widths of roads, and the gauge of chariot wheels. Degrees of penalties were assessed by precise quantities, laid down in numerical detail.

It is tempting to speculate that this kind of a puritanical-mechanistic outlook, if maintained, might have established in China a preference for the quantitative in human experience. But in fact it did not, because the humanitarian resistance to tyranny and dislike of codification for behavioral norms made it impossible. In two decades, the rule of the Legalist emperor came to an end, giving way to the milder rule of the Han dynasty. Slowly but surely, in the words of Needham, Legalism was rejected by the Chinese people as the country returned to the traditional organismic, nonabstract, human-centered, qualitative rule of law.

3. *Trouble in the Republic of Numbers*

In the West, the power of quantitative thought, built into natural science, was pressed to serve a civilization that had been instructed by the God of the Old Testament to gain dominion over the earth. Those instructions were heeded, industrial technology was born and grew to be remarkably powerful. But just as genetic errors accumulate in a living body and lead to the crises of aging and death, even so certain peculiar errors of judgment have been accumulating in the body social of the industrial lands. From those lands they have been exported to all corners of the globe, carried, like pathogenic vectors, on the backs of promises for better lives for all.

The errors I have in mind come from a neglect—even a negation—of those biological and mental functions of people that cannot at all be related to the *harmonia* and numerical order of Pythagoras and Plato. Specifically, I am talking about the fact that beneath the immense creativity of our species lies the domain of most unharmonious, and essentially unresolvable conflicts. Unless these are carefully and shrewdly managed, they make humans as immensely destructive as they can make them constructive.

Watching the events of our own days and the attendant emotions bubble over, stripped of culturally imposed niceties, I cannot help observing that contrary to the way we have been classified, homo sapiens, we are only superficially reasoning creatures. Basically, we are members of a desiring, suffering, death-conscious, and hence time-conscious species. But this model of man has no place in geometrical idealism.

One consequence of having placed all our eggs of hope in the quantitative-rationalistic basket, as if people were really reasoning and wise creatures, is the increasing loss of relevance of scientific advances to the universal need for food, shelter, health, and a modicum of dignity.

To describe the way I perceive the situation, I wish to appeal to the metaphor of a computer that uses a certain language. People handling the computer must learn to speak, or at least to write that language. In the course of time, intimate and intense work with the computer will influence the language of its operators. Through language the computer will come to mold their ways of thought, their scale of values, and, in general, their judgments of the nature of reality.

What I just called a metaphor is not a metaphor at all. There is solid and extensive evidence that computers, with their peculiar demands and capacities, have already changed the value judgments of the computer states. Problems that call for qualitative judgments are increasingly assessed in terms of numerical calculations. Human behavior itself is being increasingly interpreted in terms of computer technology and concerns that should be framed in terms of historical man are increasingly framed in terms of the ahistorical present of machinery.

Joseph Needham's comments on the Legalists in the China of twenty-three centuries ago are uncannily valid for the scientific-computerized states of our own epoch.

> It is in connection with mathematics, geometry and metrology that we come upon the fundamental philosophical flaw in Legalist thinking. In their passion for uniformisation, in their reduction of complex human personal relations to formulae of geometrical simplicity, they made themselves the representatives of mechanistic materialism, and fatally failed to take account of the levels of organisation in the universe.[20]

Our own, contemporary changes in the collective temporal umwelt, reflecting the shift from the paradigm of historical man to the paradigm of ahistorical mechanical-electronic functions, is well represented by the introduction and success of digital clocks. Whereas dial clocks are models of the continuity of the revolving sky—Plato's moving image of eternity—digital time pieces identify as significant only the present. Literature reflects similar changes. The traditional novel with its many-tiered temporal structure is being replaced by journalistic reports about the present, marketed as books. In evolutionary terms, we are adapting to a man-made–machine environment, constructed according to the inorganic naturalism of Western science.

In a 1964 paper on science and China's influence on the world, Joseph Needham remarked that

> Europeans suffered from the schizophrenia of the soul, oscillating for ever unhappily between the heavenly host on the one side and the atoms and the void on the other; while the Chinese, wise before their time, worked out an organic theory of the universe which included nature and man, church and state, and all things past, present and to come. It may well be that here, at this point of tension, lies some of the secrets of the specific European creativeness when time was ripe.[21]

The Chinese are hardly alone in their search for the organizing principles of stars, beasts, man, and society, though they are probably unique in terms of the sophistication of their organic naturalism. In stark contrast, the Western vision of "nature and man, church and state, and all things past, present and to come" is one of mathematical order, that is, the very same system of thought that is responsible for the West's scientific and industrial progress.

Many of the fundamental words in the history of Western science display the same explosive but also painstakingly elaborate character as do the writings of certain schizophrenics. They suggest mental states that crossed a critical threshold of some kind. They witness inner tensions that can be lessened only now and then, and only through the ceaseless search for increasingly abstract and, presumably, increasingly timeless ideas.

These are symptoms of alienation from the flow of human time, untoward consequences of having identified the temporal umwelt of the human mind with the temporal umwelt of the physical world.[22] They demonstrate a retreat from human reality, in analogy to the retreat of schizophrenics from the responsibilities of a partly open future, into the narrow confines of an eternal present. In different words, it is an abnegation of human freedom.

The suggestion emerges that if such features of the Western temperament as "the schizophrenia of the soul," and the withdrawal into the present (a neglect of history) were necessary for the creation of natural science in its mathematized forms, then these sciences—and others patterned upon their methods and ways of thought—cannot be exported without the same genetic features in their makeup.

4. *Faust in His Natural Habitat*

The archetype of the man with the schizophrenic European soul whom Needham spoke about is the Dr. Faustus of Marlow's play and, in a more contemporary form, Goethe's Faust. It was the social environment of this latter Faust that bore and raised to adolescence the scientific-industrial civilization. Faust sought to comprehend the timeless aspects (laws) of nature, having preferred them to the uncertainties of feelings. It is not surprising that, instead of attempting to gain access to a woman directly, he had to conjure up an evil male character as a procurer, the same personage who used to bother Luther. The tragedy of Gretchen's infanticide follows inevitably from Faust's oscillations between "the heavenly host on the one side and the atoms and the void on the other."

By embracing Gretchen, Faust left behind the divine circles and epicycles of Ptolemy and Copernicus in favor of the irregular curves of human fate. Society's sentence upon his female half then drove him to his restless search for salvation. But no salvation on earth is possible for those who believe that violating taboos of a mathematical, divine order can leave nothing for the body and soul but a lesser cartful of dung than the Ancients had had. Faust's salvation came only in the uncanny beauty of Goethe's heaven, where the Chorus Mysticus informed him that time was no more and even males and females existed only in disembodied forms.

Perhaps that is the kind of heaven we should all try to reach. We cannot do so, however, unless we give up our societies, our minds, our lives, and even our dust, and return to the atemporal state of the photon. But such a journey is prohibited by the hierarchical organization of the universe, with its stable integrative level and metastable interfaces. Long before we could reach the atemporal state of the photon, we would have ceased to be organisms capable of the enlightened feelings of the mystical choir boys. In short, and there is nothing new in this, we are stuck between heaven and earth.

It is not easy to live on earth and imitate heaven; maybe we should not try so hard. In his essay on human law and the laws of nature, Joseph Needham tells us about a cock burnt alive in Basel in 1730 for the "heinous and unnatural crime" of having laid an egg. The cock was in good company, though. One of the accusations against Joan of Arc was that she often wore male clothing which, one would presume, was also unnatural by the same law of God. Regarding the cock in Basel, Needham goes on to ask whether the state of mind in which an egg-laying cock could be persecuted at law may not be just another facet of a collective view of man and the world which, in a different setting, would produce a Kepler. Needham concludes that "historically the question remains whether natural science could have reached its present state of development without passing through a 'theological' stage?"[23]

It is a matter of personal preference whether one sees science as having passed through a theological phase or Christian theology as having been secularized into science, preaching the absolute, numerical truth of God, with the scientist as the priest in possession of the sacraments of an invincible witchcraft. I would look at both as slightly different attempts to resolve some of the unresolvable, creative conflicts of humans. The element that is common to them—to Christian theology and Western science—is the separation of noetic time experience into the temporal and the timeless.

There exists a small but distinguished body of literature on the proposition that the different directions Chinese and Western science has taken is attributable to the different assessments of cosmic-historical time. The Chinese, we learn, tended to judge historical-cosmic time as cyclic; the Christian West, as linear.[24] Curiously, as far as I could ascertain, no one has as much as hinted that the crucial element of time in the birth of modern natural science was not the issue of historical linearity, but the metaphysics of timeless number and law versus temporal contingency.

There can be little doubt that the strong teleological (that is, linear) element of Christian salvation history did contribute to the rise of the industrial West. For the hope of a final redemption from toil gave divine authority to the Platonic vision of the Republic, naturalized first into St. Augustine's City of God, and later into Marx's, Engel's and Henry Ford's factory on earth. But I do not believe that this linear view of time has in itself been the major force beneath the creation of modern natural science. That came, as I have argued, through the placing of geometry into a timeless sky, by separating it from the temporal conditions prevailing on earth, and finally by perceiving in the natural order a manifestation of the heavenly, mathematized order.

In his paper "Time and Knowledge in China and the West," Needham asserted that "in Chinese culture, history was the 'queen of the sciences,' not theology or metaphysics of any kind, never physics or mathematics."[25] Perhaps the reason why modern natural science did not arise in China, independently of the West, was precisely because the traditional focus of Chinese intellectual interest has been life and man. Their sages and their pragmatic men, with exceptions such as the Legalists, have generally refused to perceive in geometrical order patterns universal enough to control the stars and heavenly hosts above and "all the creatures here below," or even to serve as paradigms of sorts for human behavior.

In the West, Plato's universe was emulated because it was so remarkably ordered and geometrical. But the serious Greeks have also allowed for a play of immortal gods and goddesses, behaving every bit like humans. However, the divinities of Olympus were later replaced by tensor equations, as was the star-throwing god of the Hebrew prophets. The starry sky, that image of eternity, is now a universe quite unrelated to the daily concerns of people.

"The whole world, or any part of it, can now be treated as a unified system composed of nothing but dynamically curved space-time or 'super-space' or as nothing but gauge fields, or Salam's 'elementary Particles.' "[26] This enthusiasm not withstanding, however, it is not possible to erect ethical and political systems on geometry, not even on curved space-time geometry. For, logical structures are eotemporal or, using an unexamined and misleading phrase, they do not respond to the direction of time, whereas our peculiarly human needs are sociotemporal, nootemporal, or biotemporal in their character. The distinction among the types of causations characteristic of these levels can be neglected only at the cost of generating unbearable tensions in the body social.

"The certainty and predictability of low-level phenomena cannot be found in the realms of 'free-will' at the higher levels," wrote Needham, paraphrasing an earlier critique of the Legalists.[27]

If the geometrical reduction of the quote from Gal-Or is unacceptable, as it must be, so are all propositions that would completely divorce the laws of lower integrative levels from those of life, mind, and society. For we ourselves share the hierarchical organization of the cosmos.

What an ecumenical science must seek, therefore, is an epistemology that can accommodate the many ways of human knowledge in a single system, yet allow for the different ways in which the various sciences and the different departments of the humanities must present their arguments and validate their evidence. A natural philosophy of time consistent with such an epistemology would allow us to trace a continuity from the primitive temporalities of the physical sciences, through the flow of biological time to the noetic and social temporalities created and experienced by members of our species.

A dynamic reconciliation of the multiplicity of the world in the unity of a hierarchical organization should ease the mind of Faust, and make it unnecessary for him to oscillate unhappily between the heavenly hosts of his Gretchen-experience and the atoms and the void of his laboratory work. Instead, he could just commute.

5. *Legislating Order in the Republic of Numbers*

What are the reasons of the "unreasonable effectiveness" of number in natural science, to borrow a phrase from Eugene Wigner's Nobel lecture?[28] I would like to sketch a possible answer, based on detailed arguments given in other writings of mine.[29]

In Book 6 of the *Republic*, Plato has portrayed all things of the intelligible and visible world as arranged along a vertical line, which we may imagine as connecting heaven to earth. On the top of the line are the eternal, timeless ideas and unchanging forms. In post-Platonic terms, these would include the circular planetary orbits and epicycles of Ptolemy and Copernicus, and the geometry of superspace. Underneath the timeless forms are the likenesses of them, such as geometrical figures or, in our age, the geodesics of space-time plotted by a computer. Further down on the Platonic divided line come animals, plants, and, I assume, the DNA molecule. This is also the region where objects made by man belong. Everything beneath the chalk circles are temporal.

The destiny of the soul, Socrates tells us, is to climb from the dark, the sensible, and the temporal toward the luminous, the intelligible, in short, the timeless.

I do not disagree at all with the Socratic assessment of human destiny: it is, or should be, a journey from darkness to light. But if so, then I must insist that the Platonic theory of knowledge is backward, the divided line of the *Republic* is upside down.

It is the atemporal—the perpetual motion of the photon, the ceaseless vibration of the electron—that represents the absence of choice, that is, the absence of freedom and, therefore (metaphorically speaking), the darkness of the mind. From the point of view of spiritual enlightenment it is the beam of light that stands for the biblical "darkness upon the face of the deep."

Only what is temporal is open to change and hence to improvement, having this potentiality in a degree proportional to the distance of its structures and functions along a scale of complexity, from the least complex forms of matter.

In Socratic language, the liberation of the soul consists of the journey from the timeless, along the stages of increasingly sophisticated temporalities, to the noetic and sociotemporal levels of nature. In terms that avoid reference to the soul, I have called this journey "time's rites of passage." The architecture of the world as we know it demands the turning of Plato's divided line right side up. The starting point is the atemporal, the goal is the increasingly freer, the more intensely temporal regions of structures and processes.

Living matter is certainly freer than those forms of matter whose actions are determined by the laws of physics only. Thinking life, by which I mean humans, is freer than those forms of life that follow biological and physical laws only. Finally, our societies, but especially the global fraternity, is frightfully free, as demonstrated by the crises of our days.

These remarks suggest the reason why quantitative methods are so "unreasonably effective" in understanding the behavior of matter in its least complex forms, and in the understanding of life and thought in their least characteristic functions. The lower integrative levels, whether in themselves or as parts of more advanced structures, are the least free or, in Socractic terms, the least enlightened regions of the universe.

The theory of knowledge that corresponds to the revised architecture of Plato's line may be represented by a hyperbole.

Plato directed our attention to the perfect, Darwin to the imperfect. But perfect, ideal, abstract forms cannot have history. All they need is an unchanging, eternal designer. Only the imperfect, actual forms of moving matter have the potential for change and can (and therefore do) define temporalities.

A year before he died, in the midst of the ravages of the Thirty Years War, Kepler wrote to his son-in-law, the mathematician Jakob Bartsch that, "when the storm rages and the state is threatened by shipwreck, we can do nothing more noble than to lower the anchor of our peaceful studies into the ground of eternity." [30] Kepler's desire for an absence of conflict, a wish we all share when tired from the labor of survival and individuation, may be used as an entry to an understanding of the new theory of knowledge, wherein temporality is the most elevated and timelessness is the most primitive aspect of the universe.

Eternity has been the paradigm of rest, continuity, permanent identity. Mathematicians assign eternity to the rules of number, the religious to the attributes of God. But the primordial world of radiation, that self-contra-dictory, atemporal universe, possesses nothing to which the ideas of rest, continuity, permanence, or identity could be applied. Neither time, nor space, nor connectivities (causations) of any kind exist in it—yet. All these emerge only through time's rites of passage from the atemporal to the prototemporal and beyond.

Continuity, rest, and identity are features of the eotemporal level of massive, aggregate matter and not of those integrative levels that have been and remain at the fundaments of the universe. One can construct a system of relative rest from systems in relative motion, but it is not possible to construct a moving system from elements of rest and no change. Motion and change are epistemologically and, therefore, ontologically prior to rest and no change.

Slicing sensory impressions and inner needs into the categories of permanence and change is a strategy for survival of living organisms. For reasons peculiar to the human mind, this dichotomy has expressed itself in the dividing of the human experience of time into permanence (the conservative, inertial trend) and change (that corresponds to the world of need). How these categories are conceptualized is a matter of social conditioning and linguistic creation. But this division of time into the eternal and the passing is only a first, very crude approach to an appreciation of time, even though it was useful up to about our own days, just as the Ptolemaic earth-centered system was useful as a first approach to the astronomical universe.

The Platonic dichotomy of time and the timeless is the simplest, and hence very appealing attempt to analyze the hierarchy of unresolvable, creative conflicts in nature, all of which are present in our experience of human time, because we ourselves are made of matter that moves, lives, and thinks collectively with its fellows. Nothing like this may be found in the Dialogues, of course, because to every epoch its own understanding of the world appears to be obvious and just about complete.

According to the theory of time as conflict, each integrative level is associated with a set of unresolvable conflicts peculiar to that level. These conflicts become more intricate in their character with the evolutionary complexification of matter. From atoms, to planets, to life, to man and society, the unresolvable, creative conflicts approach in their nature, and eventually become our own experiential conflicts. We may judge the physical world sometimes as peaceful, or the lives of birds as idyllic, only because between their conflicts and ours there is a qualitative difference that permits a projection of our hopes and dreams upon the immensity of the sky or the lives of doves.

The intensifying conflicts and increasing degrees of imperfection (as compared with idealized, abstract conditions) along the natural scale of increasing complexity are the very conditions that can give meaning to the Socratic call for enlightenment.

6. *Ecumenical Science*

With these ideas about a continuous line of knowledge from the atemporal to the socio-temporal, and a continuity in nature according to the principles of punctuated equilibria, we may now return to the question asked in the introduction to this paper: What kind of natural philosophy, what kind of conceptual scaffolding could correspond to Joseph Needham's idea of ecumenical science?

Giving the exact sciences the respect they deserve, one may point with pride to the fact that they are spread around the globe in almost identical forms. Mathematics is universal, the laws of physics are already ecumenical. Different understandings of atomic physics and astronomy are already fused into an international system. The same may be said about those branches of biology that may profitably mimic the methods of mathematical physics. But medicine varies greatly around the globe and in certain of its branches there exists more than a single valuable approach, with no particular practica being necessarily superior to others. Going from the life sciences to the sciences of the mind, we note that opinions concerning the nature of human behavior and the desirable methodology of psychology are legion. Finally, there is hardly anything that could be called ecumenical about views of history and social theory.

The reasons for this gradation may be found in the hierarchical organization of nature. Since laws (causations) are level-specific, so must be the formal principles of inference and methods of demonstrating truth. Light waves, particles, massive matter, life, mind, and society demand different logical precepts.

The laws of the eotemporal world have generally been taken as assuring precise pre-dictability. This view is correct because in the eotemporal domain of pure (directionless) succession—in the world of the classical physicist's t—the direction of time can have no meaning. Nothing in that world can correspond to before-after relationships. Inductive generalization, which is the foretelling of the future, and deductive generalization, which is the summing up of the past, are indistinguishable. This privilege is limited, however, to the macroscopic behavior of inorganic matter.

The first breaks in the hegemony of mathematical predictions in physics came with the extension of physical science into the domain of particles where discrete mathematics had to replace calculus, and quantum logic had to replace classical logic.

Going upward from the eotemporal in the direction of organic processes, deductive and inductive reasoning separate. For living matter defines a present, a now, in terms of its necessary internal coordination and, with respect to that now, time acquires futurity and pastness. Rising from the biotemporal to the noetic and sociotemporal levels the ecumenical natural philosophy appropriate to Needham's vision must allow for an increasingly larger pluralism of scientific principles because the increasing complexity of structures and functions become increasingly unpredictable. By the time biologists, psychologists, and sociologists will be able to depend on mathematical models to the same degree as, for example, astronomers depend on them today, the queen of the sciences will include in her domain such methods that will allow for increasing undeterminacy of prediction and even for a range of ambiguity in logical relationships.

From these considerations on a natural philosophy for ecumenical science, we may now draw some speculative conclusions concerning the issue of exporting Western science to non-Western cultures. Again, we begin with the inorganic and work our way up toward the organic integrative levels.

The sciences of the inorganic were created by and seem to demand for their continued success the kind of collective personality that is usually associated with Protestant pragmatism: high esteem for order and fear of ambiguity. Physics, especially, demands strict uniformity and allows little or no variation in the precision of its principles. It is a thoroughly cross-cultural science because it deals with the least complex integrative levels of nature: elementary particles and gravitating masses behave the same way whether they function as parts of animals or people, and they certainly do not respond to differences in social environment.

The situation changes as one begins to deal with the sciences of the more complex stable integrative levels of nature. In the handling of their peculiar problems, the sciences of life, mind, and society must allow for an increasing plurality of methods and ambiguity in their statements of truth. Since this pluralism is not a sign of human ignorance but a symptom of levels of complexity, admitting them in the methodologies in the sciences of the organic is necessary for their healthy growth.

It follows that biology, psychology, and sociology, if freed from methodological commitments to physics, should be able to flourish in many and different ethnic, historical, and national forms as parts and parcel of Needham's ecumenical science.

7. Faust on the Road

We left the Faust of old in his laboratory, thinking about Gretchen and bargaining away the future of his soul. To make his character a useful metaphor, we must send him on two journeys. First he must go on a diachronic travel to the West of our epoch; then he has to take a synchronic trip to make him become a member of the worldwide community.

The life of Faust in its original setting was informed by a conflict between, on the one hand, his boundless search for knowledge, his love and fear of woman, and his desire for power, and, on the other hand, the ethical assets of his society which by today's standards were backward and icy.

At the end of his diachronic journey, approaching the turn of the twentieth century, he will find himself facing equally difficult though different problems. His new world is inundated with data, which is often equated with knowledge; his West possesses almost completely liquid ethical assets; and his new fellows have enough power to be classed with Plato's Demiurge as the creators of bodies and souls.

The search for knowledge changed from a qualitative to a quantitative proposition: more is better. This brought with it a new form of the Malthusian principle, mentioned earlier in its economic-biological significance. In an evolutionary developmental step, the principle crossed the noetic-sociotemporal interface and surfaced in a new context.[31] In complete analogy to the biological teachings of the theory, the rate at which information-as-knowledge is generated and the rate at which its transfer is demanded outrun by far the rate at which information can, in fact, be communicated and processed. Metaphorically speaking, more brain children are begotten and delivered than society can feed, house, educate, and integrate. The hefty tomes of Faust the alchemist are replaced by the information storage facilities of Faust the data banker. Withdrawal from those banks is performed by the read-out functions of computers. The processing of knowledge read out is also done by computing devices, now approaching their well-advertised "fifth generation." It is through the computer and communication world that the new form of the Malthusian principle enters.

In the United States, Japan, and western Europe one is continuously treated to the exhibit of faster, larger, and increasingly sophisticated machines which prove themselves inadequate to decrease the information backlog or break the traffic jam in data and instructions, because the amount of information the machines were supposed to have organized and processed has increased in quantity and scope while the devices were being made, installed, and tested.

Computer programs designed to facilitate the production and distribution of goods and services or the running of vast organizations often need hundreds of thousands or millions of instruction lines. These programs, unavoidably, come with genetic ailments which demand specialized computers for their repair. The scenario is analogous to the necessary complexification of organic evolution, with the introduction of unreducible, statistical uncertainties.

In the second part of Goethe's Faust the hero travels around the world. Alienated from his own age and from antiquity, he learns of the problems of his species (mostly through symbolic events) so that he can prepare his redemption and that of humanity. This enterprise is analogous to the synchronic journey that the contemporary Faust must take.

Getting on the road he will note, among other matters, that while some segments of the global society cry out for more knowledge in every field of endeavor, some others are choked by incoherent and therefore useless knowledge. He will also note that in spite of the tight control that some highly centralized governments have over the behavior of their citizens, the ethical norms of humankind are in a three-phase disequilibrium. Some are frozen, some liquified and hence fluid, some vaporized. From a distance he is likely to have a glimpse of his Gretchen, trying to find a dignified yet also practical leitmotiv for her and her child's life. And, if he examines the statistical surveys of the United Nations he will learn that Wagners,[32] witches kitchens, fighting soldiers, and slinking Mephistos are becoming democratically distributed over the surface of the earth.

It is in this world that the National Science Congress of 1978 in the People's Republic of China declared a new epoch: "Springtime for people, springtime for science." There followed a period of wild enthusiasm which subsided, however, as the immensity of the problems became evident. It was also realized that the importation of Western know-how has brought with it certain ways of thinking and doing that had to be naturalized before they could become as effective in China as they have been in the West.

In an essay written four years ago, the China correspondent of the British *Nature*, Tong B. Tang, examined the influx of Western know-how into China and concluded that, "at the present there is a dynamic balance between the ideal of indigenous Chinese scientific culture and the influence of Western scientific ideas; only in the next five years, as these influences are absorbed, will the future pattern of the world's largest new scientific force become apparent." [33] The time scale of five years is obviously too short; twenty years may be a more reliable sampling period.

The "springtime of science" in the West was the eighteenth century. It was then that the philosophes, those early propagandists for the age of reason began to explore the social significance of the (then) "new natural philosophy." They identified it in the open horizons which science has offered for the control of man's own destiny. The change from wild enthusiasm to a realistic assessment of their problems that took the People's Republic of China only a few years was a fast-motion replay of the corresponding sobering up in the West that took over two centuries. It began with the Enlightenment and stretched to our own days when the realization that "Never has man held within his grasp so much technology beneficial to his welfare; never has he been so far from applying it to that end" became a broadly held opinion among responsible observers of the contemporary international scene. [34] Thus, while the Chinese are laboring to integrate the Faustian way of seeing and doing things into their non-Western civilization, the West itself, in a parallel task, must also integrate industrial productivity and new knowledge into its own humanistic tradition, if the forces of industry and science are to be constructive rather than destructive in their long-term effects. The many descendants of Faust must be educated and guided so that they can become useful members of a community that is more heterogeneous than that literary ancestor of modern Western man could have imagined.

The reasoning of this paper suggests, in sum, that in spite of its immense advances in technology and science our epoch remains uninformed because it has not yet established a way of addressing itself. In terms pertinent to our theme, there is a need for a coherent framework within which the significance of time can be traced from the atemporal roots of the universe to the peculiar freedoms of noetic and social time.

The contribution of this conference to the education of Faust's intellectual and cultural heirs is the exploration, through selected examples, of the relationships between science and society. This we propose to do by examining a few of the very many ways along which the reasoning and passionate faculties of twentieth-century people meet the challenge of noetic time. The foregoing arguments are intended to form a part of that examination.

Notes

1. An example of criminal optimism is a forty-two-page supplement to the May 9, 1983, issue of *U.S. News & World Report* entitled, "What the Next 50 Years Will Bring." Many of its glorious predictions are plainly contradicted by other reports in the same issue, recording contemporary facts. The reader cannot help wondering how we are supposed to get from here and now, to there and then.

2. Joseph Needham, "The Roles of Europe and China in the Evolution of Oecumenical Science," *Advancement of Science* 24 (1967–68): 11.

3. J. T. Fraser, *The Genesis and Evolution of Time* (Amherst: University of Massachusetts Press, 1982); "Toward an Integrated Understanding of Time," in *The Voices of Time*, ed. J. T. Fraser, 2d ed.

(Amherst: University of Massachusetts Press, 1981), pp. xxv-xlix; *Of Time, Passion and Knowledge* (New York: Braziller, 1975).

4. Ludwig Feuerbach, *Principles of the Philosophy of Future*, trans. M. H. Vogel (Indianapolis: Bobbs-Merril, 1966), par. 59, p. 71.

5. Joseph Needham, "The Roles of Europe and China in the Evolution of Oecumenical Science," p. 1.

6. N. Sivin, "Why the Scientific Revolution Did Not Take Place in China—or Didn't It?" *Chinese Science* 5 (1982): 60.

7. Benjamin Farrington, *Greek Science* (Baltimore: Penguin Press, 1969), pp. 48–49.

8. Joseph Needham, "Integrative Levels: A Revaluation of the Idea of Progress," in *Time: The Refreshing River* (London: Allen and Unwin, 1944), p. 237.

9. Augustine, *On Free Choice of the Will*, trans. A. S. Benjamin and L. H. Hacksfatt (Indianapolis: Bobbs-Merril, 1964), bk. 2, sec. 11: "How are the rules of number and wisdom related." The quote is from verse 129.

10. Johannes Kepler, *Gesammelte Werke*, ed. Walter von Dyck and Max Caspar (München: C. H. Beck'sche Verlagsbuchhandlung, 1938–75), 8: 30 n. 8, and 6: 223.

11. Albert Einstein, "Autobiographical Notes," in *Albert Einstein, Philosopher Scientist*, ed. P. Schilpp (New York: Tudor, 1949), p. 7.

12. C. W. Misner, K. P. Thorne, and J. A. Wheeler, *Gravitation* (San Francisco: Freeman, 1973), p. 779.

13. J. A. Wheeler, "Frontiers of Time," in *Proceedings of the International School of Physics, "Enrico Fermi", Course* 72 (Amsterdam: North Holland, 1979), p. 438.

14. On the relationship between individual and collective personalities and preferred ways of knowledge, see the chapter on "Epistemology and the True," in Fraser, *Of Time, Passion, and Knowledge*, pp. 321–60, and its extensive references.

15. G. J. Whitrow, *The Natural Philosophy of Time*, 2d ed. (Oxford: Clarendon Press, 1980), p. 1.

16. Kepler, *Gessammelte Werke*, "Briefe," 15: 141–42. Free translation.

17. Max Weber, *The Protestant Ethic and the Spirit of Capitalism*, trans. Talcott Parsons (New York: Scribner, 1904), p. 249 n. 145.

18. Sir William Petty, *The Petty Papers* (London: Constable and Co., 1927), 1: 193–98.

19. See Joseph Needham, *Science and Civilisation in China*, vol. 2, *History of Scientific Thought* (Cambridge: Cambridge University Press, 1956, "The *Fa Chia* (Legalists)," pp. 204–15.

20. Ibid., p. 210.

21. Joseph Needham, "Science and China's Influence on the World," in *The Legacy of China*, ed. Raymond Dawson (Oxford: Oxford University Press, 1964), p. 308. For a penetrating analysis of that intense and peculiar anxiety that came to inform post-Reformation Europe, to favor quantity substituted for quality, and to create the social temperament that was to build science and industry, see William J. Bouwsma's "Anxiety and the Formation of Early Modern Culture," in *After the Reformation*, ed. B. C. Malament (Philadelphia: University of Pennsylvania Press, 1980), pp. 215–46.

22. The reference here is to the generalized umwelt principle of the hierarchical theory of time. See *The Genesis and Evolution of Time*, esp. sec. 2.1. See also John Michon, sec. 2.3, in this volume.

23. Needham, *Science and Civilisation in China*, "Human Law and the Laws of Nature," 2 : 582.

24. For an entry to this debate, see Joseph Needham's essay, "Time and Knowledge in China and the West," in *The Voices of Time*, pp. 92–135.

25. Ibid., p. 104, repeated in his message to this conference, included above.

26. Benjamin Gal-Or, *Cosmology, Physics, Philosophy* (New York: Springer-Verlag, 1981), p. 41 (Gal-Or's italics).

27. Needham, "The *Fa Chia* (Legalists)," p. 211.

28. Eugene Wigner, *Symmetries and Reflections* (Bloomington: Indiana University Press, 1967), p. 222.

29. See *The Genesis and Evolution of Time*, pp. 156–63; *Of Time, Passion and Knowledge*, pp. 294–99; *Time as Conflict* (Boston and Basel: Birkhäuser, 1978), index entries under "number"; and "Out of Plato's Cave: The Natural History of Time," *Kenyon Review*, n. s., 2 (1980): 143–62.

30. Max Caspar and Walter von Dyck, *Kepler in Seinem Briefe* (Berlin: Oldenburg, 1930), 2: 308.

31. In the hierarchical theory of time, the sociotemporal umwelt is not identical with "society," that

is, a group of interacting people. It comprises, instead, the objects and processes generated by the symbolic transforms of human experience: the artifacts of industry and science (as structures and as functions), the creations of the arts and letters, and the myriad other forms that human communication can take.

32. In Goethe's *Faust*, Wagner is the name of the protagonist's assistant, a character of mediocrity in spirit and mind.

33. Tong B. Tang, "Will China Be Tainted by Western Science?" *Nature* 280 (1979): 100. By the same author, "China: Where the New and the Historical Materialism Interact"; "Research Centres, Libraries, Journals Flourish in New China"; and "How the Popularization of Science Narrows the Polarization of the People," ibid. 283 (1980): 423–24; 516–17; 616–17. See also the unsigned editorial, "Planting a Tall Tree," ibid. 301 (1983): 280–84; and Joseph Needham, "Science Reborn in China," ibid. 274 (1978): 832–34.

34. From an address by Belisario Betancourt, President of the Republic of Colombia, to the United Nations, October 5, 1983.

Part I

Time

Introduction

The first four volumes of *The Study of Time* series contain over a hundred papers (*The Study of Time*, 4 vols. [New York: Springer Verlag, 1972–81]). They may, and ought to, serve as a general background for the specific issues addressed in the present book. Nevertheless, it was felt appropriate and courteous to the reader who may see only this volume, to begin with essays that deal with the general concept and experience of time.

In the opening paper, Nathaniel Lawrence is concerned with the roots of time in human experience. He considers four well-known metaphors which translate time felt into time understood: number, space, action, and purpose. None of these alone nor the four together map the complete wealth of time, but from among them telos is sufficiently powerful and general to be preferred.

Conrad Dale Johnson critically examines the ontological implications of the evolutionary theory of time. He does so by relating the theory to the strategy of explanation warranted, in his view, by modern science.

John Michon argues that certain structural aspects of the evolutionary theory of time may be treated, from the point of view of experimental psychology, as cognitive representations.

J. T. F.

The Origins of Time

Nathaniel Lawrence

Summary The temporality of our experience is not an item in that experience, but rather an aspect of it. Our experience is so diverse that pervasive aspects of it cannot be framed in a way that is both comprehensive and literal. Instead we use metaphorical concepts of time for which there is no corresponding "literal" language. These metaphors gain their generality in that they mutually refer, each one invoking the others when we pursue them critically. They perform their task of description not as colorful substitutes for precise statements, but rather by recalling or embodying aspects of the experience of temporality where that experience is put to some particular use. For example, we translate time into space in temporal charts, calendars, appointment pads, and so on, where temporal sequence is presented as spatial seriality.

The paper discerns four metaphors embodied in concepts of time: time as number, time as space, time as activity, time as telos. I aim at making these metaphors, collectively, as comprehensive of temporality as is possible. The procedure is to use both small-scale expressions in English speech and large-scale conceptions in systematic thought. There is a suggestion, at the end of the paper, that the least familiar metaphor, time as "telos," may be a kind of *primum inter pares*.

1. *The Sense of Temporality*

Below all our refined and reflective concepts of time there is a basic sense of temporality, something felt rather than thought. It pervades experience and is usually no more attended to than is the background hum of machinery in the basement, which we also accept and for the most part ignore. This sense of temporality is the raw material from which we derive, by a kind of extraction, the various concepts of time that serve us so well in limited ways. In physics, for instance, when we concentrate on the analogy between space and time in describing motion, we cover only a fraction of our direct experience of temporality. Success in this area tempts us to stretch such concepts beyond their original useful function and to reduce all the aspects of temporality to the one in hand. Our temporal experience is too rich, however, to yield a single systematic view.

The history of the idea of time is punctuated by efforts to make one aspect of temporality do for all. Monocular approaches to the subject are the rule. Even before the Christian era, philosophers had begun to create single—or at most dual—aspect models of time which physicists would later adapt to their particular needs and interests. In Parmenides, for instance, we are told that our ordinary idea of time is a mistake, an impossibility, since time continually changes and would therefore come from something that is not and must pass into something that is not. We are, Parmenides urges, therefore talking about the existence of nonbeing, a manifest contradiction. This argument can be made more difficult to get around than you might suppose. The point is, however, that it focuses on logical consider-ations alone. Parmenides rejects what cannot be clearly and logically conceived. Even if his argument were not vulnerable, it would be mistaken, since he chooses to rule out felt temporality, with its change and passage, in behalf of a conceived time, required, he thought, by the logical law of unchanging identity.

Nevertheless, Plato saw the problem and saw that a revision of our notions of reality cannot conform merely to simplified logical form. Plato's teacher Socrates, in his most famous role, had taught that the unexamined life was not worth living. It is a noble sentiment, one which is usually understood to mean that if you do not hold yourself up to critical self-examination, you lose the essence of life itself—namely, the possibility of self-betterment. Plato's use of this Socratic theme is not merely a matter of morality, however. He sees the cosmos also as, in its way, alive. For us who are alive within living nature, perception cannot be completely delusive. Rather, Plato holds, the world sensed and perceived is furnished with imperfect copies of ideal entities, changeless in an eternal (nontemporal) world. As we penetrate nature, we ascend a ladder of reality, beginning with the lowest rungs of shadows and reflections, going on to physical objects, and then to the mathematical objects which physical objects embody. In the end, the path of knowledge terminates in a domain of ideal forms, eternal and timeless. The world of time, in which we live, is neither fully real nor a realm of Parmenidean nonbeing. "Time," says Plato in a passage which I shall comment on shortly, "is the moving image of eternity." Where Paremenides, on logical grounds, says of time that it is an illusion, Plato says it is an imperfect image. Paremenides makes the vault from error to truth by the use of a single rigid logical pole. For Plato, on the other hand, it is necessary to consult the whole of experience, not merely lifeless logic. Plato saw time as both conceived (as in his formula) and felt (as in our experience).

Aristotle inherits Plato's breadth. Further, he takes into account the rise in technology that has funded physics ever since, namely the measurement of space and time. Aristotle takes motion as a fundamental given, not to be argued out of existence as a logical impossibility or a poor copy of some more genuine existence. Time is an aspect of the great motions of the cosmos, embodied in numerable years, numerable months, and numerable days. These all recur rhythmically, circularly, and according to number. The regularity of astral motion was known long before Aristotle's time, but he is mindful that the regularity of time stretches from the rhythms of the heavens down to the small vibrations of a plucked string. This pervasiveness of numerability was also common wisdom for the Phythagoreans. Their response, however, was to regard number as the fundamental stuff of reality, much as a modern physicist might say the electron *is* this equation. But for Aristotle the stuff of reality and its numberability are obviously distinct. The stuff of reality is changeable, necessarily and essentially so. Numbers, on the other hand, must be wholly unalterable in order to be reliable. We shall return to Aristotle for a closer look later. At present we note his most familiar, but not his only, identification of time. It is, he says, the "number of motion," but he explains that he means not that by which we count—that's a Pythagorean confusion; rather, it is that *in* the phenomenon of motion which we can count.

Here, then, are three classical models for time drawn from the history of "time." First, time is an illusion attending our mode of perception. Second, time is not wholly unreal, but only a moving representation of what is itself unchanging. Third, time is the numerable component of motion, that which can be counted. At this point let me remind you that each of these descriptions grasps something important about time, conceptualizes it, and undertakes to close the concept of time by a definition. This passion for a unitary definition of time has ultimately done much to put the whole inquiry into confusion. Alfred North Whitehead frequently warns us of the dangers of single-minded systematics. He insists that philosophy should be the critic of abstractions and that, though we must seek simplicity, we must also distrust it. He is famous for his analysis of the unwisdom of what he called "The Fallacy of Misplaced Concreteness," that is, the taking of a systematically useful abstraction for a concrete representation of reality. The rest of these remarks are written with a constant eye to these warnings, but without any necessary commitment to Whitehead's view of time.

2. The Language of Temporality

The ways in which we express our sense of temporality are many. Small verbal capsules are as old as poetry, as various as philosophies, and as momentary themselves as the brief situations that provoke them. Time is a river, a flame, a thief, and a bestower of gifts. It is a god, a revealer of secrets, and a burier of secrets. It flies, it flows; it sometimes stops or drags or rushes. Behind each of these identifications lies some purpose and feeling of the speaker. His descriptions are as much autobiographical as they are representative. But collectively they show how many aspects this unseen elephant has—a rope, a tree, a wall, and so on.

Temporality seems to be refracted by language into its component aspects, selected according to quite special purposes. The problem is to bring order to this mélange of meanings. The common error is to make of time some kind of entity. It is isolable in language as a noun: *time*, when we refer to the concept; *temporality*, if we deal with it as an aspect of experience. I've chosen the term *temporality* because it emphasizes the adverbial and adjectival nature of time. Number may function adjectivally. For example, in some parts of Japan house numbers in a given sector do not specify a spatial location, but a temporal one—namely, when the house was built. Or we may derive our notion of temporality adverbially from the flowing of historical events or the recoveries of memory, as in *before* and *after*. The general idea of *temporality* as an abstract noun derives both from activities like processes and from things that endure. We commit another abstraction when we detach "time" from its origins and try to resolve it into a property of mind or to reify it into some sort of *thing*, with a beginning and an end. To say of time that it is a spontaneity of consciousness, as some existentialists do, or that it "began" ten billion years ago, as some physicists do, is to say something important about what we know of temporality and why we want to pin it down, but we should get clear about the particular purposes behind inquiries with such different conclusions. Time as spontaneity of consciousness seems to ignore the independence of a world of fact. As for the *beginning* of time, doesn't *beginning* implicitly prerequire a time "in" which the beginning occurs? We need both aspects and maybe more.

The problem lies in the uniqueness of temporality. It submits to useful analogy, but it simply is different, essentially different, from anything else. To simplify it in behalf of one of its aspects is to declare an ontological position, unwittingly, sometimes half-wittingly. Time is neither just a spontaneity of consciousness nor merely a value for a mathematical variable that can be extrapolated to a zero or infinity.

Perhaps fully to understand time systematically we must develop a total ontology. In this paper I suggest a prefatory approach. Let us begin by not treating a pseudoentity as some kind of thing. We will not brush aside troublesome claims about this or that treatment of time as "subjective" or "merely scientific" and so on. We will go instead to the language of temporality and study the linguistic *expression* of our temporal sense as itself requiring analysis. We are challenged to find an underlying rationale in the puzzling diversity of our partial insights. Why are there such widely differing claims? Professional bias and religious disposition interfere with decent answers. In a word, we should let time—or temporality— literally speak for itself without prejudgment. By "literally," I mean that one of our sources for insight into temporality is the *language* of temporality, both in unreflective idiom and in systematic thought.

The search for a definition, accordingly, is not the beginning point. Rather, it is the target, the end in view, as in the Socratic method. Two of the best definers in the business, Aristotle and St. Augustine, ran into obstacles trying to define time. Each of them found that he had to modify his aim, each in his own way. It is instructive to consider them both briefly.

Aristotle says that time is an affection of motion, knowable from mental motion alone, pervasively present everywhere, the measure of both movement and rest and the countable thing in measurement as well as the cause of decay.[1] The familiar comment that Aristotle holds time is "the number of motion" ignores his many-sided treatment, one which he never reduces to single formula. He remarks, supplementarily, that it is reasonable to assume counting requires soul and thus that time may prerequire mind for its existence. In Aristotle there is nothing so clear and beautiful as Plato's "time is the image of eternity." He never tries to complete his multifarious thoughts into one systematic scheme. We shall see, however, that Plato too is not so incisive or single-minded as he is usually presented. As for Aristotle, he seems to be conducting advanced students to the untidy frontier of his own probings.

St. Augustine, in a famous passage, says that he knows what time is until he is asked to define it, and then he finds that he cannot. In the distinction with which we began, Augustine knows what temporality is—like anybody, he is familiar with it in his experience. But to transform this experience into a comprehensive concept of time overwhelms him. Instead he deals with some main problems in the *use* of the concept of time. Time, he says, is not only internally sensed, but internally *measured*. In effect, he treats time as a sort of process.[2] In the same discussion he tells us that time was created with the world, thus treating it more as a kind of entity. He thereby leaves us with the odd idea—which he shares with the Big Bang Theory—that the creative process does not itself prerequire time, a kind of Cheshire grin without the cat.

In both Aristotle and St. Augustine, then, the challenge to be comprehensive has been met by shifting away from a unitary definition of time to an examination of the multiple guises in which it appears. We may well take a cue from Aristotle and Augustine. Both are brilliant a priori practicing definers. But they give us no great formula to which we can refer all our sense of temporality. Their method is to go first to what is said of time, however diverse; not to try to enforce a single, all-encompassing concept. The language of temporality is a richer source of understanding than can be derived from individual experience or professional bent, scientific, humanistic, psychological, or whatever.

3. *Metaphor and Mesophor*

Unique as it is, time is but one of a set of concepts that have a common difficulty when we come to define them. The difficulty is this: we have no literal language by which to approach them. Traditionally objective abstract terms like *space* and subjective ones, so-called, like *love* encounter the same difficulty. They refer to aspects of our experience that are insistent but diffused throughout that experience. To talk about them we abstract them from our familiar and fugitive experience. How we define these abstractions is determined in part by the reasons for inquiry. Freudian inquiry into love is concerned with its pathology; that of the poet looks to it for inspiration. It is this multiplicity of meanings that both Augustine and Aristotle sense in the effort to bring temporality under a single concept. Spatiality is similarly multifarious. For example, there is space in this room, there is space in "the organization," there is space in the painting. There is space between the stars, and there is always space at the top. What are we to say of the "spatiality" that embraces them all?

We are often inclined to say that "real" space is what astronauts encounter—or, strictly, don't encounter. The other uses of "space" are more or less metaphysical. But hold on—who distributes the license for what is real? With many concepts we have no trouble; there is a botanical tree in my garden, a family tree in the genealogy on my desk, and a grammatical tree in the book on comparative linguistics in the bookcase. A widespread convention binds me to the first "tree" as literal; the others are, properly, metaphorical. In the domain of the nonphysical, things are not quite so easy. Consider the concepts of love, notoriously diverse—for example, sexual love, religious love, humanitarian love. Each concept is identifiable by a definition, somewhat as follows:

1. Love is the phenomenon, overtly or covertly sexual, where another person or thing is the object of desire;
2. Love is God's message, his will, and his nature;
3. Love is the raising of care for another, or others, to the level of total priority.

Each of these definitions swings the spotlight in a different direction, picking out only items of a special kind. Each begins with a presupposition of importance, that is, with a purposeful preconception of what the appropriate data are. The neo-Freudian likely has reservations about the religious claim. He might grant the humanitarian account of love, but only as analysis of a secondary phenomenon, a sublimation of more primal urges located in the biology and autobiography of persons. The humanitarian, on the other hand, may or may not accept the religious view, and might think of the neo-Freudian as obsessive in a way that is not entirely harmless. And so on. Now is any one of these accounts of love literally true, the other two being metaphorical? Is there a single general quality of our experience, a "lovingness," so to speak? We seem to lack the experiential term. Have we a self-affirming standard that declares literalness for one of these definitions, but denies it to the others? Where is the irresistible convention that we may universally rely on, the literal term to which the others all refer? Nowhere, I think.

Each of the definitions given above defines a large-scale metaphor, represented in a ruling concept, indefinitely explorable. Consider how far the sexual metaphor for love has carried a whole profession. It may be that the term *metaphor* should be reserved for simpler things like grammatical "trees," a "flowering" culture, and so on, where there are no disputes about what the "real" meanings are. I prefer to use the term *metaphor*, nonetheless, for more overarching conceptions, because of its meaning, which is "to carry across." Even today in modern Greece a closely cognate word is used on a small truck that conveys goods and produce through busy streets. Our conception of a metaphor is itself metaphorical in respect of these trucks. The trucks do their work and the metaphors of love do also. To think of lovingness in sexual terms has saved minds tormented by both love and sex. But to think of it in terms of a divine nature has also provided illumination where no other light falls. Each of these is a conveyance at least a little way into the heart of a mystery. But each, I think, ultimately requires the others (and likely more) for balance. Lacking a common literal referent, they require one another. To use one is to be "carried across" to another domain ultimately.

Freud, it is said, on being asked what the great fulfillments are in life, replied, "To love and to work." It's not likely he was talking of just gratification and toil. However, though large-scale metaphors, well understood, will take us to others whose central topic is the same, the purposes for their use will be different. The common element in our experience to which these metaphors refer I call a "mesophor," since it lies in the *middle* of a net of metaphors. The metaphor is the linguistic entity; the mesophor is a widespread feature of our experience, pervasive but not well marked out. It is to this level of the mesophor, the constituent of experience, that we must repair when some metaphor, however large its scope, is necessarily incomplete, by reason of the purposes underlying its use.

Mesophors themselves comprise a class needing explanation, a task not possible in this paper. We deal here with only one of them, temporality. But a rough identification of a "large-scale" metaphor for these metaphors would have two properties. First, when pressed, it will require reference, conceptually, to other metaphors to supplement it, or else fall short of generality. Second, within the field it defines, the distinction between literal and metaphorical may reappear, but subordinately. The first characteristic that a large-scale metaphor has, namely that it carries you to others like itself in what they are intended to do, I shall explore, as much as time allows, in the analysis of four major metaphors for temporality.

The second characteristic, that "metaphorical" and "literal" reappear in a restricted domain, can be illustrated in the above example of love, one example for each of the three concepts we've considered. I once heard a young psychologist who had, I think, spent a bit too much time at Bellevue, say of a former patient, "He literally loved candy; he got an erection when he ate it." Or consider the humanitarian view of love; I had a colleague who said of a scientific friend, "He literally loved his research; he completely ignored his family and his health for the sake of it." Or I can imagine a religious person saying, "I take St. Augustine literally: namely, 'Love God, genuinely love Him, and do as you please.'" Kierkegaard in the same spirit criticizes the mystic who withdraws from the world, putting aside the flesh, the devil, and therefore society. "He doesn't love God," says Kierkegaard, "he's *in* love with him."

Literal and *metaphorical* are good words, and they are often properly paired. But there are large-scale factors in our experience which often cut across clearly defined points of view. Let us take another look at spatiality, to see how *literal* and *metaphorical* function in a constrained field. Depending on my physics, I may argue that empty space is impossible or that it comprises ninety-nine plus percent of the universe. But either way, if the physicist qua physicist hears about empty space in an oriental work of art, he will likely regard the term as being metaphorical. For him, real empty space is astral or submicroscopic or both. But if an art critic says, "There is a large empty space in this picture," he does not deny that there are actually representations of a brook and stones and so on, but simply that they lack interest. And he would agree that he is speaking metaphorically. So also the drama critic may say, metaphorically, "For the first twenty minutes of this drama, nothing happens."

As I've tried to revise the notion of metaphor, then, the conclusions are: *Small-scale metaphors invoke something literal to which they implicitly refer. Large-scale metaphors find their balance in other metaphors which serve to complete the meaning they partly support.*

4. *The Metaphors of Temporality*

A total theory of metaphor, like a total theory of time, is probably coextensive with a large-scale philosophical system; so we must make only very brief mention of metaphor as it bears on the present problem. There are small-scale metaphors that immediately appeal to the senses, like saying of the edge of a storm that it is a "lock blown forward in the gleam of eyes." There are metaphors that don't survive translation, like the backwoods "If that don't take the rag offen the bush." There are others that do, like the Latin *via*, the German *Weg*, and the English *way*, all three of which can mean a road or—metaphorically, we say—a method. And there are quite large-scale metaphors, such as "the stream of time" or its "flow." These stretch a visible or sensible feature of our experience to cover other features less demarcable but still pervasively present in it. Although metaphors are linguistic creatures, if they survive translation into a variety of languages, we regard them more as creatures of mind than mere language. No doubt the separation of mind from its ways of communication is somewhat arbitrary, but if a metaphor is itself deep in historical time and broad in the compass of its languages, we find it hard to judge it as arbitrary.

Accordingly, I shall approach the metaphors of temporality on a dual basis: first, in terms of what I shall call four "master" metaphors, those of such depth as to appear in distinct and often widely separated times, fields, and languages; and second, in terms also of commonplace expressions in English, reflecting the above master metaphors while not themselves laying any claim to universality.

This procedure is doubly empirical. First, it goes to experience generally for its warrant; and second, it appeals to linguistic experience in particular, that is, language experienced, for its specimens. No doubt language and experience intermingle, perhaps even essentially so, if they remain lively; but watching a building collapse is different from writing or speaking about it. Yet both have a temporal base. Being empirical, this method can hardly guarantee that what I've called "master metaphors" are complete and exhaustive. They are intended, rather, to show how to loosen the grip of the would-be definers, the simplifiers who search for the one right key, the all-inclusive formula, in the analysis of temporality. But though the method I employ is empirical, it is still too narrow, since i include all but nothing from the civilized languages and philosophy of the Far East, and nothing of the diverse intimations of time in the so-called contemporary primitive cultures. In a broader treatment these could not be omitted.

The four great metaphors for temporality are very like bridges which separate cities but also join them. I shall show that, as we press any of these metaphors to the limit in its own terms, it invokes others. In addition to their generality, therefore, they share a peculiar kind of cohesiveness: they require one another. This is not surprising, since they have, as I've said, no common literal language of temporality to refer to. They are, from the point of view of the literalist, as anchorless as the plants of the Sargasso Sea.

The four very general metaphors I've discerned are as complete as I can make them at present. They are temporality metaphored as number, temporality metaphored as space, temporality metaphored as activity, and temporality metaphored as telos. I shall exhibit each of them, both in popular modes of English speech and in a systematical context, that is, as it appears in an overall philosophical view.

Time represented as number. Let's begin with time conceived as number. Suppose I say, "I am forty-eight this month, and I was born in 1936." Both statements are elliptical; the first omits the unit of measurement, the other omits reference to the zero point, namely, Anno Domini. Indeed, most statements about time *are* elliptical, harmlessly if we do not suppose them to be general. Let's look now at systematic treatments of time conceived as number.

Our oldest evidence of temporal awareness may be a marginal case. There is a bone of about 30,000 years ago, on which are marks that could be tiny pictures of the sequential phases of the moon.[3] Each mark resembles the shape of the moon at some time, new, quarter, half, and so on. And there are other carvings, somewhat more recent, marked in a series of mere dots or strokes, also possibly dating the passage of days. The controversy about these carvings is necessarily speculative. But suppose they are calendrical. If they are, they might be called "progenitors of number" rather than numbers. Suppose, for example, that an imprisoned man knots a string to keep track of days, one knot for each day. He juxtaposes three series: the days themselves, the knots on the string, and the series of positive integers by which he counts the knots. But that's us. What about our ancestor? He may well have had no counting names to apply to the marks. Their correspondence may well have involved only the matching of two sequential sets, the string of days and the string of marks in which the concept of number *simpliciter* is only embryonic.

The first reliable evidence of time conceived as number appears in the haze of thought we call "Pythagorean" and then quite explicitly and clearly in Plato, who launched so much rationalized Pythagoreanism into our current thinking.

Plato is direct. He speaks to Aristotle, who speaks to Newton, who speaks to us. The messages differ, but they have a common undertheme, namely, the exhibition of time as pure number, a pure sequence construed as an ordinary series. Plato, however, suffers from superficial popularity—and misunderstanding. He is subtler than those who quote him. So, if you will bear with me, let me give you the whole of a familiar but glossed-over passage. The creator, says Plato, "planned to make, as it were, a moving likeness of eternity; and at the same time that he ordered the Heaven, he made, of eternity that abides in unity, an everlasting likeness moving according to number—that to which we have given the name Time."[4] At the risk of examining his text more closely than the author himself has done, let us look at the change from *moving* to *everlasting*. The creator "planned to make, as it were, a moving likeness of eternity," says Plato, but what he did was to make an everlasting likeness, moving according to number. It would be silly to claim a contrariety here, but there is an important shift in emphasis. In the former phrasing the emphasis is on moving, i.e., on *change*; in the latter it is on the *unchanging* quality of time, its everlasting-ness. Plato may well be facing the superficial dilemma I mentioned above. In *experience* temporality is given as change; in *concept* time is given as having invariant meaing, something shareable and discussable. Notice also that Plato says that the "everlasting likeness" is that to which we've "given the *name* Time." The temporality of experience is continuous passage; but time as concept is embodied in a name. We remember St. Augustine's momentary paralysis on this point: if no one asks him, he knows very well what time is, but if he's asked to define it, he doesn't know what to say. The *sense* of temporality is of something fugitive, chimeric. We can represent it conceptually in suspended animation, but the outcome is deceptive and superficially paradoxical. In Sartre's novel *Nausea*, Roquentin apparently encounters Augustine's dilemma in a very simply way. He can't, he says, "catch time by the tail." And isn't that what we are tempted to think a definition ought to do?

We have already noticed diversity in Aristotle's account of time. The numerable aspect of motion, which is its centerpiece, is revised by Kant in an interesting way. "Arithmetic," says Kant, "achieves its concept of number by the successive addition of units in time." [5] As in Aristotle, so also in Kant, the clearest accounts seem to be those that do not define time, but discuss instead how it functions. However, Kant says something else that brings us closer to time metaphored as space. "Time," he says, "does not itself alter, but only something which is in time." [6] Space doesn't alter either. Moreover, we measure space as well as time. The analogy is tempting, both to popular speech and to systematic thought.

Time represented as space. When we appeal to popular language, which is under no obligation to systematic thought, we find many uses of space to represent time. We speak of the "near future," the "distant past," and events which are a "long way off." We even find time given in rather two-dimensional terms. We say that two events are separated by a "broad expanse of time." It is an appealing expression, one which permits visualization of contemporaneity, for example, namely of events differing in space but identical in time location. The spatial representation of time overextends language, however. A common way of treating time as space is to present it diagrammatically. The geology chart runs from top to bottom, thus allowing for the "descent" of man and other creatures in a stratigraphy of fossils. Economic texts chart the fluctuations in the Gross National Product, for instance, along a horizontal line, left to right, year by year, quarter by quarter. The appointment calendar on my desk, left to the passage of time, begins as a declaration for the future, but becomes a record of the past, no doubt with alterations. It changes by not changing, and that too is worthy of a digression, but not here. Finally, nonlinguistic representation of time as space does not even have to be visual. Unsighted animals learn space as a fusion of permissions to move, and I remember well the blind student who led me to my office in a darkened library, faultlessly. But for his guiding hand I would have bounced around like a rat in a maze. He had memorized a sequence of movements and had distilled space from that remembered temporal motion.

Again the bone of 30,000 years ago with problematic "moon markings" on it is a representation of time as space hybridized with time as ordinal number, rather like the geologic and economic charts mentioned above. Is there any way to treat time as pure space? No, but a valiant attempt was made in the early phases of the relativity theory to do something like that. It has historical charm, and it meshes nicely with popular expressions we've just noticed. But even physicists no longer use it. They've become much more interested in the dynamics of time.

Two early relativity men developed what might be called a "static" of time. Herman Minkowski, speaking for the new recognition that great spaces could not be meaningfully measured apart from coordinate measurements of time, proposed to represent the physical universe as a rigid and invariant structure, a kind of four-dimensional tinker toy in which physical events are given as to location and extent, together with derivable intervals between the events, stated so as to account for variations in measurement for different frames of reference. Minkowski says that this assimilation of time to space under the single title of *dimension* in effect destroys the uniqueness of each: "Henceforth space by itself, and time by itself, are doomed to fade away into mere shadows, and only a kind of union of the two will preserve an independent reality."[7] Ironically, by a kind of Cartesian transformation of space-time in relativity theory, any event can be represented as a set of numbers on a four-dimensional graph. So the spatial metaphor tumbles backward into a numerical one.

Minkowski, however, is not interested in metaphysics. A famous disciple, Hermann Weyl, was. He describes this immovable universe as the "objective world" and says of it that it does not "happen"; it simply "is." Change, says Weyl, is a purely subjective phenomenon revealed "to the gaze of my consciousness, crawling upward along the life line of my body."[8] I've dealt with these claims elsewhere and cannot expand on them here.[9] Briefly, calling change "subjective," a something known to consciousness as "crawling" up the life line, is not only mysterious but rather useless. Metaphor we must have, but how consciousness "crawls" seems more a datum for psychology than for physics. In addition, is this any better than Newton's time "flowing up"? We will discuss time as activity shortly, but it is important to mention Newton here, since his understanding of time was supposed to have been surpassed. Less figurative in Weyl, more instructive? Finally, isn't crawling a kind of change, and doesn't that change also presuppose a lapse of time? Calling it all "subjective" solves nothing; it only creates a new kind of Cartesian dilemma, two times instead of one, magically in some kind of correspondence.

To summarize: Minkowski, presenting time in a spatial way, falls back into the number metaphor; Weyl, presenting change as "merely subjective," must nonetheless account for the reality of the appearance of change, just as did his forebear Parmenides. Weyl falls "forward" into the dynamic metaphor, the one that cannot dispense with alteration. Let us go to this third metaphor for time.

Time represented as activity. Time as number rests on the activity we call "counting" or "measuring." Aristotle, St. Augustine, and Kant all make this point, each in his own way. The two older philosophers emphasize measuring, which means measuring *something*. Not surprisingly, Kant, living at a period when formal conceptions of both time and mathematics were becoming more and more abstract, writes of a "synthesis"—a successive addition of units of time, i.e., "counting." We like to think that counting can just be a counting of numbers, but a little reflection will show that this is the enumeration of a system, with no other reference to actuality. It's a bit like the self-referential act of saying, "I thank you," without any other activity which would give the speech act more concrete significance. Counting per se has meaning because it is abstracted from counting something, and ultimately all arithmetic operations are grounded in counting, whatever sophisticated abstraction it may create as a consequence.

Time as space has a similar implicit appeal to activity—else the spatialization is without meaning. We *read* our geological chart from top to bottom and our economic chart from left to right. In this activity we reinvest static time with something like its original temporality. The calendrical chart is more complex: it follows the serpentine track of a river, running for seven days from left to right and then snapping back to an eighth position directly below the first day. The meaning of the chart prescribes an order of action. These readings are all abstract, functional reconstructions of the form in which temporality was sequentially given originally, before the static metaphors took over, either numerical or spatial or both.

Our purest systematic example of the metaphor of dynamic time is Newton's masterful description—not definition—of "absolute, true, and mathematical time" as that which "of itself, and from its own nature, flows equally without relation to anything external." [10]

Newton is, of course, discussing time in physics, which was focused on the observed world as an array of objects moving in space. Later physicists, as I've indicated, wanted to get rid of the idea of flowing, but for Newton it was vital. Creation for him is God's handiwork; it is conceived as a machine, something that works in a regular and predictable way. Activity in nature is thus basic, as it was for Aristotle. The physical world is matter in motion, continuously, and its time is the absolute measure of that motion. Newton was puzzled, like Aristotle before him, that we measure motion by time and time by motion, but his confidence in absolute motion remained unshaken.

The "flowing" of Newton, however, has no relation, he says, to anything external: the flowing of time requires neither space nor matter in order to be what it is. To measure physical objects and events, we must clearly have space. Ordinary experience also includes certain kinds of temporality that are easily dissociable from space, for instance, in the flow of conversation or in the movement of thought in a discussion. You may elect to say of "He changed his mind" that it is metaphorical, but I see no necessity to do so; and in the "stream" of music there may be the shadow of metaphor, but who could call "change of tempo" metaphorical?

After Newton there followed a surge of something close to protest against the "absolute, true, and mathematical time," which was devised as backdrop for the motions of particles in space. His contemporary, the physician John Locke, asked himself about time experienced, something close to what I've called temporality. Locke points out, much in the Augustinian vein, that the idea of time ultimately depends upon the succession of ideas in the mind, underlying all apprehension, whether of change or persistence. Berkeley and Hume agree, with some modifications. Berkeley says, "Time *is* the train of ideas succeeding each other," and Hume says that the *idea* of time is "derived from the succession of our perceptions of *every* kind, ideas as well as impressions" both sensory and reflective.[11] Hence, says Hume, time is nothing but the "manner" in which we receive such data, thus summarizing a century-long reaction which led Kant, accordingly, to spell this theme out in detail: time is neither thing, nor concept, nor process, but rather the mode by which we apprehend data both from beyond ourselves and from within the self itself as well; that is, it is the "condition" of both "inner" and "outer" sense. Kant spends much of the *Critique of Pure Reason* in showing that one aspect of experience, either inner or outer, can have little meaning without the other.

Kant's effort to heal a dichotomy between the two views of time was unintentionally undermined by his own work in ethics. In his ethical study he treats will, which belongs to our inner sense, as reason in action; "practical reason" he calls it. "Theoretical reason," on the other hand, deals with time in the outer world systematically, without regard to problems of action. Those who followed Kant in the nineteenth century knew better. In Schopenhauer, in Marx, and in Nietzsche, will is neither dependent upon, nor an alternate mode of, reason. Radical humanists that they were, they insisted on the primacy of will over reason. Will comes first, with life, from its very inception, continuing through every level of existence, developmentally and logically. "Reason," says Schopenhauer in a passage I tremble to distinter, "is feminine in nature; it can only give after it has received." The subordination of reason to will, a watchword for the nineteenth century, takes an explicit and extreme form in Schopenhauer. It is will that has the generative power to create what reason can only put in order retrospectively. This is not just humanism for Schopenhauer; it's metaphysics: "The concept of will has hitherto commonly been subordinated to that of force, but I reverse the matter entirely and desire that every force in nature should be thought as will." We know causal force only inferentially, says Schopenhauer, but volitional force at first hand from within ourselves, and he sticks to the conclusions that follow: "the name *will* denotes that which is the inner nature of everything in the world, and the one kernel of every phenomenon"; and action is nothing but the "*temporal objectification* of the will." [12] In short, where Kant's time was the manner of apprehending the world and the self, Schopenhauer's time is the manner of the acting of them both.

Nietzsche's originality here is not marked. Like Schopenhauer, who so strongly influenced him, he fell under the spell of Eastern philosophy. His struggle to deal with repetitious circular time in conjunction with unique and self-making individuality, and its time, was never completely resolved.[13] But Nietzsche closes the nineteenth century with the same basic conception, largely devoid of its early metaphysical foundation. "Our intellect," he says, 'is not contrived to understand becoming; it strives to demonstrate the universal cold inflexibility of everything." [14] One understands the world through volition, by concrete doing, not through universal, unchanging concepts.

In between Schopenhauer and Nietzsche there stands another giant, a strange companion, but also a thinker who regards real time as concrete activity. For Marx, the political economist, livelihood is life, and it shapes our entire view of the world. Educated in the cosmic philosophy of Hegel, he turned his attention to things human; and as Nietzsche did after him, he philosophized not about how things are, nor merely about how they ought to be, but also about how to bring them about. He saw that, whereas before the Industrial Revolution the craftsman sold his skill, his technique, and his commitment, now industry has swept all this away with production-line assembly and repetitious efficiency. The nineteenth-century worker sells himself at the level of neither pride, skill, nor experience, but according to the least common denominator: labor time measured in hours and days. Labor time is very concrete time, but it's pretty abstract humanity. The product the laborer makes is his by rights (strictly, some part of it is), but not by law, not in a capitalist polity. It is not his to sell. It is permanently taken from him and sold in terms of market demand. Marx's man in his public standing *is* his labor time. Slavery and theft are thus combined.

Time as activity is a bulging category, perhaps needing division. It's a far cry from the Afton-like serenity of Newton's flow to the struggle for survival in the sweat shops. The range is reflected in our ordinary speech. "Events," the historian may say, from his timeless tower, "moved swiftly that day." Close-in time, however, is a volatile commodity, e.g., "Everything happened at once this morning! I don't have much time; I can give you more tomorrow." So also the Latin expression, *Carpe diem*. But the *diem* is not twenty-four standard hours; it's the moment, the right time, and that brings us close to time as telos. The rightness of a time implies a telic order.

Before we turn to that final category, we need to observe briefly the current phase of the systematic treatment of time as activity, where it has returned to metaphysics. Only a short time before Nietzsche left off publishing, Henri Bergson wrote a brilliant study called *On the Immediately Given in Consciousness*. Translated as *Time and Free Will*, this book distinguishes between time as concrete *dureé* and the "homogenous" time which science confuses with experience. The present essay is indebted to this work for not only viewpoint but substance as well. Coming from the side of psychology, Bergson's early work emphasizes the primacy of human experience. In the early twentieth century Alfred North Whitehead, turning from mathematical physics to a general cosmology, stretched terms like *organism* and *feeling* to refer to the basic events of the world process and the constitutive relations binding them together. From these concrete events there can be abstracted the spatiotemporal continuum of physics, but it has no standing save as a construct. Whitehead's magnum opus, *Process and Reality*, works out an entire cosmology, undertaking to bring the deliveries of physics and the doctrine of evolution into comprehensive conjunction with macroscopic human experience. Both these authors have been heavily commented on. Even a superficial reading of them will show, if it is not already clear, their influence on my own thinking, especially in the critical vein. If there is some independence in the present remarks it lies in the emphasis on language, the multiaspectual approach, and the willingness to lean on classical philosophy.

Time represented as telos. The metaphor of time as telos is a natural companion of the previous one. The first two metaphors are static. Presented as number or space, time is unchanging, satisfying the demand that concepts be self-identical. Time as activity or telos is less abstract, closer to the temporality from which it is drawn, satisfying the sense of time experienced better than the idea of time thought about.

However, what is meant by *telos*? It reminds us of the much abused idea of "teleology," associated with a proof for the existence of a God. This proof argues that the universe exhibits a fitted-togetherness explainable only as the outcome of a divine conscious plan. But "telos," borrowed from Aristotle, does not necessarily involve the idea of conscious intent. Its apposite verb *teleo*, "accomplish," "complete," "bring about," is not limited to what is human.

Telos is commonly represented in the idea of a "telic cause" and is best understood in contrast with "efficient cause." An efficient cause is an antecedent thing or event that brings something else to pass. In Aristotle's way of looking at cause, efficient cause is "that on account of which." To search for it is to look at the beginning of a series of events in order to understand what follows. Why did the bridge fall down? Its pilings were weakened by floods, which came from rains, which dropped because warm air encountered a cold front, and so on. Telic causation looks to the completion of a series rather than to its origins. Why do these chocolates taste so funny? Efficient cause answers, "Because poison was included in them." Telic analysis says, "Because someone wanted you dead." The meaning of the series is found telicly, in its future.

However, consciousness need not be involved. To understand a biological process we must see that in it as Aristotle says, as in conscious planning, "each step is for the sake of the next," what it tends *toward* rather than *from*. To understand the heart, we analyze its structure, its energy sources, its nerve-"wirings," and so forth, but also its function, what it is "for." Before we go further into the idea of function, let us look at some commonplace presentations of telic time.

"The fullness of time" can refer to the point of closure of a pregnancy and the opening of a separate life. It may also identify the maturity of a design in the order of things, divine or impersonal. "The time is wrong for us to have an honest president" may be referring to events set in motion by human purposes, but presently quite beyond human intervention. "Reform will come in due time" clearly points to a telic series of occurrences at least partly involving human purpose, but perhaps also identifying the kind of suprapersonal organization that we find in a Hegelian theory of history. "Time alone will tell" almost suggests that historical agency is the creator of human agency rather than the outcome of it. As these examples show, human purpose may be the familiar model for telic order, but with modification it may extend to the collective behavior of social and political groups, to the course of history unfolding, and even to divine ordination.

In systematic thought, however, the stronghold of telic time is the life and behavior of organisms. We should perhaps include the *structure* of organisms as well. However, if we accept the theory of random genetic variability, we require not an account of function for all structures, but only the capacity of the organism to tolerate anomalies when they arise.

Our first three metaphors—arithmetic, geometrical, and mechanical (as opposed to end-directed) causal—give us the counting, positioning, and sequencing of temporal units in our experience. All are required for us to get a concept of the time of organisms, but they are not sufficient. Consider the networks of time and timing in natural history. The great migrations of animals, for instance, some going from arctic to antarctic and back, are the joint product of seasonal cycles outside the animal and endogenic hormonal cycles within. Returning swallows "count" the days of the year more accurately than the ancient astronomers did—but without numbers. Small mammals whose gestation cycles are so short that they would be forced to raise their young in lethal weather, go into an incubational stall. The zygote floats free, in suspended animation, without development and then, six months later, when the time is ripe, implants for a total pregnancy of about the same length of time as our species. Born in springtime, some of the off-spring will live. The minimal telos of organisms lies in preserving their individual lives and that of their kind. It clearly is end oriented without reference to consciousness. There are also species of plants where the individuals migrate centrally and collectivize into a single individual for reproductive purposes. So also with so-called colonial animals. In time conceived as telos, the line between individual and group is often blurred.

After Darwin, organs that are "for" as well as organisms whose behavior is "for" both come under a single telos, that of survival. It's a sad little telos, very cautious, but it is a telos all the same. The times and the timing of organisms cannot be explained sheerly in terms of their past. It is indeed the telic organization and behavior that distinguishes organisms from the inorganic world.

Even where the distinctions between organ and organism and between individual and colony are sharp, the struggle for survival continues in behalf of the species. The aged, number-one stag is vanquished by the young warrior, who then becomes the hero of the tribe, sending a shock of virility through his descendants, enabling them better to cope with their environment, living and nonliving. It's something of a male legend, but what is important is that here once again we see that the one telos in nature that survived the Darwinian revolution is—ironically—survival. Nonetheless, to extract from nature "red in tooth and claw" a portrait of the natural scene in general is like trying to derive an adequate conception of pre-Classical Greek culture from the *Iliad*—dramatic, but lopsided.

The Procrustean effort to cram all natural history into so rudimentary a telic explanation leads me to two observations. One is familiar, but it bears repetition: that something has to survive in order to have a structure and to manifest behavior is so close to tautological that it verges on the vacuous. It seems to point to hardly more than the survival of the fittest to survive. If survival is the "unconscious purpose" of all organisms and of the species they embody, does it follow that all structures and behaviors are shaped by this ground condition? The other point is that modern biology has of course moved toward greater subtlety in its analysis of the paths of evolution, from the time of W. H. Thorpe's *Purpose in a World of Chance* to the present studies of Stephen Jay Gould and others.

All the same, the world of our experience includes a vast panorama of organs, organisms, and organic continuities of colonies where the events that comprise the existence of these entities are telicly organized, incapable of being wholly understood as mere outcomes of previous events.

5. *The Metaphors Reviewed*

This essay has been concerned with the origins of time in human experience. Its theme is that temporality permeates this experience, so that temporality is part of its texture or structure, rather than an isolable item *in* experience. When we undertake to render that temporality into a concept of time, we abstract from our experience certain elements of it while ignoring others. What is left behind, so to speak, is not nontemporality alone, but other aspects of temporality that do not fit the purpose of the abstraction in hand, whatever it may be. I have undertaken to show that none of these "metaphors" is dispensible for the understanding of the underlying "mesophor" of temporality, and—further—that one leads to the others when we ask persistent questions about temporality as a whole. They are metaphors lacking any complementary literal expressions that collectively express our total sense of temporality.

In identifying these metaphors I have followed two lines of examples for each: first, those appearing in popular expressions in English, whose function, in many cases, would not survive literal translation into other languages, and second, those occurring in systematic thought which seem to transcend the peculiarities of some particular language and thus lie closer to human thought generally.

The first two metaphors, time as number and time as space, are static. They satisfy in a very simple way a demand that if we deal with concepts, those concepts must be unambiguous and unchanging. The latter two concepts, time as activity and time as telos, stand closer to the demand of a concept of temporality, namely that it incorporate the element of passage which is so familiar in our awareness of time. The stability of the concept should not be interpreted without further ado as the concept of stability, i.e., unchangingness. Change in the observed world can be accounted for by analyzing it in terms of physical law and prior state conditions. But where living things are observed, we find them structured and functioning toward some end, at least the end of survival. When we suppose ourselves to share a common ancestry with other forms of life evolutionarily, we lay the ground for the hypothesis that like ourselves they strive, or struggle. And this presupposition is supported by its power to explain. What we observe intimately and inwardly in ourselves we attribute to other creatures outwardly observed, at least the telos of survival. Here, in the domain of the biological, we find a restricted license for anthropomorphism in the analysis of temporal process.

The anthropomorphism is, however, much more prevalent than we suppose. All of our metaphors are, one way and another, anthropomorphic. We are, after all, dealing with human experience, and the human tint—some would call it "taint"—remains in our abstractions. What sticks is the purpose for making the abstractions, together with such additional purposes as we may discover for them. The presence of telos in our interpretation of our experience may lie, accordingly, at two levels. First, purpose is embodied in each of the four metaphors for time. The purpose is a consciously directed telos that selects certain kinds of temporal data and presents them collectively—for example, the fluctuations of stock-market quotations given as a line in visual space. What is wanted here is quantities in a time order, nothing more. Second, in the fourth metaphor, however, the telos is not only presented as the function the metaphor serves; *telos* itself is the metaphor for time.

Being anthropomorphic is natural to *anthropos*. Just how far the general range of the telic element in nature goes is a subject well beyond the scope of this paper. It would take us, for example, into the delights of alleged "altruism" serving the fitness to survive in the haplodiploidy of hymenopterous insects. As restricted to temporal considerations, however, the question is not how to avoid anthropomorphism, but how intelligently to use it. To specify the values of the different aspects of our inevitable anthropomorphism requires an evaluation of the ends they serve, their nature and their limits. Such an investigation may not be a matter of epistemology or metaphysics. It may lie closer to aesthetics or ethics.

Notes

1. πάθος τι κινήσεως *Physics* 251b29. See also 219a1; 218b12–13; 221b1 passim; 219b9–10.

2. St Augustine *Confessions*, Bk. II passim.

3. Alexander Marshack, *The Roots of Civilization* (New York: McGraw-Hill, 1972), pp. 44–49.

4. *Timaeus* 37d in *Plato's Cosmology*, trans. with commentary by F. M. Cornford (New York: Harcourt, Brace, 1937), p. 98. I have rendered επινοετ as "planned" instead of Cornford's "took thought to make," following R. G. Bury's translation in the Loeb Library, *Timaeus*, etc., *Plato With an English Translation* (Cambridge: Harvard University Press, 1942), 7: 77.

5. Kant, *Prolegomena to Any Future Metaphysics*, ed. L. W. Beck (Indianapolis: Bobbs-Merrill, 1950), p. 30.

6. Kant, *Critique of Pure Reason*, trans. N. K. Smith (New York: Macmillan, 1953), p. 82.

7. Minkowski, "Space and Time," in H. A. Lorentz et al., *The Principle of Relativity* (New York: Dover, 1923), p. 75.

8. Weyl, *Philosophy of Mathematics and Natural Science* (New York: Atheneum, 1963), p. 116.

9. See Lawrence, "Temporal Passage and Spatial Metaphor," in *The Study of Time II*, ed. J. T. Fraser and N. Lawrence (New York: Springer-Verlag, 1975), pp. 196–203.

10. Newton, *Mathematical Principles of Natural Philosophy*, ed. F. Cajori (Berkeley: University of California Press, 1934), 1: 6.

11. *The Works of George Berkeley*, ed. by A. C. Fraser (Oxford: Clarendon Press, 1901), 1: 58; David Hume, *A Treatise of Human Nature* (Oxford: Clarendon Press, 1896), pp. 34–35.

12. Schopenhauer, *The World as Will and Idea*, trans. R. B. Haldane and J. Kemp (London: Kegan Paul, Trench, Trübner, 1907), 1: 65, 144, 153, 289.

13. See the penetrating study by Dorothea Dauer, "Nietzsche and the Concept of Time," in *The Study of Time II*, pp. 81–97.

14. Quoted in Karl Jaspers, *Nietzsche* (Chicago: Henry Regnery Company, 1965), p. 212.

Scientific Explanation and the Evolution of Time

Conrad Dale Johnson

Summary   Since the origins of Western science, it has been generally assumed that to be intelligible, the cosmic order must have a foundation that is both timeless and determinate. This assumption is not arbitrary; it follows directly from the dominant role of causal explanation in our scientific tradition. But in view of the discoveries of quantum physics, it has become necessary to rethink the ontological assumptions implied in this kind of explanation.

In fact, today it is only in the physical sciences that causality and determinacy still play an indispensable and primary role. Biology, for example, has been revolutionized by an evolutionary theory that operates with an entirely different explanatory strategy, the ontological implications of which remain largely unexplored. Between biology and quantum physics we can draw no direct analogy; but, as J. T. Fraser has shown, the evolutionary mode of explanation can be extended throughout the range of the natural sciences by means of the notion of "the evolution of time" and of temporally constituted modes of being.

This paper sketches such an extended evolutionary schema, to the point where a significant analogy to the structure of quantum physics appears possible. It suggests that explanation in the quantum realm may depend upon the very absence of any timelessly given, determinate foundation, since the lack of such an a priori ground of determinacy sets powerful constraints on the evolution of primitive temporal structure.

The most basic presupposition of any form of science is that the world somehow makes sense: that it constitutes an intelligible order. This is an ontological presupposition, an assumption about the ultimate nature of "what is." But how we make this assumption depends on something else, namely, what counts for us as intelligible. In the Western scientific tradition stemming from the ancient Greek philosophers, the intelligibility of the world was construed in a very particular way, and the whole array of fundamental ontological concepts evolved in the course of that tradition reflects this basic sense of what it means to "make sense." The essence of this orientation is summed up in the concept of *determinacy*, which in turn presupposes a very particular way of conceiving *time*.

What I want to suggest in this paper is that the kind of science that grows out of this ontological orientation, governed by the equation of intelligibility with determinacy, has definite limits to its scope and explanatory power. Today we are coming up against these limits quite explicitly and dramatically in theoretical physics, the traditional stronghold of "exact science" and the deterministic view of reality. But what is more important than merely recognizing these limits is to find a way beyond them—to find an alternative approach to explanation, grounded in another sense of what it might mean for the world to be intelligible—and such an alternative seems especially difficult to envision within the domain of physics, taken in isolation. Elsewhere, in biology and the other historically oriented disciplines, the principles of ancient Greek ontology have already been more or less radically compromised, as Western science gradually outgrew the limiting perspective of ancient thought. Taken as a whole, the contemporary scientific view of the world already demonstrates the superior power of a kind of explanation very different from the Greek, involving conceptions of time and determinacy that are at least implicitly quite distinct from the concepts that still hold away in the physical sciences. But this broader understanding of what there is in the world and how the world makes sense has yet to be worked out explicitly in a new structure of fundamental ontological concepts adequate to replace the obsolete determinism of the Greeks. In part this is because for us, as for the Greeks, physics still defines the core of what we consider real and scientifically valid. And the result is that even when the traditional ideas of time and determinacy have broken down in the quantum theory of the subatomic realm, physicists have hardly availed themselves of clues to a new understanding that lie in a wider perspective on the phenomena of nature. The sort of intelligibility exhibited in the biological domain, for example, is generally considered irrelevant to the current perplexities of physics, just because it does not correspond to the way we traditionally expect the physical world to make sense. That physics should supply crucial insights to biology we take as a matter of course, physics being the essence of what we esteem as "scientific"; but we look for no reciprocal contribution from the historically grounded disciplines to physics.

The work of Dr. Fraser, on the other hand, does represent a pioneering effort at a general ontology for the sciences based on an overview of the natural world, rather than of the particular domain of (classical) physics. The procedure adopted here is essentially that of Fraser's writing on "the evolution of time," i.e., a survey of natural phenomena with specific attention to their various temporal structures, leading to some general ideas about the nature of "what is" and how it can be explained. Like Dr. Fraser, I shall describe the world as a hierarchy of temporal levels that can be extended down below the traditional base level of classical physics to interpret the bizarre phenomena of the quantum realm as well. The focal point of my discussion, however, is the conceptual system of Greek ontology and its breakdown in contemporary physics, which leads me to a different thematic emphasis and (perhaps) to a somewhat different construction of the hierarchy of temporal evolution. Since limitations of space preclude a point-by-point comparison with Fraser's studies, I offer the following simply in the hope that the reader will find the two perspectives mutually illuminating.

The first section below presents a concise formulation of the ancient Greek interpretation of being and time, and an outline of the manifold failure of this ontology in the domain of quantum theory. The second section undertakes the survey of temporal levels mentioned above, in a necessarily cursory sketch, while the third deals with the problem of applying concepts derived from the historical/evolutionary view of nature to the apparently timeless, ahistorical groundwork of the physical cosmos.

1. *Atemporal Identity and Causal Happening*

The concept of determinacy has a twofold range of significance. On the one hand it refers to the *identity* of what exists in the world, in the sense of the logical notion of identity ($A = A$). The world is determinate in this sense insofar as whatever exists *is* whatever it is precisely and definitely, excluding ambiguity. In a determinate world, something either exists in a completely well-defined state or it does not exist at all. This aspect of determinacy was first articulated by Parmenides and later epitomized in the Platonic conception of "forms." On the other hand, determinacy also refers to the way things *happen* in the world, in accordance with the principle that nothing happens without a definite cause that completely determines and accounts for it. We have then a determinacy of being and a determinacy of becoming. The two senses are linked in a way that subordinates the latter to the former, on the basis of the fundamental assumption that the world is scientifically intelligible.

The underlying rationale for both notions of determinacy runs essentially as follows, here distilling a line of argument that begins in Plato and Aristotle and becomes the common property of Western thought thereafter. If anything is allowed to happen in the world spontaneously, without a sufficient determining cause, then there is no way in principle to explain that event, in that scientific explanation means accounting for things in terms of their causes. Further (as Aristotle argues), the chain of causes must not regress infinitely, for then all causes would be ultimately arbitrary. There must therefore be some absolute foundation that is simply given as the sole and sufficient causal ground determining all that happens. This is the point at which the argument shifts to the first and primary sense of determinacy; for if the ultimate causal ground is to determine all phenomena, completely and unambiguously, it must be completely determinate "in itself." It must be precisely definable, and it must be precisely self-identical everywhere and in everything, since any ambiguity or variation would call for a further explanation. This foundational structure being itself the final goal of scientific explanation, it cannot itself be explained; it can only be known. And we can only know what something is, genuinely and scientifically, if the thing itself really is and continues to be exactly what it is. So without causal determinacy explanation is impossible, and without determinate identity there can be no certain knowledge. If we presume the possibility of science, then we must presume the world to be determinate, in both senses.

Now there is an interesting difference between the way this kind of argument was applied by the Greeks and the way it appears in modern philosophy—in Leibniz, for example, or in the determinism of Laplace. Despite the apparent exception of the Stoics, whose thoroughgoing determinism stemmed from ethical rather than scientific considerations, it is doubtful that any ancient thinker seriously believed that *everything* in the world could be grasped and accounted for scientifically. As a rule, the Greek philosophers wanted only to assert the existence of an absolutely determinate core of "real being," which alone would be susceptible to genuine knowledge. They assumed that at the level of empirical phenomena, the determinate "reality" of things was inextricably mixed with "unreality"—spontaneous accident and ontological ambiguity. Only the foundational level of the cosmos was conceived to be truly determinate, absolutely self-identical and therefore knowable; only what was "essential" in nature was thought to be causally accountable in terms of this foundation. The much more radical claim that *every* aspect of natural phenomena, down to the minutest detail, must be scientifically explicable—that causeless happening is impossible in principle, that indeterminacy of identity is inconceivable—belongs uniquely to modern thought, reflecting the resolute empiricism of modern science. For, of course, if our access to the foundations of the world is to be by way of sensory experience, then all the data of experience must share in the determinacy of the foundation: every event, no matter how insignificant, must take place in a precisely definite way that accords precisely with the underlying structure of reality. Only if this strict determinism holds will precise quantitative measurement of phenomena reveal the ultimate nature of things.

On this point the more radical presupposition of modern thought has proved far more illuminating than the partial determinism of the Greeks. Contemporary physics uncovers meaningful, nonarbitrary patterning at an astonishingly minute range of measurement; the structure of the physical world is almost unimaginably exact, both as to what things are and how things happen. The irony in the situation is that indeterminacy does show up, not at the level of gross sense experience, where the Greeks expected it to be, but at the most fundamental level of reality. The world described by the quantum theory presents us with a strictly causal, utterly unambiguous structure paradoxically built upon a basis that is quite "unreal," in the sense of Plato or Parmenides. As we cross a certain threshold of measurement, quantitative precision becomes impracticable in principle. But this reflects something more than the inadequacy of our tools of measurement. Below this threshhold "the things themselves" cease to *be* themselves determinately, and cease to behave in causally predictable ways. The laws of the quantum realm determine the character of events only to the extent of forbidding certain kinds of events to happen, while assigning relative degrees of probability to others. What actually takes place in a given instance is, within these limits, simply up to chance. Moreover, except in the context of an interaction capable of determining (in the sense of "finding out") what actually took place, there appears to be no uniquely factual event, no definite "actuality" at all. Quantum physics describes the microcosm as a coexistence of more and less probable "virtual" or potential objects, states, and events. This spread of potentialities gets narrowed down to something approaching determinate actuality only when and to the extent that a determining interaction takes place— "determining" now *both* in the sense of measuring and finding out what is there, and in the sense of making what is there *be* some definite thing in some definite state. (Whether such "determining interactions" take place only when we make an actual observation of a system, or whether they occur all the time in nature apart from the activity of observers, is one of the remarkable issues debated today; fortunately it is not an issue we need consider here.)

The ancient Greeks, then, were doubly mistaken; first in believing the groundwork of the cosmos to be absolutely determinate, and second in believing that without an absolutely determinate groundwork, the cosmos could not be determinate or intelligible at all. Somehow an extremely well-ordered and predictable, quite definite reality does exist on the basis of the indeterminacy of the quantum realm, and the laws of that realm, limited as they are, do enable us to account for phenomena within the more familiar ranges of measurement more comprehensively and with far greater precision than has ever before been possible. In other words, the traditional procedure of causal explanation still works, and works far better than its inventors ever expected it to. The problem is only that it does not lead us back to something we can consider ultimately intelligible "in itself," something strikingly simple and transparently logical. The problem is, in fact, that the foundation in terms of which all phenomena can be explained itself calls for explanation; the thing that makes everything else make sense does not make sense itself. It refuses to be knowable in the way we traditionally expect it to be, as something absolutely and intrinsically determinate. But there may be other ways of making sense, even scientific sense. We do not explain the phenomenon of life or the morphology of an organism either by recourse to causal determinism or by appeal to the determinate, intuitively knowable identity of Aristotelian genera and species. The strategy of biological explanation is very different from the strategy of the ancients, still operative today in the field of physics. But to see its relevance to the quantum problem we must pass through several stages of argument, beginning with the link between determinacy and time.

It is arguable that virtually all the peculiarities of the quantum realm can be traced back to the one crucial fact first uncovered by Max Planck, which historically gave rise to the quantum theory—the fact that nothing takes place in nature *continuously*. All transitions between states, all forms of interaction occur by way of discrete "unit happenings" in which single quanta of energy, momentum, spin, and so on, are exchanged. This graininess of happening is the reason why, on the one hand, measurements cannot be made indefinitely precise; it is also apparently the reason why the things that exist in the quantum realm cannot *be* what they are with indefinite precision. To have a certain mass, for example, means to be accelerated in a certain way in interaction with other bodies; but if this interaction does not take place smoothly and continuously, then the quantity of mass a body possesses can be only approximate. By the same token, causally determinative laws can be only approximate. It is simply meaningless to speak of the path of a body, its mass or anything else about it "in between" these discontinuous interaction events. Only at a sufficiently gross level of measurement, where so many discrete events are involved that a process can appear to take place continuously, do classical concepts have unambiguous meaning. Essentially the universe consists of a complex patterning of individual "atoms" of occurrence, stitched together somehow to make up what appear as waves and particles moving through space and time according to certain laws of physics.

Now the idea of "happening," even in this strange and primitive form, has something fundamentally *temporal* about it. But we cannot conceive quantum events in terms of the classical conception of time, because unlike the continuous events of classical physics they have no temporal duration. Nor, on the other hand, can we conceive them as "point events" taking place instantaneously, since they have no precisely determinate location in space-time. The traditional idea of time as a continuum—that is, as a continuous sequence of instants—simply does not fit the temporal nature of the quantum realm, composed of units that are neither continuous with one another nor instantaneous in themselves. But at this point it may be well to recall how questionable, from a logical standpoint, the continuum concept is. As strange as the notion of a web of quantum events may be, can it be any more paradoxical than the notion of something continuous that is nevertheless made up of durationless moments? Zeno's paradox of the flying arrow which must nevertheless be "at rest" at each point along its path nicely illustrates the forced combination of static and dynamic concepts taken for granted by the Western mind for so many centuries. This combination, however, was not at all arbitrarily fixed upon; it is inherent in the ontology of a determinate world.

Determinacy in the causal sense certainly seems to imply continuity of happening in time, and therefore the continuity of time itself. The state of things at any moment must be directly accountable in terms of the state of things in the previous moment, with no intervening gap to break the temporal chain of connection. A discontinuous change appears impossible to account for in terms of a causal principle that does *not* change, that applies equally at all times and places. Whether we think of something like the classical law of gravitation, or of some sort of substance that remains substantially the same while undergoing superficial change, or of the self-identity of a particle continuously being itself while moving in relation to other particles—in each case the constant, changeless element operates to make change continuous. If a particle is here, and then suddenly, discontinuously elsewhere, our sense of it as a self-identical entity breaks down. So determinacy implies continuity in time, both for the sake of causal connectedness and for the sake of ongoing self-identity; but it equally implies the instantaneity of time. If time were pure "flow," in the sense perhaps intended by Heraclitus, then nothing could be grasped as being in any determinate "state." We could not speak meaningfully of the distance between two moving bodies, for example, or of the velocity of an accelerating body; all the dynamic laws of classical physics would become incomprehensible, since they all depend on such notions as the position or momentum of an object "at a given instant." Paradoxical as it may be, the continuum concept is undoubtedly profoundly rooted not only in the way we think about the world but in the way the world actually works—above the threshold of quantum indeterminacy.

Obviously, where it is useful and appropriate, we do not want to abandon the classical interpretation of time. But we do need to fit that interpretation into a broader understanding of temporality that can encompass all that we know to exist in the world. Quantum theory points in a particular direction by showing that the most fundamental "building blocks" in the cosmic structure are not entities that maintain a certain identity continuously through time, existing in a certain state at any given instant of time. At least according to one conception of the quantum realm, the fundamental units are elemental events, ontologically prior to every sort of continuously determinate self-sameness, prior even to the continuum structure of time as classically conceived. The traditional ontology treats happening always as some sort of change in or between changelessly self-same beings, in accordance with changeless causal laws, within the changeless framework of space and time. All these aspects of changeless, atemporal identity are given prior to the temporal phenomena of happening. Even the course of change itself is described as a continuous succession of instantaneous states, in each of which the dynamic of existence is "frozen" into atemporal determinacy. What I am aiming at here, on the contrary, is a way of conceiving determinate self-sameness temporally, as a dynamic process that sustains an approximate continuity of identity on the basis of underlying happening, spontaneous and discontinuous, not subject to any timeless law or static definition. As I mentioned above, it is particularly difficult to imagine what this might mean in the context of physics. Even though quantum theory seems to call for a conception of "primordial happening" prior to the self-identical entities "between which" this happening takes place, prior to the determinate space-time frame "within which" it occurs, we simply have no developed conceptual vocabulary for it. Even though quantum theory shows us a determinate order built upon something much less determinately ordered, we find it extremely difficult to imagine how this can be the case. For this reason I suggest we approach the problem analogically, by considering the temporal constitution of order and identity elsewhere in the natural world.

2. *Temporal Identity and Happening at Random*

Let us take as a particularly simple example of temporally constituted identity the orbit of a planet. This is a structure that persists through time, maintaining an essential self-sameness while also perhaps undergoing change—in its period or its shape, for instance.

But in other respects the orbit fails to correspond to the assumptions of the classical ontology, particularly in that it has no instantaneous existence. At any given moment there exists a star and a planet with a certain angular momentum and so forth; but the orbit takes time to exist as such. There is no underlying substance existing constantly from moment to moment, for the very being of the orbit consists in the cyclical recurrence of the planet's motion, i.e., in a certain pattern of happening. Any sort of wave phenomenon exhibits a similar type of identity, constituted by the rhythmic repetition of events. Systems of dynamic equilibrium also belong to this category—the structure of a star, for example, balancing the infall of matter with the outflow of energy—and are also characteristically subject to cyclical fluctuations. In all such cases we can distinguish two levels of change or happening: that which constitutes the ongoing self-sameness of the system itself, and that which impinges on this system from without, whether to bring about a temporary perturbation, a permanent alteration, or even the complete disruption of the system's self-recurrence.

At the very least then, our ontological understanding should make room for two kinds of self-identical being. Besides classical entities that subsist beneath the flux of happening, in apparently timeless constancy, there are also entities that arise spontaneously on the basis of this flux, wherever events happen to fall into rhythmic cycles or homeostatic equilibria between opposing dynamic tendencies. The evolution of time and temporal identity does not end here, however. With the appearance of this second kind of being, and in the interaction between such self-recurrent systems and the rest of the world, the possibilities of change are also raised to a new level, as just mentioned. With regard to the classical kind of identity only, there is no such thing as coming-into-being or going-out-of-being. A stone may be worn away by wind and water, but its ultimate constituent atoms are (we presume) immortal. On the other hand, something like a planetary orbit can certainly come into existence in the course of the random motion of bodies through space, and can just as well cease to exist altogether. From the classical viewpoint this is justification for treating such entities as "not really real"; as epiphenomena of no ontological significance. In fact, however, this new and more radical level of change can give rise—again spontaneously, in the course of random events—to yet another kind of temporal identity, the kind that belongs to living beings.

Considered individually, living organisms are essentially beings of the same type we have just been discussing—made of vast numbers of interlinked cycles of molecular interaction, maintaining homeostatic equilibrium simultaneously at many levels of organization. They are, however, incomparably more complex than any nonanimate self-recurrent system; and this greater complexity is of course made possible by the fact that each individual organism does not have to come into existence by chance in the random interplay of atoms and molecules. The complex structure of the organism is reproduced from generation to generation—in other words, the characteristic structure of living things is that of a self-reproducing self-recurrent system. It is a type of self-identity that subsists on the basis of the coming-into-being and going-out-of-being of individual organisms; and one that can arise by chance, though only under very special circumstances, when a chance disruption of some relatively simple cyclical system of molecular interaction happens to give rise to two or more similar systems. As long as this process of replication continues, it not only preserves the self-identical structure of the species beyond the death of any individual organism; it also makes possible the new level of change we call biological evolution. Over time random variation, coupled with different rates of coming-into-being and going-out-of-being on the part of the variant strains, tends to improvement in the structural form that is reproduced from generation to generation—improvement in its internal coordination and stability, in its reproductive capability, and in its adaptation to the environment.

Is there still another kind of temporal identity constituted on the basis of this sort of change? As a great variety of distinct species emerge and interact, competing for environmental resources and also adapting to one another's presence in the common environment, they give rise to increasingly complex structures of interdependence, sometimes called "ecosystems," that possess a unique sort of integrity, subsisting on the basis of the development and extinction of individual species. Their self-identity is even more fundamentally dynamic than the evolutionary self-identity of a species for at any given point the transformation of the structural form of a species is always directed by adaptation to an existing environment. That is, evolution at the species level is essentially "conservative," operating only to ward off threats to the survival of the species. Ecological evolution, in contrast, is profoundly "progressive": by constantly changing the nature of the environment to which each particular species is adapting, it places a premium on the speed and flexibility of the evolutionary process itself. Species survival comes to depend not merely on adjusting to a fixed set of constraints, but on a capacity to generate variation for natural selection to operate on, so that the species can continue to evolve at least as rapidly as its potential competitors. This seems to be the major reason, for example, for the widespread success of sexual reproduction. The ecological dynamic, promoting the evolution of the evolutionary process, tends also to develop the capacities with a wide range of potential usefulness, such as locomotion, a central nervous system and sensory apparatus, or the social coordination of behavior among individual organisms. It likewise encourages flexibility of response and the capacity for learning, so that individual organisms can adapt to new conditions behaviorally while their species structure adapts genetically. So again we find the emergence of a new level of temporal identity fostering a change in the nature of change, or making possible a new level of happening.

We have so far surveyed three kinds or levels of temporally constituted identity, i.e., modes of being that "take time" to exist, instead of subsisting as constantly self-same from moment to moment. A simple cyclical pattern of recurrence is not definable in a space of time less than its full period. In biological forms we see many such cyclical patterns connected together in a higher-level identity of species, the characteristic evolutionary structure of which can only be observed and defined over the course of many generations. And the temporal identity of ecological systems, composed of many interlinked evolutionary destinies on the part of many species, is still further from being graspable as something present "in the here and now." At each step we have moved further away from the concrete, tangible, continuously present objects envisioned in the classical ontology, capable of existing in a definite "state" at any given instant in time. Yet waves, orbits and dynamic equilibria, biological species and ecological systems are not merely mental constructs, not abstractions from "what is really there" in terms of the classical ontology, i.e., material objects. They are real and crucially important in the structure of what exists in the world, even though they are not "there" at any point in space and time: without them there would be no stars, no living organisms, and in particular no human beings in the universe.

But let us consider for a moment human beings, and the sort of temporal identity we represent. We noted above that the temporal dynamic of ecological interaction promotes the evolution of evolutionary flexibility. This dynamic is still limited, however, by its basis in genetic reproduction: only what gets built into the genetic makeup of a species by chance mutation can reliably be transmitted from one generation to the next, although transmission via learned behavior does undoubtedly occur here and there among nonhominid species. This is why the emergence of symbolic communication represents a temporal breakthrough of such magnitude, since it enables extremely complex and powerful systems of culturally transmitted meaning to evolve at a rate far surpassing anything taking place in the genetically based sphere of ecology. Here what happens throughout the lifetime of an individual—even what happens from moment to moment, sometimes—can be encoded and interpreted symbolically as a significant piece of the cultural heritage, and so help determine what human beings become. People talk with one another about their experience, and so develop both a public realm of commonly acknowledged fact and private individual realms of conscious awareness. In short, this next step up the ladder of temporal identity suddenly brings us back to a kind of entity—the kind we are ourselves—that exists most concretely here and now, within a continuous flow of instantaneous "present moments" constituting our subjective consciousness. We experience ourselves, in fact, as continuously self-same identities beneath the flux of change that surrounds and pervades us; and we also perceive the rest of the world as composed of constantly subsisting beings, always in some definite state from moment to moment.

Is the classical system of ontological concepts, then, simply an explicit rendering and refinement of the world of human awareness? No, it is something more, for it involves the ontological identification of two modes of being that are only *structurally analogous*: the kind of being we experience subjectively and the kind of being that is supposed to make up objective reality. Let me try to make this point clear, since it is pivotal to my argument concerning quantum physics. The world we subjectively perceive is, in a sense, an illusion. What is going on objectively, in association with the processess of human perception and consciousness generally, is an exceedingly complex babble of neuronal impulses, to some extent causally related to the state of things in the world at large, to some extent spontaneous and random. These impulses are ordered sequentially, also in many superimposed cyclical rhythms, and doubtless also in higher-level temporal patterns we have not yet learned to analyze in the functioning of the nervous system. But we do not consciously perceive any of this. What we perceive, or what we imagine we perceive, are "things" out there in the world, and also "ourselves" here in our bodies. Somehow the crazy semi-spontaneous crosstalk taking place among the trillion individual neurons of the brain gives rise to an experienced order of self-identical objects in space and time—an order incomparably simpler and more clearly delineated than the substrate of cerebral happening that underlies it. Now this experienced order of things, this "subjective illusion," is obviously very much like the real physical order of things in our immediate environment, a likeness both of general structure and specific detail. It is not difficult to understand why our mental "picture" of the world should have evolved to be as closely analogous to the objective reality around us as it could manage to be. Nevertheless, it is still only analogous: there is nothing in the physical world, for example, corresponding to the self-identical "I" of our inner experience. We construct this psychical identity by analogy to the continuous self-sameness of physical objects; we confuse the subjective experience of living through a continuous series of "nows" with the objective reality of objects subsisting through the classical continuum of instants. And the classical ontology is based upon this confusion between the order of the physical world and the order constituted within our minds, treating them both on the same temporal level, leaving out of account the entire hierarchy of evolved temporal structures that lie between them.

With the evolutionary breakthrough into human consciousness, then, a kind of temporal identity appears that recapitulates the structure of physical self-identity, in its apparently atemporal character. A human "self" and a classical particle are worlds apart; yet unlike the other modes of self-identity discussed above, they are both continuously present from moment to moment, always in some definite state of being, at each moment "fully themselves"—or at least so they seem to be. Perceptual experiments reveal that in fact the structure of conscious awareness is not truly continuous, as we would in any event expect from the discontinuous coding of information in discrete nerve impulses. The basis of awareness is a temporal patterning of unit events, so complexly organized as to give a sense of absolutely constant self-same existence. But if this is the case with the human "self," may it not also be the case with the analogous structure of the classical particle? Quantum theory presents us with an abundance of prima facie evidence to this effect, that the seeming self-sameness of macroscopic objects—indeed the seeming continuity of classical space and time as well—are actually founded on a very complex, multileveled patterning of discrete unit happenings. And this suggests that there may be some way to *explain* the patterning of events in the quantum realm, by analogy to our understanding of the multiple levels of temporal structure described above.

3. *The Evolution of Determinacy*

Certainly the evolutionary hierarchy we have been discussing constitutes an intelligible order, even though it is by no means fixed and given, independent of time and history, like the sort of intelligible order we have traditionally sought at the basis of the physical universe. It is intelligible, not because it is absolutely simple, definite, and logically transparent, but because we can understand *how it comes about*, historically, through the random interplay of randomly generated forms. Given the basic laws of physics and the basic elements of the physical world, at the classical level, it is easy to see how such things as waves and orbits can arise. The leap from this level to that of biological self-reproduction is extremely improbable, statistically, and correspondingly difficult to imagine; yet we know roughly how it must have occurred, and again once the leap has been made it is easy to understand the evolutionary process that tends to the gradual improvement and complication of living organisms. The next stage, that of ecological "meta-evolution," comes about with no such sudden breakthrough as the natural consequence of ramifying forms of life; while the emergence of human self-identity by way of symbolic communication represents another radical leap, still very little understood today but doubtless comprehensible in principle. Now if the structure of the quantum realm is essentially analogous, we should expect to understand it not by resolving all its phenomena into a single dimension of order, a "unified field theory" for example, but by sorting them out into a hierarchy of levels, each of which should be comprehensible as an opportunistically emergent level of identity coming about on the basis of the random flux of happening at the level beneath. Quantum physics would become a kind of *archaeology* of temporal patterning, in which the task is to establish a demarcation of strata, to recognize which aspects of the pattern of events that constitute the physical world belong to which evolutionary level.

There are certain key questions that must be answered, however, before such an approach can be attempted. One such question is: Where does the evolution of temporal forms *begin*? Another one, closely related, is: *Why* should such an evolutionary process take place; and also, What sort of fundamental presuppositions must we make about the ultimate nature of being, in order to make the evolutionary emergence of the physical universe comprehensible? Finally, how does this process take place at all, if not as something that occurs *in time*, and so presupposing the classical framework of universal, changeless, continuous time as the arena for historical emergence? By way of conclusion I would like to sketch, very briefly, the kind of answer I think might be appropriate to these questions. The key to all of them, I believe, lies in the concept of determinacy, and in taking seriously the possibility that the deepest ground of being is radically *in*determinate.

Suppose that we define the starting point of the evolutionary process simply by revoking the ancient axiom "nihil ex nihilo," a principle designed to guarantee the causal determinacy of all happening. Let us assume rather that in the beginning absolutely anything can happen, or at least that nothing is prohibited; so that we have to begin with a superabundant plenum of spontaneous occurrence, utterly without constraint. But what exactly are these primordial happenings? Unless we introduce some sort of arbitrary structuring principles—for example, an absolute space-time frame, or some other regularity of relation among these events—we can ascribe to them no definite characteristics at all. The most we can say of them is that they are essentially discrete; and we say this solely because we lack any common context or connecting order in terms of which to link them together in any sort of continuity of happening. So this absolute permission for occurrence is also a most effective bar to any *determinate* occurrence. The very lack of a priori constraining principles functions as a powerful constraint, for in such a chaos of unrelated events it appears impossible to define even a minimal degree of self-identical order.

The possibility of evolution on this basis depends, however, on the possibility that some minimal structure *is* after all definable without reference to any context outside itself, or to any a priori ordering principle. For example, it may be that one particular event is capable of providing a universal reference point by which certain other events might be oriented, even in the absence of any prior definition of space-time structure. It has occurred to me that what we call "the expansion of the universe" might in fact be such a universal event, if we conceive it as a single momentary happening encompassing the entire history of the cosmos; for at this very primitive level of temporality duration would have no meaning. Then, within this initial, extremely simple context of definition, another kind of self-defining temporal structure might become possible; providing in turn the basis for a still more complex and determinate order of events. But it is important to recognize that this evolutionary emergence of more and more restrictive definitions of happening *is not itself something that happens*, in some a priori time context. I think we must imagine the process by assuming that all the events that constitute our universe, throughout its entire history, are all "there" in the initial plenum of occurrence, along with indefinitely many other events. Nothing happens, at this primordial level, to pull some of these happenings out and promote them to a state of determinate reality. It is simply that only certain of these spontaneous events happen to form among themselves a determinate pattern of relations; and that for this pattern of related events only those participant events are "real" and significant. To put it another way: the reason all the events we actually observe in the universe are "lawful," fitting into determinate patterns of relation in space and time that we call "laws of physics," is that all events that do *not* do so are ipso facto not determinate events—at least within this universe. To fit into the universal patterning of events *is* to have a determinate place in space and time, and to be determinate as well in whatever respect elemental events may be determinate in this cosmos. Not to fit the patterning is not to be able to have any definite location, not to be able to transmit any definite amount of spin, momentum, or energy. It is interesting that the "virtual events" of quantum theory fall into place very nicely within this scheme, as events that fulfill some of the requisites of determinacy but not all of them, and that therefore occupy a kind of half-way state of being between the definite reality of actually observed events and the complete "unreality" of those events that do not fit the determinative patterns of our universe at all.

It is difficult to tell, at this point, whether the process I am trying to describe really makes sense—or rather, whether our sense of what it means to "make sense" will evolve in this direction. Essentially it amounts to envisioning a deep dimension of history prior to time and temporal happening—something like a step-by-step crystalizing of the cosmos and its temporal dynamic out of a timeless suspension of pure chaotic indeterminate occurrence. The timelessness of this primordial depth is not that of static self-sameness, but of its opposite: too much is going on here, too freely and unrestrainedly, for any time structure to exist as such. So the evolution of time does not mean the setting-in-motion of something still and changeless. It means the self-selection through a sequence of increasingly stringent definitions of a relatively stable, orderly, self-same kind of happening—the kind we observe in the realm of classical, macroscopic physics, the kind of happening that takes place, seemingly at any rate, between constantly self-identical physical particles. These particles are, of course, "illusory," but only in the same sense we ourselves are illusions, identities constituted in the temporality of consciousness. No sort of determinate self-identity is absolutely "real," in the sense of the ancient Greeks. Every being, from so-called elementary particles on up, owes its being to the free play of happening and its remarkable fertility in generating new ways of being a "self."

If something like this speculative approach eventually bears fruit in the interpretation of the quantum underworld, then nature will turn out to be intelligible in a much more radical way than we have traditionally supposed. And its intelligibility will lie precisely in its lack of any absolute, eternally given groundwork of determinate reality, explaining everything but remaining inexplicable itself. We may well be able to understand not only why there exists a well-defined set of universal "timeless" facts and principles, at the level of classical physics, but also why these structures are not absolute, why they break down in peculiar ways in the depths of the microcosm. We may even be able to explain in detail just why *this* particular system of physical principles "works" to constitute a determinate universe—in effect, to account for each element in this system in terms of its function in defining the self-sameness of the whole. Most intriguing of all, an insight gained into the workings of the quantum world might show us a way into the analogous mysteries of mind and brain, explaining something of the underground of our psychic existence.

J. T. Fraser's "Levels of Temporality" as Cognitive Representations

John A. Michon

Summary An interpretive proposition, made and examined in J. T. Fraser's natural philosophy of time, is called the principle of temporal levels.* It maintains that each stable integrative level of the universe manifests a distinct temporality and that these temporalities coexist in a hierarchically nested, dynamic unity.

This paper argues that the hierarchy of temporalities of the principle of temporal levels may be treated as cognitive representations that derive from a fundamental set of subjective interpretations of reality, known in cognitive psychology as worldviews or basic metaphors.

After a sketch of some of the crucial features of Fraser's hierarchical theory of time, the paper discusses two major views of basic metaphors. In particular, it demonstrates that basic metaphors qualify as *interpretation functions* by means of which knowledge about the world is accessed and organized into cognitive representations.

Quantitative relations appropriate to each basic metaphor specify a particular type of measurement scale. If the metaphors are then taken in their temporal context, the temporal levels of Fraser's theory emerge. His five levels of temporality appear to be related to five distinct, canonical scales of measurement. The formal properties of these scales correspond closely to the properties of temporal levels specified in Fraser's natural philosophy of time.

1. Introduction

In this paper I shall discuss the metatheoretical status of J. T. Fraser's theory of time as a "hierarchy of creative conflicts" as it has been proposed in his recent work (particularly Fraser 1975, 1978, 1982). As a descriptive system Fraser's levels of temporality (hereafter referred to as FLT [singular]) has gradually matured and expanded over the past fifteen years. At the same time, Fraser's theoretical and ontological claims have become more explicit. "Time," says Fraser, "had its genesis in the early universe, has been evolving, and remains developmentally open-ended," and—well aware of the fact that this is not an easy view to accept—he continues: "The notion of time as having a natural history is difficult to assimilate with received teachings or even to express in noncontradictory statements. Yet [a] detailed inquiry . . . reveals that the evolutionary character of time is already implicit in the ways time enters physical science in particular and natural science in general" (Fraser 1982, 1).

This is no trivial matter; in fact, Fraser claims a straightforward material status for time.

* This research was supported, in part, by a grant from the Netherlands Organization for the Advancement of Pure Research under project number 15–23–15.

But should we indeed adopt such a realist stance toward time and assume that temporality in its various manifestations derives from the intrinsically temporal properties of matter? Or should we, instead, opt for a constructivist stance by maintaining that temporality is an interpretation of observed phenomena that have no intrinsic temporal structure or perhaps only a rudimentary one (Davies 1981; Michon and Jackson 1984 V, 1985). Unfortunately the epistemological status of FLT is not yet entirely clear, and consequently no unambiguous answer to this question can be derived from it immediately.

However, the least one can admit about FLT as a theoretical structure is that it constitutes a highly complex taxonomy or classification scheme, deriving from the idea that time has too many faces to fit a single descriptive mode such as the conventional time of clock and calendar. The question, then, is whether or not FLT is more than just such a taxonomy. Is it, or does it represent, a genuine theoretical structure in the sense that a mathematical group or a formal grammar or quantum mechanics is a structure? Does it, in other words, have intrinsic rules of operation that determine the explicit forms it can take? And if so, what do such descriptive terms as *hierarchical, stable levels, evolutionary open-ended* imply in that context? In short, is FLT a system that can generate empirically testable hypotheses about the world, and does it therefore qualify as a scientific theory? Or, in terms of the most appropriate metaphor available in this case: What makes FLT tick? Some answers to this question may be found by considering the cognitive roots of FLT.

First, I wish to propose that there is *at least* one domain of discourse in which FLT specifies or instantiates aspects of an implicit but in principle testable theory about the world. This will be achieved by showing, in the first place, that FLT emerges from a more general cognitive basis. The domains of discourse associated with FLT will be seen to constitute a system of basic metaphors or "world models." A basic metaphor, in this context, will be understood as a generative cognitive structure or as a set of symbolic rules that can produce mental representations or concrete "images" of the world. Metaphors in this sense are not just analogies. They behave somewhat like genuine scientific theories and models: they are generative in that they represent or mimic part of reality, the principal difference being that they do not refer *literally* to the objects and relations they represent.

Next it will be argued that the five levels of temporality distinguished within FLT are, in a general way, related to certain types of measurement scales derived from the (abstract) theory of measurement. These scales, moreover, represent the proper level for expressing quantitative relations between the entities within each of the metaphorical domains of discourse under concern.

2. *FLT in Outline*

A detailed exposition of FLT is, of course, beyond the scope of this paper. Fortunately Fraser himself has produced several clear and simple summary statements about what I perceive as the three core concepts of his system: the *levels of temporality*, the corresponding *stable integrative levels of nature*, and the *extended umwelt principle* connecting the other two.

2.1. THE LEVELS OF TEMPORALITY   Fraser distinguishes five separate levels of temporality (e.g., Fraser 1982, 29–31). The first level, *atemporality*, constitutes a kind of baseline: it is characterized by the absence of time as a meaningful attribute of events. It corresponds closely to our concept of chaos, and in an atemporal world, relations between events can be qualified only in terms of coexistence, or simultaneous presence or absence. Only at the second level, *prototemporality*, can temporal order relations between pairs of events be specified in terms of before and after. But prototemporality is a restricted, local form of time. "Disconnected fragments of time" will prevail in a prototemporal universe and "temporal positions may only be determined probabilistically" (ibid., 31). *Eotemporality* is the next higher level in the hierarchy; it is "the time represented by the physicist's *t* in equations usually described as not responding to the direction of time" (ibid., 30). In other words, eotemporality is essentially straightforward Newtonian time: it is metric—even isometric—and it is reversible. It is a mere fourth geometric coordinate having no other intrinsic merit than simplifying the equations of classical dynamics, the domain of discourse comprising the inorganic world of Newtonian mechanics. Although it is possible to specify a kind of zero-point (t_0) in physical time, this point is essentially arbitrary (Davies 1981) and does not have the privileged position of the *now* or *present* which emerges at the next level in FLT, *biotemporality*. For a *present* to exist, the capacity for self-organization is a prerequisite. In biotemporality, the temporality that evolved with life, "the physiological present is the phenomenological witness to the simultaneities of need which must be maintained if the autonomy of a living organism is to be assured" (Fraser 1982, 30). Organisms are, somehow, capable of displaying organized behavior on the basis of reasonably accurate predictions about what is going to happen, which they derive from an internalized model of the environment. The physiological present represents the necessary "tuning" interface between the sequence of outer world events and those in the simulated, inner world (Michon 1978, 1985). This "tuning" is essential for survival. What chance of survival would an organism stand if it were out of tune most, or even some, of the time! Biotemporality is characteristically the time of irreversible processes: the organic world constitutes the principal battlefield against the increase of entropy. Thus biotemporality has a direction, although it has only very vague "beginnings" and "endings." *Nootemporality* finally, in Fraser's conception, is the unique form of time of the human mind: it has the clear present of consciousness of self and definite beginnings and endings. Events retain their singular meaning and position in time relative to each other: someone's identity is uniquely defined by the sequence of events called *personal history*.

Fraser stipulates that the five levels are structurally stable: any conceivable temporal phenomenon *can*, and *can only*, be described in terms of these temporalities.[1] They form a nested hierarchy, which means that a higher level retains all the properties of the levels below. Biotemporality and nootemporality thus offer richer descriptive frameworks than do proto- and eotemporality.

2.2. THE STABLE INTEGRATIVE LEVELS OF NATURE   A second central idea in Fraser's system is the concept of *stable integrative levels of nature*. The phenomenal world partitions "naturally" into five large theoretical domains. "It is postulated that these levels of organization are distinct, stable, and bear a hierarchical, nested relation to each other" (Fraser 1982, 29). "They are successive forms of order that differ in their complexity, organization and relative independence" (Fraser 1978, 21). Physically the stable integrative levels of nature are identified as the domains of special relativity theory, quantum mechanics, general relativity theory, biology, and physiology, and the sciences of mind, knowledge, and society, respectively (Fraser 1982).

Table 1. The Relations between F L T and the Stable Integrative Levels of Nature

Level of Temporality	Temporal Judgment	Stable Integrative Level of Nature (extended umwelt of ...)
Atemporality	Simultaneity	Particles with zero rest mass (photons)
Prototemporality	Order (partial/complete)	Particles with nonzero rest mass
Eotemporality	Duration (distance)	Aggregates of matter
Biotemporality	Now, timing	Organisms
Nootemporality	[Personal] History (beginnings/endings)	Minds

2.3. THE EXTENDED UMWELT PRINCIPLE   The third core concept invoked by Fraser is the "extended umwelt principle." This principle is derived from the concept of *Umwelt* as it was defined by the biologist Jakob Von Uexküll early in this century. Animals, according to Von Uexküll, live in a world that is species-specific and optimally "fit" to their anatomical and physiological apparatus. The umwelt concept appears also valid with respect to knowledge: "whatever is known is known according to the manner of the knower" (Thomas Aquinas; quoted in Fraser 1978, 21). The extended umwelt principle, as proposed by Fraser, is an extension of the umwelt concept to entities in general: not only butterflies, dolphins, and people have their own species-specific universe, but photons, galaxies, and daffodils have one too.

The relevance of the extended umwelt principle is that it expresses the intrinsic relations between the stable integrative levels of nature and the levels of temporality. Table 1 summarizes these relations. (For further details see Fraser 1978, 1982).

In its simplest, fairly trivial interpretation, the extended umwelt principle states that certain phenomena require their own domain of discourse and have no status outside that domain. There is, however, a deeper meaning to the extended umwelt principle which appears to be related to the concept of *intentional system* as defined by Dennett (1978). A system, according to Dennett, is intentional if we can predict its behavior by *ascribing* rationality, opinions, emotions, or intelligence to it. Whether the system "really" possesses those attributes or not is immaterial; the only point is whether the assumption that it is endowed with rationality, intelligence, and so on allows us to correctly predict its behavior to a sufficient extent (ibid., 236–39). In my view the extended umwelt principle should be interpreted in this sense. Thus, photons are *ascribed* the potential to behave rationally in their proper umwelt, that is, in the world of special relativity. This allows physicists to make predictions about their behavior without knowing what photons "really" are or "really " think. If we adopt this intentional stance toward the entities within each stable integrative level of nature and thereby *ascribe* the appropriate temporality to them, we arrive at a position where it essentially does not matter whether or not such an entity "really" possesses a particular "natural" level of temporality. As long as we can validly predict its temporal behavior we cannot falsify our assumptions.

This position, which occupies a central position in contemporary discussions about the metatheoretical foundations of psychology (see e.g., Dennett 1978; Healy 1981; Biro and Shahan 1982; Newell 1982; Michon 1984), implies the explicit introduction of an *observer* into the description of a behaving system (whether photon, galaxy, daffodil, or J. T. Fraser). It also indicates the necessity of clarifying what precisely *is* attributed by the observer to such behaving systems.

Perhaps the approach outlined here may answer such questions as why there are just five levels of temporality and why the properties at each level are what they are. Until now, these questions have remained unanswered. Are the levels of temporality therefore simply to be accepted as contingent matters of fact? In my opinion the answer is *No*, and the remainder of this paper will explain why.

3. *Cognitive Representations: Root Metaphors and World Models*

World model, worldview, root metaphor, and *basic metaphor* are different terms for the same thing: in psychological theory they stand for so-called schemata, abstract cognitive structures that enable intelligent beings to represent and summarize their knowledge of the world in a coherent way. Schemata are rule-based, generative procedures that guide perception, thinking, and action (for an introduction, see Anderson 1980 or Johnson-Laird 1983). Such schemata are necessarily present in any system of "sufficient complexity" (Wonham 1976)—and any definition of "systems of sufficient complexity" is likely to include human beings.

What role do such generative schemata play in the functioning of a complex system such as the human mind, and what epistemological status do they have? This role can be described as providing access to the unbounded field of potential, uninterpreted knowledge that constitutes the environment in which this complex cognitive system—the mind—can operate as an active agent (Newell 1982). The operations of the system can only be performed through representations, namely by generating hypotheses about the effect of certain operations, testing these hypotheses mentally, and subsequently verifying the outcome of these tests by actually executing the operations in the real world. Representations are therefore to be considered as realizations of a body of knowledge. As such they are necessarily approximative: knowledge cannot be embedded exhaustively in a representation. Such a view of knowledge and cognition has undeniably certain Kantian overtones. In particular the conception of knowledge as a cognitive environment faintly echoes Kant's world of the *Ding an sich*. The relation between knowledge as understood here and the cognitive symbolic structure that carries the representation of this knowledge has been adequately summarized by Newell (1982) in the following functional relation:

$$\text{representation} = \text{knowledge} + \text{access}$$

This equation stipulates that there may be many (approximative) symbol structures in which one and the same body of knowledge may be represented. On the other hand, the structural requirements for a representation fulfilled only if an access or interpretation function is defined. The interpretation or access function is an ensemble of rules acting as a filter, but it is an active, self-organizing filter since the rules adapt to the requirements of the environment and to the previous experiences (history) of the subject.

Knowledge as it is defined in this context refers not only to simple facts, but it also includes the underlying (abstract) principles or laws of nature from which these facts derive. Such principles may sometimes take the form of formal, axiomatic scientific theories. Probability theory in its axiomatic form (Kolmogorov), linguistics (Chomsky), and geometrical optics (Luneburg) are examples of such abstract theories. They constitute what is known as *competence theories*, or prescriptive theories. Competence theories are essentially theories without agents. Thus, probability theory is a theory about betting without bettors, linguistics is a theory about language without speakers or listeners, and geometrical optics is a theory of visual perception without perceiver. Only when given a concrete interpretation do such structures come to life: probability, for instance, may be interpreted in terms of relative frequency, as a gamble, or as a "natural cause" (Cohen 1981). Such interpretations are known as *performance* theories.

With knowledge as such we appear to be in a similar position: in principle epistemology constitutes a theory about knowing independent of a knower, while metaphors are interpretations, performance theories of knowing (as, incidentally, are logics [Newell 1982]). Such a view allocates a crucial role to "metaphors" or "world models." It does, however, not require an unusual interpretation of the concept of metaphor. Black (1962), whose epochal *Models and Metaphors* generated most of the recent discussion about metaphorical language, pointed out that the role of metaphor is not that of an analogy, viz., substitution of terms from one domain into another domain or comparison. Metaphors of the kind that are called *generative* allow the use of their "associated implications" or intrinsic meaning for structuring the topic to which they are applied. As Boyd pointed out in a recent discussion of the role of metaphor in scientific theory, "the use of metaphor is one of many devices available to the scientific community to accomplish the task of accommodation of language to the causal structure of the world" (Boyd 1979, 358).

I wish to extend this point of view, by proposing that some metaphors are not accidental but rather derive from structural properties of the human mind. Ultimately this suggests that such basic metaphors cannot just take *any* conceivable form but, instead, constitute a finite number of what may perhaps be called "stable integrative levels of *mind*." Mental structures might, in other words, display considerable morphological stability. This position is, in one form or another, prominent in several modern theories of cognition (e.g., Chomsky 1980; Fodor 1981; Piaget 1977; see also Haroutunian 1983).

3.1. THE MORPHOLOGY OF BASIC METAPHORS   Several authors have attempted to establish a "minimal" set of basic metaphors. Although these attempts were originally not made in the context of the search for rule-based cognitive structures, they have recently become of great importance to the field of cognitive science. The level of intelligence displayed by computers and robots is almost entirely determined by the quality of the world model they maintain, that is, in the terminology used above, by the set of rules that enables them, as agents in a knowledge environment, to organize their "experiences" into coherent representations of the situations in which they operate.

The number of basic metaphors encountered in the literature turns out to be rather limited and fairly consistent among authors. In what follows I shall restrict the discussion to two schemes. One was proposed, quite long ago, by Pepper (1942) and the other much more recently by De Mey (1982).

Pepper, in a book that has recently been gaining new prominence (see e.g., Tyler 1981), distinguished six basic or root metaphors (see table 2).

First of all, according to Pepper, the world may be interpreted in terms of spiritual forces, animistically or mystically, depending on whether (many) individual, personal spirits are

Table 2. Basic Generative Metaphors as Identified by Pepper and De Mey

Cognitive Structure (Generative Metaphor)		Principal Domain of Discourse	Movements and Topics in Science (De Mey)		
Pepper (Root Metaphor)	De Mey (World Model)		Philosophy of Science	Psycholinguistics Artificial Intelligence	Perception Pattern Recognition
Animism	–	Individual personal spirits	–	–	–
Mysticism	–	Absolute spirit	–	–	–
Formism	Monadism	Facts	Positivism	Word-to-word translation	Template matching
Mechanism	Structuralism	Relations	Logical positivism	Syntactical analysis	Feature analysis
Contextualism	Contextualism	Functions	Sciences of science	Indexical expressions	Context analysis
Organicism	Cognitivism	Self-organizing structures	Paradigm theory	World models	Analysis-by-synthesis

postulated as causal agents or one general or one absolute world spirit. Animism and mysticism as root metaphors are essentially prescientific, unlike the four that follow.

Formism, Pepper's third root metaphor is a way of interpreting the facts and relations in the world in terms of items and categories, in classificatory schemes and orderings based on rational principles (e.g., Ramon Lull), or systematic observation of natural phenomena (e.g., Tycho Brahe or Linnaeus).

Mechanism, the next root metaphor, deals with the world in terms of interrelations and interactions between elements conceived as components of a mechanical system. This was the dominant worldview of the eighteenth century and most concisely expressed by the mechanical clock.

Contextualism differs from the mechanistic view by acknowledging the dependence of a system's functioning upon the environment. The exemplary system of contextualism is the thermostat, and the exemplary science is cybernetics.

Organicism, finally, acknowledges the structural and functional interdependence of system and environment. It supposedly accounts for development and learning, recognizes the uniqueness of personal history, and centers on concepts related to self-organization.

Pepper's metaphors were originally not meant to stand in a hierarchical or sequential relation to each other. In the present context, however, I prefer to emphasize the hierarchical character they appear to have at closer inspection. Organicism, for instance, apart from dealing with the generative aspects of structure, must incorporate the feedback principle that is central to contextualism if it is to account for the interrelations among parts of a unified, organismic entity. Contextualism in turn retains the dynamic interactions among components that are central to the mechanistic metaphor, and so on.

De Mey (1982) recently proposed a taxonomy for the "natural" development of scientific theories. Although his is an independent conceptualization, placed in the context of cognitive science, there is a striking correspondence between Pepper's *root metaphors* and De Mey's *world models.* De Mey, however, only deals with structures having formal scientific importance and providing a framework for the philosophy of science and for empirical research in cognitive science, in particular psycholinguistics (artificial intelligence) and pattern recognition (see table 2 for a summary).

Monadism, like Pepper's formism, deals with facts and classification. Philosophically it is disguised as positivism. It is recognizable in the word-to-word translation approach to machine language and in template matching theories of visual perception.

Structuralism, equivalent to mechanism in Pepper's taxonomy, deals with context-independent systems. In philosophy it is represented by logical positivism, and in cognitive science by syntactical analysis and feature analysis.

Contextualism recognizes that science and its objects are influenced by the environment in which they operate, an insight that figures prominently in the "sciences of science" movement, and is also central in the concepts of indexical expression in psycholinguistics, and data-driven processing or context analysis of perceptual information.

Finally, *cognitivism*, the equivalent of Pepper's organicism, is found in Kuhn's paradigm approach to the philosophy of science. According to this view, science is not only influenced by external factors, but at least as much by the (self-organizing) pressures from within the scientific community. Research topics at this level are the world models or root metaphors themselves, as bases for knowledge-based data systems and automatic translation, and for analysis-by-synthesis or "top-down" processing in perception. This point of view recognizes that subjects bring their knowledge and experience to bear upon their perceptions and actions.

As in the previous discussion it should be understood that these worldviews are considered in terms of a hierarchy. They are not necessarily exclusive but the "higher" forms retain aspects of the "lower" ones. Thus, for instance, perception in the cognitivist perspective entails both top-down and bottom-up elements.

Thus we seem to arrive at a set of four "stable" root metaphors, whose prominent characteristic is the fact that they may serve as interpretation functions (or access functions) for a body of uninterpreted knowledge.[2] In other words, we may recognize the basic metaphors as ensembles of theory-constitutive (Boyd 1979) or generative rules that, when applied to a particular domain, will produce representations of reality in terms of certain more or less complex systems ranging, for instance, from a sophisticated, but essentially formist or monadic description of the phyla of life on earth (Margulis and Schwartz 1982) to equally sophisticated but essentially organismic or cognitivistic arguments about self-organization in systems far from thermodynamic equilibrium (Prigogine 1980, e.g., xvii and chap. 9). It should be emphasized, perhaps unnecessarily, that the hierarchical relation stressed in the foregoing discussion does not imply a qualification or disqualification of the scientific value of any of these metaphors: each has its proper own domain.

The choice of interpretation will sometimes be suggested by the nature of the data that are to be accommodated in a particular representation. More often than not, however, this choice will be determined by the needs of the observer, rather than by the entity under concern.

3.2. THE RELATION BETWEEN FLT AND THE BASIC METAPHORS   It is now possible to state the relation between FLT and the basic metaphors described in the previous section. The argument in what follows is that the stable integrative levels of nature as Fraser describes them should be understood as specific representations of knowledge. Each of these stable integrative levels is generated by, or derived from one of the basic metaphors

Table 3. The Relations between Fraser's Levels of Temporality, Pepper's "Root Metaphors" and Corresponding Measurement Structure.*

Level of Temporality	Root Metaphor	Representative System	Measurement Structure	Scale Type
Atemporality	Animism/ mysticism	Magic wand	Elements, wholes	Nominal
Prototemporality	Formism	Library	Monotonic	Ordinal
Eotemporality	Mechanism	Clock	Linear	Interval
Biotemporality	Contextualism	Thermostat	Dedekind Complete	Ratio
Nootemporality	Organicism	Self-organizing system (organism)	Identity	Absolute

* For an explanation of the left three columns see Section 3.2; the right two columns are explained in Section 4.

defined above. The resulting connections are summarized in the first three columns of table 3.

Although in some of Fraser's most recent work—particularly his study on the genesis and evolution of time (1982)—the levels of temporality are presented in a purely physical and therefore seemingly nonmetaphorical context, the theory, in fact, is supposed to deal with the grand total of all phenomena, physical as well as mental. "The temporalities of nature are paradigmatic. Although they may be recognized as emerging in the history of complexifying matter, they may also be identified in the structural organization of the mind" (Fraser 1981, 5). The following two quotations, one dealing with the emotions of participants in the French Revolution and the other taken from a discussion about modern art, may help to illustrate the mental ramifications of FLT.

> The participant becomes an *enfant de la patrie*, a child of the almighty fatherland. His self definition lessens as he turns into an indistinguishable member of the mob whose actions may only be described statistically. Drives appropriate to the bio-, eo- and prototemporal umwelts cathect the mental representation of objects and produce the corresponding temporal feelings: that of the abiding present and/or fragmented time, the eternal *jour de gloire*. The significance of future and past lessens or vanishes. The temporal world of the child emerges into consciousness as a rediscovered reality. (Fraser 1981, 8)

> The following are representative examples from the arts which I have found as inducing, in my experience, the peculiar moods that correspond to hallmarks of temporalities. Aleatory paintings, novels whose pages may be fully exchanged, radio and television programmes put together from unrelated fragments exude the atmosphere of the atemporal and the prototemporal, depending on their degree of incoherence. (Ibid., 20–21)

Analysis of such examples reveals their thoroughly metaphorical character. Following the lead of the second example, for instance, a field full of football players would *exude* the atmosphere of prototemporality, or perhaps eotemporality, or even show the hallmarks of one of the higher temporalities. But we should realize that the choice of temporality depends on those characteristics of the situation that strike the observer most: "chaos for the atemporal; fragmentation for the prototemporal; directionless continuity for the eotemporal; directed continuity for the biotemporal; future-past-present, self *vs.* other, guilt, anxiety, and human freedom for the nootemporal" (ibid., 20).

What actually does strike the observer most depends on his or her ability or willingness to adopt a particular intentional stance toward the event, that is, to recognize a particular extended umwelt. If I am not able to *ascribe* intelligence to what happens in a football stadium (because I do not know the rules of the game), or if I am not willing (because I simply loathe football), I impose temporal chaos or prototemporal fragmentation on the situation. On the other hand, if I am enthusiastic about football I intentionally *ascribe* intelligence and rationality to the players and perhaps even to the team as a whole.

Whatever I ascribe, though, appears to be consistent, not only with the hallmarks of the various levels in FLT, but more generally also with the abstract generative rules of the basic metaphors. If I am ignorant of football, I can only adopt a formist, that is, counting, classifying, and fact-gathering stance toward the game, not capable of seeing the forest for the trees. As a football coach, on the other hand, my generative metaphor will more likely be of an organismic nature, although I may at any time regress to a hierarchically lower worldview.

In short, an extended umwelt, with its corresponding temporality, is to be considered as a particular case of intentionality on the part of the observer who ascribes certain (metaphorically dressed) system properties to that entity. This implies that we may conceive of Fraser's stable integrative levels of nature specified in FLT as cognitive representation, that is, as instantiations of the basic metaphors described before. In this light we are able to understand why on occasion subsuming certain types of events under the appropriate level of temporality may be difficult.

Of course, Fraser is quite aware that the stable integrative levels of nature and the corresponding levels of temporality are necessarily fuzzy at the edges, for instance, when he writes: "The theory of time as conflict assumes that the human mind, beyond displaying its peculiar nootemporal features also subsumes functions that are appropriate to the lower temporal umwelts" (Fraser 1978, 25). But some problems appear to have deeper roots. I shall mention two of them. The first is that many social or psychological attributes or events can only be subsumed under discrete, classificatory schemes: motherhood, for instance, or academic degree obtained, or membership in the International Society for the Study of Time. Although there can be no doubt that these characteristics refer to the biosphere or noosphere, they can of course only be discussed at the formistic, that is, at the prototemporal level. (Actually, the difficulty lies at the core of the relative impenetrability of sociological phenomena for scientific analysis.) With respect to FLT this means that "functions that are appropriate to the lower temporal umwelts" are not necessarily relics of the objects and events that constitute the natural kinds of these lower temporal umwelts but mental or biological properties that have no prototemporal or eotemporal ancestors at all. In other words, the fact that I happen to be a member of said Society is not in the least a consequence of the prototemporal properties of the elementary particles that I consist of, and yet requires a prototemporal description.

The second and more problematic difficulty is that the fuzziness of the various levels of temporality actually works in both directions: not only do lower temporalities appear in higher-level phenomena, but the reverse appears to occur as well. This, in my opinion may create serious problems for an interpretation of FLT as a *physical* theory. At the prototemporal level, for instance, according to Fraser (1982, 29), "temporal positions may only be specified probabilistically." However, if probability density functions are locally defined on the order of (pairs of) events, then the prototemporal character would seem to be automatically lost, simply because these probability functions impose a metric over the whole range of observation points (Thurstone 1927; see also Torgerson 1958). Consequently, genuine prototemporal phenomena may indeed display eotemporal properties, depending on the chosen interpretation!

In this interpretation then, FLT can be considered as a particular—namely, time-oriented—set of cognitive representations derived from, or generated by a well-established, perhaps fundamental set of basic metaphors, and a systematic and consistent test of the "associated implications" (Boyd 1979, 364) of these metaphors in the chosen universe of discourse.

The implications that concern us most in the present discussion pertain to the levels of temporality. We may conceive of a level of temporality as the representation of the proper temporality associated with, and generated by one of the basic metaphors. This implies that part of each basic metaphor is a measurement structure, a necessary or at least preferred way of quantifying relations within the context of that metaphor and of the representations derived from it.

The reason is simply that if metaphors are to qualify as theory-constitutive in a quantitative sense, they must have an internal structure that provides consistency, completeness, intransitivity, internal validity, and so on. The question is, therefore, whether the various temporalities as defined in FLT can be derived from the internal structure of the basic metaphors and, more specifically, from the characteristic measurement structures associated with these metaphors. And, in the second place, we should find out whether these measurement structures do indeed produce a stable and exhaustive set of temporalities. The latter requirement is to be met if we accept Fraser's claims that the five levels of temporality are exhaustive and that mesoforms do not appear often and are unstable if they do.

4. *FLT and Measurement Theory*

4.1. MEASUREMENT AND FORMAL SPACE   The proper frame of reference for answering these questions is suggested by Fraser (1982) in a chapter that focuses on the measurement of time. Time measurement, according to Fraser, is an experiment, a controlled observation. It requires two "clocks" or repetitive processes, one of which is assigned the status of master clock. It also requires two pairs of events—one pair in each process domain, as well as a rule of correspondence.

Within this framework we can conceive of each temporality as a particular *type* of measurement, each one obeying the generic rules set by a formal theory of measurement, but each providing a different interpretation of these rules. Measurement theory, in the terminology of my earlier discussion, is a theory of surveying without a surveyor, and metaphor-specific measurement structures are interpretations of that abstract theory which generate the properties of the various levels of temporality. Measurement is usually defined as the "consistent assignment of numbers to states of an empirical variable" (Torgerson 1958), and we may observe that the more regular of the two processes required by Fraser's definition of time measurement serves essentially the purpose of the required number scale. That process is conceptually treated as true Newtonian time for lack of an absolute reference, and as such it formally has exactly the properties that the number system has in formal measurement.

The systematic assignment of numbers to observed states of the world produces a particular type of representation called *measurement scales*. Because measurement theory is a formal theory, measurement scales are void of empirical content and can, therefore, handle any kind of information including *time*. This, incidentally, refers to one basic tenet of the psychophysics of time, which took form as the "equivalence postulate" in my contribution to the first conference of this Society in 1969 (Michon 1972). If time behaves like any other psychophysical dimension such as brightness, loudness, itch, or sweetness, then the levels of temporality are correctly looked at as *representations* generated by particular measurement structures.

Measurement can be considered as the formal specification of relations between objects and events within any given domain of discourse. But when it comes to the actual interpretation of these formal relations it seems hard to avoid spatial terms. In experimental psychology perceived relations between, for instance, colors, speech sounds, emotions, or facial expressions are frequently expressed in terms of vectors (directions and distances) in formal, multidimensional space. The spatial metaphor is apparently a very powerful means of expressing quantifiable relations.

Temporal relations are no exception to this rule. Clark (1973), Miller and Johnson-Laird (1976), and others have pointed out that expressions for temporal relations are indeed also based largely on spatial terminology. Clark in particular has argued that this is not a coincidence but, on the contrary, refers to the existence of "a thoroughly spatial metaphor, a complex cognitive system that space and time expressions have in common" (Clark 1973, 62). Thus it is not surprising that temporal relations should fit the requirements of the formal space of measurement theory.

4.2. MEASUREMENT SCALES AND FLT We must now show that each of the five temporalities does indeed correspond to an appropriate measurement scale type with its underlying measurement structure. This amounts to imposing a formal structure on FLT from which it must then be shown that (a) five levels of temporality do indeed exhaust the possible forms of time, or nearly so, and that (b) the mutual (hierarchical) relations that characterize FLT do indeed follow from the properties of this structure. Empirically this seems fairly straightforward and in figure 1 a suitable, widely accepted typology of measurement scales is given.

Scales may be classified hierarchically according to whether they are ordered or not, whether distance is defined or not, and whether a zero-point and/or a unit are defined or

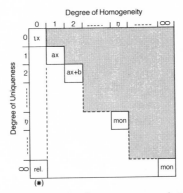

Figure 1. Hierarchy of measurement scale types

not.[3] These distinctions produce a set of five scale types, exactly the number we would need for showing that they do indeed meet the requirements of FLT.

Unfortunately, the classification displayed in figure 1 is based on empirical and ad hoc considerations; scientists have simply found that when numbers are systematically assigned to the states of an empirical variable they hardly ever need to construct a scale type that is not one of these five. Recently, however, Narens (1981) has shown that if we disregard for the moment the unordered nominal scale, the remaining four canonical scale types can also be derived from a rational mathematical argument. Narens's analysis is quite involved and the following paragraphs offer only a bare outline of his arguments.

Scales are generated by measurement structures which can be described in terms of automorphisms. Automorphisms specify what transformations a scale may undergo before it will lose its type-identity and become something different. Thus a nominal, unordered scale may be subjected to any transformation that will leave the identity of the "measured" objects or events unchanged. Postal account numbers, for instance, may be altered without changing the properties of the system. They serve only for individual identification and it suffices that no two distinct accounts have the same number. Ordinal scales, at least the completely ordered ones, will accept any monotonic transformation, including sign reversal. Interval scales preserve relative distance; they are essentially linear metric scales of the type $y = ax + b$ in which both a and b are free parameters. Ratio scales of type $y = ax$ remain invariant only under transformation of the unit parameter a, while their origin is fixed. The absolute scale, $y = \iota x$ finally, accepts only the identity transformation: every point on an absolute scale is fixed.

Narens (1981) was able to show that the automorphisms that characterize the ordered scale types are exhaustively described by two fundamental properties of the underlying measurement structures: uniqueness and homogeneity. The degree of uniqueness of a scale type specifies the number of points that must minimally be determined to see whether two scales are automorphically identical. The degree of homogeneity can loosely be described as specifying the number of points that may be varied together in one scale, without destroying the properties of that scale. Uniqueness and homogeneity may both in principle vary between zero and infinity. It can be shown, however, that the degree of homogeneity can be at most equal to the degree of uniqueness and that, moreover, the degrees of uniqueness and homogeneity must be smaller than 3, except when certain requirements are relaxed. This reduces the number of possible scale types considerably, as is shown in figure 2.

The most important, that is canonical, measurement structures are those that have equal degrees of uniqueness and homogeneity. If both have zero degree, we have an identity structure for which the absolute scale is the proper scale type. Uniqueness and homogeneity both of degree 1 define the so-called Dedekind Complete Structure, which generates ratio scales.[4] Uniqueness and homogeneity both of degree 2 specify the linear structure and the corresponding interval scale. For the monotonic measurement structure which determines ordinal scales, certain requirements need to be relaxed. In the resulting so-called η-uniqueness and η-homogeneity, η stands for the number of distinctly ordered points on the scale and consequently may vary between 2 and infinity. Among the noncanonical scales that can be found below the main diagonal of the diagram in figure 2 are, for instance, scales with an invariant constant. These scales, marked by the asterisk (*) in figure 2, all have zero degree of homogeneity. The best known species of these "funny" scales is found in this category, namely the relativistic addition theorem $x \oplus y = (x + y)/(1 + xy/c^2)$. It is

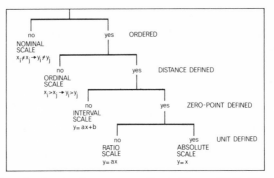

Figure 2. Classification of ordered scale types according to Narens (1981). The *canonical* or *natural* scale types appear on the main diagonal of the diagram, their degrees of homogeneity and uniqueness being equal. Increasing degrees of homogeneity and uniqueness determine the absolute scale ($y = x$), the ratio scale ($y = ax$), and the interval scale ($y = ax + b$), plus any number of ordinal scales (*mon*). The position of the latter on the diagonal depends on the number of elements being scaled. Since the degree of homogeneity is at most equal to the degree of uniqueness, the upper-right half of the matrix is void. In the lower-left half below the main diagonal one will find miscellaneous, spurious, but sometimes important scale types. An example is the addition theorem of relativity theory $x \oplus y = (x + y)/(1 + xy/c^2)$, which is characterized by an invariant constant c (the velocity of light).

an example of a scale that has an important and highly sophisticated meaning, but is not canonical in the sense of this paper; in particular, the relativistic sum $x \oplus y$ will be different for different values of x and y for which the ordinary sum $x + y =$ constant. So much then for Narens's arguments.

It seems appropriate to argue that the scale types which derive from measurement theory show the desired properties that make it possible to relate them to FLT. First, if we include the nominal scale, the number of canonical scale types is precisely the required number, five—no more, no less. These scale types comprise the vast majority of all empirical measurement relations and as such may certainly be called *stable*. The five scale types, moreover, are related hierarchically in the sense that the more highly structured, transformation-resistant types preserve the properties of all lower types. Thus points on an absolute scale are well ordered, while their relative distances as well as their distance to the scale's non-arbitrary zero-point are both meaningful.

It appears that these measurement structures and their associated measurement scales can be mapped in a one-to-one fashion with the levels of temporality distinguished in FLT (see table 3, columns 1, 4, and 5). At the temporal level the possibility of identifying events or classifying them in a categorical fashion is restricted to essentially unordered elements or ensembles. No metric can be imposed at that level. At the prototemporal level the "formism" of time is established, implying that order relations can be established between events, though not necessarily a total ordering. Thus fragmentation, the hallmark of prototemporality, may reign supreme, total ordering being only a limiting case. Eotemporality, the time of classical mechanics, is adequately described by the interval scale of linear measurement structures: both unit of measurement of such a scale and its zero-point, the physicist's t_0, are arbitrarily chosen (Davies 1981). At the biotemporal level the restrictions imposed by ratio scaling acquire an intrinsic meaning: a true zero-point is a necessary prerequisite in the biotemporal Umwelt. Finally nootemporality with its "beginnings and endings" and its recognition of personal history implies that the course of events in human existence is unique: if events would take a different course we would become a different person altogether. Such a temporality requires the particular unique absolute scale derived from the identity structure. Consequently, the measurement structures as defined above do indeed qualify as structures that display the required formal properties of the levels of temporality in Fraser's system.

5. *Conclusions*

Although the preceding discussion does in no way claim that it has covered more than a small part of the implications of FLT, it has shown that Fraser's system can be given at least one consistent interpretation. FLT may be treated as a set of representations generated by a small, and indeed perhaps minimal, set of root metaphors. More specifically the five levels of temporality derive from the measurement structures that seem to be the appropriate relational structures attached to each of these basic metaphors (see table 3).

Metaphors are not just comparative or substitutive images. As many authors have argued (see Ortony 1979) they can also be theory-constitutive, representing "one strategy for the accommodation of language to as yet undiscovered causal features of the world" (Boyd 1979, 364). In this sense FLT appears to describe the many features of the strategies people adopt to cope with a complex temporal reality. One crucial strategy is that of intentionally *ascribing* certain properties to entities in (part of) that reality and then *assuming* that these entities will behave rationally in their umwelt, i.e., in accordance with their given rules (natural laws) and their initial conditions.

Metaphors have particular significance in such a context, because they constitute, once more in Boyd's words, a "nondefinitional mode of reference fixing which is especially well suited to the introduction of terms referring to kinds whose real essences consist of complex relational properties, rather than features of internal constitution" (ibid., 358).

Notes

1. Fraser sometimes introduces yet another level of temporality: sociotemporality or the time of human society and culture. The properties of this level are not very well defined, however, and do not differ very clearly from nootemporality.

2. To this quartet we may then add one, or perhaps two, additional root metaphors which accommodate the *absence* of formal systemic characteristics.

3. The interesting case of partial versus complete ordering will not be discussed here. It would, however, not change the general line of my argument.

4. Narens (1981) deals with the point that strictly speaking the scales deriving from a Dedekind Complete Structure are defined over the positive real number domain, R^+.

References

Anderson, J. R. 1980. *Cognitive psychology and its implications*. San Francisco: Freeman.

Biro, J. I., and R. W. Shahan, eds. 1982. *Mind, brain, and function: Essays in the philosophy of mind*. Brighton, Sussex: Harvester Press.

Black, M. 1962. *Models and metaphors*. Ithaca, N. Y.: Cornell University Press.

Boyd, R. 1979. Metaphor and theory change: What is "metaphor" a metaphor for? In *Metaphor and thought*, ed. A. Ortony, 356–408. Cambridge: Cambridge University Press.

Chomsky, N. 1980. *Rules and representations*. Oxford: Blackwell.

Clark, H. H. 1973. Space, time, semantics, and the child. In *Cognitive development and the acquisition of language*, ed. T. E. Moore, 27–63. New York: Academic Press.

Cohen, L. J. 1981. Can human irrationality be experimentally demonstrated? *Behavioral and Brain Sciences* 4: 317–31.

Davies, P. C. W. 1981. Time and reality. In *Reduction, time and reality: Studies in the philosophy of the natural sciences*, ed. R. Healy, 63–78. Cambridge: Cambridge University Press.

De Mey, M. 1982. *The cognitive paradigm*. Dordrecht: Reidel.

Dennett, D. C. 1978. *Brainstorms: Philosophical essays on mind and psychology*. Hassocks, Sussex: Harvester Press.

Fodor, J. A. 1981. *Representations: Philosophical essays on the foundations of cognitive science*. Brighton, Sussex: Harvester Press.

Fraser, J. T. 1975. *Of time, passion, and knowledge*. New York: Braziller.

———. 1978. *Time as conflict: A scientific and humanistic study*. Basel and Boston: Birkhaeuser.

———. 1981. Temporal levels and reality testing. *International Journal of Psycho-Analysis* 62: 3–26.

———. 1982. *The genesis and evolution of time: A critique of interpretation in physics*. Amherst: University of Massachusetts Press.

Haroutunian, S. 1983. *Equilibrium in the balance: A study of psychological explanation*. New York: Springer.

Healy, R., ed. 1981. *Reduction, time and reality: Studies in the philosophy of the natural sciences*. Cambridge: Cambridge University Press.

Jackson, J. L. 1985. Is the processing of temporal information automatic or controlled? In *Time, mind, and behavior*. See Michon and Jackson 1985.

Johnson-Laird, P. N. 1983. *Mental models*. Cambridge: Cambridge University Press.

Margulis, L., and K. V. Schwartz. 1982 *Five kingdoms: An illustrated guide to the phyla of life on earth*. San Francisco: Freeman.

Michon, J. A. 1972. Processing of temporal information and the cognitive theory of time experience. In *The study of time*, ed. J. T. Fraser, F. C. Haber, and G. H. Mueller, 242–58. New York: Springer-Verlag.

———. 1978. The making of the present: A tutorial review. In *Attention and Performance VII*, ed. J. Requin, 89–111. Hillsdale, N. J.: Erlbaum.

———. 1984. Tijdbeleving en tijdbegrip. *Intermediair* 20 (13): 33–37. (Also to be published in G. A. M. Kempen and C. Sprangers, eds., *Kennis, Mens en Computer*, Amsterdam: Intermediair, 1984.)

———. 1985. The compleat time experiencer. In *Time, mind, and behavior*. See Michon and Jackson 1985.

Michon, J. A., and J. L. Jackson. 1984. Attentional effort and cognitive strategies in the processing of temporal information. In *Timing and time perception*, ed. J. Gibbon and L. Allen. *Annals of the New York Academy of Science* 423: 298–321.

———. 1985. *Time, mind, and behavior*. Heidelberg: Springer-Verlag.

Miller, G. A., and P. N. Johnson-Laird. 1976. *Language and perception*. Campbridge: Cambridge University Press.

Narens, L. 1981. On the scales of measurement. *Journal of Mathematical Psychology* 24: 249–75.

Newell, A. 1982. The knowledge level. *Artificial intelligence* 18: 87–127

Ortony, A., ed. 1979. *Metaphor and thought*. Cambridge: Cambridge University Press.

Pepper, S. C. 1942. *World hypotheses: A study in evidence*. Berkeley: University of California Press.

Piaget, J. 1977. *The development of thought: Equilibration of cognitive structures*. New York: Viking Press.

Prigogine, I. 1980. *From being to becoming: Time and complexity in the physical sciences*. San Francisco: Freeman.

Thurstone, L. L. 1927. A law of comparative judgment. *Psychological Review* 34: 273–86.

Torgerson, W. S. 1958. *Theory and methods of scaling*. New York: Wiley.

Tyler, L. E. 1981. More stately mansions: Psychology extends its boundaries. *Annual Review of Psychology* 32: 1–20.

Underwood, B. J., and R. A. Malmi. 1978. An evaluation of measures used in studying temporal codes for words within a list. *Journal of Verbal Learning and Verbal Behavior* 17: 279–93.

Wonham, W. M. 1976. Towards an abstract internal model principle. *IEEE Transactions on Systems, Man, and Cybernetics* 6: 735–40.

Part II

The Non-Chinese World

Introduction

Through selected topics from non-Chinese thought and literature, this part addresses the intricate relationships that tie the notion and experience of time to social structures and to different modes of knowing.

Denis Corish seeks to identify, in the witness of Greek language and intellectual labor, the metamorphosis of the concrete experience of time into the abstract idea of time which came to infuse Western thought.

Francis C. Haber suggests that certain time-related value judgments, fostered by Christianity, entered into the promotion of early modern science and technology.

The increasing consciousness of time, tied to the idea of unlimited progress, came under attack after the English horological revolution, in the view of Samuel L. Macey. First represented by the literary-political struggles between the Ancients and the Moderns, a body of belief was born that saw in uncontrolled growth more social evil than virtue.

Anindita Niyogi Balslev maintains that the notion of cyclic time, perceived by Western scholars in Indian philosophy, is an unwarranted generalization from patterns of cosmic recurrence, present in Indian thought.

We learn from Ruth M. Stone that African music tends to emphasize qualitative notions of time as distinct from the linear, calculated progress exemplified by Western music.

With Jonathan Kramer we return to Europe, to examine European music in terms of the distinction between two conceptual extremes in the nature of musical time: linearity and nonlinearity.

J. T. F.

The Emergence of Time: A Study in the Origins of Western Thought

Denis Corish

Summary   In early Greek literature time is represented in terms of temporal experience. The word *time*, χρόνος, always signifies for Homer and Hesiod a *length* of time. The poet Pindar was the first Greek to use *time* to signify an instant as well. From Homer to Aristotle time gradually emerges from the realm of concrete experiential description to become an abstract entity that can be discussed in terms of its own properties. It is possible to trace some stages of this emergence—for example, Pherecydes and other sixth-century writers personified time, and Parmenides used expressly temporal argument. The emergence of time as an abstract entity, the "abstractification" of time was not the work of a single thinker or school. It appears to have been a gradual expression, through the medium of many minds, of the genius of the Greek language itself.

What I want this paper to convey is some notion of how time became transformed for the early Greeks from an experience or group of experiences to an abstract object to be studied scientifically. Time was made into an abstract entity, became abstractified. Time started out as an experience, or rather as a multiplicity of experiences; at first, it did not exist as a single entity with a single name. But that group of experiences coalesced into that entity with that name—or rather, that name became singled out as the name for that group of entities. Indeed not only did *time* become a label, a general term, in the course of that process; it also, by that same process, became an entity to be studied in its own right, in terms of its own properties. Time, as opposed to temporal experiences, which had always existed, was gradually discovered.

I am using the emerging discovery of time as an example of the growth of scientific thinking, of the growth of the scientific mind, in the West. The example is a particularly apt one for our Society—but I must begin by saying something in general about that early growth of scientific thinking so that the example can do its proper work.

Bruno Snell says in *The Discovery of the Mind* that "European thinking begins with the Greeks. They have made it what it is: our only way of thinking; its authority, in the Western world, is undisputed."[1] Snell is certainly right. There were influences on the Greeks themselves, Egyptian and Babylonian, for example. And there were non-Greek additions vital to Western thought, for instance the Indian mathematical inventions of place notation and the number zero. There were also genuinely modern, non-Greek sciences, such as dynamics. But there is no doubt that the original Western formative force of that knowledge we call scientific is Greek. The influence felt at the beginnings of specifically modern

Western science, in the Middle Ages and the Renaissance, is more Greek than anything else—though we owe an incalculable debt to Islam for the presentation, growth, and transmission of that influence.

The Greeks invented science—as opposed to art or technology, which both go back to the beginnings of the human race, or even, in the case of technology, beyond that. Technology is in essence knowledge of technique, knowledge of how to do or make things. It may be organized knowledge; it may be very elaborate; it may even, as in our own day, be scientific in the sense of depending upon a scientific view—a Newtonian dynamics or a post-Newtonian theory of energy. But the purpose to which such knowledge answers is practical. In this essential respect modern scientific technology is not different from primitive technologies of hunting or gathering, of farming or making war. And such technologies go back far beyond anything we can call Western science, and existed sometimes in a very elaborately developed state (consider, for example, the bronze-casting technology of China, c. 1500 B.C., or the building technology of the Egyptians or of the Aztecs).

Art is to be found in one form or another among all human races, and it too goes back much further than any activity that can be called scientific. In Greece itself, Homer, the great artist, appeared before any of the great scientific thinkers, or, indeed, before any scientific thinker at all.

What was it, then, that occurred in historical Greece and that is to be deemed scientific rather than technological or artistic? The obvious answer is that what occurred was organized abstract knowledge—geometry, let us say, rather than the rule-of-thumb land-measuring practices of the Egyptians, algebra rather than the computations of the Babylonians, metaphysics rather than the myths of Homer or Hesiod. But what makes the difference; what makes something scientific rather than technological or artistic?

Here we can only be descriptive and brief, but that will serve our purpose. The pre-Greek technologies had been concerned with answering specific, practical questions (e.g., "How does one construct a pyramid?"). The adequate answer to such a question was the thing done (the pyramid built). Similarly, in the nonpractical realm, artistic statements (e.g., "Chaos first came to be") were satisfying by their own nature, and they still are, in the sense that our typical reaction to them is to sit back and listen to the statement uncritically. What the Greeks did was to pose a specific question (to that extent, like a technological one), but this question was not in the practical realm, so the answer to it was not something done or made, but a statement (to that extent, like an artistic statement). One question was: "What is everything made of?" and the answer was: "Water." That is, it was a quite specific answer to that question, and not a story. The immediate result was criticism (which is not the typical reaction to a story, or to a successful technical achievement, although in an already scientific society like our own, scientific criticism may go hand in hand with technology).

It is the refinement of knowledge through criticism that typifies the Greeks' scientific spirit, and our own. With the Greeks the refinement passes beyond criticism itself to the awareness (or should we say invention?) of abstract entities and their existence in (or elaboration into?) ordered schemata of knowledge. We shall speak of the bare emergence of one such entity: time. But first let us continue with the briefest sketch of the whole picture; of what the new critical spirit could, for the satisfaction of its own urgings, prompt or goad the Greek mind into achieving—and in a remarkably short time.

Around 600 B.C., someone (tradition has it that it was Thales of Miletus) proposed that water is the primal stuff of all things. Others immediately began to come forward (we have their names but they are not needed here) to propose other candidates: some sort of boundless chaos, air, fire, also called change, and so on. We have few texts from this period, but it is clear that the proposal of one candidate for primacy meant the rejection of another. It is clear, that is to say, that some sort of critical spirit took hold—and before long it began to extend beyond the question of the primal stuff. Homer and Hesiod were criticized for making the gods seem liars and cheats like men. It began to be suggested that one man's knowledge was not as good as another's; that there was a way of mere opinion held by the many but a more difficult way of truth available to those who would think. And after not much more than two hundred years Socrates, facing his own death for the belief, could say that the life uncriticized was no fit life for a man to live. After less than three hundred years, by the time of the death of Aristotle in 322 B.C., we had many areas of human knowledge mapped out by and for critical examination: geometry and number theory, logic, cosmology, astronomy, physics, biology, psychology, history (considered as a science), metaphysics, ethics, politics, rhetoric, the theory of art. This is what the critical, scientific spirit could do in so short a time.

Snell has suggested that the Greeks "discovered the human mind." He qualifies the statement by saying: "In spite of our statement that the Greeks discovered the intellect we also assert that the discovery was necessary for the intellect to come into existence." This way of thinking "did not come into being until it was discovered; it exists by grace of man's cognizance of himself." [2] What the Greeks discovered, or began to discover—for of course the process has a history and a development—was man's own self-conscious mind. And out of that developing discovery there arose and developed the critical habit and the awareness of the abstract—the entities that come out of, or inhabit, the mind itself.

Now I should like to take one such entity—time—and relate how it developed into discovery; how it came to be through that development.

The early Greeks had no problem with time as an experience, or group of experiences, to be expressed in language—in the tenses of verbs, temporal nouns, adjectives, adverbs, and prepositions. And probably there were no such problems in Indo-European languages earlier than the Greek either. What may be possible, though, is that such specifically temporal expressions got refined into specific form from some cruder primitive utterance. In Otto Jespersen's view of language, the more primitive states of language consisted of elaborate but not very definite expressions, rather like the speech of young children, which had to evolve into more simple and concise utterance. This was against the prevalent theory of Jespersen's day, which had it that language evolved from simple elements that then had to be combined together to form more complex expressions—in which expressions we find traces of older simplicities that we identify as roots. Jespersen held, to the contrary, that "the evolution of language shows a progressive tendency from inseparable irregular conglomerations to freely and regularly combinable short elements." His views here were influenced by the monosyllabic, combinatorial character of such developed languages as Chinese and English. He also saw the more developed languages as being more capable of handling abstractions. "The more advanced a language is," he says,

> the more developed its power of expressing abstract or general ideas. Everywhere language has first attained to expressions for the concrete and special. In accounts of the languages of barbarous races we constantly come across such phrases as these: "The aborigines of Tasmania had no words

representing abstract ideas; for each variety of gum-tree and wattle-tree, etc., they had a name; but they had no equivalent for the expression 'a tree'; neither could they express abstract qualities such as 'hard, soft, warm, cold, long, short, round' ' "; or, The Mohicans have words for cutting various objects, but none to convey *cutting* simply. The Zulus have no word for 'cow' but words for 'red cow,' 'white cow,' etc.[3]

It is not surprising then to find that the common Greek word for time, χρόνος, occurs in Homer not in the abstract sense of *time* but in the more concrete sense of *a length of time*. That is, when Homer uses the word *time* (always, it seems, in a special way, in the accusative case—χρόνον) it is always in some such phrase as "for a time," " for a long time," and never in such an expression as "the first time I saw you," in which *time* would indicate an instant, a point of time and not an interval. (I do not raise here the philosophical question whether there really exists such a thing as a durationless instant. It suffices that there are words—in many languages—that refer to points rather than to intervals of time. For interesting observations on an enduring aesthetic instant, see Frederick Turner, "Space and Time in Chinese Verse," in this volume.) The concept of the instant can be handled, but not by use of the word *time*, χρόνος. In the *Odyssey* when Penelope asks pardon of Odysseus for not welcoming him at first sight, the expression she uses for that instant is the adverbial neuter τὸ πρῶτον, *at first* (which of course, since it is neuter, excludes the possibility that there could be a suppressed masculine accusative, χρόνον)[4]. Also in Hesiod's *Works and Days*, time, χρόνος, again appears to be a length of time, and the word does not occur at all in the *Theogony*.[5] This in spite of the fact that there are all kinds of temporal expressions in both authors, and both deal extensively with temporal narrative—and Hesiod's works may be said to be inherently temporal besides, since they deal with successions of gods, succession of days and seasons, and so on. We have in these early authors all the concrete details of temporal experience but not yet time as an abstract entity.

As Snell points out:

> In Greece the verbal—and that is to say: the intellectual—seeds of scientific language are of a very ancient date. To take one example: we could scarcely imagine the existence of Greek science or Greek philosophy if there had been no definite article. For how could scientific thought get along without such phrases as τὸ ὕδωρ (water), τὸ ψυχρόν (the cold), τὸ νοεῖν (thought)? If the definite article had not permitted the forming of these "abstractions" as we call them, it would have been impossible to develop an abstract concept from an adjective or a verb, or to formulate the universal as a particular.[6]

Such use of the article, Snell says, allows Homer to speak of the present, future, and past, not in quite that abstract way but more concretely, as the things being, the things that will be, and the things being before, τά τ' ἐόντα τά τ' ἐσσόμενα πρό τ' ἐόντα. "The plural number," says Snell, "shows that Homer does not yet 'abstract' permanent being, but merely draws together the sum total of all that is now, and distinguishes it from all that will be."[7]

Another step in the production of the abstract was personification—that is, things that would eventually emerge as abstract entities, such as time, first became gods, such as Time. Snell says:

> Many words which were later regarded as abstracts began their career as mythical names. In Homer, e.g., fear appears as a demon, as the Frightener, the *Phobos*. The extent to which these words were understood as names, even after their mythic connotation had long worn off, is evident from the use of the article. Aeschylus, for one, does not use the article in combination with ... those nouns which, like proper nouns, describe something existing only once, as γῆ, ἥλιος, οὐρανός, σελήνη:

earth, sun, heaven, and moon. . . . Nor does Aeschylus attach the article to abstract nouns. Lessing once observed that in the language of the German 17th-century poet Logau the abstract nouns were, by the omission of the article, given the status of persons. He thought that this was a poetic artifice; in reality the presentation of abstracts as proper nouns had once been the general practice.[8]

Time is not an abstract noun, in the sense in which *temporality* is (and for such abstracts the omission of the article in most contexts is standard practice in English), but *time* is the name of an abstract entity (and it also often appears without the article; note the difference between the expressions *time* and *the time*). Time is not personified in either Homer or Hesiod, but in the sixth century it becomes so; it becomes a god; it begins to become an entity to be noticed in itself. "The idea of time as a divine power occurs, not only in Iranian religion, but in other Greek sixth-century writers as well as, probably, Anaximander."[9]

About the possible Iranian influence in the personification and deification of time, G. S. Kirk says: "Time, χρόνος, as a primary cosmogonical figure may derive from the Iranian hypostatization *Zuran Akarana* (unending time). But this Iranian concept finds its earliest testimony in a late 4th-century B.C. Greek reference, by Eudemus as reported in Damascius, and there is no reason to think that it was formulated as early as the Greek archaic period."[10] M. L. West, on the other hand, thinks that there is reason to believe this. Speaking of the ccurrence of the god Time at Sidon, in Iran, and in India, as well as in sixth-century Greece, he says:

> Time is not personified by other peoples. Personification of months, seasons, etc., is fairly widespread, but time in the abstract appears as a god only in the regions we are considering. In Greece and perhaps in India it appears in the sixth century B.C. In Iran and at Sidon it is established by the fourth century at the latest, and our evidence is so incomplete that there is no difficulty in the idea of its being a couple of centuries older. It appears in all four places in a remarkably similar form. The uniformity is the more remarkable in view of the fact that the progenitor Time appears combined with quite different national traditions: Kala with the Vedic creator Prajapati, Zurvan [Kirk's *Zuran*, above] with Zoroaster's creator Ahura Mazdah, Ulom with the old Semitic wind and water cosmogony.

All this might be evidence in favor of Greece's being the original personifier of time, but West pleads the case that "a period of Iranian influence stands out sharply in the development of Greek thought from c. 550 to c. 480 B.C."[11] The general judgment of his reviewers however seems to be that he has failed to prove his case.[12]

Personified time also appears, also under possible oriental influence, in the so-called Orphic cosmogonies of the Greeks. Whether these are early or late, though, is a matter of much scholarly debate, with the weight of authority coming down generally for the late dating. I have spoken of this in my last paper before this Society, and I refer those interested to that paper.[13]

The earliest Greeks from whom we have personifications of time are Pherecydes of Syros, Solon, the law giver of Athens, the philosopher Anaximander, and, possibly, the philosopher Heraclitus. What Pherecydes has to tell us about time is that it, or rather he, together with the sky god Zas (Zeus) and the earth goddess Chthonie, always existed, ἦσαν ἀεί—the first use of this particular formula, I think.[14] I quote here a directly relevant passage from my previously mentioned paper:

> Pherecydes also evidently identifies [Time] with Kronos, the father of Zeus in what may be called the standard myth, the God who swallows his own children. The great classicial scholar Wilamowitz thought that Time was too abstract a God to be found in the 6th century, and therefore this god

must be identified as Kronos, not Chronos, but many scholars now agree with Werner Jaeger that the identification of Chronos, Time, with Kronos, swallower of his own children, is a "patent bit of etymologizing." ... As G. S. Kirk puts it in *The Presocratic Philosophers*, "χρόνος, which is widely supported in the sources, is almost certainly correct; the other two figures [Zas and Chthonie] are etymologizing variants of well-known theogonical figures, and we naturally anticipate a similar case with the third figure." The abstraction objected to by Wilamowitz need not be of a very high level. As Kirk suggests: "Pherecydes probably took the Kronos of legend, asked himself what the etymology was, and arrived at the obvious answer, Chronos or Time—a familiar and simple concept."[15]

I still think Kirk is right in his general answer to Wilamowitz, but wonder now if he can be altogether right in his reasoning at the end. If we accept Snell's suggestion that personification is a step toward abstraction, which seems reasonable enough, then we can hardly accept Kirk's suggestion that *time* was already available to Pherecydes as "a familiar and simple concept"; it becomes that only later, after the step of personification has been taken and left behind. But it is still possible that some sort of etymologizing went on; that Chronos, who as Time is really a very different, much more abstract sort of god (more abstract than the sky or the earth), became a god by the resemblance of the word to the name of the god Kronos. Wilamowitz had a point—but there are enough other sixth-century instances of the personification of time to make likely enough its personification by Pherecydes too.

One of these personifications is from Solon, who speaks of Earth (some of whose boundary stones he has removed, thus in some sense freeing her) being his witness "in the court of Time," ἐνδίκη χρόνου.[16] Jaeger says of Solon: "throughout his poetry, the thought recurs that injustice can maintain itself only for a brief time and dike always comes sooner or later."[17]

Similarly, the famous fragment from the philosopher Anaximander speaks of things paying for their injustices retribution to each other according to the ordering of time—κατὰ τὴν τοῦ χρόνου τάξιν. Now τάξις is a common Greek word for *order*, so we are tempted to think that τὴν τοῦ χρόνου τάξιν refers simply to the order of time—which would however be an extremely abstract notion to expect from the sixth century B.C. The fact that we have not up to this point found a clear-cut use of χρόνος to indicate time in that kind of abstract sense should make us cautious. Again, the similarity of Anaximander's phrase to Solon's, in which time is clearly personified, should constitute a prima facie case for personification here too. And Theophrastus, the source for the quotation, describes the words themselves as being "rather poetic," which certainly the bare phrase *the order of time* is not. Kirk comments: "Theophrastus certainly used similar phraseology himself, notably τάξιν τινὰ καὶ χρόνον ὡρισμένον [a certain order and a definite time]. ... But this is very different from the bold personification of τὴν τοῦ χρόνου τάξιν."[18] The χρόνος of Anaximander is very generally considered a personification. The use of the article with the word here is not decisive (Snell's comments above notwithstanding), because the use of the article with proper names, though not invariable, is common in Greek.

The word τάξις here, as Charles Kahn points out, is not attested before Anaximander[19]— which again should warn us not to take the passage too abstractly. Jaeger gives us a translation of τάξις more likely than mere "order":

From our Greek text-books, it is true, we learn that τάξις means 'order', and so Diels understands it in this passage [of Anaximander's]. But in Greek we say the judge τάττει δίκην [ordains justice] or τάττει ζημίαν [ordains a fine] or τιμωρίαν [retribution]; for instance, τάττει θάνατον [he ordains death]; that fits the situation best, since it is with the penalty (τίσις) which things have to pay for their ἀδικία [injustice] that the fragment of Anaximander is concerned. τάξις must therefore have the meaning 'ordinance' here and cannot mean order. In this old judicial sense the noun is used by Plat. *Laws* 926b; τάξις is, more generally speaking, every rationing or assessment.[20]

Given the probable personification of time then, and the general atmosphere about the text of court justice, as also in the fragment of Solon, it seems quite reasonable to suppose that Anaximander used the word τάξις, but with the meaning *ordination* or *assessment*, as Kirk gives the translation. There is no reason to suppose that Anaximander had progressed so far in abstraction as to be able to refer more or less casually to the order of time.

It may be that the philosopher Heraclitus also personifies time. There is some question here because the word he uses is not χρόνος but αἰών, which is related to the Latin *aevum* and from which our own *aeon* is derived. The Greek term can mean *lifetime* or simply *life*—and so we only note the personification in Heraclitus and move on. What Heraclitus does show is a strong working consciousness of time, but in concrete, not abstract, terms: in the multiplication of detail in the reiteration of a temporal message (whether that message is one of constant change, as the traditional view has it, or one of a certain stability, is something that the scholars argue about, but we shall not go into it here). Different and again different waters flow;[21] day and night, living and dead, young and old—all things in temporal succession, as well as being opposites—are "the same," for "these things having changed round are those, and those things having changed round again are these ones";[22] the god is day and night winter and summer, ... changing as a fire changes when different incenses are added to it.[23] The opposites also come into a simultaneous (which, of course, is also a temporal) unity, as in the tension of string against frame in the bow or lyre.[24] We are not yet talking of simultaneity as such, that is, in the abstract, or succession as such; we are talking rather of generalizations expressed in terms of instances of succession or simultaneity. Of the fragment: "Cool things warm up, warm cools, moist dries, dry becomes wet,"[25] Kirk says:

> Snell, *Hermes* 61 (1926) 356 ff., strongly contended that these oppositions are not stated in an abstract way, but that the epic words show that here as elsewhere in Heraclitus the connexion between opposites is chiefly deduced from the realm of personal experience. Words which describe the behaviour of things, and which were invented before abstract thought was practised, tend to describe those things in terms of the individual's reactions to them. Thus Heraclitus had himself observed that his body varied between hot and cold, and so on; from this he derived, not a logical principle, but a generalization about the behaviour of *things*, regarded as living entities with the power of self-change. A great deal of this is correct, and especially this warning: 'Gar zu leicht überhören wir, wie sehr seine Worte von dem Erleben ihre Kraft erhalten, und sind immer wieder versucht, seine Gegenüberstellungen als nur logische Gegensätze aufzufassen.'[26]

We have seen that Homer and Hesiod used χρόνον, the accusative case of χρόνος, to indicate a period of time. The poet-philosopher-critic Xenophanes uses the dative case, χρόνῳ, which may be translated *in time*.[27] Such temporal expressions, using the accusative or the dative, become common in the fifth-century historian Herodotus. He also uses the genitive, in phrases such as ὀλίγου χρόνου, *in a short time*, but, more tellingly from our point of view, in χρόνου περιιόντος, *as time came round*, where *time* occurs in a position that in Homer would be filled by something more concrete, such as *the year*.[28] So here we seem to be getting closer to an abstract notion of time—time is being regarded as an entity, like a year or a season, that can come round.

χρόνος in the nominative case occurs in the poet Pindar (who was a generation older than Herodotus) in contexts where it is personified, but with the same sort of lively consciousness of the entity time that is to be found in Shakespeare's sonnets. So Pindar calls Time "the father of all," and "he who alone tests genuine truth." [29] But Pindar also uses χρόνος in the nominative and dative cases to indicate a moment of time, for example in Pythian Ode 12, line 30: ἔσται χρόνος, "there shall be a time [when . . .]—and this, according to Fränkel, is original to Pindar: "Neu ist, und vor Pindar überhaupt noch nicht nachweisbar, die Verwendung von χρόνος für den Zeitpunkt" [The use of χρόνος for the instant is new; it is not at all traceable before Pindar].[30] Homer used the word only for intervals; now it can also be used for instants; the instant as well as the interval is a time; time is becoming an abstract entity.

In speaking of the early period of the history of the concept of time one should mention the Pythagoreans. It is somewhat difficult to date their discoveries because their custom was to attribute all of them to their founder, Pythagoras. Aristotle asserted that the Pythagoreans held that the heaven drew in time, breath, and void from the surrounding infinite; he also asserted that "some" identified time with the sphere of the heaven itself, and these are generally understood to be the Pythagoreans. But we find nothing here to help our particular examination of the emergence of time as an abstract entity. We do however find something helpful when we turn to the philosopher Parmenides—we find an argument being couched in temporal terms.

Parmenides does not talk about time as such; he talks about reality. As is well known, he argues that all that one can truly say about reality is "It is," because anything else, any plurality, any distinction, depends upon the attempted statement "It is not" (in the sense at least that if A is other than B, then A is not B), which attempted statement is unintelligible and not reflective of any genuine state of reality. Parmenides has not come to the point of recognizing theoretically the difference between the negative existential statement "A is not" and the negative nonexistential statement "A is not B," which latter is quite unproblematic. In Parmenides' forbidding as wrong a negative statement form that people had always correctly used we see an instance of abstract, theoretical consideration lagging behind concrete expression. Other, more positive, instances can be seen in the late emergence of the sciences of logic and grammar from the actual logical and grammatical practice of people speaking. And of course our present topic, tracing the emeregence of time as an abstract entity from the temporal experience of people, is witness to yet another instance.

As far as time is concerned, Parmenides argues, in what is one of the earliest real arguments we have anywhere (as opposed, for example, to strong, sometimes strongly critical, declarations, such as one finds in Heraclitus or Xenophanes or Anaximander) that his subject is unbegotten and indestructible. "It was not, nor will it be," he says,

> since it is now, all at once, one continuous. For what kind of origin could you seek for it? How and from what did it grow? "From something which is not" I will not allow you to say or think. For it is not to be said or thought that anything is not. And what need could have made it grow later rather than earlier if it came from nothing? Therefore it must either be completely or not be at all. . . . How could what *is* afterwards perish? How could it become? For if it came into being it *is* not, nor if it sometime is to be. So coming to be is done away with, and passing away unthinkable.[31]

We attend only to the temporal aspects of this subtle argument. Only *Is* is real; *Was* and *Will be* are not. (From this we shall get later on, with Plato, the notion of a present, tenseless eternity, of which time with its tenses is merely an imitation). We are asked: Why should something, if it comes from nothing, appear later rather than earlier? (This argument will reappear in history. Leibniz will use it against Newton's view of time, asserting that in that view there is no sufficient reason why God should create the universe at one time rather than another.) And we are asked: Why should what *is* perish afterwards? We are dealing then with *is*, *was*, and *will be*, with *earlier* and *later*—but we are dealing with them not as reports of experience, as one might find them in Heraclitus, or as elements in experienced-based narration, as one might find them in Homer; we are dealing with them as elements in an argument, elements that draw attention to themselves and their properties, in terms of which the argument proceeds. That argument, according to one view of it, denies the reality of time altogether. But there is no doubt that insofar as it is a temporal argument, it sets temporal entities before the mind as things that can be dealt with in an abstract way. And there is also no doubt that those entities, *Is*, *Was*, *Earlier*, *Later*, are being tied together in a bundle, so to speak. And the name of that bundle, as will be explicitly recognized by Plato and Aristotle, is *time*.

Here we near the end of our quest, and begin to run into too much detail to follow it as we have been doing. When one nears the city the roads become many. Through the arguments of the disciples of Parmenides, Melissus, and Zeno, and through the cosmological views of subsequent philosophers, Empedocles, Anaxagoras, the Atomists, and others, and through the mathematical views of the Pythagoreans, sets of temporal data were handed down until, in the philosophy of Plato, time was ready to be given extended treatment as a scientific subject.

To take our story through the philosophies of Plato and Aristotle would take much longer than the time we have already spent on it. But it should be remarked that in the *Parmenides* of Plato we find, to mention the topics almost at random, some account of time flow, of linear time, of static temporal relationships (of the earlier-later variety), of dynamically changing temporal relationships (of the past-present-future variety), and of the instant. It is clear, as F. M. Cornford remarks, that Aristotle's account of time in the *Physics* owes much to Plato's account in the *Parmenides*.[32] In the *Timaeus* of Plato we get another and different account of time, a cosmological account, where that of the *Parmenides* might be said rather to be concerned with the internal logic of time. And in the *Timaeus* we get the famous depiction of time: "a moving image of eternity . . . moving according to number, while eternity itself rests in unity."[33] Aristotle's definition of time as the "number (or measure) of motion in respect of before and after"[34] certainly owes something to that concept of Plato's in which time moves according to number.

But finally, what we have seen, the transformation of time from a multiplicity of experiences to a single abstract entity to be defined and discussed, to hold the attention of the mind as an object in its own right, was the work of no one mind, school of thought, or even group of people (philosophers, let us say, as opposed to poets or historians), but was, through all those different minds certainly, the work of the Greek language itself.

Notes

1. Bruno Snell, *The Discovery of the Mind: The Greek Origins of European Thought*, trans. T. G. Rosenmeyer (Cambridge: Harvard University Press, 1953), p. v.

2. Ibid., pp. v, vi.

3. Otto Jespersen, *Language: Its Nature, Development and Origin* (New York: W. W. Norton and Co., 1964), p. 429.

4. Homer *Odyssey* 23. 214.

5. Hermann Fränkel, *Wege und Formen frühgriechischen Denkens* (München: C. H. Beck'sche Verlagsbuchhandlung, 1960), p. 10. For a general account of time in the early Greek period see the essay "Die Zeitauffassung in der frühgriechischen Literatur."

6. Snell, *Discovery of the Mind*, pp. 227–28.

7. Ibid., p. 228.

8. Ibid., pp. 230–31.

9. Edward Hussey, *The Presocratics* (London: Gerald Duckworth and Co., 1972), p. 24.

10. G. S. Kirk and J. E. Raven, *The Presocratic Philosophers* (Cambridge: Cambridge University Press, 1969), p. 39.

11. M. L. West, *Early Greek Philosophy and the Orient* (Oxford: Oxford University Press, 1969), pp. 35, 389.

12. See the review by W. J. Verdenius in *Mnemosyne* 32 (1979): 389. Verdenius refers to reviews by G. S. Kirk, *Classical Review*, n.s., 24 (1974): 82–86, and Miroslav Markovich, *Gnomon* 47 (1975): 321–28.

13. Denis Corish, "The Beginning of the Beginning in Western Thought," in *The Study of Time IV*, ed. J. T. Fraser, N. Lawrence, D. Park (New York: Springer-Verlag, 1981), pp. 34–45.

14. Hermann Diels, *Die Fragmente der Vorsokratiker*, 10th ed., ed. with additions by Walther Kranz (Berlin: Weidmannsche Verlagsbuchhandlung, 1960–61). Pherecydes frag. 1.

15. Corish, "The Beginning of the Beginning," pp. 39–40.

16. Solon frag. 24. 3–7 Diehl.

17. Werner Jaeger, *Paideia*, 2d ed. (Oxford: Basil Blackwell, 1945), 1: 144.

18. Kirk and Raven, *Presocratic Philosophers*, p. 118 n. 1.

19. Charles H. Kahn, *Anaximander and the Origins of Greek Cosmology* (New York: Columbia University Press, 1960), p. 170.

20. Werner Jaeger, *The Theology of the Early Greek Philosophers* (Oxford: Oxford University Press, 1947), p. 207 n. 59.

21. Heraclitus frag. 12 Diels-Kranz. I have found it more convenient here and in the following passage to paraphrase rather than quote. The paraphrases have no quotation marks.

22. Heraclitus frag. 88 Diels-Kranz (trans. Kirk).

23. Ibid., frag. 67.

24. Ibid., frag. 51.

25. Ibid., frag. 126.

26. G. S. Kirk, *Heraclitus, the Cosmic Fragments* (Cambridge: Cambridge University Press, 1954), p. 151.

27. Xenophanes frag. 18 Diels-Kranz.

28. See, for example, *Odyssey*, 1. 16: "But when the year came with the revolving of the seasons. . . ."

29. Olympian Ode 2. 17; 10. 53–55.

30. Fränkel, *Wege und Formen*, p. 10.

31. Parmenides frag. 8. 5–22 Diels-Kranz.

32. F. M. Cornford, *Plato and Parmenides* (London: Kegan Paul, 1939), p. 185.

33. Plato *Timaeus* 37d 5–7 (trans. Jowett).

34. Aristotle *Physics* 4. 11. 219b2.

Time, Technology, Religion, and Productivity Values in Early Modern Europe

Francis C. Haber

Summary   This paper is concerned with the emergence of a set of values that supported machine manufacture and increased economic productivity in connection with a tradition in the Christian West of justifying technology on religious grounds.* The tradition took on new importance in the early seventeenth century. Against a prevalent expectation of an impending catastrophic end of time for this world with the advent of the Apocalypse, a group of writers advocated a gradualist redemption of mankind from the damage of the Fall by using the surviving spark of reason to develop the arts and sciences. They argued that this would lead to a better understanding of the works of God, make the earth more fruitful, and benefit mankind. Francis Bacon and a later circle of Baconians centered around Samuel Hartlib were influential in transforming the religious justifications into a utilitarian program, articulating a set of values that emphasized modernization and increased productivity.

The mass production of goods with machinery driven by the natural forces of wind, water, or steam was an essential element in the emergence of industrialism. It is an idea that was developed into a social goal with particular intensity in modern Europe. The practice, however, is very old. Joseph Needham has found ample evidence of the use of water mills for industrial purposes in ancient and medieval China, with striking examples of the use of complex spinning machinery driven by water mills in the production of textiles in the early fourteenth century.[1] He has demonstrated beyond question that the Chinese were incredibly gifted in mechanical inventiveness and that technology found significant support inside and outside the imperial governments. Yet, the Industrial Revolution took place in eighteenth-century England, not in China, despite its technological proficiency. The Romans were producing flour with water mills by the first century B.C. The construction of machines for such mills was described by Vitruvius in his *Ten Books of Architecture* (c. 27 B.C.). The largest industrial complex of the Roman Empire appears to have been at Barbegal, near Arles, and Jean Gimpel estimates that it could produce twenty-five tons of flour a day.[2] However, the Romans did not adopt a policy of extending the mechanization of the production of goods.

Because the Ancients did not take the step toward industrialization, Benjamin Farrington has argued that their science was a "failure." They considered science only as a knowledge of nature, not as the means of power over nature, he said, noting the similar

* Support for this paper was provided by a grant from the General Research Board of the Graduate School of the University of Maryland at College Park.

observation of Francis Bacon and his conclusion that if you make a vestal virgin of science you must not expect her to bear fruit. With a remarkable present-centered and utilitarian arrogance, Farrington stated: "The failure of ancient science was in the use that was made of it. It failed in its social function." His explanation that the Ancients did not apply science to economic production because they relied on "the muscles of slaves" [3] is widely accepted, and there is some evidence for it. However, the "failure" of the Ancients to become like us is not quite so simple. If the experience of trying to develop industrialism in traditional societies is any clue, economic "modernization," among other things, requires the presence of favorable values and attitudes as well as the use of hardware.[4] More than an abundance or scarcity of labor appears to be involved in adopting a policy of mechanization.

In Europe, by the tenth century, perhaps beginning at Roman sites, water mills for powering machine processes were widespread.[5] In the next few centuries the mills were used not only to grind grain; through cams and other devices, they performed hammering operations, drove bellows, and sawed wood. Monastic establishments had an active role in building and operating complex mills. The fulling of cloth was done by machine in the eleventh century. The mechanical processing of textiles was so productive by the thirteenth century that Carus-Wilson called it "an industrial revolution." [6] By the fourteenth century, water mills were being used to produce paper and in the fifteenth century an assortment of other mechanical tasks had been adapted to the mill, such as the making of copper pots and weapons of war, spinning silk, and shaping materials. Windmills were used to drive machinery by the fourteenth century. The invention of the compass and technological improvements in shipbuilding, full-rigged sails, and stern-post rudders made it increasingly possible to harness the wind to drive ocean-going vessels. The inventiveness of the late medieval period was also applied to extending human powers: the labor saving of the spinning wheel, improved vision with spectacles, better timekeeping with the mechanical clock and watch, and greater force on the battlefield with explosives and firearms.[7]

Values favorable to mechanization appear to have been in place early in the European West. Although water mills may have substituted for a scarcity of human labor, it may be presumed that many societies with a scarcity of labor did not turn to mechanized economic production. Conversely, abundance of labor did not deter technological innovation in China.[8] The pervasiveness of the technological bent in the West, so early in evidence and so relentlessly pursued, prompted the economic historian Carlo M. Cipolla to ask: "Why *was* Western Europe so receptive and favorable to change? Why did medieval Europe obsessively dream of mastering nature? Why was it looking for mechanical solutions?" He was not satisfied with the stock answer that invention was "a response to need," since so many of the inventions and uses of machines or gadgets were responses to wants rather than needs. Why they were wanted, even when they were not needed, is part of the problem. "Necessity," he said, "explains nothing; the crucial question is why some groups respond in a particular way to needs or wants which in other groups remain unformulated and unfilled." [9]

Some part of the explanation for this early mechanism in the West must be sought in the area of favorable attitudes, beliefs, and values. In the modern industrial nation, growth in productivity is an article of faith, a measure of economic health, and a criterion of value that permeates the whole fabric of life. Indeed, growth in productivity is often an end in itself that needs no further justification. Economic "modernization" depends upon replacing the authority of tradition and customary ways of the past with an acceptance of innovation and an openness to future change, and thus entails a progressive attitude toward the future. The goal of growth in productivity assumes that the past and the status quo must ever give way to the new and improved, but internalizing this goal meets resistance in traditional societies. How this goal emerged in Europe and provided favorable values for industrialization is complex and poorly documented. In this paper I want to touch upon some aspects of how the social goal of productivity was formulated by writers who espoused the development of the arts and crafts as a means of justifying religious belief and/or realizing future-oriented visions. Interpretations of the meaning of time are intimately involved in the particular expressions of future orientation.

The Church in medieval society had a dominant position in the areas of attitudes, values, and belief, but many matters of belief were subject to debate, ambiguity, and differing interpretation or emphasis. There were, for instance, differences of opinion on the balance that should prevail between the pursuit of the spiritual and the worldly in the goals of life. There has been a powerful mystical and ascetic tradition throughout the history of Christianity opposed to worldly activities, but there has also been a strong tradition defending them. I would like to point to a complex of tenets, what I have termed "technological idealism," used to bridge the eternal and the temporal that gave value to human invention and productivity.

Technological idealism centered on the idea that in the art of "making" things, the hand is guided by a model, or pattern, or design, present in the mind. This anthropomorphic paradigm was projected to the conception of God as Maker, to the world as an artifact of God's making, to a design that God followed in making his works, and to God's purpose in making as the incorporation or incarnation of his eternal ideas in the temporal substance that comprised the world. Some aspects of these ideas were present in the thought of Plato and Aristotle. The Stoics developed out of Platonism the idea of God as Architect who made the world in accordance with a design. Cicero used the example of Archimedes making mechanical celestial globes from a design in his mind as an imitation of divine making. The idea of God as Maker was also set forth in Genesis, and was supported in other texts, several of the psalms, for instance, and the Book of Wisdom (11:21), where it was asserted that God made the world by number, weight, and measure.[10] However, it was St. Augustine who put pagan and biblical sources of technological idealism into a Christian form that exerted an influence that lasted through the seventeenth century.

St. Augustine argued that God made the world *and time* in accordance with a design that was in his mind prior to the act of creation. To St. Augustine God was an activity, not only in creating, but also in sustaining the world, and he criticized Plato for removing God from the created world. He also argued that God revealed himself by his works, as well as by his word in the Holy Scriptures, therefore we must contemplate and admire the handicraft of the Architect of the world. St. Augustine provided a justification for the study of nature as a devout exercise. In his *City of God*, he also made the unfolding of the temporal plan of history a part of God's design. He held that in this temporal plan the godly had to take an active role that involved more than contemplation and prayer, important though they were, and this had been laid down in Genesis 1:26;28: "And God said, Let us make man in our image, after our likeness: and let them have dominion over ... all the earth, ... God said unto them, Be fruitful, and multiply, and replenish the earth, and subdue it: and have dominion over the fish of the sea, and over the fowl of the air, and over every living thing that moveth upon the earth." He put forward God the Architect as model and inspiration for human beings in their making; he gave artisan examples of human making to demonstrate that some small divine spark of reason still remained in mankind after the Fall; and he suggested that God had provided this spark to cope with the fallen condition by using it in the arts and sciences.[11]

The analogy of God as Artisan or Architect was popular in the Middle Ages, and in the fourteenth century, after the invention of the mechanical clock, God was also pictured as the Great Clockmaker.[12] The idea of an architect who makes material things in accordance with a design in his mind, that is, technological idealism, was conspicuous among Augustinians, including St. Bonaventure,[13] Henry of Langenstein,[14] and Nicholas of Cusa.[15] The idea of man imitating God as Maker was used to elevate and justify human creativity and invention in the arts and sciences. The clockwork analogy of divine making was especially apt because a clockmaker had to have a design in mind in order to make and assemble parts to produce a mechanism that would indicate an abstraction like the time of day. In this technological idealism element of Christian thought, the machine was not considered an alien thing and the water-driven machinery in Augustinian monasteries could easily be justified. Technological innovation has, of course, advanced at the hands of artisans without any reference to the world of learning. However, the use of machines and invention in the high culture of the West to illuminate ideas in philosophy and religion, and to justify the ways of God, gave social sanction to the pursuit of mechanical invention. The injunction from Genesis that man should make the earth fruitful was a standing sanction to put the machine to practical productive use. And the tendency in Christianity to think in terms of universal mankind and universal purpose provided a favorable environment for projecting machines and productivity to a cosmic role, rather than just the everyday experience of making ends meet.

The practical potential of Christian technological idealism was drawn out in the more secular environment of the Renaissance. A number of humanists, artists, and artisans rejected the attitude sometimes expressed by the Ancients that the mechanical arts were base and demeaning.[16] Humanists interested in classical science and mathematics argued that mechanics, along with the other arts, was honored in antiquity, even if manual labor was despised. They elaborated the mathematical and mechanical traditions of Archimedes and Vitruvius and tried to recapture the mechanical theory developed by the Ancients. In sixteenth-century Italy the theory and practice of mechanics was also promoted by self-taught engineers, active heads of state, and officials of the Church, and the argument was often made that mechanics was worthy and noble, inseparable from the other higher activities of the human spirit. The brilliant successes of Galileo in mechanics in the early seventeenth century took place in a society that had already put mechanics in a position of high value.

Out of these interests in mechanics and technology a new type of artisan literature emerged in the sixteenth century that was a mixture of the practical manual and a justification for promoting the practical arts. The old arguments of technological idealism were brought to bear in the justifications, and these were given new force among Protestants from supporting comments by Calvin. Jesuits who took up the same arguments could draw on the long-established Augustinian tradition. A strong support in the artisan literature came from the French Calvinist Petrus Ramus (1515–72), who assaulted the authority of the Scholastics and claimed that the artisan was the discoverer of a true knowledge of God's works. William Ames (1576–1633), a Ramist whose works were used as textbooks in New England in the seventeenth century, fully expressed technological idealism in his interpretation of God as the Architect whose art could be imitated in the practical as well as the higher arts.

In the high culture of the seventeenth century, the mechanical traditions were taken over and used as the basis for the idea of technological progress in the literary battle of the Ancients versus the Moderns. At a somewhat lower level, the artisan literature of the sixteenth and seventeenth centuries rehearsed the theological justifications for the pursuit of technology, with supporting citations from the Bible. Ansgar Stöcklein has analyzed about a hundred of those books dealing with machines.[17]

In the prefatory material of the machine books, the authors showed a familiarity with the traditional arguments justifying the pursuit of invention and making. Recurring themes, illustrations, images, and ideas drawn from the Bible were used to show that progress in making machines was in accordance with God's will and example. God was the Great Architect and the Great Mathematician who had made all things by measure, number, and weight. The argument was often repeated in the machine books that man should imitate God as Maker by ordering both his work and his life by measure, number, and weight. It was said that Plato did not recognize that the ideas of geometry should be applied to practical uses and, as a result, in his account of creation by an artificer, he left the world of ideas separated from the world of matter. By contrast, it was claimed, when the biblical God created the world, the ideas of geometry were applied to matter, since God made the world as a machine, and mechanics was applied geometry. One writer said that the union of ideas and matter had higher value than ideas alone, and because this union is complete in mechanics, it is the most honorable of all the arts. Another writer, a disciple of Ramus, said that the creation and maintenance of the world is the carrying on of mechanics, since the world is a machine, and the great Mechanic willed that man imitate him exactly in his proper activity, lending him mind and hand for it. Man is a mechanic because God is, since man is in the likeness of God.[18]

The argument was often made in the machine books that the mechanical art is an extra help for fallen mankind. Through use of mind and hand in the arts and sciences mankind could survive in the hostile postlapsarian world and progress out of the animal condition. Beyond this, however, the idea of toil as punishment was contrasted with working at discovering God's art, which was enjoyable because it offered the possibility of understanding natural things and thereby recovering the lost knowledge of God's works. Although man had limited powers and his originality was dependent upon God, to some degree his having original ideas was like creating out of nothing. One writer claimed that discovery of a useful and necessary thing is a creation by the human understanding, and that discovery in the mechanical arts comes nearest to the work of God.[19] Discovery of the principles of mathematics and the invention and building of ingenious machines were hailed as triumphs of the spirit.

Even the medieval tradition of making a garden as an image of Paradise with natural plants and animals was changed to an image of Paradise in which automatons and mechanisms were used to replace natural things, symbolizing the mechanical art in the creation and man's ability to imitate it. The Fall itself became what A. O. Lovejoy recognized in Milton's *Paradise Lost* as "The Fortunate Fall,"[20] that is that, unfortunate as the Fall was, it was also fortunate because it left man with a desire for knowledge and the possibility of rising to new heights through his own efforts. The machine books used this idea in praising the development of technology. Some claimed that through technology, instead of just restoring the lost Paradise, mankind could make and manage a new Paradise that would surpass the original.[21]

Behind this religious justification of productivity in the late sixteenth and early seventeenth century there was a sense of urgency prevalent in the age about the end of worldly time. The age was preoccupied with time. Ancient theories of cyclical time had been popularized in the Renaissance, and many writers were convinced that they lived in a cycle of the decay of the earth. This bleak prospect was intensified in the Reformation by the widespread expectation that the Kingdom of God was near at hand and would be ushered in with a sudden and violent overthrow of the mundane world. With the Apocalypse and the Second Coming of Christ there would be an end to the time of this world and all the righteous would enter into eternal life.

The Apocalypse, the Millennium, and a New Jerusalem remained prominent in religious consciousness through the seventeenth century. Thomas Burnet in his very popular *Sacred Theory of the Earth* wrote: "He that does not err above a Century in calculating the last period of Time; from what evidence we have at present, hath, in my opinion, cast up his accounts very well. But the Scenes will change fast towards the Evening of this long day, and when the Sun is near setting, they will more easily compute how far he hath to run." [22] A scholarly industry arose from calculating chronology and the conjunctions of heavenly bodies in order to predict the day of the final catastrophe. It was against these prevalent expectations of an impending catastrophic end of worldly time that a group of writers developed a program of technological progress. Step by step, they transformed the vision of the sudden coming of a New Jerusalem, in which the righteous would sit idly at the feet of the Lord, to the vision of the gradual coming of a New Atlantis, in which the godly would be engaged in science, technology, and productive activity. The road to this earthly paradise was the development of the arts and sciences through use of the divine spark left to mankind after the Fall. By this road, man could progressively come to know and admire the works of God and at the same time fulfill the injunction in Genesis to be fruitful, multiply, replenish the earth, and subdue it. For some of the writers, improvement was also an act of atonement, repairing the damage to the earth itself that occurred with the Fall. It was assumed, of course, that God would not bring the world and time to an end as long as we were putting our shoulders to the wheel. The writers thus argued for a gradualist self-redemption, not just through the traditional moral improvement, but also through active participation in bringing to fruition God's injunctions to mankind about care of the earth itself.

Francis Bacon (1561–1626) brought the mechanical tradition into the mainstream of European thought. He presented a program that held out hope for a steady and rapid improvement in human welfare, if science and technology were rationally developed and applied to understanding and mastering nature. He proposed that the slate of tradition should be wiped clean of all error resulting from the "idols" of the mind. Action, invention, utility, and working for posterity were necessary ingredients in his program for progress. Bacon in effect outlined a blueprint of modernization for an industrial society, so it is understandable that he became the patron saint of utilitarians and advocates of material progress down to the twentieth century. Actually, he appears to have been a visionary who wrote within the religious and apocalyptic milieu of his age.[23] The reputation of Bacon has been haunted with charges of opportunism and worse, and it has been easy to assume, especially by the philosophes who made him father of modernity, that he was worldly and his references to Scripture were only concessions to his age. However, the abundant biblical references in his works have a structural place in his philosophy, and this was understood and appreciated by many early readers who took his works at face value. They saw a reformer who wanted to clear away obstacles to a new path toward the redemption of man through the conquest of a natural world that was the divine artifact of God. Bacon's program was based on seeking the revelation offered in the works of God, separately from the revelation given in the word of God in the Holy Scriptures.

Bacon dedicated more than twenty-five years, in office and out, to his *Instauratio Magna*, or *Great Renewal*, aimed at the regeneration of mankind through a New Philosophy. It was never completed, but parts were published: *The Advancement of Learning* (1605), *Novum Organum* (1620), and *De Augmentis Scientiarum* (1623), an expanded version of *The Advancement of Learning*. Not a part of the *Instauratio*, but closely associated with it, was his uncompleted and very popular utopian piece, *The New Atlantis* (1627). In his works Bacon expressed the belief that his own times stood on the threshold of a great restoration and renewal (instauration). He struck a note of urgency about the need to start mankind on a new road, which he expressed in several instances through the use of the prophecy of Daniel in connection with the Pillars of Hercules.

In an early fragment, *Valerius Terminus*, Bacon wrote that all knowledge was a plant of God and its bearing fruit was appointed to the autumn of the world. He said that this was indicated, not only by general providence, but also in the prophecy of Daniel (12:4), "where, speaking of the latter times, it is said, 'Many shall pass to and fro, and science shall be increased;' as if the opening of the world of navigation and commerce, and the further discovery of knowledge, should meet in one time or age." [24] In the *Novum Organum*, the frontispiece shows a ship, flying a banner bearing the words from the prophecy of Daniel, sailing out between the Pillars of Hercules. The pillars signified the restraints that had been placed on the advancement of learning. Bacon thought that Columbus had fulfilled the first part, the "to and fro," of the prophecy of Daniel by sailing through them, and that this was the sign of a turn in history. In the text, arguing that in all divine works the smallest beginnings lead to some result, he said the prophecy of Daniel plainly hinted "that Fate (which is Providence) would cause the complete circuit of the globe, (now accomplished, or at least going forward by means of so many distant voyages,) and the increase of learning, to happen at the same epoch." [25] In connection with the voyages, he wrote: "It would indeed be dishonourable to mankind, if the regions of the material globe, the earth, the sea, and stars should be so prodigiously developed and illustrated in our age, and yet the boundaries of the intellectual globe should be confined to the narrow discoveries of the ancients." [26]

The Pillars of Hercules metaphor was used by Bacon not only as a promise of progress in his own times, but also as an indictment of the past. In the *Advancement* he asked why a few received authors should stand up like the columns of Hercules, beyond which there should be no sailing or discovering.[27] In the *Novum Organum*, after complaining that men do not attempt anything new, he wrote, "The sciences have thus their own pillars, fixed as it were by fate, since men are not roused to penetrate beyond them either by zeal or hope." [28] It was with this sense of the autumn days of the world that Bacon hoped to provide the key to fulfilling the second part of the prophecy of Daniel about the increase of knowledge.

The apocalyptic sense of a great turning can be seen throughout Bacon's works. In the early *Valerius Terminus* Bacon distinguished between two kinds of knowledge in Paradise, the evil kind of ambition toward divine powers, which led to the Fall, and the good kind of contemplation of the works of God.[29] The latter also provided the necessary knowledge of nature for human well-being after the Fall. Bacon elaborated this idea in the *Advancement*, claiming that there was no restraint on pursuing knowledge of secondary causes, since the original temptation that led to the Fall was the aspiring for moral knowledge of good and evil, not natural knowledge. At the conclusion of the *Novum Organum* Bacon wrote:

> For, man, by the Fall, lost at once his state of innocence and his empire over creation, both of which can be partially recovered, even in this life, the first by religion and faith, the second by the arts and sciences. For creation did not become entirely and utterly rebellious by the curse; but in consequence of the divine decree, "In the sweat of thy brow shalt thou eat bread," she is compelled by our labours, (not assuredly by our disputes or magical ceremonies,) at length, to afford mankind, in some degree, his bread, that is to say, to supply man's daily wants.[30]

Bacon said that man's recovery by means of the arts and sciences of the sovereignty and power that he had in his first state of creation must extend from the discovery of all operations and possibilities of operations of the immortal works of God down to the meanest mechanical practice. If man would restore his kingdom, he must use his mind for discovering, imitating, and adapting the principles upon which God's works operated. This knowledge could only come by the sweat of the brow. It was not a knowledge for our pleasure, but for "fruit or generation." [31] The task of gaining this knowledge, however, was doubly difficult. First, the inner spark of reason had been dimmed by the Fall so that now a knowledge of nature is largely dependent upon the senses. Second, "the mirror of the mind is no longer a clear and polished surface for receiving the true rays of things, and we must seek a remedy for this also." [32]

Because the mirror of the mind was dimmed, Bacon thought that the understanding became prepossessed with false idols. These must be cleansed away and the mind purified so that the natural light from God's works can be seen clearly. When this has been done, Bacon said, "and it has at last been clearly seen, what results are to be expected from the nature of things and the nature of mind, we consider that we shall have prepared and adorned a nuptial couch for the mind and the universe; the divine goodness being our bridesmaid." [33]

Holding that the true source of natural knowledge can only come from the works of God, Bacon said that we must fix our mind's eye steadily in order to receive their images exactly as they exist. Then, with God's kindness, we can have "a revelation and true vision of the traces and stamps of the Creator on his creatures." But to find the real divine stamp in nature would necessitate that nothing in nature, however lowly, should be exempt from investigation. Bacon expected objections by philosophers and divines, who "will say, that the contemplation of truth is more dignified and exalted than any utility or extent of effects: but that our dwelling so long and anxiously on experience and matter, and the fluctuating state of particulars, fastens the mind to earth, or rather casts it down into an abyss of confusion and disturbance, and separates and removes it from a much more divine state, the quiet and tranquillity of abstract wisdom." [34] But we must fasten the mind on the earth, he said,

> For we are founding a real model of the world in the understanding, such as it is found to be, and not such as man's reason has distorted. Now, this cannot be done without dissecting and anatomizing

the world most diligently; but we declare it necessary to destroy completely the vain, little, and as it were apish imitations of the world, which have been formed in various systems of philosophy by men's fancies. Let men learn (as we have said above) the difference that exists between the idols of the human mind, and the ideas of the Divine mind. The former are mere arbitrary abstractions; the latter the true marks of the Creator on his creatures, as they are imprinted on, and defined in matter, by true and exquisite touches. Truth, therefore, and utility are here perfectly identical, and the effects are of more value as pledges of truth than from the benefit they confer on men.[35]

Bacon said that his goal was not to raise a pyramid to the pride of man, but to "rear a holy temple in his mind, on the model of the universe, which model therefore we imitate." To Bacon, utility was the test of truth about nature. Of all signs of the advancement of knowledge, he wrote, "there is none more certain or worthy than that of the fruits produced: for the fruits and effects are the sureties and vouchers, as it were, for the truth of philosophy."[36] Since the practical arts dealt with the concrete things of the world, they were at once the most decisive demonstration of true effects. A machine can work only if it is made in conformity with the laws of nature and therefore the more the art of man invented machines, the more nature was revealed.

Invention, however, did not come from the unassisted hand, Bacon said, and the understanding left to itself possessed little power. Both the hand and the understanding needed the assistance of instruments to be effective.[37] Bacon left help for the hands to others. He was concerned only with help for the understanding. First it was necessary to wipe the mind clear of error, and this is what he concentrated on in *Advancement of Learning*. Then, when the pure light of nature could be received, it would be possible with the aid of instruments and proper methods to discover the operations of nature. Bacon thought that his own most important contribution to the advancement of knowledge, and the key to the restoration of the Kingdom of Man, was his invention of the method of invention. He propounded an experimental method for the physical sciences, methods of observation and systematic classification for natural history, and methods of sifting language to separate truth from falsehood. He also gave primacy to the aim of discovering nature's secrets and applying them to the mastery of nature for the benefit of mankind.

In the system of Bacon, as in that of Ramus, and in the tradition of technological idealism, theoretical science and the practical arts were interactive and reinforcing. Bacon emphasized the force and effect of printing, gunpowder, and the compass, which, he said, "have changed the appearance and state of the whole world; first in literature, then in warfare, and lastly in navigation: and innumerable changes have been thence derived, so that no empire, sect, or star, appears to have exercised a greater power and influence on human affairs than these mechanical discoveries." The empire of man over things, he said, is founded on the arts and sciences alone, and nature is only commanded by obeying her. How much more exalted, Bacon said of his own invention of the method of invention, it will be as it leads to the easy discovery of everything else! And this would lead to the contemplation of things as they are, which is much more dignified than all the advantage to be derived from discoveries. "Only let mankind regain their rights over nature, assigned them by the gift of God, and obtain that power, whose exercise will be governed by right reason and true religion."[38]

The practical arts held out the highest promise for restoration of the Kingdom of Man in Bacon's vision, because they brought into close connection the mind, things, and utility. References and allusions in Bacon's works suggest that he was familiar with the tradition of technological idealism and the earlier writings on the biblical justification of technological progress, but he changed the emphasis from a glorification of what had been achieved by mankind in technology to a recognition that much of what had been achieved was the result of time and chance, rather than conscious, rational pursuit. When Bacon contrasted the mechanical arts with philosophy, he found them to be progressive, but when he considered them by themselves, he was impatient with the lack of attention given to making them flourish even more. He complained that we spent too much time admiring what we had, rather than lamenting our poverty in the face of what we should have.[39] He said that the lack of goals, the lack of rewards, the lack of leisure to hound nature for its truths, and the lack of support from governments were serious obstacles to the advancement of the arts and sciences, but the greatest obstacle was to be found in men's despair and the idea of impossibility.

Reflecting the then-popular belief that the world was in a cycle of decline, Bacon said that people think "that in the revolutions of ages and of the world there are certain floods and ebbs of the sciences, and that they grow and flourish at one time, and wither and fall off at another, that when they have attained a certain degree and condition they can proceed no further." Therefore, he said, it is necessary to emphasize hope, "for without it, all that we have said tends rather to produce a gloom than to encourage activity or quicken the industry of experiment." Because the way was mistaken in the past, it shows that "the difficulty does not arise from things themselves, which are not in our power, but from the human understanding, its practice and application, which is susceptible of remedy and correction."[40] He argued that we should, "according to the Scriptures, look unto that part of the race which is before us, than look back to that which is already attained."[41] He said that the old age and increasing years of the world should be considered as antiquity. The Ancients are older in respect to us, but in respect to the age of the world they are younger and lived in a less advanced age. Therefore, we have reason to expect much greater things from our own age than from antiquity, "since the world has grown older, and its stock has been increased and accumulated with an infinite number of experiments and observations."[42]

In his vision for a program of progress, Bacon elevated utility from the category of despised labor into the region of divine truth. To increase the productivity of labor, Bacon called for collaboration and the division of labor in research. With "Solomon's House, or the College of the Six Days' Work," in *New Atlantis*, Bacon presented a model of a research institute for natural history, experiments, and invention. He had the head of this House say: "The end of our foundation is the knowledge of causes and secret motions of things, and the enlarging of the bounds of the human empire, to the effecting of all things possible."[43] Bacon promised a New Jerusalem that was a technological society. He promised the restoration of the Kingdom of Man through the redemption that would come from using reason to understand and appreciate the works of the Great Architect, and to make nature productive for the benefit of mankind. Bacon thought that his age was the turning point in time for the fulfillment of knowledge in the unfolding of the divine providential plan of history. In his work can be seen the future time of mystical Christianity transmuted into the time of secular progress in productivity through technology.

The apocalyptic mentality survived Bacon with even more vigor in the next half century, but before his thought was taken over in the Enlightenment on behalf of a materialist utilitarianism, it was used in the millennialist climate of Puritanism. Although Bacon was in eclipse in the 1630s, his philosophy and a vigorous revival through the influence of Samuel Hartlib (c.1600–1662), who dedicated his life and fortune to realizing Bacon's program of technological progress.[44] Hartlib and his close associates, John Dury and Jan Amos Komensky (the famous Comenius), began as Apocalypse men, but became rabid Baconians, or gradualists. The reverses of Protestantism in the beginning of the Thirty Years' War had sharply intensified Apocalypticism. Joseph Mede at Cambridge, the tutor of John Milton and an influence in Cambridge Platonism, for instance, published a "Key to the Apocalypse" in 1627, and biblical prophecy was rampant among the Puritan gentry as well as the learned community. In this climate, Hartlib had considerable influence in Parliament. According to Hugh Trevor-Roper, Hartlib, Dury, and Comenius provided the philosophy of reformation in education, science, and models of government for the Puritans throughout the changes of fortune of their leadership down to the Restoration. He said of their late influence that "the intellectual world which surrounded Cromwell was very largely the world of these three men, the 'invisible college' of which they were the centre."[45] After the Restoration, the influence of Hartlib continued, though altered, through a younger generation that he had sponsored, befriended, or influenced. Hartlib believed that he had been the inspiration for the founding of the Royal Society. He could at least claim as his friends and disciples Robert Boyle, William Petty, John Pell, Christopher Wren, John Wilkins, all of whom were members of the Society, and many others who were the Baconians of a new age.

Hartlib made many proposals to advance the Baconian program. He supported inventors in mechanics and he carried on a thirty-year campaign, supported by the Puritans when they were in power, for the advancement of the practical arts as well as his many other reformist activities. Among his proposals was a college for the advancement of husbandry and the trades. He claimed that husbandry was the mother of all other trades and scientific industries, therefore a collegial way of teaching the art would be of infinite usefulness.[46]

Charles Webster said of Hartlib: "He shared Bacon's confidence that a great co-operative effort to marshal empirical knowledge would lead to an intellectual regeneration, a return of man's dominion over nature which had been sacrificed at the Fall." Hartlib and his colleagues, he added, "were convinced that England lay under a special dispensation, designed to be a focal point in the *Instauratio magna* of learning as one aspect of the complete reformation of religion. They saw education as the key to the reform of religion and society. In the words of Dury, 'without the reformation of the wayes of education in the schooles, it will not be possible to bring any other reformation to any settlement or progress of the whol Commonwealth.'"[47] And education included, in the words of Hartlib, "Exercises of Industrie not usuall then in Common Schooles." Hartlib prided himself on having supported "the best experiments of Industrie practised in Husbandrie and Manufactures; and in other Inventions and Accomodations tending to the good of this Nation, which by printing he hath published for the benefit of this Age, and of Posterity."[48]

Walter Blith was one of the Hartlib circle and a Baconian. In his book *The English Improver; or, a New Survey of Husbandry* he gave specific information on drainage, conditioning the soil, and making and using tools and instruments. He also wrote on the necessity for improving husbandry. Taking a well-established liberty, Blith designated God as the Great Husbandman, who had made all things for man, therefore man must "husbandize the fruits of the Earth, and dresse, and keepe them for the use of the whole Creation." Blith said that God, having given man a pattern and precedent for his encouragement, made man Lord of all until the Fall; "and after that God intending the preservation of what he made, notwithstanding the great curse upon Adam, Eve, and Serpent, the Earth not going free, but a curse of Barrennesse cast upon it also, yet Adam is sent forth to till the Earth, and improve it. In the sweat of his face he must eat bread untill he returne to the Earth again." [49]

Blith praised the usefulness of husbandry in maintaining our "Lives, Estates, this Common-wealth, and world, and the Improvement, or Advancement of the fruits and profits of the Earth by ingenuity," which, he said, "is little less than an addition of a new world; for what is gained hereby either above the naturall fruitfulnesse of the Earth, or else by reducement of that which is destroyed, or impoverished from his naturall fruitfulness, to great fertility, is a cleere Augmentation or Addition to the Common-wealth." Husbandry, he said, has first place in "omnifying" God, and husbandry required invention to increase the yield of the land, or its fruits would only end in the workman's belly. Believing that the English people were not very active in searching after improvements, he warned, "misery and penury will follow if we doe not rouze the sluggard, and post after Industry, pursue all advantages of Improvement whatsoever." [50] Blith's program was well known. Robert Trow-Smith claims that Blith was the greatest of the mid-century writers on agriculture and set the pattern of good husbandry until the time of Jethro Tull in the eighteenth century, that his analysis of the theory of plough design was still standard down into the Victorian period, that his principles of ley farming are still followed, and that all the many surviving copies of his works are well thumbed.[51]

Another of the many people supported by Hartlib was Gabriel Plattes, an inventor of farm implements and an advocate of both rational planning and the use of machinery to increase agricultural production. Also a Baconian, he had a vision of making England the Paradise of the world. One of the curious things about the work of Plattes and the whole Hartlib school was that these men perceived the inertia of those who possessed the nation's agricultural capital and recognized the need for education to rouse them to enter upon private enterprise for the good of the commonwealth. They kept driving home the idea that an investment in improvements would dramatically increase personal profits, to the advantage of all. Plattes went into considerable detail about ways of increasing productivity. He attacked the "hot apocalypse men" running around expecting miracles instead of working for improvement through new inventions. Repeating Blith, he said "all workmanship without invention, resolveth it selfe into the workman's belly, as may be manifestly seene." Like the other Baconians, Plattes argued that it was a religious duty to increase the productivity of man and the earth, and he expressed the hope that others would profit from his inventions. He wrote: "I shall help to bring to ripenesse certaine seeds of knowledge, planted in their hearts by the Finger of God in their creation." [52]

The program of technological progress developed by this group of writers translated a biblically justified road to a reformation and a restoration of man to the powers he enjoyed before the Fall into values favorable to increased secular productivity. They attacked traditions that stood in the way of innovation and invention. They moved the Golden Age of the Ancients from the past to the future. They relegated the pastoral Garden of Eden to a primitive early state of mankind and projected a future Paradise enlarged by the arts and sciences. They supplanted the ancient cycles of growth and decline of culture with the steady progression of the arts and sciences. They relieved providential history of its burden of work as a punishment for sin and glorified creative and inventive work in the advancement of the arts and sciences. They did not do all these things alone, but by focusing on practical productivity, they appear to have launched social values favorable to industrial modernization.

The program of these writers paralleled the emergence of protoindustrialism, but the connections between the literary justifiers and those in the field and shop are by no means clear. Motivations of long dead actors in historical movements are not easy to establish. Would they have fought so hard against tradition and for technological progress if they had not felt the urgency of reformation, restoration, and redemption as preparation for the last stage in the great plan of providential time? Did their vision of redemption through productivity go underground, leaving behind the unstated assumption that the goal of increased productivity needed no justification? It is clear that they left an articulated social goal and justification of values favorable to economic modernization in the foreground of industrialization.

Notes

1. Joseph Needham, *Science and Civilisation in China*, vol. 4, p. 2, sect. 27, "Mechanical Engineering" (Cambridge: Cambridge University Press, 1965), esp. pp. 330–435, and fig. 627a, facing p. 404.

2. Jean Gimpel, *The Medieval Machine: The Industrial Revolution of the Middle Ages* (New York: Penguin Books, 1977), p. 9. See also Needham, *Science and Civilisation*, 4: 408–10.

3. Benjamin Farrington, *Greek Science*, 2 vols. (Harmondsworth: Penguin Books, 1949), 2: 165–66.

4. A pioneering attempt to measure motivation values was made, for instance, by David C. McClelland, *The Achieving Society* (Princeton, N. J.: D. Van Nostrand Co., Inc., 1953). See also Benjamin Higgins, *Economic Development: Principles, Problems, and Policies* (New York: W. W. Norton and Co., 1959).

5. Gimpel, *The Medieval Machine*.

6. E. M. Carus-Wilson, "An Industrial Revolution of the Thirteenth Century," in *Essays in Economic History*, ed. E. M. Carus-Wilson, vol. 1 (London, 1954), cited in Carlo M. Cipolla, *Before the Industrial Revolution: European Society and Economy*, 1000–1700 (New York: W. W. Norton and Co., 1976), p. 162.

7. Cipolla, *Before the Industrial Revolution*, chap. 6. See also Gimpel, *The Medieval Machine*. Needham points out that most of these developments had occurred earlier in China.

8. See Needham, *Science and Civilisation*, 4: 27–29.

9. Cipolla, *Before the Industrial Revolution*, pp. 173–74.

10. Ernst Robert Curtius points to the importance of this verse from Wisdom in *European Literature and the Latin Middle Ages* (New York: Harper and Row, 1963), pp. 544–46.

11. See esp., *The City of God*, 22.24.

12. See F. C. Haber, "The Cathedral Clock and the Cosmological Clock Metaphor," in *The Study of Time II*, ed. J. T. Fraser and N. Lawrence (New York: Springer-Verlag, 1975), pp. 339–416.

13. St. Bonaventure, *De Reductione Artium ad Theologium*, trans. Emma Therese Healy (New York: St. Bonaventure College, 1955).

14. See Nicholas H. Steneck, *Science and Creation in the Middle Ages: Henry of Langenstein (d. 1397)* (Notre Dame: University of Notre Dame Press, 1976).

15. Nicholas of Cusa, *The Vision of God*, trans. Emma Gurney Salter (London: J. M. Dent and Sons, 1928). See also F. C. Haber, "The Darwinian Revolution in the Concept of Time," in *The Study of Time I*, ed. J. T. Fraser, F. C. Haber, and G. H. Müller (New York: Springer-Verlag, 1972), pp. 390–91.

16. See, e.g., Paoli Rossi, *Philosophy, Technology, and the Arts in the Early Modern Era*, trans. Salvator Attanasio (New York: Harper and Row, 1970).

17. Ansgar Stöcklein, *Leitbilder der Technik: Biblische Tradition und Technischer Fortschritt* (Munich: Heinz Moos Verlag, 1979).

18. Daniel Mögling (1629) and Henri de Monantheuil (1599), cited in ibid., pp. 71–72.

19. Georg Philipp Harsdörffer (1653), cited in ibid., p. 64.

20. Arthur O. Lovejoy, "Milton and the Paradox of the Fortunate Fall," *Essays in the History of Ideas* (New York: George Braziller, Inc., 1955), pp. 277–95.

21. See Stöcklein, *Leitbilder der Technik*, pp. 46–48.

22. Thomas Burnet, *Sacred Theory of the Earth*, 3d ed. (London, 1697), bk. 3, p. 29.

23. See also Paoli Rossi, *Francis Bacon: From Magic to Science*, trans. Sacha Rabinovitch from the Italian (London: Routledge and Kegan Paul, 1968).

24. Basil Montague, ed., *The Works of Francis Bacon, Lord Chancellor of England. With a Life of the Author*, 3 vols. (Philadelphia: Parry and McMillan, 1859), 1: 82 [3: 221]. The references in the edition of the works of Bacon edited by James Spedding, Robert Leslie Ellis, and Douglas Denon Heath (1859) are added in square brackets for convenience.

25. Bacon, *Novum Organum*, in *Works*, 3: 362 [4: 92].

26. Ibid., p. 358 [4: 82].

27. Bacon, *Advancement*, in *Works*, 1: 184 [3: 321].

28. Bacon, *Novum Organum*, in *Works*, 3: 334 [4: 13].

29. Bacon, *Valerius Terminus*, in *Works*, 1: 81 [3: 217].

30. Bacon, *Novum Organum*, in *Works*, 3: 425 [4: 247–48]. See also 3: 337 [4: 20].

31. Bacon, *Valerius Terminus*, in *Works*, 1: 81 [3: 222].

32. Bacon, *Novum Organum*, in *Works*, 3: 340 [4: 27].

33. Ibid.

34. Ibid., pp. 342, 367, 369 [4: 32, 106–7, 110].

35. Ibid., p. 369 [4: 110].

36. Ibid., pp. 367, 354 [4: 106–7, 73].

37. Ibid., p. 345 [4: 47].

38. Ibid., p. 370 [4: 114–15].

39. Ibid., p. 358 [4: 83].

40. Ibid., pp. 361, 362 [4: 90, 92].

41. Bacon, *Advancement*, in *Works*, 1: 185 [3: 323].

42. Bacon, *Novum Organum*, in *Works*, 3: 358 [4: 82]. See also *Advancement*, 1: 172 [3: 291].

43. Bacon, *New Atlantis*, in *Works*, 1: 266 [3: 156].

44. See G. H. Turnbull, *Samuel Hartlib* (Oxford, 1920).

45. H. R. Trevor-Roper, *The Crisis of the Seventeenth Century: Religion, the Reformation and Social Change* (New York: Harper and Row, 1968), p. 281.

46. Samuel Hartlib, *An Essay for Advancement of Husbandry-Learning: or Propositions for the Erecting Colledge of Husbandry* (London, 1651), Preface. See also *Samuel Hartlib His Legacy of Husbandry*, 3d ed. (London, 1655).

47. Charles Webster, ed., *Samuel Hartlib and the Advancement of Learning* (Cambridge: Cambridge University Press, 1970), pp. 3, 4.

48. Hartlib, *Petition*, in ibid., p. 5.

49. Walter Blith, *The English Improver Improved* (London, 1649), Preface.

50. Ibid.

51. Robert Trow-Smith, *English Husbandry from the Earliest Times to the Present Day* (London: Faber and Faber, 1950), pp. 107–17.

52. Gabriel Plattes, *A Discoverie of Infinite Treasure, Hidden Since the Worlds Beginning* (London, 1639), Preface [pp. xvi, xxx].

Literary Images of Progress: The Fate of an Idea

Samuel L. Macey

Summary I shall concentrate on some of the ways in which Western technology and its associated modern sense of time consciousness have affected the development of the idea of progress during the past three hundred years.

The British horological revolution of 1660–1760 was at the cutting edge of Western technology and resulted in an increased consciousness of time in the English language. Among other words, *progress* itself changes its meaning during the seventeenth century from a progress through space (as in *Pilgrim's Progress*) to a progress or advancement through earthly time, in which, for example, bourgeois financial aspirations are satisfied through navigation and trade. This newer meaning of progress is reflected in the many novels of Defoe.

Chronological awareness also becomes much more acute during the seventeenth century. It is clearly related to the new meaning of *progress* and is well illustrated in Condorcet's utopian vision of man's social and moral progress in the future. Ironically, however, the ultimate eighteenth-century clock in the form of the chronometer contributed greatly to the improvement in navigation and mapping. This brought an end to utopias (or even dystopias) placed in unknown distant lands. As a result, many of the more recent dreams of progress (as occurs with Condorcet, Marx, or Huxley in contradistinction to *Utopia*, the *New Atlantis*, or *Gulliver's Travels*) had to be projected into the future.

In the age leading up to Darwinism, the rigidity of the clockwork in Newton's universe meant that the model was doomed. The organic model, foreshadowed in Humes's *Dialogues* (1779), would be more appropriate to the evolutionary connotations with which progress was to become associated. In the nineteenth century this sense of progress through time motivates not only Darwinian evolution but also the dialectics of Hegel and Marx. In our own Einsteinian century the newly discovered expanding universe is similarly based on the model of an evolutionary progress through time.

Three hundred years ago, the idea of making a worthwhile progress in terms of our time on this earth allowed us to break out from an enclosed world inhibited by transcendental values and the fear of an Armageddon to be produced by God. Today, our quickening sense of future doom, particularly among the young, warns us that Western technology could create its own Armageddon. The next generation may well refuse to pay the price that unrestricted progress would now appear to demand.

Those of us who are from the Western world and more than forty years old have spent the greater part of our lives in a society where the idea of progress was equated with virtue. Progress was clearly good. There were, of course, such earlier indications that all might not be well with the idea of progress as the fin de siècle disillusion with material progress and the post–World War I despair with progress.[1] During the middle of the 1960s, however, progress—and more specifically material progress through technology—came to be questioned on a scale that had not occurred for some three hundred years. Since the questioning of the idea of progress involves an agonizing dilemma that will remain with us for the rest of our lives, we must surely benefit from understanding how the idea itself, as epitomized in the battle between the Moderns and the Ancients, came to be part of our civilization.

Until the definitive work of R. F. Jones, it was generally thought that the battle in the latter part of the seventeenth century between the Moderns, who sought progress, and the Ancients, who admired the past values of Greece and Rome, was essentially a literary one.[2] The survey of French literature, for example, from which I drew my early rudiments of literary knowledge, felt that the "querelle des Anciens et des Modernes" began with Perrault, a Modern, who in 1678 defended "Le Siècle de Louis le Grand."[3] Though Boileau entered the lists for the Ancients, the Moderns won. That, of course, is what happened in real life, but in fiction the results could be different. In Swift's *Battle of the Books*—written less than ten years after Perrault's poem, though not published until 1704—the Moderns are routed in an imaginary battle in England's St. James Library between the books of the Moderns and the books of the Ancients.

Since in real life the Moderns and the idea of progress were gaining the ascendancy, one might well ask why in literature the Augustan ideas of the writers who defended the Ancients were generally respected until the middle of the eighteenth century. Even in England the control of drama through the unities of time, action, and place—which were supposedly derived from Aristotle's *Poetics*—was not finally overthrown until Dr. Johnson's *Preface to Shakespeare* (1765).

R. F. Jones has demonstrated in his *Ancients and Moderns* (1936) that although the literary quarrels have tended to retain the headlines, they are only a later reflection of the more important quarrels between the proponents of ancient and modern science. In science, Bacon enunciated and Galileo, Torricelli, Stevin, Boyle, and Newton proved the merits of the experimental philosophy. Such activities clearly demonstrated the advantages of their methods over some of those used by Aristotle and his followers. By the third quarter of the seventeenth century, therefore, the authority of Aristotle in physics and cosmology had succumbed to modern scientific method. Aristotle the literary critic, however—whose *Poetics* reflected the glory of such writers among the Ancients as Aeschylus, Sophocles, Euripides, and Homer—was able to retain his hegemony for a further hundred years.

Until the idea of progress became fully accepted, men had thought of their ancestors as giants and themselves as pigmies. W. Jackson Bate, in his *Burden of the Past*, shows how such ideas tended to inhibit neoclassical authors and encourage them toward imitation rather than original composition.[4] It is understandable that the reactionary neoclassical writers should satirize extensively the scientists and Moderns who were promoting progress through their own ideas, experiments, and projects. We find such satire in Swift's "Voyage to Laputa" or Pope's *Dunciad*. As R. F. Jones puts it at the conclusion of *Ancients and Moderns*, "humanism won the day in the literary world and later directed much of its satire against the 'men of Gresham' [the Royal Society]. So we have a neo-classical rather than romantic period in literature."[5]

The founding of the Royal Society in London, in 1662, however, had been well supported by what we would now call the intelligentsia. It provided a focus for the experimental philosophy and the new science. The planning for the Royal Society consciously followed the plan for Solomon's House that Bacon had set out in his *New Atlantis* almost forty years earlier. Bacon's experimental philosophy used inductive reasoning in which all hypotheses were tested by practical experiments. His followers avoided the deductive method that involved logical deductions without experiment from statements made by such Ancients as Aristotle. The idea of progress is implicit in the very title of Bacon's great work, *The Advancement of Learning*.

Though the idea of progress is implicit in Bacon, it is much more explicit in the writings of his followers—like Glanvill, Webster, and Power—during the third quarter of the seventeenth century. For the new scientists, to borrow Wordsworth's felicitious phraseology, "Bliss was it in that dawn to be alive." Their writings demonstrate that they celebrated the birth of progress with an almost evangelical joy. Their joy was understandable, since progress had been so long impeded by conceptions such as the inevitable decay of nature and the inevitable superiority of the Ancients who had been giants. We may take Henry Power's *Experimental Philosophy* (1664) as a typical example. He claims that in the past the greatest impediment to the potential for progress in "the promotion of the Arts and Sciences ... is the Universal Exclamation of the World's decay.... That both the great and little World have long since passed the Meridian, and, That the Faculties of the one doe fade and decay, as well as the Fabricks and Materials of the other." [6]

Power concludes his *Experimental Philosophy* with a paean of praise to the progress in science achieved by the Moderns, despite the hindrances of the Peripatetics, who were followers of Aristotle:

> And this is the Age wherein all mens Souls are in a kind of fermentation and the spirit of Wisdom and Learning begins to mount and free it self from the drossie and terrene Impediments wherewith it hath been so long clogg'd, and from the ... useless Notions, from which it hath endured so violent and long a fixation.
>
> This is the Age wherein (me-thinks) Philosophy comes in with a Spring-tide; and the Peripateticks may as well hope to stop the Current of the Tide ... as hinder the overflowing of free Philosophy: Me-thinks, I see how all the old Rubbish must be thrown away, and the rotten Buildings be overthrown, and carried away with so powerful an Innundation. These are the days that must lay a new Foundation of a more magnificent Philosophy.... I think it is no Rhetorication to say, That all things are Artificial; for Nature it self is nothing else but the Art of God. Then, certainly, to find the various turnings, and mysterious processes of divine Art, in the management of this great Machine of the World, must needs be the proper Office of onely the Experimental and Mechanical Philosopher. [7]

I have quoted from Henry Power at length because he conveys the joy in progress that a minor natural philosopher or scientist like him was then experiencing, in this case through experiments with the microscope. In addition, three of the images in the quotation from Power have a part in our story on progress: first, the imagery related to the sea or navigation; second, the image of the world as a great machine or piece of clockwork; and, finally, the image of the old philosophy or science being like old buildings or rubbish that must be swept away. In the second half of the seventeenth century all three images are to be found in great writers like Boyle and Locke, as well as in a host of minor ones.

Let us look first at the sea and navigation, which were essential to the rise of Britain's leadership in the Western world. David W. Waters points out, in *The Art of Navigation in England*, that "as late as 1568 probably only one English seaman was capable of navigating to the West Indies without the aid of Portuguese, French or Spanish pilots. Yet, by the time of the Armada ... Englishmen had gained a 'reputation of being above all Western nations, expert and active in all naval operations....'" [8] Though Galileo and Torricelli, among others, first successfully took the leadership in experimental science in Catholic Italy, the smuggling of the manuscript of Galileo's last great work, the *Discorsi*, out to the Netherlands is symbolic of the movement of science in the direction of the Protestant North. This movement was reinforced during the period leading up to France's revocation of the Edict of Nantes by the emigration of Huguenots to the Netherlands, Prussia, and England.

During the seventeenth century, the Netherlands took over from the Catholic countries much of the leadership in world shipping and mapmaking. Yet that leadership was soon going to be challenged successfully by another Protestant country. Under Cromwell, the first Navigation Act of 1651 had specified that no goods could be imported into England except in English vessels. This symbolized a movement that was to break the supremacy of the Netherlands both at sea and in America.

The new scientists consciously drew a parallel between progress in exploration and progress in intellectual powers. It had been claimed that in classical times the words *ne plus ultra*—indicating that one could go no further—were inscribed on the Pillars of Hercules at the exit to the Mediterranean. Four years after Power's *Experimental Philosophy* and a year after Bishop Sprat's eulogy to science entitled *The History of the Royal Society*, Glanvill wrote *Plus Ultra* (1668) whose very title points to the limitations of the knowledge of the Ancients. In his work, Glanvill claims that in intellectual and experimental knowledge there is still "an *America* of secrets, and [*sic*] unknown *Peru* of Nature" waiting to be investigated by the new scientists. Like Power, Glanvill has an almost evangelical optimism concerning progress: "Me-thinks this age seems resolved to bequeath *posterity* somewhat to remember it: And the glorious Undertakers, wherewith Heaven hath blest our Days, will leave the world better provided then [*sic*] they found it. . . . It may be some Ages hence, a voyage to the *Moon*, will not be more strange then one to *America*." [9]

Let us move on to the second image from Power, that of the world as a machine. The relationship between navigation and the image of the world or the universe as a machine is much closer than may at first be apparent. When Power wrote his *Experimental Philosophy* (1664), relatively accurate clocks had only been invented seven years earlier by the astronomer Huygens. Huygens had mistakenly thought (and Newton was at first no wiser) that his pendulum escapement might be used for ascertaining the longitude at sea. [10] It was another hundred years before the Englishman John Harrison produced a sufficiently accurate chronometer for sea-going purposes. Huygens's escapement reduced the inaccuracy of portable clocks from about five minutes per day to as many seconds, but by 1761 Harrison's fourth chronometer erred by no more than fifteen seconds after a five-month journey to the West Indies and back. The century between 1660 and 1760 (which I have called the British horological revolution) [11] laid the foundation not only of British hegemony at sea, but also of much important progress in such aspects of engineering as metallurgy, machine tools, and batch production. This progress led into Britain's subsequent industrial revolution. [12] In the eighteenth century, Power's image of "this great Machine of the World" could only refer to clockwork. It is clearly no accident that the horological model inherent in Newton's clockwork universe and its corollary of the watchmaker God is most frequently found concurrent with the British horological revolution when Thomas Tompion and George Graham, the two fathers of English clockmaking, were both considered worthy of burial in Westminister Abbey. [13]

Let us now look at the third and last of Power's images, before we return more specifically to the idea of progress. In 1664—two years after the founding of the Royal Society—Power (restating, as he frequently does, the ideas of Bacon) glories in the weakness of the Ancients before the oncoming flood of science. Power writers about the value of sweeping aside the rubbish and rotten buildings of Aristotelian philosophy. Unwittingly, he was foreshadowing another important stimulus for material progress. In the following year, at least sixty-five thousand Londoners died in the Great Plague, and a year later, in 1666, thirteen thousand houses in the heart of London were razed to the ground in the Great Fire. In his *Journal of the Plague Year*, Daniel Defoe—the Dissenting Modern and evangelist of progress—celebrates the subsequent advances in industry and commerce: "It is incredible what a trade this made all over the whole kingdom, to make good the want and to supply that loss . . . in short, all the manufacturing hands of the nation were set at work. . . . All foreign markets also were empty of our goods . . . so that there was never known such a trade . . . for the time as was in the first seven years after the plague and after the fire of London." [14]

Elsewhere in his works, Defoe celebrates the hegemony of London over England nearly as much as he does the increasing progress in British navigation and trade.[15] If we stand in London, therefore, in the middle of the 1660s and look forward, we can see a vista of almost exactly three hundred years of virtually unquestioned material progress associated with Western technology, and the three images of Henry Power tell us a great deal about how the idea of progress was nurtured in England through science, navigation, and industry.

We have noted the relationship between England's industrial revolution and the revolutionary increase in the accuracy of clocks and watches during the third quarter of the seventeenth century. During much the same period a more acute sense of chronology was also developing, or, in other words, of time horizons on the large scale. Not only the Greeks and Romans but Englishmen as recently as the Elizabethans, as can be seen in the plays of Shakespeare, lacked our modern sense of chronology. Indeed, the modern chronological meaning of the term *century* did not begin until the first half of the seventeenth century. By 1650–54, however, Bishop Ussher in his *Annales Veteris et Novi Testamenti* had even superimposed a modern form of chronology on the Bible. It was now possible to date one's chronology from the precise moment at 9:00 A.M. on Sunday, October 23 in 4004 B.C. when the Creation occurred.[16]

Though our discoveries in chronology and horology during the seventeenth century were surely sufficient for the needs of urban man, we have, during the last three hundred years, maintained an exponential rate of progress in our measurement of time in ever larger and ever-smaller dimensions. The eighteenth century gave us the beginnings of geological time, but also chronometers and stopwatches. The nineteenth century gave us progress through time in the evolution of all species, but also the tying together of virtually simultaneous time through telegraphs, time zones, and electric clocks. Our own century has given us the progress of a universe that has been expanding outward for billions of years, but also atomic clocks and hydrogen masers that measure time to an accuracy of far less than a second in thirty thousand years. Clearly, in these developments, as in many others, our progress in the measurement of time is closely related to both our material and our intellectual progress.

During the Renaissance there were, of course, the beginnings of the idea of progress as it relates to Western technology and bourgeois dreams of establishing a personal dynasty.[17] Ultimately, however, the laws from the past and the need to ensure a future in heaven tended to inhibit progress. One purpose of this paper is to stress the extent to which the third quarter of the seventeenth century in London represented a watershed insofar as the development of the idea of progress was concerned. My purpose will be further advanced by considering the way in which the meaning of the word *progress* itself (like the meaning of the word *century*) began to change during the first half of the seventeenth century. The change insofar as *progress* was concerned was from a term related to space to a term related to time.

Though the *Oxford English Dictionary* does not yet reflect some of the pejorative connotations associated with the word *progress* during our own time, it does show us that during the seventeenth century the term acquired its modern meaning. The earlier meaning associated with a journey through space is still found in Shakespeare's idea that "a king may go a progress through the guts of a beggar,"[18] or even in Bunyan's *Pilgrim's Progress from This World to That Which Is to Come* (1678). That previous meaning, however, is now an anachronism. During the seventeenth and eighteenth centuries, as a result of conditions related to the British horological revolution, there was a marked increase in the use of English words related to time. The term *anachronism* itself—which presupposes an understanding of chronology—was, for example, first used in 1646.[19]

It is not unusual for spatial and temporal words to be derived from one another. The term *atom* derives from the Greek *atmos*, or twinkling of an eye, while the minute and second (or second minute as it was earlier called) are clearly related to a minute measurement in size. Thus it is not surprising that in the seventeenth century (which was beginning to be so concerned with time) the conception of a progress or advancement through space should become transferred to the conception of a material progress or advancement through time. The first recorded use of the verb in this sense seems to be in Shakerley Marmion's little-known play *Holland's Leaguer, an Excellent Comedy* (1632): "I began betimes and so progresst from less to bigger." As early as 1603, Richard Knolles, in his *Generall History of the Turkes*, had used the noun in the modern sense: "If you consider the beginning, progresse and perpetuall felicitie of this the Othoman Empire."

The older meaning of the word *progress* also encompassed Roman-type triumphal progresses as found in Petrarch's *Triumphs* (c. 1356–74), in which Love is conquered by Chastity, Chastity by Death, Death by Fame, Fame by Time, and Time by Eternity. From the second quarter of the fifteenth century, no theme, other than the cycles of Old and New Testament story, gave more frequent employment to artists and craftsmen than did the illustrations of Petrarch's six *Triumphs* as progresses through space.[20]

We have already noted that in the title of *Pilgrim's Progress* Bunyan still uses the term in its old sense. Bunyan's Christian and Christiana make a progress through space that is noticeably unrelated to chronological time. Their progress bridges the temporal values on this earth and the eternal values in the New Jerusalem. That Bunyan was conscious of the relationship between time and eternity is demonstrated by the quatrain entitled "Upon Time and Eternity" in his *Book for Boys and Girls* (1686).

Defoe deals with the subject of time and eternity at much greater length in the rarely read didactic part 3 of *Robinson Crusoe*. His novels, however, are progresses of a very different kind than the works of Bunyan. Despite the claims of the protagonists and their author, Defoe is read for evidence of a form of progress quite unlike that in Bunyan. Defoe's errant protagonists all progress through a readily ascertainable chronological time on this earth, and they all seek material advancement. Their ultimate goal is the opportunity to live out their old age comfortably in or near London, that great metropolis where Western technology was being engendered.

Defoe's idea of progress, rather than Bunyan's, allowed Hogarth—seven years after the completion of Defoe's novels—to use the term *progress* in an ironic sense. Hogarth, however, is not questioning the idea of progress itself. In 1731, *The Harlot's Progress* shows in six pictures a reverse progress through time in the fortunes of the young woman Moll Hackabout. Shortly afterwards, *The Rake's Progress* does much the same for a young man. In the following decade, Hogarth produced, in a series of twelve pictures, the didactic *Industry and Idleness*, which combines a normal with a reverse progress. In this series, Goodchild, the good apprentice—by applying himself both to his work and to his master's daughter—finishes up as lord mayor of London; while Tom Idle, the idle apprentice (who symbolically had the ballad of Moll Flanders pinned to his loom in plate 1), finishes up on the gallows at Tyburn, after being betrayed by his whore.

The image of the good apprentice who combines industry with an accumulation of capital has remained one of the elements in the idea of progress up till our own times, but the image of the clockwork universe has not. Organic images provided more suitable models in the period leading up to Darwin's theory of evolution. Darwin's theory itself is closely connected with the idea of a successful progress through time in which only the fittest survive. The essential elements of Charles Darwin's theory already existed in the latter part of the eighteenth century. By 1779, Hume's *Dialogues Concerning Natural Religion* had downgraded the mechanical metaphor in favor of the organic one; by 1794–96, Charles's grandfather Erasmus Darwin had published *Zoonomia* with a chapter on the evolutionary principle; and by 1798 Malthus had published *An Essay on the Principle of Population*, from which Charles Darwin suggested that he had obtained the essential clue for basing his theory of evolution on the survival of the fittest.[21]

The head start in material progress that England gained through the experimental philosophy in the latter part of the seventeenth century was naturally envied by writers in other lands, and particularly by the French. In the latter half of the eighteenth century, the French philosophes were exacerbated by the restrictions of the ancien régime. They sought to emulate British progress in the industrial arts, as Diderot does in his *Encyclopédie* (1751–76). But they also expanded the British model to suggest that people could go beyond material progress, since they had, in addition, the capacity to achieve social and moral progress.

Condorcet's *Esquisse d'un tableau historique des progrès de l'esprit humain*, published posthumously in 1795, is probably the best example of a work showing the evolutionary nature of man's social and moral progress. Its sense of chronology should be compared with Buffon's successive geological stages in *Époques de la nature* (1779). Condorcet takes a chronological historic overview, reflecting the heightened interest in chronology that had been developing since the second half of the seventeenth century. The *Esquisse* of Condorcet divides human history into ten epochs, and demonstrates man's perfectibility by showing how the human spirit progresses from the first epoch when men worked together in small hordes as hunters and fishers. The ninth epoch—which ends with the moral and political revolution of 1789 that Condorcet had supported—is an illustrious period that begins with Sir Isaac Newton's discovery of the true nature of the universe and John Locke's discovery of the true nature of man. The most original part of Condorcet's treatise is the tenth epoch. In that epoch, Condorcet moves into the future when inequality between both nations and classes will be destroyed, and the indefinite perfectibility of man himself will be demonstrated on the physical, intellectual, and moral levels.

Philosophical utopias, as well as literary utopias and dystopias, tend by their very nature to be concerned with the question of progress in one form or another. Although Condorcet's goals are not necessarily the same as those of Hegel or Marx, we can see a comparable sense of progress through historical time motivating the Hegelian dialectic, which celebrates the modern German nation state, and the Marxian dialectic, which celebrates a future classless society. Where, as occurs in Condorcet or Marx, the society being celebrated differs greatly from the present that is being endured, it became natural for the author's utopian society to be projected into the future. Thomas More had simply provided an exotic setting for his *Utopia* (1516), just as Bacon did for his *New Atlantis* (1626). Because as late as 1700 almost half the world was still unknown to travelers and mapmakers from western Europe, Swift, in 1726, could still quite credibly place the land of Brobdingnag—six thousand miles long and three thousand miles wide—in the general area of Vancouver Island. However, the chronometer, which John Harrison had perfected by 1761, soon made a great deal of difference to both mapping and navigation in the hands of such progressive sea captains as Cook, Bligh, and Vancouver. Though both their titles mean "Nowhere," Samuel Butler's *Erewhon* (1872) is constrained by a world that had been much better surveyed than that of More's *Utopia*.

By the end of the eighteenth century, the realism of time and place with which Defoe had influenced the novel became reinforced by an increased knowledge of the surface of the earth. As a result, it was more and more necessary for writers of both utopias and dystopias—while remaining concerned with the present—to project their ideas into the future. This is true of those who write utopian treatises like Condorcet or Marx, and of those who as long ago as the second half of the eighteenth century gave us literary utopias like L.S. Mercier's *Year 2440*. Though Huxley's *Brave New World* (1937) and Orwell's *1984* (1949) are both projected into the future, they are anti-utopias or dystopias, which oppose the type of ordered society seriously proposed by Mercier in *The Year 2440*. They suggest that at the very least such utopias involve the loss of one's personal freedom.

The idea of material progress has, however, become so completely integrated into our thinking that we frequently find both our dystopian and utopian writers implicitly debating not so much progress itself as whether our future is best served by progress through free enterprise or progress through the centrally organized state. Despite our protests to the contrary, the material progress that has resulted from Western technology has now made us all much more concerned with our time on this earth than with our preparations for eternity. It matters little whether we are atheists or Christians, Communists or capitalists; our concern is only with which system leads most directly to an earthly happiness based on material progress. And much the same is true of the so-called Third World countries. Though they condemn the rapacity of Western technology, they are as eager to share in the products of its progress as are the "have" nations of the left or the right.

We in the West can readily accept that our sense of progress relates to free enterprise and Western technology; and that to a great extent this derives from what occurred in the England of the seventeenth century. We may find it more difficult, however, to understand that Communist doctrines derive from exactly the same idea of progress. Engels makes quite explicit the relationship between the Marxian and Hegelian dialectic and the idea of progress when he writes, in *Ludwig Feuerbach*, that the "great basic thought that the world is not to be comprehended as a complex of ready-made *things*, but as a complex of *processes*. . . . in which, in spite of all seeming accidents and all temporary retrogression, a progressive development asserts itself in the end." And Engels adds: "this great fundamental thought has, especially since the time of Hegel, so thoroughly permeated ordinary consciousness that in this generality it is scarcely ever contradicted." [22]

Though free enterprise certainly initiated the material progress associated with Western technology, Western technology itself is by no means inimical to meritocracy in a classless society. Western technology may have been founded in part on a rape of labor and resources, but it has long since passed beyond that stage. It now provides a leveling of incomes far greater than we generally recognize. In North America today, there is rarely more than a threefold differential between a unionized laborer and a management executive. These income differentials have been dropping steadily since the days of Defoe when a servant earned three pounds a year and the minimum income of a squire or gentleman was almost two hundred times as much. As Western technology has progressed from the subdivision of labor into automation, and house work as well as industry has been largely mechanized, human beings have become more important as consumers and less important as laborers. Three hundred years ago, our forefathers were almost all peasants. Yet now most of us in the Western world expect to enjoy material standards of food, clothing, transport, entertainment, housing, and heating comparable to those of at least a squire at the time of the Restoration.

What we now in the West expect, the rest of the world proposes to emulate in less than fifty years. By that time the world's population is projected to reach some ten billion, which is twenty times what it was at the Restoration in 1660. If everyone demands the same material standards that we enjoy in the West, each person will be requiring at least fifty times the material standards of the average individual at the time of the Restoration. When one allows for the increase in both population and the demands of the average individual, we can reasonably project that in fifty years the world's requirements for manufactured goods of all kinds will be of the order of one thousand times what they were in 1660.

The magnitude of the problem that derives from material progress is such that even those most devoted to the idea must sense an urgent need to control population or consumption or both. The idea of progress has served us well since the time when we obeyed the biblical injunction and set out to increase and multiply not only ourselves but also our material possessions. Indeed, the population of the world, which had by 1660 only doubled to five hundred million since the time of Christ, has already increased a further eightfold in the past three hundred years. Yet the projected acceleration in the rise of population and material consumption is now both greater and more immediate. It matters little whether unrestricted progress will kill us through carcinogens, polluted water, or a nuclear holocaust. Both the sense of an ending and the lack of a concerted will to deal with it are clear enough. Today, we no longer need a god to produce our Armageddon.

What can be concluded? When I began this paper, I said that—despite certain earlier warning signals—during the middle of the 1960s material progress came to be questioned in the West on a scale that had not occurred for some three hundred years. Many of the young people who questioned progress at that time are today much less vociferous. Perhaps they have understood that progress cannot be reversed without a price being paid in terms of their own material comfort. Nevertheless, and as a result of what has occurred, people are now far more conscious of ideas like energy conservation, environmental controls, and zero population growth—all of which can be related to the reversal of the idea of unlimited material progress.

I said at the beginning of this paper that those of us who are more than forty years old have spent the greater part of our lives in a world where the idea of progress was equated with virtue. Our desire for material well-being has given us a vested interest in supporting the idea of progress at almost any cost. In a curious reversal of the battle between the Ancients and the Moderns that took place three hundred years ago, we descendants of the victorious Moderns have now become the new Ancients who want to conserve the idea of progress. Like the aristocrats of the ancien régime, we hope that the deluge will come after our deaths. But we must understand that the younger generation, the new Moderns whose lives are at greater risk, may well subscribe to a new idea of world order and control whose configurations we cannot yet delineate.

We are too close to the battle lines to be sure whether the controls of the new Moderns or the continuing progress of the new Ancients will prevail. It may take another generation before we know the outcome, but if we do move toward a global order, Huxley's *Brave New World* might well provide an indication of the future model. In that model the world population is controlled at two billion, where it was when Huxley wrote the book; progress is no longer desirable, because all necessary inventions already exist; and all social classes are preestablished to ensure stability.[23] Indeed the whole fabric of society is controlled as precisely as are the four thousand electric clocks in the four thousand rooms of the Central London Hatchery and Conditioning Centre, which simultaneously strike four when the main day shift hands over to the second day shift.[24]

For those of us in the West who are over forty the prospect of living in Huxley's Brave New World seems bleak enough. But it may not appear entirely unpleasant to some of our Chinese friends who already have a population of over one billion. The new Moderns among us, too, may prefer a serious version of Huxley's satirically conceived utopia to the extinction or decimation of our species in the twenty-first century. Perhaps we must develop a new model with finite population in which those who have are obliged to support the material progress of those who have not.

If the model of a finite global society such as Huxley's should prevail, the idea of unrestricted material progress will almost certainly change from a virtue to an evil. During the past three hundred years, we have worshipped Progress as a many-faceted god and particularly as a god who could bring us material advancement during the course of our time on earth. Progress has been our chief deity and we have worshiped it far more ardently than the watchmaker God or the old man with a white beard. Though the signs are not yet entirely clear, this paper has suggested why, like all deities who are deposed, Progress may one day become the great Satan or Antagonist, the devil in an age that is just now waiting to be born.

Notes

1. George L. Mosse, *The Culture of Western Europe: The Nineteenth and Twentieth Centuries* (Chicago: Rand McNally, 1962), pp. 220–22, 289 passim.

2. Richard Foster Jones, *Ancients and Moderns*, 2d ed. (Berkeley: University of California Press, 1965), pp. 267, 342 passim. Despite recent revaluations, the essential merit of Jones's work would seem to remain. See, for example, Joseph M. Levine, "Ancients and Moderns Reconsidered," *Eighteenth-Century Studies* 15 (Fall 1981): 72–89.

3. R. P. L. Ledésert and D. M. Ledésert, *Historie de la Littérature Française* (London: Edward Arnold, 1946), 1: 274–76.

4. W. Jackson Bate, *The Burden of the Past and the English Poet* (New York: Norton, 1970), pp. 37–38, 111 passim.

5. Jones, *Ancients*, p. 272.

6. Henry Power, *Experimental Philosophy* (London: John Martin and James Allestry, 1663), pp. 183–92, and preface.

7. Ibid., pp. 192–93.

8. David W. Waters, *The Art of Navigation in England in Elizabethan and Early Stuart Times* (London: Hollis and Carter, 1958), p. 101.

9. Joseph Glanvill, *The Vanity of Dogmatizing* (London, 1661), pp. 181–83.

10. Samuel L. Macey, *Clocks and the Cosmos: Time in Western Life and Thought* (Hamden, Conn.: Archon Books, 1980), pp. 28–29.

11. Ibid., pp. 11, 17–18, 21, passim.

12. Macey, "The Horological Revolution and the Industrial Revolution," *Clocks*, pp. 33–44. For a more traditional view, see T. S. Ashton, "The Technical Innovations," *The Industrial Revolution 1760–1830*, rev. ed. (London: Oxford University Press, 1962), pp. 58–93.

13. For these and earlier references to the clock metaphor see Macey, "The Clock Metaphor in Philosophy and Theology," *Clocks*, pp. 65–101. See also F. C. Haber "The Darwinian Revolution in the Concept of Time," in *The Study of Time*, ed. J. T. Fraser, F. C. Haber, and G. H. Müller (New York: Springer-Verlag, 1972), pp. 383–401; and F. C. Haber, "The Cathedral Clock and the Cosmological Clock Metaphor," *The Study of Time II*, ed. J. T. Fraser and N. Lawrence (New York: Springer-Verlag, 1975), pp. 399–416.

14. Daniel Defoe, *A Journal of the Plague Year* (New York: New American Library, 1960), pp. 217–18.

15. For a discussion of Defoe's concern with navigation, projects, and financial institutions, see Samuel L. Macey, *Money and the Novel: Mercenary Motivation in Defoe and His Immediate Successors* (Victoria: Sono Nis, 1983), pp. 17–46. Until 1700, London, with approximately six hundred thousand inhabitants, had no less than twenty times the population of any other town in England.

16. J. T. Fraser, *Of Time, Passion, and Knowledge* (New York: George Braziller, 1975), pp. 371–73, 149, 469.

17. Ricardo J. Quinones, *The Renaissance Discovery of Time* (Cambridge: Harvard University Press, 1972), pp. 9–10, 25, 349, passim.

18. William Shakespeare, *Hamlet*, 4.3. 32–33.

19. Herman L. Ebeling, "The Word *Anachronism*," *Modern Language Notes* 52 (1937): 120–21. According to the *Oxford English Dictionary*, the word *synchronism* was first used in 1588.

20. Francesco Petrarch, *The Triumphs* (London: John Murray, 1906), Mr. Colvin's Notes upon the Engravings.

21. The question of what Darwin really learned from Malthus has been much debated. For a useful discussion on the subject, see Peter Vorzimmer, "Darwin, Malthus, and the Theory of Natural Selection," *Journal of the History of Ideas* 30 (1969): 527–42. See also Howard E. Gruber and Paul H. Barrett, *Darwin on Man* (New York: E. P. Dutton, 1974), pp. 161–63, 172–74; and Loren Eiseley "Darwin and Malthus," *Darwin's Century* (New York: Doubleday, 1958), 178–82.

22. Frederick Engels, *Ludwig Feuerbach and the Outcome of the Classical German Philosophy*, ed. C. P. Dutt (New York: International Publishers, 1941), p. 44.

23. Aldous Huxley, *Brave New World* (Harmondsworth: Penguin, 1955), pp. 39, 44, 173–78 passim. This paper does not consider the "craft"-oriented society—as reflected by William Morris's *News from Nowhere*—which might be thought a desirable new form of social progress. Our present predilections suggest that we continue to be seduced by Western technology and its related lifestyle. One cannot ignore the ever-increasing and world-wide hunger for mechanical transportation, domestic electrical equipment, electronic gadgetry, and fast foods.

24. Ibid., pp. 37, 119—22.

Reflections on Time in Indian Philosophy: With Comments on So-Called Cyclic Time

Anindita Niyogi Balslev

Summary The enigmatic character of the time experience has challenged the human intellect without regard to cultural boundaries. A survey of the history of Indian philosophy reveals a deep involvement with the problem of time. It is possible to identify several distinct and often contradictory conceptual models of time put forward by different schools of Indian philosophy. In an intercultural framework, however, it seems commonplace to maintain that a predominant feature of Indian thought is the notion of cyclic time. This appellation ignores the great diversity in the views of time within the Indian traditions. Moreover, the notion of cyclic time has never been an issue for debate, nor can it be identified as the view of any particular school. The conceptual model of cyclic time, derived from the Hellenic tradition, apparently has resulted in misinterpretations of the Indian position, because both traditions have certain features in common. In this connection it is important to understand the true meaning of the pattern of recurrence that is woven into the texture of Indian thought. It is equally significant to grasp the philosophical function of the symbol of the wheel in Indian culture.

The problem of time, as the history of ideas bears witness to, has challenged the human intellect across the boundaries of disciplines and cultures. The deep involvement with this problem is evident Indian philosophical traditions.[1] One can trace from the early texts—at the level of myths and allegories—ideas about time that are impregnated with suggestions influencing the formation of later theories. Fully developed views about time, however, belong to that stage of philosophical growth where speculations crystallized and took the shape of distinct schools of thought.

It is possible to identify several conceptual models of time in the history of Indian philosophy. The contrast of ideas is awe inspiring—at one end of the scale there is a unitary view of time and at the other end there is a pluralistic view. Some have maintained the objective, independent reality of time, whereas others counteract this stand, pointing to its phenomenal character. The *reader* even encounters the startling inquiry regarding whether being and time coalesce ontologically and hence their separation is to be attributed to an arbitrary linguistic convention.

In an intercultural framework, however, this diversity of conceptual models is generally overlooked. Thus, for instance, it seems commonplace to maintain that the notion of cyclic time is a characteristic and predominant feature of Indian thought. In this connection it is striking to observe that upon closer study of the sources there is no evidence for this contention. The notion of cyclic time, as will be clear from the following survey, has never been an issue for debate, nor can it be identified as the view of any particular school. We shall return to this theme later, after an exposition of the distinct views regarding time in the philosophies of India.

At the outset, let us make some important preliminary observations. The different views on time can be seen to be worked out in accordance with the total vision of reality that is expressed in the metaphysical commitments of the various schools. It is, therefore, important that a particular view of time be studied from within the framework of a given a system, as it influences, and in turn is shaped by, other major concepts such as being and causality. This puts into relief the fundamental role that the view of time plays in the making of a system, because it cannot be replaced by another view without seriously affecting or even endangering the entire conceptual structure. This is why a deeper understanding of the problem of time in the philosophies of India also requires a proper grasping of the conceptual models concerning the problems of being and causality, amongst others. With this in mind, let us first observe the principal characteristics of the three philosophical-religious traditions of India.

Brahmanism bases itself on the Upaniṣadic intuition—expressed in the doctrine of Ātman—of the identical, immutable reality underlying all change and becoming. In the course of the history of the Brahmanical tradition there emerged different schools exhibiting pluralistic, dualistic, monistic, and nondualistic conceptual structures. It is within these metaphysical frameworks that one has to grasp the diverse views about time.

The Buddhist tradition, on the contrary, represents the vision of reality as flux. In radical opposition to Brahmanism, one finds no idea of being that is exempt from change. In the Buddhist universe what does not change does not exist. This is expressed in the doctrine of momentariness (*kṣaṇikavāda*). Although the doctrine was subjected to different interpretations, it is discussed in all three phases of the history of Indian Buddhism. The impact of Buddhist thought can be said to have been revolutionary in the field of Indian philosophical thinking. This was achieved through a rigorous formulation of the idea of "being as instantaneous."

The Jaina tradition exemplifies an attempt to build a conceptual structure that compromises the extreme views by making room for both identity and difference, permanence and change. It puts forward a metaphysical pluralism and advocates an atomic conception of time, which is indeed peculiar to this tradition.

We shall now examine in some detail the distinct conceptual models of time that developed within these traditions and identify them as views of specific schools.

Within the framework of the Brahmanical tradition itself one encounters an interesting diversity in the treatment of time. The Nyāya-Vaiśeṣika schools, for instance, propounded a view of absolute time. Time is characterized as an independent existent, as all pervading, and as having no beginning or end. It is a unitary conception, where all pluralistic usages are explained as merely conventional, made with the help of standard external adjuncts, e.g., solar motion. Time is conceived as static, although any change is conceivable or possible only with reference to or in conjunction with it.[2]

However, other Brahmanical schools of thought are in opposition to this interpretation of time. Thus, the Sāṅkhya school refuses to accept time as a distinct ontological category.[3] Although the school agrees with Nyāya-Vaiśeṣika in maintaining the reality of change, in the Sāṅkhya conceptual structure this does not necessitate the notion of an empty time. It is in the concept of Prakṛti as dynamic nature that Sāṅkhya combines time and matter in the same principle.

The Yoga school agrees with Sāṅkhya in rejecting the reality of an absolute, unitary time but advocates a discrete view. It maintains the reality of time as instant. But "no two instants can be said to exist simultaneously," which implies that such notions as a collection of moments or an objective series is a mental structuring, a subjective construction, devoid of any reality.[4]

In the school of Advaita Vedānta the Brahmanical tradition saw the most rigorous formulation of being as timeless. In the Advaita ontology there is no room for plurality or movement. Here one comes across a refutation of the reality of time as well as change, denying them independent ontological status.[5] The problems of change qua time are reduced in this scheme to problems of appearance.

It is significant that these views of time, developed in the pluralistic Nyāya-Vaiśeṣika, the dualistic Sāṅkhya-Yoga, and the nondualistic Advaita Vedānta metaphysical structures, make room for a conception of being as unproduced and indestructible. This category of thought, in the spirit of the *ātmavada* of the Upaniṣads, remained central to the philosophical systems of all the Brahmanical schools.

With this basic intuition in common, the Brahmanical philosophers naturally also had to face the problems of change and becoming, generation and destruction, and so forth. In order to understand the philosophical positions taken on these issues, the various doctrines of creation and theories of causality, developed in harmony with their views of time, must be taken into consideration. Let us briefly outline the principal ideas.

In the Nyāya-Vaiśeṣika scheme, the production of the contingent entity (*kādācitka*) as an effect (*kārya*) is conceived as a new beginning (*ārambha*) of something that was not existent (*asat*) prior to the causal operation. Hence, the doctrine of creation is called *ārambhavāda* and the theory of causality is termed *asatkāryavāda*. The production and destruction of an entity is conceived as its conjunction and disjunction with the absolute time (*mahākāla*). Thus, the ontological reality of time is the very presupposition for any movement or change. It is precisely for this reason that it is described as that which has itself no beginning or end, but is the substratum of all that has beginning and/or end. But according to the Sāṅkhya theory of causality—*satkāryavāda*—also shared by the Yoga school, the interpretation is different. Here the effect is said to be potentially existent (*sat*) in the cause, which is actualized in and through the causal operation. The idea of an absolute time as a frame of reference is not required in this structure. Creation is manifestation (*abhivyakti*) of what was unmanifest, hence the doctrine of creation is termed *abhivyaktivāda*. The contrast of ideas is evident. The view, that the effect is a new beginning, marked by its prior nonexistence (*prāgabhāva*), has for its prerequisite the notion of an objectively real, absolute time, as in the case of the Nyāya-Vaiśeṣika. On the contrary, the Sāṅkhya view, where the effect was considered a manifestation, an actualization of that which was potentially present in the cause, could do away with the notion of an empty time as a category of existence. In the school of Advaita Vedānta, however, the main focus is on the ontologically real, discerned as nondual (*advaita*), as being-consciousness-bliss (*sat-cit-ānada*). The doctrine of *vivartavāda*, advocated by the school, expresses the idea of cause and effect in a reality-appearance formula. This introduces the concepts of empirical reality (*vyavahāra sat*) and the reality per se (*paramārtha sat*). In this awareness of distinctions—involving a shifting of standpoint—multiplicity, change, and time are granted empirical reality. The Advaita Vedānta, in prodounding this doctrine of *vivarta-*

vāda, clearly demarcates its own distinct position, refuting the *satkāryavāda* of Sāṅkhya-Yoga and a satkāryavāda of Nyāya-Vaiśeṣika.

Brahmanism, in tune with its spiritual foundation in the Upaniṣadic vision, has maintained, in and through all its variations in the understanding of time, a category of thought that provides for a conception of being as uncaused. The rise of Buddhism brought forth a serious challenged to this conceptual pattern.

With the idea of causal efficiency (*arthakriyākāritva*) as the criterion that distinguishes the real from the fictitious, the Buddhists introduced a novel conception of being and time in the field of Indian philosophical speculations. What the Buddhists demonstrated with great logical skill is that the real has to be necessarily momentary in character. Their arguments aimed at establishing that causal efficiency cannot be predicated of the permanent entity and consequently the latter is nothing but fictitious. The classical Buddhist arguments,[6] which were to remain famous, aimed at supporting the idea of reality as flux— where at no two moments can a thing be said to remain identical.

The Buddhists thus denied any conception of being as uncaused, as permanent, as universal, as substance. They also rejected all ideas about time as an all-embracing receptacle à la Vaiśeṣika. The drastic Buddhist conception that emerged is that the so-called separation of being and time is in the last analysis to be attributed to a linguistic convention.

The principal schools of Indian Buddhism are Vaibhāṣika and Sautrāntika (first phase), Mādhyamika (second phase) and Yogācāra-Vijñānavāda (third phase). There are important differences in the philosophical tenets, in the light of which these schools have interpreted the doctrine of momentariness (*kṣaṇikavāda*) and the doctrine of dependent origination (*pratītyasamutpāda*), i.e., the Buddhist theory of causality. An awareness of these internal differences enables one to obtain a deeper insight into the Buddhist universe of thought and to evaluate the eventual implications for the problem of time.

The Sautrāntika understanding of the doctrine of momentariness is for example distinctly different from that of the Vaibhāṣika school. According to the position of the Vaibhāṣika school, termed *sarvāstivāda*,[7] all the elements exist in all three times, i.e., past, present, and future. These were conceived as momentary, as they were subject to constant change and mutation. The Sautrāntika and the Vijñānavāda schools found this interpretation wholly unacceptable. They pointed out that to maintain the reality of all the elements in all three times is as good as holding them to be permanent, which amounts to giving up the idea of momentariness. The Vaibhāṣika philosophers defended their position, leading to interesting exchanges, throwing light on the Buddhist critique of causality.[8]

In the second phase of Buddhism the doctrine of momentariness received a novel treatment by the school of Mādhyamika Śūnyavāda. The method of dialectical analysis, characteristic of this school, was used to show the untenability not only of the idea of time as unitary, but also of the idea of time as instant.[9] The motive for this dialectical approach of the Mādhyamika school was to expose all claims of speculative metaphysics as dogmatism. Some have considered this development as a "dangerous crisis" for the doctrine of momentariness,[10] which was to regain its supremacy in the third phase of Buddhism with the rise of the school of Yogācāra Vijñānavāda. In this school of Buddhist idealism an important question raised concerns the status of momentariness—whether it is an ultimate metaphysical truth or is to be accepted as belonging to the realm of the empirical. It is not possible here to go into further details of these debates recorded in the history of Indian Buddhism.

In the *anekāntavāda* or the many-sided view of reality in Jainism, we find another conceptual model of time. Insofar as the Jaina outlook makes room for both change and permanence and opposes any one-sided extreme view (*ekānta*), the question of time has been a matter of philosophical concern. The reality of change has in this structure a natural sequel, the idea of reality of time. Again, a division is introduced into the concept of time as absolute (*niścaya*) and relative (*vyavahāra*). The real, objective time is conceived in the form of time atoms (*kālāṇu*). These are held to be real and objective, arranged in a monodimensional order. It is said that unlike the space atoms, the time atoms are not capable of combining. The conventional time periods, of which there is an extensive list in the literature, are said to be relative concepts formed with reference to any arbitrary standard of motion.[11]

A careful investigation of the diverse conceptual models in all their different aspects leaves no doubt about the serious concern with the problem of time in the philosophies of India. It is also essential that such a study takes full account of the polemics found in the Brahmanical, Buddhist, and Jaina literature. The impact of a specific view of time on other major philosophical issues in a given structures becomes evident from the records of these controversies.

The Brahmanical thinkers, for example, were fully aware of the challenges that the radical Buddhist idea of being as instantaneous brought to each of their systems. They therefore launched a massive attack against this view. The main charges brought by Brahmanical thinkers against the Buddhist doctrine of momentariness can be classified under three principal headings: (1) the theory is incompatible with the idea of causal efficiency; (2) it cannot do justice to such phenomena as perception, memory, or recognition; (3) it renders ideas concerning moral retribution and salvation meaningless. This shows the wide-rangeing consequences of the idea on such branches of conceptual inquiry as logic, epistemology, psychology, and metaphysics.

The Buddhists, firmly rooted in their conviction, were equally exemplary in the precise formulations of their replies, which were worked out consistently with their conception of reality. The controversies between the schools went on for centuries.

The Jaina contributions are also significant. On the one hand, they challenged the Nyāya-Vaiśeṣika conception of a unitary time; on the other hand, they raised objections against the Buddhist one-sided emphasis on change alone. The records of these sharp exchanges are illuminating for a proper appraisal of the different views on time.

With this broad outline as a background, let us now proceed to the question of cyclic or circular time, a designation that is often associated with Indian thought.

The first thing to observe is that this inquiry is pertinent only in an intercultural context. Seen within the framework of Indian traditions alone it is needless and meaningless to get into any such discussion. As is clear from the above survey, there have been several distinct conceptual models of time in the history of Indian philosophy. There are also many records of controversies touching upon various issues concerning time. There are, for example, exchanges about whether time is real or appearance, whether it is unitary or pluralistic, or about how time is known, e.g., by perception or inference, but there is no record of any debate regarding whether time is cyclic. In short, in Indian philosophical literature, although one comes across detailed enumeration of various properties and characteristics of time in the context of specific views, nowhere is there any mention of cyclic time.

Faced with this situation, our next task is to inquire into the source of this appellation of *cyclic time*, the context where it is used, and its underlying implications.

A search for the source of such a designation leads to the intercultural perspective of the problem of time. In a confrontation of the Indian, the Greek (pre-Christian), and the Judeo-Christian traditions reference is made to their respective understanding of time. A common appraisal of the situation is reflected in the coinage of the term *cyclic time* characterizing the Indo-Hellenic positions and *linear time* expressing the Judeo-Christian stands. It is not, however, easy to find clear-cut formulations that enable one to grasp unambiguously the conceptual contents that are intended by these designations. It remains nevertheless necessary to understand the implications of the notions, where time is qualified by such epithets as *cyclic* and *linear* in the analogy of geometrical figures. The general observations are: if exact recurrences and repetitions are features entailed by cyclic time, uniqueness and unrepeatability are those of linear time. Moreover, in the Judeo-Christian tradition, the linear notion of time involves the idea of beginning and end,[12] whereas the cyclic notion does not warrant that. Some interpret cyclic time as advocating reversibility, others say that the order of events is irreversible, but, as the image of cycle indicates, a future event is also a past event, which renders history meaningless.

For an interesting document concerning the notion of circular time and what it implies, consider the polemical writings of St. Augustine. In his *City of God* he confronts this Greek model: "as those others think, the same measures of time and the same events in time are repeated in circular fashion; on the basis of this cyclic theory, it is argued, for example, that, just as in a certain age the philosopher Plato taught his students in the city of Athens and in the school called the Academy, so during countless past ages, at very prolonged yet definite intervals, the same Plato, the same city, and the same school with the same students, had existed again and again. Heaven forbid, I repeat, that we should believe that. For Christ died once for our sins, but rising from the dead he dies no more, and death shall no longer have domain over him."[13]

An analysis of this significant passage leads to the discernment of certain important elements that are part and parcel of the notion of cyclic time. It involves an exact repetition of cosmological processes along with recurrences, over and over again, of the same individuals with their indentical destinies. Theologically viewed, the conceptual structure makes no room for salvation.[14]

Turning to the Indian scene, one comes across a grandiose cosmological model in the *Purāṇas* where the universe is conceived as undergoing repeated creation and dissolution. It is probable that the idea is closely related to Vedic astronomy. The age of each world cycle (*kalpa*) is measured in astronomical figures, in terms of billions of human years. Each world cycle is then divided and subdivided into periods called *manvantara*, *mahāyuga*, and so on. The epic *Mahābhārata* and the Bhagavad-Gītā use the same idea. It can be observed that this notion of repeated creation and dissolution is very largely accepted by the major schools of Indian philosophy. It may even be said to be a feature of the Indian culture in general.

It is, however, important to note that the Indian mind uses this idea in a soteriological framework. The philosophical literature contains elaborate discussions where one can trace the considerations and argumentations[15] for accepting the idea of repeated creation and dissolution of the cosmos. No Indian tradition has attributed absolute beginning to creation. The idea of beginningless creation (*anādi sṛṣti*) can be traced in the very old text of RgVeda-Samhitā. All cosmological speculations are in conformity with the principle of ex nihilo nihil fit.

It is to be further observed that the recurrences of world cycles do not in the Indian context involve any idea of exact repetition of the particular, and that instead the emphasis is on the similarity of the generic features. There is no equivalent of the Greek model, which St. Augustine is confronting, in the philosophical-religious traditions of India. The doctrine of Karma, a pan-Indian concept, is a rebuttal of any idea of mechanical recurrence of human destiny.

Yet this Greek model seems to have created misunderstandings in the interpretation of Indian thought.[16] Note the following passage of Arnold Toynbee: This philosophy of sheer recurrence, which intrigued, without ever quite captivating, the Hellenic genius, came to dominate contemporary Indic minds." He points to the "cyclic theory of time" which the "Hindu thinkers had evolved," and refers to the Purāṇic idea of *kalpa*. Toynbee further comments:

> Are these "vain repetitions" of the Gentiles really the law of the Universe, and, therefore, incidentally the law of the histories of civilizations? If we find that the answer is in the affirmative, we can hardly escape the conclusion that we are the perpetual victims of an everlasting cosmic practical joke, which condemns us to endure our sufferings and to overcome our difficulties and to purify ourselves of our sins—only to know in advance that the automatic inevitable lapse of a certain meaningless measure of time cannot fail to stultify all our human exertions by reproducing the same situation again and again *ad infinitum*, just as if we had never exerted ourselves at all.[17]

These lines remind one of the polemical words of St. Augustine facing the Greek idea, also from his *City of God*: "From this whirligig they are quite unable to free their immortal soul even though it has attained wisdom, for in its own uninterrupted circular course it moves back and forth between false happiness and genuine unhappiness."[18]

If these are the implications of the appellation of cyclic time, they are evidently far from the spirit of Indian thought. It is therefore necessary to grasp the philosophical significance of the pattern of recurrence that is weaved into the texture of this culture. A deeper acquaintance with these philosophical traditions reveals that the ideas concerning Karma, transmigration, world cycle, and salvation are all interconnected parts of a given conceptual system. It is not possible to go into the wide variety of views concerning these ideas that have emerged in the history of Indian thought.

But, as it is directly relevant for the present discussion, one would like to draw attention to the fact that the idea of world cycle represents a cosmological model accepted by the different schools of Indian philosophy, which otherwise have distinctly different views about time. As an example, one could mention that both the Vaiśeṣika and the Sāṅkhya schools accept the idea of repeated creation and dissolution in their cosmology, although their metaphysical schemes operate with very different conceptions of time, as already pointed out. In other words, to accept the idea of world cycles as a cosmological model (or the idea of transmigration, for that matter) is not equivalent to resorting to any idea of time as cyclic or circular. These are, philosophically speaking, different issues however intimately related.

Apart from the cosmological models of repeated creation and dissolution, which in the

Vāyu Purāṇa is compared to the cycle of day and night of Brahma (the deity), Indian culture makes profuse use of the image of the wheel (*cakra*). The philosophical schools also use the symbol of the wheel in different ways. To cite an authentic example of the function of the symbol in the Brahmanical tradition, reference could be made to the commentary of Vyāsa on the *Yoga-Sūtra*. It is said that from virtue arises happiness, from impiety, pain, from happiness, attachment, from pain, aversion, attachment and aversion lead to efforts, which result in action. This in turn gives rise to virtue or impiety, happiness or pain, attachment or aversion, and so on and on. Thus revolves "the six-spoked wheel of the round of the rebirths" (*saḍaram samsāracakram*).[19]

The Buddhist tradition also, stemming from the same cultural soil, makes the symbol a vehicle of Buddhist thought. In Buddhist philosophical literature as well as in sculpture one comes across the imagery of Buddha's "setting in motion the wheel of law" (*dharmacakra-pravarttana*). The pictorial image of the wheel of becoming (*bhava-cakra*) is used in the service of the Buddhist idea of "the different stages in the transmigration of the individual."[20] Evidently, these are not expressions of any idea of mechanical repetition of individual destiny, externally imposed. On closer examination it can be seen that the emphasis is on the inexorability of the moral law, Karma, involving the idea of transmigration, with salvation as the final goal.

This symbolic representation of the wheel, when understood as intended by the culture from which it stems, is no "counsel of despair for humanity."[21] It is important not to lose sight of the soteriological dimension.[22]

It is now clear that the spectrum of views concerning time that has emerged in the philosophical-religious traditions of India is also of interest for an understanding of Indian culture in general. To make an incorrect assessment of the treatment of time in the philosophies of India is to project a false image of the culture. A philosophy of time forms an integral part of a coherent picture of human existence and remains indispensable for a worldview.

Notes

1. See, for example, Anindita Niyogi Balslev, *A Study of Time in Indian Philosophy* (Wiesbaden: Otto Harrassowitz, 1983).

2. *Praśastapādabhāṣya with commentary Nyāyakandalī of Śrīdharabhaṭṭa* (Varanasi, 1963).

3. See *The Tattvakaumudī*, Vācaspati Miśra's commentary on Sāṅkhya-Kārikā. Text and trans. Ganganath Jha (Poona, 1965), Karika 33 and commentary thereon, pp. 111–13.

4. *Yoga-Sūtra of Patañjali with the Bhāṣya of Vyāsa, the Tattvavaiśāradī of Vācaspati Miśra and the Vṛtti of Bhoja* (Benares, 1972), a commentary on Yoga-Sūtra, 3: 52. See also the translation by J. H. Woods (1914; reprint ed., Delhi: Motilal Banarsidass, 1972).

5. *Tattvapradīpikā* of Citsukha (Benares, 1974), pp. 510–14; and *Khaṇḍaṇakhaṇḍakhādya* of Śrī Harṣa, Chowkhamba Sanskrit series, 1970, pp. 682–84.

6. S. Mookherjee, *The Buddhist Philosophy of Universal Flux* (1935; reprint ed., Delhi, 1975), pp. 1–37.

7. *Abhidharmakośa and Bhāṣya of Vasubandu with Sphuṭārthā, commentary of Ācārya Yasomitra*, vols. 1, 2, ed. Swami Dwarikadas Shastri (Varanasi: Bauddha Bharati, 1971).

8. *Tattvasamgraha of Śāntarakṣita, with the commentary Pañjikā of Kamalaśīla*, ed. Swami Dwarikadas Shastri (Varanasi: Bauddha Bharati, 1968), pp. 613–32.

9. *Mādhyamika Kārikā* of Nāgārjuna, ed. L. de la Vallée Poussin (St. Petersburg, 1907), chap. 19, "Kālaparīkṣā."

10. Theodore Stcherbatsky, *Buddhist Logic*, (New York: Dover, 1962), 1: 110.

11. *Pañcāstikāyasāra* of Kundakundāchārya, The Sacred Books of the Jainas, vol. 3 (New York: A.M.S. Press, 1974), pp. 21–24.

12. Some hold that linear time without any beginning or end is a secularization of the biblical idea.

13. St. Augustine, *De Civitate Dei*, trans. P. Levine (London: Heinemann; Cambridge: Harvard University Press, 1966), bk. 12, chap. 14, p. 63.

14. For an analysis of another example of the idea of eternal return, see D. W. Dauer, "Nietzsche and the Concept of Time," in *The Study of Time II*, ed. J. T. Fraser and N. Lawrence (New York: Springer-Verlag, 1975), pp. 81–97.

15. See Śaṅkara's commentary on *Brahma Sūtra* (2.1.35); for translation, see G. Thibault, *Sacred Books of the East*, vol. 34 (Oxford, 1890).

16. Greek philosophy evidently contains several conceptual models. The idea of exact repetition has been attributed to the Pythagoreans.

17. Arnold Toynbee, *A Study of History*, rev. and abridged by the author and Jane Caplan (New York: Oxford University Press, 1972), pp. 157–58.

18. St Augustine, *De Civitate Dei*, bk. 13, chap. 13, p. 61.

19. *Yoga-Sūtra of Patañjali*, 4: 11.

20. E. J. Thomas, *History of Buddhist Thought* (London, 1933), p. 70.

21. Toynbee, *A Study of History*, p. 487.

22. Mircea Eliade discusses the soteriological aim of "the myth of the cosmological cycles" in his "Time and Eternity in Indian Thought," *Man and Time: Papers from the Eranos Yearbooks* (New York: Pantheon Books, 1957), pp. 173–200.

The Shape of Time in African Music

Ruth M. Stone

The time is now.
All days are not equal.
AFRICAN TAXI MOTTOES

Summary   For a century, comparative musicologists and ethnomusicologists studying African music have marveled at and speculated about the rhythms by which performers organize their musicmaking. This study examines the implicit ideas of temporality in the work of these scholars, relating these ideas to broader concepts of African time and suggesting that their configuration represents an alternative to Western linear quantitative time. While the focus is song time, other time levels are briefly considered as they relate to song time: event time, biographical time, life-cycle time, stylistic time, and historical time.

The study of African rhythm seized the imagination of scholars from the earliest European scrutiny of African music, and an important issue has been the search for an organizing principle. Whether identified as the downbeat of the big drum by W. E. Ward, the motor activity of the body by Erich M. von Hornbostel, the metronome sense by Richard Waterman, or handclapping by A. M. Jones, all assume an underlying equally spaced beat or pulse, as Alan P. Merriam aptly pointed out. Such an assumption should not surprise us because Western clock time, as well as much Western art music of the eighteenth through early twentieth centuries, is based upon the homogeneous division of time.

During my own research of Kpelle music in West Africa, particularly the Wọi* epic, I determined that the idea of a single organizing beat with equally divisible units is quite obscure in Kpelle conceptualization. A multiplex basis appears to ground the organization for the Kpelle.

Recent work on hemiola, inherent rhythms, the time line, mnemonic syllables, and transaction suggests that African music emphasizes qualitative over quantitative elements, the delineation of a three-dimensional space, and motion. A consideration of other aspects of time in African societies supports such conclusions.

African music compels not only the people who create it, but also those scholars who have tried to study it. The rhythm—apparently special and unusual—arrests our attention as we wonder how these artists achieve such constellations of sound, of movement. In this paper I will explore both scholarly and indigenous concepts used to explain time in African music and identify the most interesting and powerful ideas in light of data available. I will argue that African rhythm is organized on a multiplex basis derived from a motion-filled, three-dimensional spatial conceptualization with a qualitative focus.

African musical performance is an exciting and often dazzling mélange of singing, dancing, speaking, masquerading, and acting. In a closely intertwined event these modes of communication fuse in a way that makes it difficult to separate and analyze. Ethnomusi-

---

* In the orthography, ọ = ɔ, ŋ = ŋ, y̧ = ɣ, and ẹ = ɛ. ọ is pronounced "aw" as in awful; ŋ is pronounced "ng" as in sing; y̧ is pronounced "ch" as in the German ach; ẹ is pronounced "eh" as in let.

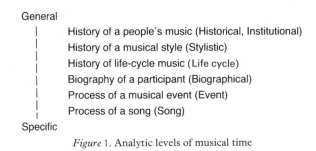

Figure 1. Analytic levels of musical time

cologists have traditionally scrutinized songs—items of performance—and song time. The study of musical rhythm is essentially the study of song time.

Many other levels of time interact with song time and also require consideration. The second level, more inclusive than song time, is event time, the flow characteristic of a musical event. The pauses and speeches between songs, dance, and drama all constitute a great deal more than music sound. Instrumental playing, singing, speaking, dancing, and dramatization contribute to the complex. At the third level of specificity is the life trajectory of a musician or other participant—biographical time. Fourth, life-cycle time encompasses the stereotypic life span of a group of people. Fifth, the history of musical style affects the sound performance. At the most general level, the broad history of music influences a particular song-time level. As we move from song time to historical time, each of these time levels not only possesses a unique character but is also increasingly broad and more inclusive. The overarching category is what J. T. Fraser has termed *nootemporal umwelt*, the temporality that is "unique to the human mind" (Fraser 1981, xxxii).

To understand the temporality of a musical performance, we need to understand something of the levels of time and their integration. Because ethnomusicological study has focused on song time, I wish to concentrate on that area, drawing on the other time levels to illustrate relationships among them.

One of the earliest reports of time in African music comes from Ibn Batuta, the great Arab traveler who left Morocco in A.D. 1352 to cross the Sahara and visit the kingdom of Mali. His account indicates a multisensory experience of which musical sound was but one part: "In front of the Sultan go the singers holding gold and silver rattles; behind him are about three hundred armed slaves. The Sovereign walks leisurely.... Finally he slowly mounts the platform in the manner of a preacher mounting his pulpit: as soon as he is seated, they beat the drums, and sound the horn and trumpets" (Batuta 1858, 406,411, in Jones 1957, 8–9). Some observers of African rhythm did not appreciate the sound. Father Denis de Carli on a journey through the Congo in 1666–67 remarked, "This harmony is grateful at a distance, but harsh and ungrateful near at hand, the beating of so many Sticks causing a great confusion" (Angelo and DeCarli 1704, 694). Others, however, were struck by the precision of rhythmic coordination. Of the Kafir in southern Africa it was said, "Their notion of melody is very slight, while their time is perfection itself, and the very fact that several hundred men will sing the various war songs, as if they were animated by a single spirit shows that they must all keep the most exact time" (Wood 1868, in Wallaschek 1893, 4).

The careful study of musical rhythm by comparative musicologists—as ethnomusicolo-

Double Bell	x	.	x	.	x	x	.	x	.	x	x	.	
Beats	x	.	x	.	x	.	.	x	.	x	.	.	
Pulses	x	x	x	x	x	x	x	x	x	x	x	x	
Grouping	2+		2+		3+			2+		3			= 12

x = struck
. = rest or sustained

Figure 2. Double bell pattern

gists were earlier known—began with the advent of the cylinder recorder, for expeditions became capable of bringing back recorded samples of music, much the same as they collected specimens of the flora and fauna. These recordings could be examined and studied in the laboratory.

Although researchers espoused a variety of explanations for African rhythm, Alan P. Merriam observed that all scholars assumed, implicitly if not explicitly, an equal pulse base with its homogeneous quantitative linearity (1977). Merriam did not point out, however, that although the basic underlying pulses were considered equal, at a higher analytic level these pulses were sometimes grouped into beats of unequal length. Additive rhythm as described by Curt Sachs (1953) often contained beats of asymmetrical proportions, though they were composed of pulses all equally spaced. Sachs's ideas represented a breakthrough for ethnomusicologists, allowing for the possibility of nonequal groupings. The prominent pattern in African music, sometimes called the *time line*, could in Sachs's terms be analyzed as in figure 2.

Approaches to Rhythm

In 1952 Richard Waterman suggested an organizing principle called the *metronome sense*. Drawing on his experience in Afro-American jazz rather than on fieldwork experience in Africa, he proposed that Africans created a basic framework of equally spaced beats. Within the grid, the participants embellished the scheme as they liked. Even if all the beats were not aurally sounded, the musician filled in the unsounded beats mentally. Waterman further reasoned that in African music "off-beat" phrasing occurred when the music emphasized rhythms that occur off, rather than on, the beat (1952, 207–18). The contribution of Waterman's theory rests in its assertion that rhythm is more than what is heard, and that what takes place in the mind of the listener is important even if it is not audible.

Waterman's description of African music as offbeat is an idea that other scholars have utilized as well—sometimes using *syncopation* interchangeably (Locke 1978, 349; Chernoff 1979, 47–48). The consequences of employing these terms are profound. Both offbeat and syncopation imply that a steady and equally spaced beat underlies the performance. In relation to that beat, another is sounded, playing against the equal beat. The conception is important, for one might ask whether the two parts could be better analyzed as each moving in its own rhythm, each conceived with its own beat, two beats that do not necessarily coincide? Such a question is not trivial for it asks whether two parts form a single rhythmic conception, as might characterize syncopation, or whether they are independently conceived rhythms sounded in conjunction, as might be the case with hemiola.

Rose Brandel, among others, has maintained that what has been identified as syncopation or off-beat phrasing is better described as *hemiola*. Following the lead of her mentor Curt Sachs she commented, "The African hemiola style is based on this play of two and three, which is much like the Middle Eastern additive style of rhythm with its far greater diversity of durational contrast" (1961, 15). Pulses are grouped together in units of two or three and they can exhibit the 2: 3 ratio horizontally over time or vertically between parts. An example of horizontal hemiola can be seen in figure 3.

```
        x   .   x   .   x   .   x   .   .   x   .   .
        2+      2+      2+      3+          3           = 12

or

        x   .   x   .   x   .   .   x   .   x   .   .
        2+      2+      3+          2+      3           = 12
```

Figure 3. Horizontal hemiola

Vertical hemiola, on the other hand, might be realized as in figure 4.

```
        2+      2+      2+      2+      2+      2
        x   .   x   .   x   .   x   .   x   .   x   .   = 12


        x   .   x   .   x   .   .   x   .   x   .   .
        2+      2+      3+          2+      3           = 12
```

Figure 4. Vertical hemiola

Such a conception allows the possibility of unequally spaced beats without the implication that the asymmetrical beats are offbeats in relation to a central beat. Beats may be unequal in length without involving syncopation. John Blacking has commented on a 6/8 rhythm pattern, noting that "when it is played in Europe it is always conceived as the product of a single agent—with very few possible exceptions.... In the African context the rhythm expresses the perfect cooperation of two performers who nevertheless pursue their individuality by maintaining different main beats" (1969, 18).

Arthur M. Jones, a missionary and one of the most persistent researchers of African rhythm, coined the term *cross-rhythm* to describe a phenomenon similar, but not identical to hemiola (1934). "The melody being additive, and the claps being divisive, when put together they result in a combination of rhythms whose inherent stresses are *crossed*. This is the very essence of African music: this is what the African is after. He wants to enjoy a conflict of rhythms" (1959, 21–22). He suggested not only different rhythms but different principles of constructing the rhythms.

Inherent Rhythms

Gerhard Kubik identified a related phenomenon in East and Central African music (1962). In numerous performances the gestalt of the rhythm is quite different as perceived by the listener than as organized by the individual performer. Resulting rhythms are not only those played by individual performers but are also the result of a configuration of parts. The seventeen-key *akadinda* xylophone from Uganda, for example, is played by three men with the song "Basibira malaika" (Moslems are fasting). Kubik shows the three parts, as well as an inherent rhythm, which is not represented by what any single part plays. Thus the rhythmic intricacy draws not only from single parts conceived independently but also from the unit.

Time Line

The organizing principle in song rhythm has been identified by a number of researchers as the pattern often sounded by the clapperless double bell (*gankogui* in Ewe). The pattern is typically notated in 12/8 and can be realized in a number of ways.

```
Ewe (Ghana)   12
Gangkogui      8    x   .   x   .   x   x   .   x   .   x   .   x
```

Figure 5. Standard pattern

This distinctive and pervasive pattern has been labeled time *line* (Kubik 1972, 169–76) and *timekeeper*, for Kwabena Nketia comments, "The rhythm pattern is therefore a guiding principle and it is in this sense that the gong may be referred to as timekeeper" (1958, 21). James Koetting, however, cautions that this relationship not be overextended when he says that "while the function of the gong as a basic ensemble timing center must not be questioned, it would be a mistake to analyze all the patterns of a piece as though they had a primary timing relation to the gong" (1970, 137).

Speech syllables may be used to differentiate the pattern for African musicians. The Yoruba, for example, use the following mnemonic device:

```
Drum     x   .   x   .   x   x   .   x   .   x   x   .
Speech   kon     kon     ko- lo      kon     ko- lo
                                           (King 1960, 52)
```

Figure 6. Yoruba mnemonic syllables

Kubik discovered that the Fon of Togo incorporate a "silent complementary pattern" he also refers to as a "negative mirror image" of the sounded pattern. The singer simultaneously sounds the time line with his right hand (RH) and silently taps the complementary part with his left hand (LH).

```
Pattern (RH)    x   .   x   .   x   x   .   x   .   x   .   x
Grouping        7+                      5                    = 12

Inaudible
complementary
grouping (LH)       .   x   .   x   .   .   x   .   x   .   x   .   = 12
                5+                  7
```

Figure 7. Silent complementary pattern

Kubik maintains that even though not heard, the part must be considered part of a total complex characteristically used in Central Africa (1972, 171–72). Aside from P. Augier who feels that the seven and five are symbolically important for the Tuareg (1971, 217–33), most researchers acknowledge that the seven and five are concepts of the Western analytic perspective rather than of the African point of view.

Hewitt Panteleoni, using data of the Ewe of Ghana, points out that the time line occurs in the highest pitch range, quite in contradistinction to Western ensembles where the underlying rhythm comes from the lowest pitched instruments. He conceives of this placement as the top layer from which come "timing and gait" (1972, 50). He further cites drummers who claim one must always be with the bell pattern. In arguing for the time line as the regulative principle, he points out that the timing pattern is asymmetrical and that against the timing pattern every other pattern has but one placement. He says that this scheme has an advantage over using equidistant beats as the regulators in which case without change in timbre or dynamic stress, these beats can "serve to place a pattern in only the most general way" (58–59).

If one holds that this time line forms a fundamental part of the regulative system, then there are several implications. First, asymmetry is prominent, at the level both of the individual strokes and of the larger groupings that are inferred. Second, if the time line is a fundamental unit, with each of the instruments placed in only one specific way against it, perhaps the focus on more specific units such as beats that constitute it misses the more important focus of the time cycle.

Motor Patterns

A number of scholars have asserted that motor patterns must be studied in order to understand the basis of African rhythms. Erich M. von Hornbostel, one of the earliest to make this claim, maintained that "what really matters is the act of beating; and only from this point can African rhythms be understood" (1928, 49). Though a number of people have argued with the details of his theory, the idea is significant in that it broadens the approach to studying African rhythm.

In the last twenty years, Kubik has contributed more than any other ethnomusicologist to the motor-based analysis of African rhythm. He has worked from the premise that the act of musicmaking involves both an acoustic and visual-motor aspect. From film analysis of rhythmic patterns, Kubik discovered that both East and West African performers require two-thirds of the time between impact points to reach the vertex (the highest point of raising the arm) and only one-third of the time to strike the next impact. Therefore a 2: 1 ratio exists between upswing and downbeat. European students of the *akadinda* xylophone, on the other hand, tend to divide the distance between impact points in half (1965, 33–34). His finding is all the more stunning when he claims that not only does this generalization hold for musical performance, but it also obtains for millet pounding, bellow pumping, and bark cloth beating. If one concludes that equally spaced impact points reflect an equally spaced beat, one has ignored the vertex pattern that introduced a perfect hemiola between silent and audible beats and therefore unequal beats between the motor and acoustic. Kubik also argues that the stereotypic repetition, which is so often cited as a major feature of African music, is, in fact, nonexistent if one takes into account the motor as well as the sound patterns, for in combination one finds subtle variations to be an important feature (40).

Timbre Text

A recent and interesting direction in rhythm analysis has been of the timbre and verbal text within rhythmic patterns. Many African musicians learn rhythmic patterns, including the time line, through mnemonic phrases consisting of syllables that convey not only timing but also timbre.

12/8 pattern	x	.	x	.	x	x	.	x	.	x	x	.
Yoruba-Nigeria	kon		kon		ko̩	lo		kon		ko	lo	

(King 1960 : 52)

| Bamenda-Cameroon | ko̩ | | ko̩ | | ko̩ | yo̩ | | ko̩ | | ko̩ | yo̩ | |

(Kubik 1972a : 174)

| Akan-Ghana | kon̩ | | kon̩ | | ko | kon̩ | | kon̩ | | ko | kon̩ | |

(Ibid.)

Figure 8. Mnemonic syllables

As Kubik points out, the syllables can distinguish timbral subtleties to an extent that Western staff notation cannot. In the first example in figure 8, although the *ko̩n* and *lo̩* are notated exactly alike as quarter notes in staff notation, the player of the *kanango* (hourglass drum) uses more energy to strike *ko̩n* than *lo̩*. *Lo̩* is a legato stroke (Kubik 1972, 170, 176). Roderic Knight, who has studied Mandinka drumming in Gambia says that "one may conclude that [the drummer's] abilities are at least in part attributable to learning each rhythm as a pattern of timbres—different timbres produced by four basic strokes on the drum" (1974, 29).

Transaction

As we examine these various approaches to rhythm, note that each one takes into account the way African musicians themselves conceive of time. In the transactional explanation of time we center on the interaction between at least two parts. Kubik observes that two players of Mangwilo xylophone in southeastern Africa sit opposite one another and share in playing the same instrument. They are referred to as *Opachera* (the starting one) and *Wakulela* (the responding one) (1965, 36). Similarly, Paul Berliner shows that even with a solo instrument like the plucked idiophonic *mbira* of Zimbabwe, the Shona people designate the first part as "*kushaura* (to lead the piece, to take the solo part)" and the second part as the "*kutsihira* (to exchange parts of a song; to interweave a second interlocking *mbira* part)" (1978, 73).

Kubik identifies what he calls "interlocking" style in Mangwilo xylophone music: each player feels his own pulse and the two mesh when heard as one in yet another unity (1965, 39). The rhythms then exist with both individual and combined identity.

The idea that drums converse in their interactions is a prominent theme among African musicians and can be conceived as a call-and-response pattern (Chernoff 1979, 53). Thus, rather than consider African rhythm as focusing on one beat to which all other parts fit, we need to explore the possibility that the organizational principle rests within the dynamic tension between two parts, which converse through time. John Blacking highlights the notion of transaction by showing that musicians use it, not out of necessity, but for aesthetic quality: "Thus, performances by combinations of two or three players of rhythms that can, in fact, be played by one are not musical gimmicks: they express concepts of individuality in community, and of social, temporal, and spatial balance, which are found in other features of Venda culture and other types of Venda music" (1973, 30).

Relations among Levels

I will now explore the next higher level, event time, and show some common threads of time organization evident in this more inclusive analytical area. Because ethnomusicologists have done little study in this area, I draw primarily on my own fieldwork among the Kpelle of Liberia, West Africa, that began in 1970, continued during 1975–76, and to which I returned most recently in the early part of 1983.

The complex movement of time can be studied in the epic that centers around the superhuman hero Wọi. In this event, drama, narrative, and music integrate in the creation of time.

Wọi-mẹni-pele, as this event is known among the Kpelle, is one in which the narrative never concludes. As one singer told his audience, "the head of an epic does not come out. You just keep bouncing." The singer realizes this goal of endless narrative by constructing each episode so that a neat conclusion is never reached. Rather, in the midst of one episode, the elements of another episode are inserted. The effect is achieved musically as phrases of an upcoming episode are sung briefly before an episode has ended. The temporal shifts that occur are evident even in the narrative text, for the teller, as often as sentence to sentence, moves to various times (i.e., tenses) to reveal the action of the story. The temporal style contrasts with other Kpelle genres such as the *chante-fable* (mẹni-pele) where each song episode concludes with a dramatic high point. As Kpelle people readily articulate, the epic, however, must not end.

The epic event is created, first and foremost, by a storyteller-singer. Like the Southeast Asian *dalang* or puppeteer, he also serves as the conductor of the entire event. He keeps himself aware of all that is happening and communicates the need for adjustments to the musicians. A chorus provides a background of music for the storyteller, performing continuously throughout the narration of each episode and singing short interlocking ostinato phrases, constructed of a short pattern that is repeated without variation. Between the end of one choral ostinato and the beginning of the next, a supporting singer may also perform an ostinato. In addition, two instrumentalists play interlacing rhythmic patterns on glass bottles. A questioner prods the storyteller at crucial points, asking who is speaking or questioning whether such a fantastic thing could have actually happened. All the people serve to make this event a series of transactional parts combined into a unity.

Significantly, the Wọi epic has neither a precise starting nor a precise concluding episode. Unlike the Mwindo epic, recorded by Daniel Biebuyck and Kahombo Mateene among the Nyanga people of the Congo Republic, the Wọi epic does not proceed from the birth of the hero through his various lifetime adventures (1971). Rather, from all evidence, the teller is free to begin and end with any episode. The absence of a necessary linear progression between episodes in some African epics is very reminiscent of the situation Alton L. Becker describes for Javanese shadow theater (*wayang kulit*). A *wayang* plot is built on coincidence and may begin at any temporal point in the story. It must, however, begin in certain locations. That is, space rather than time is constrained (1979, 225). In a related vein, Robert Plant Armstrong's textual analysis of the Nigerian musical drama, *The Palm Wine Drinkard*, identifies the episodes as "sequential" rather than "consequential" in what he terms "intensive continuity" created by the "density of multiple, discrete parts" (1971, 168).

The Wọi epic takes place in the distant mythic past as implied by the episode in which all living things—plants and animals—are born to Wọi's wife. It is also in a time of fighting and conflict as Wọi moves from one battle to another. The episodes recorded move between earth and various parts of the sky: the part of the sky upon which one can sit (*yele kọlọn*) and the distant sky that exists behind the sky proper (*yele-polu*).

The central characters are Wọi and his family—his wives, his sister, his daughter, Maa-pu, and his two sons, Zu-kpeei, the elder, and Wọi-boi, the younger. Divinities include two monster spirits who oppose Wọi: Yele-lao who appears also as a bitter rattan plant and Mẹni-maa-fa who alternates between human and lizard forms. A number of other animals and plants act also in a human capacity. During the epic performance the storyteller also summons his tutelary spirit. Thus, in addition to human participants, physically present, we must note surrogate participants. They may be *predecessors* (beings who share neither time nor space) or *contemporaries* (beings who share time but not space ordinarily). In the performance context they are, in Alfred Schutz's terms, transformed into *consociates* (individuals who, during the event, share both time and space) (1973, 15–19).

The epic plot concerns conflicts between Wọi and various enemies. One cannot, however, identify a single climactic battle. Furthermore, dramatic moments when the enemy is defeated are downplayed and muted, again blunting linear progression.

The lack of plot movement, however, does not imply a lack of action. For movement and action are depicted with precise characterization throughout the episodes: playing the slit drum, pumping the bellows, cutting trees. Movement pervades in the onomatopoeic syllables sung by the chorus that are a kind of summary and symbolic key to each episode.

The episodes created within this epic are developed into what I have elsewhere (1982, 72) termed *expandable moments*. At a variety of structural levels, moments envelop action with variable propensity to expand outward but not linearly. Such an approach to temporality recalls Georges Gurvitch's definition of time as a "continuity of heterogeneous moments" (1964, 18). As these moments expand, they at some point reach a limit. The participants leap conceptually to another moment and they proceed to expand this new moment. The moments expand through three-dimensional space, for the Kpelle employ terms to explain development that creates such an impression.

> Raise the song.
> Cut the edge of the dance.
> Respond underneath the song.
> Lower the performance.
> The performance has gotten down.

The terms *edge* and *underneath* are locational words. The verbs indicate further aspects of location and, in addition, detail the desired action: *raise, cut, respond,* and *lower*. Through such description the action is noted with precision and placed within the moment three dimensionally, rather than in simple, linear two-dimensional spatial terms so customary to Western thinking and practice. This three-dimensional space also serves as a metaphor for explaining certain dimensions of Kpelle time in a nonmetric sense, just as in Western thought two-dimensional linearity creates a metric for time. Because the Kpelle blunt the passage of linear time (as do the Balinese), I would characterize the Kpelle notion of event time as "motionful present" rather than the "motionless present" that Clifford Geertz attributes to the Balinese (1973, 40).

Event time in African music is certainly not all of one order and I would like to distinguish Kpelle time associated with ritual from time associated with secular activity. Maurice Bloch asserts that the nonlinear time reckoning observed among various African cultures is, in fact, ritual time and that if ordinary time were studied, different results would be apparent (1977, 278–82).

From my Kpelle data, however, I would like to suggest that in practice it is difficult to isolate neatly sacred and profane time in the manner Edmund Leach suggests (1961). These two times comingle within the single epic event. Ritual time in Kpelle terms emphasizes continuity, repetition, and unity. Cut-off cues are omitted to preserve the onward flow. Nonritual or ordinary time stresses segmentation, variation, and creativity. These are associations that the Kpelle both recognize and verbalize.

The Wọi epic very deftly interweaves the ritual and secular. Segmentation of ordinary time exists in the short, multi-ostinati the chorus sings. Rather than respond in unison, they sing fragmented, interlocking responses. The storyteller-singer exercises considerable creative license as he narrates each episode, drawing on the momentary ambience for direction. On the other hand, ritual time is clearly evident as episode unit endings are obscured through foreshadowing of musical themes, story, and characters. Furthermore, continuity is demonstrated by a storyteller never singing all the episodes he knows—for his repertoire is theoretically infinite.

This analysis of time characteristics in music is further supported with examples from social and historical time levels, illustrating the themes that permeate the various time levels.

Social time is located in and defined by the social group. Temporal references are established from social event landmarks rather than from physical, personal, or clock marks (see Lewis and Weigert 1981, 433). People define actions in relation to what other people in a group are doing.

One of the most significant and long-standing analyses of social time in Africa comes from E. E. Evans-Pritchard. In his study of the Nuer (1940), his categories of "oecological time" and "structural time" both derive, in large part, from social action. Under oecological time the two main seasons, *tot* and *mai*, relate to the rainy and dry seasons, and they are also associated with a cluster of social activities. The Nuer do not travel *when* the season arrives. Rather, it arrives by coincidence when they travel (1940, 99). Thus the Nuer find *tot* in a certain place rather than going to a certain place in *tot*. Across the continent in West Africa Paul Bohannan quotes the Tiv as saying, "The first harmattan comes when we cut guinea corn" (1953, 255).

Even daily time rhythms may be socially oriented. Among the Kabyle of Algeria, Pierre Bordieu notes that the five daily Islamic prayer calls are not conceived linearly or numerically. He comments: "The islands of time which are defined by these landmarks are not apprehended as segments of a continuous line, but rather as so many self-enclosed units. . . . Each of the temporal units is an indivisible block juxtaposed to the others" (1963, 59).

Historical time encompasses the broadest perspective considered thus far. History is the concern of those engaged in formal retrospect, and history is important to African peoples, many of whom possess it in an oral rather than a written form (d'Azevedo 1962). The past for many African peoples is not static. As Warren L. d'Azevedo explains: "The Gola sense of historical time, therefore, must be considered as a multiple, compartmentalized and variable phenomenon undergoing continual change. . . . the Gola approach to the past is dynamic rather than static. Its motives are instrumental and the past is regarded as a potential reservoir of negotiable property" (1962, 33). D'Azevedo goes on to say that chronological sequence in genealogies is not stressed. Rather, "it is the quality of an event or a cluster of events which is the focus of interest" (28). Gilbert Rouget's analysis of court songs in Dahomey well illustrates d'Azevedo's assertions. In Porto-Novo the songs at court are sung not so much to reiterate and preserve facts unaltered as they are to actively reconstruct the past. Allusiveness and ambiguity are prominent features designed to present the obscure meanings of these songs of praise and insult. While the first stanza is addressed to the present king, the subsequent verses, which are addressed to past kings, vary in the kings they include (1971, 35).

From the evidence of a number of time perspectives in African music we can draw some tentative conclusions. First, time in African music emphasizes qualitative over quantitative elements. Such attention stresses timbral characteristics over the chronometric elements so often emphasized in the Western ordering of time in music. The lack of quantitative characteristics, does not, however, negate a complex system of coordination. Social and historical time levels also show similar avoidance of the chronometric while stressing various qualitative dimensions of time.

Furthermore, we should not rush to conclude that Africans are traditionally incapable of chronometric time reckoning. In Kpelle ritual performance, chronometric aspects assert an unusual importance not apparent in other types of performance. Among the Kpelle, the number three is ritually associated with a woman, and the number four with a man. Thus, a girl is brought out of seclusion three days after birth, she emerges from the Sande secret society at the end of three years, and when she dies her death feast occurs three days after burial with three gunshots fired.

One sees in these particular cases an inversion of the normal ascendance of qualitative time. Here quantitative time is viewed as re-creative and reproductive of the traditional elements of life while qualitative time is associated with the creative, progressive, and innovative.

A second salient feature of time in African music is the delineation of space. Qualitative distinctions are often made by reference to space. Music conceptually moves in a three-dimensional volume of expanding moments that contrasts to nineteenth-century Western notions of a flat, linear progression.

Third, time in African music emphasizes the concept of motion. Motion is the lifeblood and character of music, identified and noted with great precision. In Kpelle, for example, the dancer can tremble in six different ways.

The past, in African music, is dynamically manipulated within the present. While attention centers on music in the present, the past is equally essential because it provides authority and sanction, entering into the present in an active and instrumental way. The present is a context for adjusting and reproducing the past to best fit the current moment. For example, musicians manipulate relationships with deceased ancestors to enhance the performance.

The uniqueness of African musical time rests not on any one of these characteristics that

I have noted but on their total effect. The emphasis provides a subtle yet strikingly different approach to shaping music. But this very subtlety makes the blend of elements subject to misinterpretation. In the end, the differences are quite profound and we see how wispy and fragile are the concepts we seek.

Here we have a view of time that on certain levels is an alternative to linear progression calculated quantitatively. A qualitative view of time emphasizing motion and three-dimensional spatial delineation shows precision and sophistication in its organizing of music even as we now crudely understand it. In the end, alternative modes of time conception create exciting new vistas for study leading ultimately to a more cosmopolitan perspective. Only through a concern for music as created, conceptualized, and understood by Africans will we be better able to grasp what is only now roughly sketched as time in African music.

References

Angelo, Michael, and Denis de Carli. 1704. A curious and exact account of a voyage to Congo in the years 1666 and 1667. In *A collection of voyages and travels*, ed. A. and J. Churchill. 4 vols. London.

Armstrong, Robert Plant. 1971. *The affecting presence*. Urbana: University of Illinois Press.

Augier, P. 1971. La polyrythme dans les musiques du Sahara. *Libycor* 19: 217–33.

Batuta, Ibn. 1858. *Voyages d'Ibn Batoutah*. Translated by C. Defrémery and B. R. Sanguinetti. Paris.

Becker, Alton L. 1979. Text-building, epistemology, and aesthetics in Javanese shadow theatre. In *The imagination of reality: Essays in Southeast Asian coherence systems*, ed. A. L. Becker and Aram A. Yengoyan, 211–43. New York: Ablex.

Berliner, Paul. 1978. *The soul of Mbira*. Berkeley: University of California Press.

Biebuyck, Daniel, and Kahombo C. Mateene, eds. and trans. 1971. *The Mwindo epic*. Berkeley: University of California Press.

Blacking, John. 1969. *Process and product in human society*. Johannesburg: Witwatersrand University Press.

―――. 1973. *How musical is man?* Seattle: University of Washington Press.

Bloch, Maurice. 1977. The past and the present in the present. *Man* 12: 278–82.

Bohannan, Paul. 1953. Concepts of time among the Tiv of Nigeria. *Southwestern Journal of Anthropology* 9 (3): 251–62.

Bordieu, Pierre. 1963. The attitude of the Algerian peasant toward time. In *Mediterranean countrymen*, ed. J. Pitt-Rivers, 55–72. The Hague: Mouton.

Brandel, Rose. 1961. *The music of Central Africa*. The Hague: Martinus Nijhoff.

Chernoff, John M. 1979. *African rhythm and African sensibility*. Chicago: University of Chicago Press.

d'Azevedo, Warren L. 1962. Uses of the past in Gola discourse. *Journal of African History* 3 (1): 11–34.

Evans-Pritchard, E. E. 1940. *The Nuer*. Oxford: Oxford University Press.

Fraser, J. T., ed. 1981. *The voices of time: A cooperative survey of man's views of time as expressed by the sciences and by the humanities*. 2d ed. Amherst: University of Massachusetts Press.

Geertz, Clifford. 1973. *The interpretation of cultures*. New York: Basic Books.

Gurvitch, Georges. 1964. *The spectrum of social time*. Dordrecht: D. Riedel.

Hornbostel, Erich M. von. 1928. African Negro music. *Africa* 1: 30–62.

Jones, Arthur M. 1934. African drumming. *Bantu Studies* 8: 1–16.

―――. 1957. Drums down the centuries. *African Music* 1 (4): 4–10.

―――. 1959. *Studies in African music*. 2 vols. London: Oxford University Press.

King, Anthony. 1960. Employments of the "standard pattern" in Yoruba music. *African Music* 2 (3): 51–54.

Knight, Roderic. 1974. Mandinka drumming. *African Arts* 7: 25–35.

Koetting, James. 1970. Analysis and notation of West African drum ensemble music. *Selected Reports, Institute of Ethnomusicology, UCLA* 1 (3): 115–46.

Kubik, Gerhard. 1962. The Phenomenon of inherent rhythms in East and Central African instrumental music. *African Music* 3 (1): 33–42.

——. 1965. Transcription of Mangwilo xylophone music from film strips. *African Music* 3 (4): 35–41.

——. 1972. Oral notation of some West and Central African time-line patterns. *Review of Ethnology* 3 (22): 169–76.

Leach, Edmund. 1961. Two essays concerning the symbolic representation of time. In *Rethinking anthropology*, 124–43. London: Athlone Press.

Lewis, J. David, and Andrew J. Weigert. 1981. The structures and meanings of social time. *Social Forces* 60: 432–62.

Locke, David. 1978. The music of Atsiagbeko. Ph. D. diss. Wesleyan University.

Merriam, Alan P. 1977. Analysis of African music rhythm and concepts of time reckoning. Paper presented at the Society for Ethnomusicology meeting, Austin, Texas, November 4.

Nketia, J. H. Kwabena. 1958. Traditional music of the Ga people. *African Music* 2 (1): 21–27.

Pantaleoni, Hewitt. 1972. Three principles of timing in Anlo dance drumming. *African Music* 5 (4): 50–63.

Rouget, Gilbert. 1971. Court songs and traditional history in the ancient kingdoms of Porto-Novo and Aomey. In *Essays on music and history in Africa*, ed. Klaus P. Wachsmann, 27–64. Evanston: Northwestern University Press.

Sachs, Curt. 1953. *Rhythm and tempo*. New York: W. W. Norton.

Schutz, Alfred. 1973. *Collected papers 1: The problem of social reality*, ed. M. Natanson. The Hague: Martinus Nijhoff.

Stone, Ruth M. 1982. *Let the inside be sweet: The interpretation of music event among the Kpelle of Liberia*. Bloomington: Indiana University Press.

Wallaschek, Richard. 1893. *Primitive music*. London: Longmans.

Waterman, Richard. 1952. African influence on the music of the Americas. In *Acculturation in the Americas*, ed. Sol Tax. 2: 207–18. Chicago: University of Chicago Press.

Wood, J. G. 1868. *Natural history of man*. Vol. 1. London: Routledge.

Temporal Linearity and Nonlinearity in Music

Jonathan D. Kramer

Summary   Linearity is defined as "the determination of some aspects of music in accordance with expectations that arise from preceding music"; nonlinearity is "the determination of some aspects of music in accordance with expectations that arise from principles that govern an entire piece or section." * All music uses both linear and nonlinear temporal structures.

The most pervasive linearity is found in tonal music, but even tonal music displays nonlinearity in, for example, the creation of consistent textures. Nonlinearity can also operate in the realm of formal proportions—the lengths of sections and/or amounts of time spent in various tonal areas interrelate in an atemporal, nonlinear manner.

The perception of formal balances across an entire piece depends on what might be called "cumulative listening." Overtly discontinuous atonal works invite a cumulative understanding of nonlinear proportional balances. Certain works of Stravinsky, for example, exhibit the consistent use of a single ratio to determine the lengths of all sections.

Atonal linearity implies motion toward goals that are established contextually, given the absence of tonality's a priori hierarchy of degrees of stability. Linear goals in atonal music may be predictable or not. Linearity and nonlinearity can coexist on different or even the same hierarchic levels.

Total linearity and total nonlinearity are both impossibilities, but certain experimental compositions of the last quarter century have approached both these extremes.

Preliminary Definitions

Linearity and nonlinearity are the two fundamental means by which a piece of music structures its time and by which time structures a piece of music. Thus, nonlinearity is not merely the absence of linearity. It is itself a structural force. Virtually all music utilizes a mixture of linearity and nonlinearity. Since they may appear to different degrees and in different combinations on each level of music's hierarchic structure, their interplay determines both the style and the form of a composition. My aim is to show how this interaction operates in different kinds of music.

My definition of linearity is "the determination of some aspect(s) of music in accordance with expectations that arise from earlier events in the piece." Nonlinearity is "the determination of some aspect(s) of music in accordance with expectations that arise from principles or tendencies governing an entire piece or section." While these definitions serve adequately as a point of departure, they do have potential problems: the idea of "determination" requires further explanation, the term "aspect of the music" is vague, and the

* I would like to thank Margaret Barela for many fine suggestions and for an extraordinarily careful reading of an earlier version of this article.

mechanism by which expectations may or may not arise from preceding events or from general principles must be considered. How (and even whether) a listener understands the dependence of an event on preceding music must also be studied. I am not concerned with the actual process of composition, with the way the composer came to choose B-flat rather than C. Determination has to do rather with the perceived relationship between two events. If the music seems to imply B-flat as either a (linear) continuation of preceding notes or a (nonlinear) consequence of an overall logic, then the *music* can seem to have "chosen" B-flat (even if the composer actually wrote the B-flat before composing the notes that precede it).

The term "aspect of the music" is purposefully vague so that it can refer to a concrete detail (such as an individual note or interval) or to a larger unit (such as a phrase or entire section). Or aspect might be the duration of a section, the character of a passage, or even a subjective mood. In short, an aspect is virtually any characteristic of the music.

Information Theory

My definition of linearity recalls the information-theoretic methods of analysis proposed by some music theorists. The use of Markov chains to study music has been pursued by Hiller, Youngblood, Moles, Meyer, Cohen, and Knopoff and Hutchinson, among others.[1] Although information theory applied scientifically to the study of music has been problematic, it does provide a useful aesthetic framework for understanding the listening process.

A Markov chain is, lossely speaking, a series of antecedents contributing to the probability of a consequent event. In a first-order Markov chain an event is "chosen" on the basis of probabilities suggested by one preceding event. For example the chances that a C will follow a B in a passage in C major are decidedly different from the probability of encountering a C after a B in F-sharp major. In a second-order Markov chain the probability of each event depends on the two preceding events. There is, for example, a specific probability in A minor of hearing a C after a B that follows an A. The higher the Markov order, the greater the linearity. Total nonlinearity corresponds to a zeroth-order Markov chain, in which each event is generated independent of preceding events, although it may indeed be chosen in accordance with a particular statistical weighting. There is, for example, a particular probability of encountering a C in E-flat minor, regardless of what notes precede it.

Comprehensive analysis of most music would require very high-order chains, since a given event may well depend on hundreds of preceding events. This is true even when events are grouped hierarchically by the listener. Therefore, as A. Wayne Slawson has remarked, it is impossible in practice to specify a maximum order that would account for all meaningful probabilities in a given composition.[2] Furthermore, it is difficult to define just what constitutes an event, even on the level of the smallest details. Is a chord an event? Or is each note of a chord a separate event? Is the interval separating two successive notes an event? Is a duration an event? Is a motive an event or a series of events? Does a permutation of familiar notes constitute a new event or is it a variant of an old event?

Not surprisingly, information-theoretic analyses have tended to focus on isolated parameters (e.g., melody) and/or have been concerned only with lower-order Markov chains. The results have not been particularly encouraging. I seriously doubt that information theory will ever provide powerful analytic tools for entire pieces, although it can work for isolated aspects of music. But it does provide a useful conceptual framework for aesthetic understanding of linear musical time, as Abraham Moles suggests and as Leonard B. Meyer demonstrates. Events do imply later events; probabilities do exist for what will follow a given sequence of events. It may not be possible to calculate these probabilities accurately, but we do feel their force. If some event is an outgrowth of previous events, we understand that the music has progressed from antecedent to consequent. The piece moves through time from the music that implies to the music that satisfies (or delays or thwarts) the expectation. This sense of progression comes from the confluence of several interlocking antecedent-consequent relationships, from a complex interaction of implications and outgrowths that takes place across various durations.

All music exhibits both linearity and nonlinearity. But what would a totally linear piece sound like? Or a totally nonlinear work? Some composers explored these extremes during the experimental 1950s and 1960s. Their approaches to total linearity come close to excessive predictability. If every event is an outgrowth of all previous events, then the context becomes a web of implications that allows no deviation. Consider Frederic Rzewski's *Les Moutons de Panurge*, in which the performers play a sixty-five-note melody as follows: 1; 1–2; 1–2–3; 1–2–3–4; 1–2–3–4–5; and so on. After the first few notes predictability far outweighs new information. The expectation that the melody will be repeated just as it was with the addition of one note is always fulfilled. Except for the mild and lessening suspense over what the new final note will be, the linearity is total. There are no surprises, no thwarted expectations, no deviations from the compositional process.

At the opposite extreme is music in which each event is composed for itself, with no reference to preceding or following events. One of the earliest computer compositions, Lejaren Hiller and Leonard Isaacson's *Illiac Suite* for string quartet, contains some passages that were composed according to zeroth-order Markov chains. Some sections randomize pitches while others randomize intervals of succession—with markedly different results. Using zeroth-order Markov processes does not quarantee the *perception* of nonlinearity, however. As the *Illiac Suite* demonstrates, inadvertent stepwise connections and motivic similarities may strike the listener as linear relationships, despite the total nonlinearity of the composers' conception. Furthermore, statistical probabilities can change, thus producing the appearance of progression even though each event is still generated independently. The opening of the fourth movement, in fact, utilizes a changing series of probabilities, resulting in a kind of linearity-once-removed. Other passages, however, retain one set of probabilities throughout.[3] In such passages the order of notes quite literally does not matter, since they were composed only in accordance with an abstract system of probabilities.

Linearity in Tonal Music

Apart from a few recent experimental compositions, all Western music is linear to a substantial extent. The most pervasive linearity is found in tonal music. Tonality embodies a set of hierarchic relationships between tones, supported by durations, dynamics, timbres, and so on. The tonic is endowed with ultimate stability. All tonal relationships conspire toward one goal—the return of the tonic, finally victorious and no longer challenged by other keys. Thus tonal motion is always goal directed. The arrival of the tonic is never in doubt (in information theory, such inevitability is termed redundancy). Rather, the suspense, and hence the motion, are determined by just what route the music takes and at what rates it travels. Those rare pieces that end in a key other than the one in which they begin depend on the denial of this expectation for their force. The expectation of tonic return is still operative, but that implication is ultimately denied for expressive effect. Much tonal music moves toward a climax—a point of greatest tension that is usually remote from the tonic—after which it drives back toward the tonic. The return of the tonic is an event of rhythmic importance, a structural downbeat, a point of resolution, the goal.

Composers often play on the expectation of recapitulation structural downbeats by taking circuitous routes, by inserting false recapitulations, or by undermining the tonic downbeat at the start of a true recapitulation. Such subtleties do not weaken the linearity of the music—quite the contrary. They depend on carefully established expectations. The choice of when and how to undercut a recapitulation downbeat depends on contextual implications set up earlier in the piece.

Consider, for example, the first movement of Beethoven's Quartet in F Major, Opus 59, Number 1. After a long and complex development section, the following sequence of events occurs: (1) the tonic returns (in first inversion with the second theme of the first theme group) in m. 242; (2) the main theme returns in the tonic in m. 254; (3) the tonic note reappears accented in the bass in m. 279 (but as the third of a D-flat chord); (4) at long last there is a strong cadence in the tonic (root position V to root position I) finally in m. 307; and (5) we must wait until m. 348 to hear the main theme with full root-position tonic support. Beethoven is doing more than playing on our understanding of sonata form; he is dealing with the consequences of earlier events. He shapes the recapitulation this particular way because of the implications of the strange opening of the piece (see fig. 1)—not really a I chord (as Roger Sessions points out),[4] certainly not a III[6] chord, but rather a subtly unsettling incomplete harmony. This unstable chord could never serve as a point of arrival at the start of a recapitulation. Thus, the sense of resolution is spread over five time points rather than residing (in the traditional manner) in the one instant of reprise. This movement is therefore a wonderful example of tonal linearity. It is a complex and sophisticated statement of the same aesthetic that makes us expect a tonic note after a leading tone or a tonic chord after a dominant seventh. We may not understand all the implications of the unusual opening when we first hear it,[5] but we are struck by its strangeness and we wait for an "explanation"; this waiting is the essential experience of linearity.

The way Opus 59, Number 1, approaches its recapitulation is not a surprise. It is a logical, although not totally predictable, consequence of an opening that could never function as a recapitulation resolution. Surprises—events that really are unexpected and unprepared—do exist in tonal music, however. Surprise is often a product of linear thinking. For an event to be unexpected suggests that implications have been established. We need only turn to the first movement of another Beethoven quartet—the A Minor, Opus 132—for an excellent example (see fig. 2). Coming after a progression that seems to move ever more pointedly toward a definitive cadence (of which there have been precious few thus far) in C minor, there is a sudden cessation of sound (m. 92) followed by a recitativelike passage of utter newness. It is true that certain intervallic connections can be drawn between this new idea and earlier themes, but these correspondences are minimal compared with the stark unfamiliarity of this music. Particularly because it breaks a strongly linear continuum, the discontinuity is overwhelming. Furthermore, the continuation of this music does nothing to erase the impact of the discontinuity with which it arrives.

Figure 1. Opening of the first movement of Beethoven's String Quartet Number 7 in F Major, Opus 59. Number 1

In fact, the recitativelike material is never integrated into the movement. It is not heard again. It is an unrelated interruption, without precedent and without motivic outcome. Yet it has linear consequences, not literally in the music but rather in the way we hear it. Once it happens we cannot forget it. It colors our understanding of the remainder of the movement: we understand that any subsequent continuity just might be shattered.

Despite the recitative's lack of motivic precedent and despite the manner in which it interrupts a cadence-directed progression, I am not calling it a nonlinear event. This particular surprise is a *linear* occurrence. It depends on linear expectations, which it subverts. Since this type of surprise is not nonlinear, what *is* tonal nonlinearity?

Nonlinearity in Tonal Music

Unchanging contexts exemplify nonlinear determination of aspects of the music. Consider pieces in which the texture, motivic material, and rhythmic figuration are virtually constant. Chopin's Prelude in E-Flat Minor, Opus 28, Number 14, and Bach's Prelude in C Major, from the first volume of *Das Wohltemperierte Klavier*, are good examples. In such music the context is not a consequence of the way the piece begins, but rather it is

Figure 2. From the first movement of Beethoven's String Quartet Number 15 in A Minor, Opus 132

determined by the surface of the composition, which is in certain respects unchanging. The music's personality exists throughout the piece but does not grow or transform itself as the work unfolds.

It might be argued that a constant context is, in fact, heard linearly. In either prelude the second measure's similarity to the first increases our expectation that the third measure will also be similar. Eventually the probability for consistency turns into virtual certainty, and (in information-theoretic terms) the texture and rhythm become redundant. (The music's linearity resides in other aspects—melodic contours, harmonies, registers, and possibly dynamics.) We realize in retrospect that an unchanging principle of organization—not a progressive linearity—has been determining the texture and surface rhythm since the opening of the piece. Once this consistency of rhythmic and textural pattern becomes a certainty, we start to notice the nonlinearity of the texture. It is still possible for us to be surprised, of course, by an unexpected change in the texture and/or rhythm. In Schubert's song *Gretchen am Spinnrade*, for example, just such a disruption occurs with extraordinary impact. The constant texture, which represents the spinning wheel's endlessly mesmerizing motion, breaks at one point. Gretchen pauses from her work as she first remembers Faust's kiss. As in Beethoven's Opus 132, the impact of the unexpected is enormous, and we can no longer listen to the music as we did previously, despite the resumption of the spinning motive. But there is a significant difference between the Beethoven and the Schubert: the surprise in Opus 132 contradicts linear implications of harmony and gesture, while in *Gretchen* the surprise violates nonlinear consistency of texture and rhythm.

Proportions in Tonal Music

In addition to contextual consistency, formal proportions are also heard nonlinearly. How long one segment of musical time lasts with respect to another can be a significant factor in the creation of balanced structures. We hear, store, and compare durations of time spans in order to understand their relative balance. For two sections to be in a balanced proportion, it does not really matter which is heard first; similarly, for the total time spent in the tonic to balance the total time spent in other areas does not depend on where in the movement the tonic and nontonic segments are located. Neither type of balance—of section durations or of time spent in different keys—depends on progression, and thus such proportions are understood nonlinearly outside the music's time frame.

Significant studies have been made of proportions in Mozart's music. Jane Perry-Camp has discovered large sectional balances that work according to carefully (yet intuitively, it seems) controlled durations;[6] Arlene Zallman has discovered similar balances of total durations spent in various tonal areas.[7] It is interesting to compare the work of these two theorists. Consider, for example, the Piano Sonata in E-Flat Major, K. 282, which both Perry-Camp and Zallman have analyzed. There are 36 measures in the first movement (or 69, if the repeats are taken). The main structural division segments the movement into 15 and 21 (or, with repeats, 30 and 39) measures; the total number of (noncontiguous) measures in the tonic is 21 (39 with repeats); 15 measures (30 with repeats) are spent away from the tonic—an interesting balance! In the second movement the ratio of the length of Minuet II to that of the second half of Minuet II (whether or not repeats are considered) is 5 : 3, precisely the same ratio that exists between the second half of Minuet I and the first half of Minuet I. (Since both minuets do not modulate, the ratio of their respective lengths—6 : 5—is the same as the ratio of durations spent in each of the two tonalities.) Consider also the last movement. There are 102 measures (204 with repeats), subdivided at the end of the exposition 39 and 63 (or 78 and 126); the durational ratio of these two sections is 0.61905, which is remarkably close to the golden-mean ratio 0.61803 (Perry-Camp has found a large number of Mozart movements with golden-mean proportions). The number of measures in the tonic in this movement is exactly equal to the number of measures not in the tonic.

Although Mozart's music is predominantly linear, it is structured in part by nonlinear forces that contribute to formal proportions. Perception of balance depends on what might be called "cumulative" listening[8]—an all-encompassing, retrospective, atemporal understanding that lies beyond the piece's time frame. The nonlinear balance in K. 282 is a subliminal underpinning to the linearity inherent in the work's tonality.

Proportions in Atonal Music

Music that is more thoroughly sectionalized than Mozart's readily invites cumulative listening. Thus it is not surprising to find sophisticated balances at work in the music of composers such as Messiaen and Stravinsky. Much of their music is extremely sectional, with each section self-contained in some manner. When in such music an ongoing structural linearity is either disguised or nonexistent, we may look to cumulatively heard proportions for structural coherence.

I have examined the proportions in a number of Stravinsky's works that exhibit discontinuities.[9] Probably the most impressively worked out system of proportional balances is to be found in *Agon*. This ballet has puzzled commentators because of the high degree of discontinuity between sections and the apparent lack of unity of materials and procedures. Yet the work coheres, in part because of a set of sophisticated proportional balance. Following an earlier article,[10] I call self-contained sections that are set off by discontinuities *moments*; a moment is characterized in *Agon* by consistencies of texture, harmony, compositional procedure, orchestration, tempo, melodic material, and form. Moments can be subdivided by less extreme discontinuities, and they can be grouped together according to either simple adjacency or motivic similarity. Thus moment groups, moments, and submoments represent three distinct but hierarchically adjacent levels of structure.

By comparing moment durations, we find that all moments from the longest to the shortest in *Agon*—except the extremely long serial moment—have durations approximating a series of numbers in the ratio $\sqrt[4]{2} : 1$. All approximations but one are remarkably accurate. The ratio $\sqrt[4]{2} : 1$ is not as odd as it might seem: the series doubles every fourth term. Thus the n + 4th term is twice the nth term, and therefore many moments are twice as long as other moments—presumably a perceptually relevant relationship. These doublings of section durations have a decided impact on the cumlative balance in *Agon*. Proportional lengths determined by the ratio $\sqrt[4]{2} : 1$ extend beyond moment durations to lengths of moment groups, up to the duration of the entire piece. Thus the duration of almost every moment is determined by this series; many groups of adjacent moments correspond to the higher durations of the $\sqrt[4]{2} : 1$ series; even sums of durations of moment groups are determined by the series. In addition, another series, also in the ratio of $\sqrt[4]{2} : 1$, determines the lengths of all submoments of the largest moments to within remarkably close approximation. The pervasiveness of this system of proportions is impressive. Stravinsky may not have consciously calculated these section lengths, but he was clearly sensitive to proportions and he devised and executed a sophisticated system of formal balance.

This system is nonlinear. The balances of moments, submoments, and moment groups work cumulatively across the whole piece. Lengths are determined not on the basis of preceding durations but according to a single principle that prevails unaltered throughout. As *Agon* progresses, we acquire more information that enables us to perceive the balance of *unequal* sections—this is the essence of cumulative listening. The order in which we encounter the various durations almost does not matter. (I am not suggesting that the sections of *Agon* could be performed in another order without destroying the sense of the piece—although such a reordering would produce a more nearly intelligible result than would a similar experiment performed on a Mozart sonata. I am claiming only that the *durations*—not the *materials*—of sections are organized nonlinearly and understood cumulatively.) We are able to perceive identical moment lengths, lengths that are twice other lengths, and the interrelationship of all moment durations according to a single series that consistently utilizes one ratio.

Linearity in Atonal Music

I have given examples of *nonlinear* perception that depend on a cumulative processing of duration information; I have also alluded to *nonlinearity* in the textural/rhythmic domain of tonal music. The *linearity* of tonal pitch structure, on the other hand, has been well established in tonal theory. We find numerous examples of linearity in atonal music as well, despite the absence of tonality's a priori system of goal definition. Much atonal music does progress linearly through time, either toward contextually defined goals or toward goals that are understood as (relatively) stable because of rhythmic support. In the latter case we may not know what a cadential harmony is to be until it actually arrives—a situation quite different from tonal drives toward cadences.

An example of nontonal linearity can be found in the first phrase (excluding the introductory motto) of Alban Berg's *Kammerkonzert* (see fig. 3). There is no doubt that the phrase ends in m. 7. Why do we hear this measure as cadential? Although the final E-C dyad is a reasonable goal (given the preceding sustained E in the oboe and, more important, the linear approach to C in two voices), it is surely not the only set of pitches toward which the phrase could have progressed. The horn's sustained G, for example, could have signaled an upcoming goal, and stepwise motion toward other pitches is possible without greatly altering the material. The cadence is created by nonpitch parameters: the slowing tempo, the lengthening note durations, the thinning texture, the decreasing dynamics, the downward motion after an overabundance of rising figures, the less frequent change of instrumental colors, and the freshness of the subsequent music. The cadence is thus an outgrowth of the preceding music.

Granted, such nonpitch support of cadences is commonplace also in tonal music. There, however, the pitch structure carries the weight of the cadence. To confirm this claim, play the chords in the Berg in even values, and do the same with a tonal cadence: the tonal skeleton still cadences, but the Berg does not. True, the *Kammenkonzert*'s harmonic density does decrease toward the cadence, and reference is made to the motto pitches, but the E-C cadence is neither the least dense harmony nor the most referential sound.

Some atonal compositions attempt to create *predictable* goals contextually. In the first movement of Webern's First Cantata, for example, a four-note chord becomes a stable sonority by virtue of frequent emphasis in a variety of settings;[11] it comes to assume the character of a goal by reiteration and perseverance. The Berg and Webern examples both demonstrate nontonal pitch linearity; the difference is that in Webern the progression is toward a goal known in advance (as in tonal music), while in Berg the goal of motion is not predictable.

Consider one more atonal piece—Stravinsky's *Symphonies of Wind Instruments*. This piece, like *Agon*, can profitably be heard as a series of independent moments. These self-contained sections are defined by consistency of harmony, tempo, and motivic material. The durations are balanced in a manner similar to that in *Agon* (although here the ratio is simpler—3 : 2).[12] When the music moves from one moment to the next, there are stepwise connections that suggest linearity on a large scale. Within each moment, however, the harmonies are static (or sometimes alternating) and the motivic material is permuted and repeated, but it is rarely developed. Thus, the music is nonlinear within but linear between sections. Linearity and nonlinearity both operate throughout the work, but on different hierarchic levels. The background structure is linear, even to the point of having a

Figure 3. Opening of the first movement of Alban Berg's *Kammerkonzert*. Copyright 1925 by Universal Edition; copyright renewed. All rights reserved. Used by permission of European American Music Distributors Corporation, sole U.S. agent for Universal Edition.

predictable quasi-tonal goal; but the middleground level (where we find the moments) is characterized by harmonic stasis and durations understood cumulatively.

Thus linearity and nonlinearity can coexist on different hierarchic levels. But they can also operate on the same level, as several of Messiaen's works demonstrate. *Cantéyodjayâ*, for example, consists of several sharply differentiated sections, some of which are linear (since they progress toward other sections) and some of which are nonlinear (since they are harmonically static). The middleground is thus alternately linear and nonlinear.

Conclusion

I have tried to show that linearity and nonlinearity are two complementary forces in the structuring of musical time. Virtually all music exhibits both, but in different ways. The hierarchic levels on which linearity and nonlinearity exist are crucial to the temporal nature of music, as is the consistency with which they operate. The history of Western music has seen a gradual increase in the importance of nonlinearity, so that today many compositions are far more nonlinear than linear. (The extreme linearity of the 1970s' so-called process music, on the other hand, is possibly a reaction against the fragmentation of total nonlinearity. But even this music also has a strong nonlinear component. A process is a pervasive principle that determines several aspects of the music. In *Les Moutons*, for example, the additive melodic process unfolds linearly, but it is also an unchanging procedure that permeates the piece.) Even the most nonlinear music exists in time and is first heard as a temporally ordered succession. Thus linearity can never be banished totally from the musical experience.

My original definitions of linearity and nonlinearity may by now seem a little vague. I have applied the two terms both to compositional procedures and to listening modes; I have mentioned them as aspects of pitch, texture, and duration structures; I have addressed matters of their coexistence on the same and different hierarchic levels. Perhaps the following list of terms that may be associated with each will help to clarify the two concepts:

linearity	nonlinearity
progression	succession
teleological listening	cumulative listening
motion	stasis
directed change	unchanging context
temporal	atemporal

The last pair of terms requires some explanation. When certain aspects of a piece exist within the space of the music for their own sake, not because of some progression, they are atemporal. Their impact is not dependent on their position along a time continuum, but they nonetheless contribute to overall coherence. Thus, nonlinearity is an organizational force. It can be articulated by as large a variety of textures, forms, and processes as can linearity. It can interact with linearity in a variety of ways. From this interaction come many of the tensions, resolutions, and hence meanings of music.

Notes

1. Lejaren A. Hiller and Calvert Bean, "Information Theory Analyses of Four Sonata Expositions," *Journal of Music Theory* 10, no. 1 (1966): 96–137; Lejaren Hiller and Ramon Fuller, "Structure and

Information in Webern's Symphonie, Opus 21," ibid. 11, no. 1 (1967): 60–115; Joseph E. Youngblood, "Style as Information," ibid. 2, no. 1 (1958): 24–35; Abraham Moles, *Information Theory and Esthetic Perception*, trans. Joel E. Cohen (Urbana: University of Illinois Press, 1966); Leonard B. Meyer, *Music, the Arts, and Ideas* (Chicago: University of Chicago Press, 1967), pp. 15–21; Leon Knopoff and William Hutchinson, "Information Theory for Musical Continua," *Journal of Music Theory* 25, no. 1 (1981): 17–44; Knopoff and Hutchinson, "Entropy as a Measure of Style: The Influence of Sample Length," ibid. 27, no. 1 (1983): 75–97.

2. A. Wayne Slawson, "Review of *Computer Applications in Music*, ed. Gerald Lefkoff (Morgantown: University of West Virginia Press, 1967)," *Journal of Music Theory* 12, no. 1 (1968): 108–10.

3. Lejaren A. Hiller and Leonard Isaacson, *Experimental Music* (New York: McGraw-Hill, 1959).

4. Roger Sessions, *Harmonic Practice* (New York: Harcourt, Brace and World, 1951), pp. 203–4.

5. Some consequences of this unique opening are felt immediately. The initial instability is prolonged by several factors: the arrival of root-position tonic harmony on the weakest beat of m. 1, the statement of tonic harmony midway through m. 3 (rather than at its beginning), the first real change of harmony occurring on a weak best in m. 7, the inordinately slow harmonic rhythm, and the imbalance of $6\frac{1}{2}$ measures of tonic followed by $11\frac{1}{2}$ measures of dominant. Because of this instability, a tremendous sense of resolution is felt when the tonic returns unequivocally in m. 19.

6. Jane Perry-Camp, "Time and Temporal Proportion: The Golden Section Metaphor in Mozart, Music, and History," *Journal of Musicological Research* 3, no. 1–2 (1979): 133–76.

7. Arlene Zallman's Work is currently unpublished.

8. In earlier versions of this article, I tried using first the term *statistical* and then the word *stochastic* to refer to cumulative listening. While both these terms accurately label the phenomenon I wish to describe, they carry unfortunate connotations from other usages.

9. Jonathan D. Kramer, "Discontinuity and Proportion in the Music of Stravinsky," in *Stravinsky Reheard*, ed. Jann Pasler (Berkeley and Los Angeles: University of California Press, forth coming).

10. Kramer, "Moment Form in Twentieth Century Music," *Musical Quarterly* 64, no. 2 (1978): 177–94.

11. Kramer, "The Row as Structural Background and Audible Foreground: The First Movement of Webern's First Cantata," *Journal of Music Theory* 15 (1971): 158–81.

12. See Kramer, "Moment Form," pp. 184–88.

Intermezzo

With Professor George H. Ford, President of the International Society For the Study of Time (1979–83) we step away from the details of our theme and look back to see ourselves.

THE EDITORS

Humanities and the Experiences of Time

George H. Ford

Summary The study of time is is sometimes assumed to be an exclusive preserve that must be restricted to disciplines such as physics or mathematics. According to this interpretation, people committed to humanistic disciplines, such as literary criticism and history, would be misfits in the ISST. In contrast to this view, I will show that the study of literature is as involved with understanding time as the study of physics is. For evidence, this paper cites literary works that embody a variety of life-time experiences, as in novels of Sterne and Tolstoy and also as in poems of Marvell and T. S. Eliot whose *Four Quartets* links birth and death into a unit: "In my beginning is my end."

Misunderstanding of how literature can contribute to time studies occurs when humanists are required to define time or to theorize about it instead of being allowed to do what they can do well, which is to report on what living in time is like. Instead of categorization they offer concrete experiences. For example, what the Dutch psychologist John Michon has categorized as *subjective duration* can be fleshed out by "epiphany scenes" (as James Joyce calls them). A good example occurs in a novel by Margaret Laurence when the heroine's attitudes toward life and death are radically altered by her brief encounter with a great blue heron by a lakeshore in the Canadian wilderness. A second example is a passage from a sermon by John Donne in which he portrays the timeless quality of eternity. A third example, Yeats's "Lapis Lazuli," is a poem dramatizing how art enables us to confront a "tragic scene" with a kind of joyful gaiety. Although Yeats's poem is set in China, the experience it records is a universal one rather than one restricted to the cultures of East or West.

The conclusion reached is that because of the special insights into the experiences of time offered by literature, humanists are indeed qualified to contribute to the deliberations of our ISST.

There is an observation in Dickens's first novel, *Pickwick Papers*, made by a character named Roker, a guard in a London debtor's prison, who is fond of reminiscing about past events and recalling them to a person called Neddy. "You remember Tom Martin, Neddy?" says Roker on this occasion. And, yes, Neddy remembers Tom Martin, a fistfighter who had once, many years ago, got into a dispute at a tavern in which he had "whopped" a coal heaver, and Mr. Roker evokes that event of the distant past:

> "Bless my dear eyes!" said Mr. Roker, shaking his head slowly from side to side, and gazing abstractedly out of the grated windows before him, as if here fondly recalling some peaceful scene of his early youth; "it seems but yesterday that [Tom] whopped the coal-heaver.... I think I can see him now, a coming up the Strand between the two streetkeepers, a little sobered by the bruising, with a patch o' winegar and brown paper over his right eyelid, and that'ere lovely bulldog, as pinned the little boy afterwards, a following at his heels. What a rum thing Time is, ain't it, Neddy?"[1]

This delightful passage about time's rumminess is one that I should like to lay claim to having discovered myself, but it had been noticed by T. S. Eliot, who more than forty years ago considered using Dickens's passage as an epigraph to his great collection of lyrics, *The*

Four Quartets,[2] one of the most time-conscious works of literature ever written, with its meditative explorations of some of the complex experiences of time. By way of prologue to my paper, here is Eliot's account of listening to one of those bells we hear in coastal waters, bells that are attached to red buoys set in motion by sea swells:

> And under the oppression of the silent fog
> The tolling bell
> Measures time not our time, rung by the unhurried
> Ground swell, a time
> Older than the time of chronometers, older
> Than time counted by anxious worried women
> Lying awake, calculating the future,
> Trying to unweave, unwind, unravel
> And piece together the past and the future,
> Between midnight and dawn, when the past is all deception,
> The future futureless, before the morning watch
> When time stops and time is never ending;
> And the ground swell, that is and was from the beginning,
> Clangs
> The bell.[3]

"What a rum thing Time is, ain't it, Neddy?"

Both Dickens and Eliot became interested in time in their own ways and each of us, as individuals, comes to time in his or her own way, for reasons emerging from those depths of our souls to which only we, as individuals, have access. And it is here, with ourselves, that we must begin.

We all must ask, When did I become interested in time? Or, before that, aware of time? In my case, I suppose I must have had the same experience that all of us have as children, an experience recorded by autobiographers and by poets such as Wordsworth, of watching the sun go down, let us say, and acquiring thereby a sense of the diurnal round. Before childhood, of course, for all of us, time may be said to begin at the moment of conception— an event that few of us think about and very few writers touch upon. The one Western literary work dealing with that event, to my knowledge, is Laurence Sterne's novel *Tristram Shandy*, which opens not with the birth of Tristram but with a hilarious account of the moment of his conception, a moment his father always believed to have been a disaster. "My Tristram's misfortunes" said his father "began nine months before ever he came into the world." This was because of what happened on a Sunday night, the first week of March 1718. As Tristram explains for us, his father was a man of remarkably regular habits, one of them being to wind up the large household clock, on the first Sunday night of each month of the year. And on those same monthly Sunday nights it was also Mr. Shandy's regular habit to perform certain marital duties. As a result, Mrs. Shandy had become accustomed to associate winding up the clock with certain "family concernments" (as Tristram calls them), and, as illustrating the theories of John Locke, these associations worked with her the other way round as well, as was to happen on this Sunday night when Tristram was conceived. Here is Tristram's report on what happened in the bedroom of his parents:

> *Pray, my dear*, quoth my mother, *have you not forgot to wind up the clock?* ——— *Good G——*! cried my father, making an exclamation, but taking care to moderate his voice at the same time,—Did *ever woman, since the creation of world, interrupt a man with such a silly question?*

Not many of us could lay claim to such specific knowledge as Tristram Shandy displayed about that particular starting point for our individual time lines, but with or without disastrous interruption, the event is of course a universal one. As Eliot noted: "In my beginning is my end."

But there is a more special question we can ask ourselves, one more accessible to the understanding: When did we become interested in the *study* of time and begin to ask questions about the subject? For me it was no sudden epiphany—the kind of single overwhelming experience that led J. W. Dunne to write *An Experiment with Time*. Nor did I begin with books on the topic such as G. J. Whitrow's *Natural Philosophy of Time*, or J. T. Fraser's *Voices of Time*, or books on time and literature such as one by Hans Meyerhoff or the classic study of *Time and the Novel* by Adam Mendilow. These important books came later, as did the writings of Gaston Bachelard and also Georges Poulet's *Studies in Human Time*. For me, an interest in the topic was generated by works of literature themselves—from the poems and plays and novels that I had been studying (and, later, teaching) without much conscious awareness of how prominent a role time plays in such works, and how it links them all into a unity of fascinating interconnections. For me, then, there was a gradual discovery of something that is, to many, a commonplace: a discovery that the study of literature is as involved with understanding time as the study of physics is.

If I were to try to select one work that most immediately led, in my own case, to speculations about time and literature, it would be Tolstoy's *War and Peace*, a novel that could also have been entitled, as some have noted, *Youth and Age*. The actual time span in Tolstoy's novel is not long; it covers only about fifteen years. But it is long enough to make us poignantly aware of people changing, so that in the later sections of the novel we make our own flashbacks to earlier scenes—as, for example, when we see late in the story "an over-blown matron" named Natasha, we may be led to evoke "a girl dancing into a crowded room," hundreds of pages earlier. I am not the first to observe time's importance to Tolstoy, however, as we can see in the novelist Percy Lubbock's account in his fine book, *The Craft of Fiction*:

> Time is all-important in *War and Peace*. . . . Tolstoy is the master of the changes of age in a human being. Under his hand young men and women grow older, cease to be young, grow old, with the noiseless regularity of life; their mutability never hides their sameness, their consistency shows and endures through their disintegration. They grow as we all do, they change in the only possible direction.

And still further:

> Time that evenly and silently slips away, while the men and women talk and act and forget it; time that is read in their faces, in their gestures, in the changing texture of their thought, while they only themselves awake to the discovery that it is passing when the best of it is gone—time in this aspect is present in *War and Peace* more manifestly, perhaps, than in any other novel that could be named.[4]

Nor is it only novelists who can powerfully affect us with the sense of change we experience in Tolstoy; change is also a favorite topic for poets. Andrew Marvell's anthology piece inevitably comes to mind here to remind us, as the speaker says to his coy mistress:

> But at my back I always hear
> Time's winged chariot hurrying near,
> And yonder all before us lie
> Deserts of vast eternity.

This compressed image affects our response to the poem in ways that differ from our response to Tolstoy's *War and Peace*. The novel, I venture to note in passing, has special aspects concerning the reader—what a contemporary German critic, Wolfgang Iser, calls "The Implied Reader":[5] the reader who is turning the pages, an action that (we sometimes forget) is also part of a time scheme.

This issue of literary genres is one that I will return to by reviewing some of the experiences of time treated in works of literature. But first I need to explore further the question of how and why a humanist and literary person may get involved with the study of time, a pursuit that is commonly assumed to be properly reserved for experts in physics, mathematics, metaphysics, and cosmology. In effect, does the humanist who becomes engaged in time studies have any significant contribution to make? The question is urgent, for answering it requires us to suspend the commonplace that time can be understood by defining it. This necessity is wonderfully suggested by again going to Dickens, in this case his rather didactic novel, *Hard Times*.

The opening scene takes place in a schoolroom. One of the little pupils is a girl called Sissy Jupe, whose whole life has hitherto been involved with horses, for her father is a horse trainer and rider in a circus. In this scene, Sissy is asked by a visitor to the school, a Mr. Gradgrind, to "define a horse." Sissy is stunned by this question, for despite her intimate knowledge of the species she has never tried to "define" a horse. So Mr. Gradgrind gives up on her and turns to a nasty little boy named Bitzer for a definition: "'Bitzer,' said Thomas Gradgrind. 'Your definition of a horse.'" And so Bitzer offers his definition: "'Quadruped. Graminivorous. Forty teeth, namely twenty-four grinders, four eye-teeth, and twelve incisive. Sheds coat in spring; in marshy countries, sheds hoofs, too. Hoofs hard, but requiring to be shod with iron. Age known by marks in mouth' Thus (and much more) Bitzer. 'Now, girl number twenty,' said Mr. Gradgrind [to Sissy Jupe] 'you know what a horse is.'"[6]

What Dickens's satiric fable is pointing out surely is that there are two different kinds of knowledge, the one focusing on categorizations and the other upon concrete experiences. I cite Dickens's fable not to suggest that definitions *have* to be pointless ones. Indeed, to cite a case close to hand, their usefulness can be readily demonstrated in the speculative labors of J. T. Fraser in his efforts to arrive at what he calls a "seamless epistemology" for the study of time. The responsible theorist, that is, does not dismiss as irrelevant what the horse rider has to report about experiences with horses!

My simple point is that poets and novelists will be seen as dumb as Sissy Jupe if we ask them for a Gradgrindian definition of time or a theory of time, but they have much to tell us if we ask them, instead, what living in time is like, as Tolstoy tells us of the experiences of aging and the changes that time brings, or Proust tells us of the role of memory and of *temps perdu* (a time that is not, as Proust makes evident, *perdu* after all). Of course there are many kinds of experiences treated memorably by writers, but three examples are notable.

The first example is related to a human phenomenon identified by a Dutch psychologist, John Michon, as *subjective duration*. Michon's term comes from his recent paper entitled "Psychological and Physiological Aspects of the Temporal Organization of Behaviour."[7] According to Michon, *subjective duration* describes what occurs when we are impatiently waiting for a late train to arrive and five minutes of clock time seem to take fifty minutes of internal time, or, contrariwise, five minutes of clock time seem to pass in a few seconds when we are sharing in some states of happiness or ecstasy. As employed in literature, subjective duration may be a feature of events that William Wordsworth called "spots of time" when a person gains a sudden insight during some confrontation, and it is also part of what James Joyce called "an epiphany," which is some sort of transforming experience, again aroused by a confrontation. Robert Browning's term for this experience is "The Eternal Moment." To exemplify such an experience we might profitably go to still another writer—a contemporary Canadian novelist, Margaret Laurence, in whose novel *The Diviners* a forty-seven-year old woman, Morag Gunn by name, lives in a cabin beside a river in the Canadian north woods, generally alone, and much of the time in a mood of disillusionment and disappointment. A turning point in her attitudes occurs one evening when she and her friend Royland go out fishing in a small boat with a slow-running outboard motor. On the riverbank of this lonely wilderness, they suddenly come upon a bird, of a species seldom seen in that region, a great blue heron, and this confrontation has a profound effect on Morag Gunn, although the novelist does not spell out the effect and leaves us, the readers, to piece together what must have happened.

The scene is in North America, but for me it also evokes the art of China. Examples of Chinese illustrations that I have seen often feature long-legged water birds, which may have been herons, searching for fish in waters near the shoreline. I believe the portrait of experience evoked is common to us all:

> At first, Morag thought Royland had caught his line in some weed. Then she saw the huge bird. It stood close to shore, its tall legs looking fragile although in fact they were very strong, its long neck and long sharp beak bent towards the water, searching for fish, its feathers a darkbright blue. A great Blue Heron. Once populous in this part of the country. Now rarely seen.
>
> Then it spotted the boat, and took to flight. A slow unhurried takeoff, the vast wings spreading, the slender elongated legs gracefully folding up under the creature's body. Like a pterodactyl, like an angel, like something out of the world's dawn. The soaring planet's rocketing changes. The sweeping serene wings of the thing, unknowing that it was speeding not only towards individual death but probably towards the death of its kind. The mastery of the heron's wings could be heard, a rush of wind, the wind of its wings, before it mounted high and disappeared into the trees above a bywater of the river.
>
> Royland reeled in his line, and by an unspoken agreement they took the boat home, in silence, in awe.
>
> That evening, Morag began to see that here and now was not, after all, an island. Her quest for islands had ended some time ago, and her need to make a pilgrimage had led her back here.[8]

In this remarkable passage about a brief encounter in time present we may note how the novelist contrives to weave in stretches of time past and time future. Taking us back into lost geological ages is that pterodactyl ("something out of the world's dawn") and the curious reference to the flight of an angel. Taking us forward in time is the prediction of an evolution toward a probable extinction of a species of beautiful and seemingly independent creatures. And also forward looking is a recognition by the woman of her own future and her acceptance of her role in our earth's dispensations. A few moments of clock time expand for Morag into a kind of eternity.

That word *eternity* leads me to a second example of experienced time. It is in the tensions and contradictions in experience that time can be observed, yet these, in turn, can be seen as such only against the backdrop of the "experience" of eternity. Writers of literature rarely dwell upon eternity, perhaps because its "experience" must be an imagined one, but it is fundamental to many works. I offer a short passage from an earlier poet, and one who was also a preacher as well as a poet, John Donne. Here, from one of his prayers, is how Donne imagined the state of eternity:

> Bring us, O Lord God, at our last awakening into the house and
> gate of heaven, to enter that gate and dwell in that house
> where there shall be no darkness or dazzling but one equal music,
> no fears nor hopes but one equal possession,
> no ends nor beginnings but one equal eternity,
> in the habitations of thy glory and dominion,
> world without end. Amen.[9]

We may note here that Donne's magnificent prose-poem never mentions time directly, yet in every line of the passage he is referring to time by implication, for time means a world of change and contrasting pairs (noise and silence, for example). Also absent in a timeless realm, as other writers have noted, is laughter, for laughter is a time-induced phenomenon, as is literature itself. Mark Twain was not being merely funny when he observed that "there is no humour in heaven."[10] And also no literature, of course, for Lessing's formula in his *Laokoon*—that literature is a time art—still stands, and in heaven verse and prose would hence be without point or function.

A third and final example specifically relates to Chinese experiences of time and shows us how literature can stand as a corrective to received knowledge. The image of China that one encounters among many nineteenth-century writers is of a vast country that had been blocked from progress for two thousand years because of a "backward" attitude toward time. Among scientifically minded people in the Victorian age and among its writers committed to the idea of progress such as John Stuart Mill or Alfred Tennyson or Charles Dickens, this image of Chinese stagnation is a recurrent one. Mill spoke of two thousand years of Chinese history as illustrating a "collective mediocrity."[11] And the speaker in Tennyson's "Locksley Hall," discussing progress and change in the 1840s, affirms: "Better fifty years of Europe than a cycle of Cathay."[12] That these views of China and time were misinformed and wrong has been tellingly demonstrated in recent years by Joseph Needham, as he does in his brilliant discussion in *The Voices of Time* where he asks rhetorically: "How could anyone ever have imagined that the time sense of the Chinese was inferior to that of Europeans? Almost the opposite could be said."[13]

A further corrective to nineteenth-century smugness, on a much smaller scale than Needham's, is offered in a late poem by William Butler Yeats called "Lapis Lazuli." The starting point for this 1936 poem was a realization that the Second World War was coming, that bombs would soon be falling, and that mankind was doomed to suffer terrible losses. At such a time, the poet asks, is there any justification for enjoying and studying literature and art? Are they not mere frivolities? By way of answer, Yeats describes a work of Chinese art that he had recently received as a present: a piece of lapis lazuli, a hard blue stone, out of which had been carved figures of three elderly Chinese men on a journey up a mountain. The scene in Yeats's poem may remind us of the figures on Keats's Grecian urn, but Yeats's treatment of it is distinctly his own:

> Two Chinamen, behind them a third,
> Are carved in lapis lazuli,
> Over them flies a long-legged bird,

A symbol of longevity;
The third, doubtless a serving-man,
Carries a musical instrument.

Every discoloration of the stone,
Every accidental crack or dent,
Seems a water-course or an avalanche,
Or lofty slope where it still snows
Though doubtless plum or cherry-branch
Sweetens the little half-way house
Those Chinamen climb towards, and I
Delight to imagine them seated there;
There, on the mountain and the sky,
On all the tragic scene they stare.
One asks for mournful melodies;
Accomplished fingers begin to play.
Their eyes mid many wrinkles, their eyes,
Their ancient, glittering eyes, are gay.[14]

I, too, have received a little gift from China, and, although it is not a valuable item like the beautiful carved lapis Yeats received, it tells us much of the experience of time. My present was a small figure made of ordinary clay and painted in the bright colors of today. This clay figure is of a very old bald-headed man, with a long white beard, who is holding a shepherd's crook in his right hand. This little statue, which I keep on my desk top in my study at home, was given to me recently by one of my former graduate students at the University of Chicago, who had come there from China and now taught English at a university in Beijing. He tells me that this little figure is, like the bird in Yeats's poem, "a symbol of longevity." For me the statue seems a kind of Chinese equivalent to our Father Time figure in the West whose iconography has been so wonderfully sketched by Sam Macey.[15] If we looked at this Chinese figure more closely, however, we would be impressed with its differences from our traditional icon rather than with its similarities. For one thing, *our* Father Time carries a scythe; my Chinese man carries a shepherd's crook, and the symbolic implications are surely, thereby, profoundly different ones. Even more important, by way of difference, are the smiles of the two figures. If our Father Time ever smiles, it is the gruesome grin of the fleshless skeleton, whereas the Chinese time figure reassures us about time, for he has the same facial expression as those elderly men in Yeats's poem: "Their eyes mid many wrinkles, their eyes/Their ancient, glittering eyes, are gay." Yeats's lines tell us much about time and force us to an awareness of the richness and depth of the Chinese experience of time, which so often escaped nineteenth-century writers.

Perhaps there will be a large-scale awakening to what the artist can provide by way of understanding temporal experience. On May 19, 1983, there appeared a report in American newspapers about some recommendations for the improvement of space-travel programs in America, recommendations submitted by a special task force stationed in Washington. The most striking of these recommendations was that space travel should soon be opened up so that private citizens may be carried into outer space, and that the first to fly on such flights ought to be writers, artists, poets. This proposed priority in favor of the literary person may strike us as foolishly eccentric. What does a novelist or literary critic know of the extraordinarily specialized technological skills that have made possible these space programs? Could such writers even define a space shuttle to the satisfaction of today's Mr.

Gradgrinds? Clearly not; such writers would be as hopeless at that task as Sissy Jupe was when she was asked to define a horse! Why then should we waste space fuel to launch them skyward? For a reply I must rely on the arguments of the task-force people themselves. It was they who have contended that writers would "provide the public with insights into space flight and the role of the human in space." Authors could provide, we learn, "a comprehensive visual mission history as well as real-time (on the spot) reports." [16]

In any event, here again is a further experience of time and space that awaits to be memorialized by the special skills of a special kind of artist: the writer of novels and plays and poems. And finally, these contributions to our understanding of the experiences of time also await the attentions of a special kind of humanist: the scholar and critic and historian of literature who can make the literary artist's contributions more accessible and more a part of the big terrain we are jointly trying to explore. This is how I—a literary humanist—have come to the study of time. In the papers of this volume, each author, in his or her own way, reveals something of the encounter with time's rumminess.

Notes

1. Charles Dickens, *The Pickwick Papers*, chap. 42.

2. See Helen Gardner, *The Composition of the Four Quartets* (London: Faber and Faber, 1978), p. 38.

3. T. S. Eliot, "The Dry Salvages," in *Four Quartets* (New York: Harcourt, Brace, 1943), p. 22.

4. Percy Lubbock, *The Craft of Fiction* (London: Jonathan Cape, 1935), pp. 52 (see also p. 31), 50–51.

5. See Wolfgang Iser, *The Implied Reader* (Baltimore: Johns Hopkins University Press, 1974).

6. Charles Dickens, *Hard Times*, chap. 2.

7. John A. Michon, "Psychological and Physiological Aspects of the Temporal Organization of Behaviour," *Heymans Bulletins* (Groningen, 1982), pp. 22, 27.

8. Margaret Laurence, *The Diviners* (New York: Knopf, 1982), pp. 291–93.

9. Sermon cited in burial service for Sir Arthur Elton, Bt. (Clevedon, Somerset: Privately printed, 1977).

10. Cited in *Times Literary Supplement*, December 24, 1982, p. 1430.

11. See John Stuart Mill, *On Liberty*, chap. 3.

12. Alfred Tennyson, "Locksley Hall," line 184.

13. Joseph Needham, "Time and Knowledge in China and the West," in *The Voices of Time*, ed. J. T. Fraser, 2d ed. (Amherst: University of Massachusetts Press, 1981), p. 104.

14. W. B. Yeats, "Lapis Lazuli," in *The Collected Poems of William Butler Yeats* (New York: Macmillan, 1958), pp. 292–93.

15. See Sam Macey, "The Changing Iconography of Father Time," in *The Study of Time III*, ed. J. T. Fraser, N. Lawrence, D. Park (New York: Springer-Verlag, 1978), pp. 540–76.

16. See *Rochester Democrat and Chronicle*, May 19, 1983, p. 1.

Part III

China

Introduction

Through selected topics from Chinese thought and history, this part addresses the intricate relationships that tie the notion and experience of time to social structures and to different modes of knowing.

In the opening paper, N. Sivin focuses on the distinction between the predictable and the unpredictable, as perceived in early Chinese mathematical astronomy. His work reveals an epistemology quite different from its traditional Western counterpart.

Jin Guantao, Fan Dainian, Fan Hongye, and Liu Qing Feng represent in quantitative terms the evolution of traditional Chinese science and technology, in an elaboration of the type of curves and tabulations that Joseph Needham has given us earlier (*Clerks and Craftsmen in China and the West* [Cambridge: At the University Press, 1970], fig. 99, p. 414). The authors compare their graphs with similar plots, which depict the development of science and technology in the West. Then they explore some of the reasons that might account for the difference between the two sets of curves.

Qiu Renzong's essay is a qualitative assessment of those features of the social and cultural background of traditional China that prevented the merging of theoretical knowledge and craft tradition into the synthesis of modern science.

Kristofer Schipper and Wang Hsiu-huei explore the role played in Taoist ritual by the coexistence of creative and destructive time cycles, as seen by the Tao, in the nature of the universe.

Zhang Yinzhi presents a sampling from the Mohist Canons pertaining to time and space.

Hans Ågren introduces us to two forms of traditional Chinese medicine that see differently the role of time, as it enters the progress of illness and the process of recovery.

Lo Huisheng's short paper sums up a number of interlocking philosophical theories relating time to the practice of medicine.

The advantages and disadvantages of different views of time, as they enter the practice of archaeology, are examined by Synnøve Vinsrygg, in the context of China and the West. The paper gives its reader a glimpse into the complexity of issues that determine what the members of a culture tend to regard as making sense.

Frederick Turner seeks to identify the reasons that make metric poetry one of the great cultural universals. He sees the sources of that universality in the functions of the neural processes, common to all members of our species and responsible, as he sees them, for the common meters of Chinese and Western poetry.

Thus we return to the claim made earlier in this book that the experience of time, shared by all people, may serve as a suitable vehicle for intercultural studies.

J. T. F.

On the Limits of Empirical Knowledge in the Traditional Chinese Sciences

N. Sivin

Summary This essay explores a broad theme fundamental to the study of time in Chinese science, namely the persistent denial by scientists and philosophers for the past two thousand years that full knowledge of the patterns underlying physical phenomena is attainable by rational and empirical means. These thinkers maintained that empirical study must be pursued alongside other ways of knowing that in general are concerned with being and experience outside space and time: meditation, concentration, disciplined intuition, self-examination, and so on.

Statements to this effect from writings in various fields of science from about 100 B.C. to the seventeenth century are considered, but in order to pay special attention to thought about time, the essay is mainly concerned with discussions of indeterminacy in the technical literature of mathematical astronomy. Early statements reflect a crisis in the ability to reliably predict astronomical phenomena previously documented in my *Cosmos and Computation in Early Chinese Mathematical Astronomy* (Leiden: E. J. Brill, 1969). By the eighth century this argument was being used not only to explain the failure of predictive techniques but also as ammunition in attacks on innovators by conservative holders of astronomical sinecures in the imperial civil service. Beginning in the eleventh century, discourse about the limits of empirical knowledge was transformed by astronomers better prepared than their predecessors to explore methodological and epistemological aspects of their science, and by a few philosophers who made these aspects an important part of their thought. The notion of indeterminacy in their hands became an organizing center for explorations in what would now be called the philosophy of science. This seemingly obscurantist notion was fruitful in clarifying the difference and potential conflict between accuracy and precision (late twelfth century), to give only one of several examples.

For two thousand years time has been a natural focus of interest in the study of Chinese thought, and of scientific thought in particular. Of the uncountable Chinese commentaries on and studies of the Book of Changes, for instance, not many have ignored the preoccupation of that classic with time shaping the cosmos and man's perception of nature. One of the earliest commentaries, the so-called Great Commentary, interpreted the cosmic way, the Dao, in this famous passage: "As the sun moves on, the moon comes; as the moon moves on, the sun comes. As sun and moon impel each other light is produced. As the cold goes, the heat comes; as the heat goes, the cold comes. As cold and heat impel each other the year is formed. What moves on contracts; what comes expands. What contracts and what expands influence each other, producing what furthers [man's activities]."

So we see that it is the harmoniously alternating interplay of opposites that forms time; it is time that underlies cosmic process; and it is cosmic process that provides a pattern for human reflection and conduct. As a line in the next passage of the same commentary tells us, the man attuned to the cosmic order "waits for the time and acts." Right action arises from knowledge of the right time.[1]

The cyclic character of time was so obvious in philosophic writing that scholars in China, Japan, and the West, much more interested in the classics than in what was going on in the minds of living people, tended to proceed as though there were no other Chinese time sense than the cyclic. But no great civilization is so simpleminded, as anyone will agree who recalls what used to be a similar situation in the study of ancient Greek thought.

A more adequate understanding of time in China has emerged from the last half-century's research, especially out of two original and penetrating essays. In *La pensée chinoise*, published in 1934, Marcel Granet, with the eye of an anthropologist, detected within the larger cycles a finer structure of time that was discontinuous and, as he put it, "packaged" into seasons, epochs, and ritual occasions. These distinct moments were divided between the dominions of yin and yang, or alternately among those of the Five Phases (*wu xing*), so that different qualities and activities were proper to each separate link in the temporal chain. In Granet's view, based on early classical writings, time was still cyclic, but its texture as experienced moment to moment by early Chinese was not at all smoothly connected.

Joseph Needham, as part of his massive preliminary reconnaissance of all Chinese sciences and techniques, took the next major step in his 1964 lecture "Time and Knowledge in China and the West." Needham demonstrated that every conceivable premodern conception of time can be found in the historical record, especially in the actual documents of natural science that his predecessors had ignored. There was the analogical, symbolic, didactic time of the historian; the objective, regular metric of the great astronomical clocks and water clocks of the past two millennia; the inseparable continuity and discontinuity of biological process; the progress and regress found in various sociopolitical visions of past and future; and the recognition by those who did technical work that techniques improved and knowledge accumulated over the centuries.

My own interest, aroused by these contributions and by those of Chinese and Japanese colleagues that followed, has been concerned mainly with how these time senses shaped the perception of nature in general and the sciences in particular. Where exactly were the Chinese applying cyclic ideas of time? To the cosmos and to two microcosms that in their normal functioning were in perfect correspondence to it. One of these microcosms was the liturgical order of both government and religion, each with its time-bound rituals. The other was the life-maintaining order of the human body, in phase with the environment and with the individual's emotional and rational processes. This seemed to me to constitute a remarkably articulated nest of cycles, with the life trajectory of the mayfly or the diurnal rhythm of the human body representing the smallest wheel, and, as the largest, the practically infinite great cycle—from the beginning to the end of time—integrating all the astronomical periods, all the smaller cycles turning within it like a superbly complicated train of gears.[2]

What were they using cyclical ideas for? To define order—obviously a dynamic order rather than a static one. That definition later made prediction possible, as in astronomy, or pointed the way to restoring disturbed order, as in medicine—or, for that matter, to creating ideal visions of the relations of man and nature through the seasons, as in landscape painting and poetry. The point is that patterns of function through time, rather than taxonomic structures, became central in making sense of experience.

This cyclic and dynamic view of time was fully formed at the center of Confucian orthodoxy by the first century B.C. It no longer makes sense to argue about whether science was somehow the creation of Daoists or any other group of philosophers. The people who created China's technical sciences did not belong to such groups. Regardless of what the founders of these schools may have wanted them to be, by the first century B.C. their traditions had blended to provide the common tools of thought that every inquiring person shared. The cyclic time sense by that time was neither Daoist, Legalist, Confucian, nor Mohist; it had become, once and for all, the nonspecialist's mode of thinking about natural process. As in any culture, including our own, some people were not interested in natural process; but those who were thought in this mode.

The other time senses—compartmented, progressive, regressive—were not in competition with that one, but were used, often by the same people, in thinking about different ranges of phenomena, generally social rather than natural (although the difference between social and natural was not at all clear-cut). Despite claims to the contrary, the great mass of the Chinese people and the civil servants of the imperial government alike, when they thought about natural process, thought of recurrent patterns of balanced opposition, usually expressed in the language of yin and yang and the Five Phases. This is what the documents of popular thought, political ritual, magic, religion, and the sciences tell us about the past, and what those who observe old-fashioned Chinese communities report today. Cyclic thought has thus become central once again in the study of scientific traditions, but, unlike the past situation, we now pay due attention to noncyclic time senses when we consider such topics as the growth of knowledge and the legends that put the ultimate origins of every science and every invention back into the long archaic stretch of time before history began.

The study of what was is never entirely free from the historian's convictions about what should have been. But we have learned better in the last twenty years than to waste effort debating whether cyclic time is a good thing, or whether it helped or hindered the growth of science. Historians of science have learned better than to entertain simpleminded opinions about such subtle matters. We acknowledge that judgments of value are part of our work, but we have learned to suspend them until we have examined the actual use of time concepts in theories and technics. That effort has barely begun.

Again and again, in the few such studies that have been carried out, we can see that cyclic time phenomena play very different roles in different contexts. In mathematical astronomy, for instance, the two great computational systems of the first century A.D. were based on the best available assumption, namely that the celestial motions were simple cycles, intricately fitted together to form great periods. In principle, more accurate techniques could have been discovered with no more sophisticated mathematics, but they could not have been assimilated to the formal character of astronomy as a whole. Simple cyclic techniques were adequate for the mean motions of the sun, moon, and planets, but despite ingenious design they were bound to fail for long-range predictions of apparent phenomena, above all, of eclipses. The dilemma of consistency in theory *vs.* accuracy in prediction was resolved over the next few centuries, not by astronomers' building a different set of assumptions on a new foundation, but by their abandoning the ideal of a rational astronomy governed by cosmology. Instead, as we will see, they consciously tended to accept any technique that worked, and to reject it when it ceased to work.

In medicine and alchemy cyclical ideas never seemed inadequate to those who used them. There could be no crisis over the failure of quantitative prediction, since neither science offered any. Some historians have felt that such concepts should have been inhibitory, but they have never proven that the other time concepts found in very different Chinese contexts could have been more productive in medicine and alchemy, or even that they could have been assimilated. Over the whole evolution of these sciences, their technical languages have been those of cyclic process, especially those of yin-yang and the Five Phases theories, adapted and supplemented to fit their needs. Technical examples would not be appropriate here, but the point is clear enough in a passage relating the political and somatic microcosms by Ge Hong 葛洪 (283–343), physician and amateur of alchemy: "The human body is a counterpart of the state. . . . The spirit is like the monarch; the blood is like the ministers; the *qi* pneuma is like the people. Thus we know that one who keeps his own body in order can keep a state in order. Loving care for one's people is what makes it possible for a state to be secure; nurturing one's *qi* is what makes it possible to keep the body intact. When the people are dispersed the state perishes; when the *qi* is exhausted the body dies. What is dead cannot be brought to life; what has perished cannot be preserved. Because all this is so, the perfected man allays catastrophe before it happens, and cures illness before it has developed. He treats it in advance rather than chasing to catch up after it has passed him by. . . . " The time-bound character of medicine is typically clear here. The same is so true of alchemy that I once described it as "the manipulation of time."[3]

After long study of how the alchemists explained to each other what they were doing and why, I had to admit that thinking of alchemy simply as early chemistry only perpetuates confusion. We have any number of statements, again phrased in the clear technical language of yin-yang and the Five Phases, that a major aim of alchemy was constructing laboratory models of cosmic process, with its millennial great cycles shrunk down on the scale of time to a few months or a year. The aim of this effort was not knowledge but transcendence, salvation, immortality, gained through a contemplation of the cosmic Dao that mortals could not ordinarily encompass. In this endeavor, which was unambiguously religious, the alchemists discovered many chemical facts, indeed more knowledge about quantitative relations than we can find in contemporary European alchemy. Exactly how much the Chinese alchemists learned we still cannot specify, since we have not yet investigated how many of their facts, processes, and apparatus they borrowed from craftsmen and physicians. But the point is that their chemical discoveries were by-products. That may irritate some historians of chemistry who feel that alchemists, if they were competent, ought to have been trying to do modern chemistry. But once we know the difference between ends and means, we are no longer free to confuse them.

The picture that emerges from these recent outcomes of research is still very partial. All we can say is that the value of time concepts and their influence on the evolution of science are not fixed quantities, but depend on how they are applied, to what aspects of experience, and for what ends. I would now like to report on a related problem that has concerned me for some time. This is a very tentative report, because this line of research is only beginning to yield up a pattern.

My theme is the limits of scientific inquiry—that is, ancient Chinese concerns about whether nature can be comprehended fully by rational, empirical investigation. The relation of this topic to time concepts may seem indirect, but issues of change and prediction come up in every source that discusses the topic, and the temporal themes that I have just summarized will play a central part in my conclusions.

We find the limitations of observational knowledge taken up regularly in writings on astronomy, the most exact of the ancient sciences, but not in astronomy alone. Because this theme mainly appears in technical discussions rather than in writings of a general kind, we can avoid the dangerous assumption that the opinions of philosophers determined what scientists thought in China. What emerges from the writings of fifteen hundred years is an abiding interest in the idea that the scale of the cosmos is too large, and the texture of nature is too fine, too subtle, too closely intermeshed (*wei* 微, *miao* 妙, and so forth) for phenomena to be fully predictable. This proposition denies that the physical world can be fully penetrated by study, or fully described in words or numbers. This cognitive strategy evolved, and its history can be traced.

Before looking at this idea historically, let me introduce two short but typical statements about astronomy's inherent limitation as a science. Here is an early assertion of this idea, by the polymath Cai Yong 蔡邕 in A.D. 175:

> The astronomical regularities are demanding in their subtlety, and we are far removed from the Sages [who founded this art]. Success and failure take their turns, and no technique can be correct forever.... The motions of the sun, moon, and planets vary in speed and in divergence from the mean; they cannot be treated as uniform. When the technical experts trace them through computation, they can do no more than to accord with [the observations of] their own time. Thus there come to be [differences between] the techniques of various periods.[4]

Cai's lack of confidence should not be dismissed as a simple matter of the crude techniques available in the second century, as we will see when we return to that period. First let us take a passing look at a much later time, when Western astronomy was widely known. Perhaps the last such statement on the part of a scholar well qualified in astronomy comes from Dai Zhen 戴震 (1724–77), the leading philologist and in many respects the most influential intellectual of his time, in his essay on solar theory:

> In all prediction of celestial phenomena, as time passes there are bound to be errors that are due neither to inaccuracies in positional data nor to the need for periodic revision of computational methods. The sphere of the sky is so enormous that number and measure cannot get to the end of it, just as when we measure something an inch or a grain at a time, there is bound to be discrepancy by the time we have counted up to a foot or an ounce. Because this is so, we define units of time and observe phenomena so as to make the most of our techniques. Our best course is to continue using a technique so long as its inaccuracies remain imperceptible, and correct it once they have been noticed. This is a matter of indeterminacy as error accumulates over a long period.[5]

Now let us first look at some of the early philosophical ideas that may have formed the backdrop to statements about cosmic indeterminacy. Then we can consider the historical development of such statements themselves, in astronomy and other departments of knowledge. Finally we can ask what light this theme casts on the character and history of prediction as a goal of Chinese science.

It is important to look at each statement, not as a great idea that must be taken at face value, but as a reflection of the viewpoint of someone with certain interests in certain historical circumstances. I will consider only a few sources, and necessarily pass over most of them too quickly to do justice to the circumstances and interests that they reflect, but please bear in mind that this is only a rough, preliminary sketch of work in progress.

Philosophical Precursors

In the pre-Han classics it is remarkable how seldom words that later imply subtlety and indeterminacy, such as *wei, miao,* and *xuan* 玄, refer to the possibility of knowledge. One pertinent treatise is the Great Commentary to the Book of Changes, the major source of orthodox cosmology from the Han on. There the word *wei* refers to the gentleman's sensitivity to the ethical implications of a situation as soon as they begin to evolve, long before they become obvious. Its statements are clearly not about factual or theoretical knowledge of the natural world.

In the *Laozi* 老子 we find several other pertinent ideas. The Way itself in its constant and unchanging aspect, we are told, is shadowy and indistinct, and cannot be described. *Wei* and similar words are never clearly applied to the empirical world or to theoretical knowledge, but *wei, miao,* and *xuan* appear together in one line that describes the exemplary gentleman:

> Of old those adept in the Way
> Their mastery recondite, subtle, and mysterious,
> Were too profound to be known . . .

One might guess from familiarity with the book as a whole that the Sage becomes indeterminate as he models himself on the indeterminate Dao that he contemplates, but the text does not go quite that far.[6]

To sum up, by 300 B.C. certain aspects of the Dao were described as indeterminate, but these aspects are not identified with the phenomenal world, which *can* be described. Words implying indeterminacy rather than ineffability are used to describe the character of the ideal person rather than that of the cosmos. Not surprisingly, the key words above, which later appear in astronomical discussions, do not occur in any germane sense in the *Zhuangzi* 莊子. That book consistently rejects the humanistic orientation that we have found in the *Laozi* and the Great Commentary, and is unequivocally opposed to the logical description of experience.[7]

The indeterminacy of the cosmos finally appears in less ambiguous form in the *Chunqiu fan lu* 春秋繁露 (135 B.C.?), Dong Zhongshu's 董仲舒 attempt to construct for the Han a new state intellectual orthodoxy that incorporates cosmology: "The Ancients had a saying that if you do not know the future you can see it in the past. Now in the study of the Spring and Autumn Annals 春秋 statements about the past are used to clarify the future. But because its words embody the subtlety of the natural order (*tian zhi wei* 天之微), they are hard to comprehend."[8] Dong is using the subtlety of nature, its resistance to being understood, as a metaphor for the arcane language of the orthodox classic.

Indeterminacy in Astronomy

Now let us pass on to the earliest statements about the limitations of astronomical prediction. Most of these assertions appear in the Standard Histories that chronicle the affairs of each dynasty. Computing the ephemerides and interpreting ominous phenomena were matters of concern to the state, which attempted to center this activity in its Astronomical Bureau and Imperial Observatory. Once astronomy was thus tied to the imperial charisma, a succession of computational systems for predicting the positions and chief phenomena of the sun, moon, and planets was officially adopted, nearly fifty systems between the beginning of the first century B.C. and the middle of the seventeenth century A.D. Improvement in techniques did not lead to revision of the current system, but to its complete replacement by a new one. This was, at least, the principle; in practice we find occasional traces of piecemeal revision, and several replacements that were no improvement at all. New systems were sometimes ordered up to signal a new dynasty or announce a "new deal." On such occasions innovation was too much to expect.

Nearly all the judgments about astronomical systems in the Standard Histories were set down when a new system was presented for adoption, or when an old system was regularly failing to give accurate predictions. A sensible person today who plans to buy an automobile, and wants to find out about the limitations of a certain design, would not ask a salesman who sells that model, but would consult someone who had been driving one for some time. In astronomy as well, it is the prospect of obsolescence that encourages frankness. We usually find doubts about the extension of knowledge expressed not with respect to a system presented for adoption but when the shortcomings of an established system have become apparent, and all the more when a competitor in the offing suggests that its tenure is limited.

Probably the most serious period of crisis and reassessment in early mathematical astronomy began shortly before the end of the first century A.D., when the Grand Inception system (*Taichu li* 太初曆), adopted in 104 B.C. and greatly developed as the Triple Concordance system (*Santong li* 三統曆) a century later, was about to be replaced.[9] In A.D. 92, Jia Kui 賈逵 presented to the throne the first major document of this crisis, his "Discussion of Calendrical Astronomy (*lun li* 論曆)." He speaks of what we would call the imprecision of constants; even those instituted by the legendary Sages who had founded astronomy in the Golden Age,

> unable to endure unchanged [lit., "run through"] for thousands and myriads of years, must be altered and replaced. We [in later times] first determine angular measures and numerical quantities from observations made over long intervals, and select those that accord with the positions of the sun, moon, and planets.... [Our] methods will thus differ from one period to another. The Grand Inception system [of two centuries earlier] cannot give accurate predictions for the present day; nor can the new system provide correct computations back to the beginning of the Han period. The computational methods of a single school can only be applicable within an interval of three hundred years.... When the Han first attained power, it would have been appropriate to adopt the Grand Inception system [because time had come for renewal]; but there was no such reform until 104 B.C., 102 years later. Thus early in the dynasty there were lunar conjunctions the day before the last day of the month [i.e., two days before mean lunation], but by the time of Emperors Cheng 成 and Ai 袁 (32 B.C. to A.D. 1) the second day of the month was being taken as the day of lunation [i.e., the civil month was routinely set back one day] so that most conjunctions would occur on the last day of the month [which was allowable in the early Han]. This is clear proof [that calendar reform is periodically necessary].

Why cannot even the Sages discover constants precise enough to be used forever? That Jia explained earlier in his report: "The Celestial Way being irregular, lacking uniformity, there are bound to be remainders. These remainders will have their own disparities, which cannot be made uniform."[10] Imprecision is not a characteristic of the constants, that is, but a characteristic of the universe.

By the end of the second century, as my earlier quotation from Cai Yong indicates, the implications of indeterminacy had become much broader than in Jia Kui's time, and were affecting prediction in ways that did not simply depend on the precision of constants.

Although the sun moves along the ecliptic, and the moon is never more than about six degrees from it, Han astronomers measured their positions along the equator. The ability to convert mathematically from positions on the ecliptic and the lunar orbit to right ascension and vice versa was beyond the simple linear techniques then in use. This made major improvement in eclipse theory—the central problem in traditional astronomy—seem hopeless. A report on lunar eclipse prediction of the late second century outlines this difficulty at some length, and then eloquently draws a conclusion:

> In view of this [limited feasibility of mathematical solution], there is no point in rejecting any method that does not conflict with observation, nor in adopting any method whose utility has not been demonstrated in practice. The Celestial Way is so subtle, precise measurement so difficult, computational methods so varying in approach, and chronological schemas so lacking in unanimity, that we can never be sure that a technique is correct until it has been confirmed in practice—nor that it is inadequate until discrepancies have shown up. Once a method is known to be inadequate, we change it; once it is known to be correct, we adopt it: this is called "sincerely holding to the mean."[11]

The anonymous author is expressing resignation in the face of the crisis I have referred to. Imprecise constants could always be revised, but it was now clear—puzzlingly clear—that Han assumptions about the character of the celestial phenomena were beginning to break down. It was beginning to be apparent that certain phenomena, especially eclipses, could not be described by simple cyclic or linear methods. Finally, when over several centuries this difficulty could not be resolved, astronomers stopped trying. Cosmological hypotheses no longer ordered their computational techniques. They bought the power to predict in the simplest possible way, at the cost of the power to explain. This is a cost that greatly *limits* the power to predict in the long run, but that lesson did not become apparent until the seventeenth century, when the best astronomers of the time recognized enthusiastically the explanatory power of the geometric models introduced by the Jesuits.

Not everyone had reason to accept the idea of astronomical indeterminacy. We might expect people defending new astronomical systems rather than criticizing old ones to argue against it; indeed examples are not hard to find. There is the spirited and rather exasperated rejoinder of Zu Chongzhi 祖沖之, one of China's greatest mathematical astronomers, against the attack on his new system by Dai Faxing 戴法興 in or near 463. Dai had developed an extensive argument along the lines of those I have quoted. Zu's defense, pragmatic rather than theoretical, is too long to cite completely:

> The writings of the Xia, Shang, and earlier dynasties have been lost; but the historical records of the Spring and Autumn period and the Han record eclipses and lunations with care for detail; they constitute clear evidence. Testing my astronomical system by their use, I find the data entirely in accord [with my computations]. There is truly nothing speculative in it. It takes precision as far as possible, so that over a span of a thousand years there is no discrepancy; far away though it be, it can be known. Now I have studied all the ancient methods, and there I find much that is inexact. Computations are off by as much as three days, and the beginnings of *qi* periods by as much as seven hours. I know of no [ancient system] that can accurately predict the phenomena of the present time.

Tsu's claim that there would be no discrepancy in predictions over a thousand years was excessive. It did not accord with informed opinion, it could not be proven in practice, and he did not make it persuasive in principle. For reasons as much political as technical he did not carry the day. His system, despite its excellence, was not officially adopted for fifty years.[12]

In 729 Ixing 一行 discussed in his new Great Expansion system (*Dayan li* 大衍曆) the technique for predicting lunations. He politely suggested that even if the course of the cosmos were inherently too irregular to be fully comprehended—and he did not minimize its irregularity—that would be irrelevant to the work of prediction: "If the anomalies in the celestial positions [of the moon] actually fluctuated with time, providing rebukes [to the ruler] that the regularity of astronomical constants cannot encompass, and substituting for regularity a mutability [that derives] from the inaccessible [fine structure of the cosmos], this would be a matter beyond even [the ability of] Sages to assess. It can hardly lie within the scope of mathematical astronomy."

This is a more meaningful statement than its brevity and skeptical tone make it look. In the first place, it reminds us that Ixing was anticipating exactly the sort of argument that Zu Chongzhi had had to fight off. The idea that astronomical knowledge was inherently limited was now being used even against the best new systems rather than just to explain the failure of old ones. Second, for Ixing the conceptual crisis I have mentioned was long over, and a disinterest in cosmology was the norm among astronomers. They rarely took up questions of the actual spatial relations or physical realities underlying the phenomena.

It is curious, considering Ixing's lack of interest in these questions, that he remains the last great astronomer to give cosmology an important role in his computational system. His cosmology was not physical, however, but drew in a curiously antiquarian way on the numerology of the Great Commentary to the Book of Changes.[13] Still his curiosity in such matters was much narrower than that of his Han predecessors. The astronomical systems that followed Ixing's were narrower still from the viewpoint of cosmology. Decreasing interest in the physical and metaphysical patterns that underlie the phenomena is not necessarily associated with more "scientific" trends in astronomy, either in China or in the West, because in real scientific work (as distinguished from certain ideal schemes of philosophers and historians of science) analysis of data and thought about their ultimate significance interact. It was the demand for a coherent and intelligible cosmic order that motivated Copernicus, Galileo, and Kepler to innovate in directions that became decisive for modern science.

New Issues in the Song

By the Northern Song period, discussions of the sort I have summarized were either too rare or too familiar to record. Many of the difficulties that had originally suggested inherent limitations to knowledge were no longer difficulties; for instance, the time of lunar eclipses could be predicted with some confidence. The issue for the working astronomer, as I have said, had become not knowability but technical progress. Whether some day his science might reach those ultimate limits, or would always fall short, was not an urgent problem.

In the Song period the idea of indeterminacy suggested ultimate questions of a new kind. These questions came from astronomers better prepared than their predecessors to explore methodological and epistemological aspects of their science, and from philosophers who made those aspects an important part of their thought. My examples will be Shen Kuo 沈括 (1031–95) as a professional astronomer—among his enormous range of accomplishments— and Zhu Xi 朱熹 (1130–1200) and Cai Tuanding 蔡元定 (1135–98) to represent the philosophers.

In his Brush Talks from Dream Brook (*Menggi bitan* 夢溪筆談), Shen summarizes the lost preface to his Oblatory Epoch system (*Fengyuan li* 奉元曆), an innovative document:

Those who discourse on numbers [by which he means all regularities that make prediction possible], it seems, [can only] deal with their crude after-traces. There is a very subtle (*wei*) aspect to numbers that those who rely on mathematical astronomy are unable to know; [what they can know of] this aspect is, all the more, only after-traces. As for the ability [of the sagely mind as exemplified in the Book of Changes] "when stimulated to encompass every situation in the realm," after-traces can play no role in that [wisdom]. That is why "the spirituality that makes foreknowledge [possible]" cannot readily be sought through after-traces, especially when one has access only to the crudest ones. As for the very subtle traces I have mentioned, those who in our time discuss the celestial bodies depend on mathematical astronomy to know them, but astronomy is no more than the product of speculation (yi 億).

Shen proceeds to develop an epistemological point that comes up several times in his writing, namely that in order to know, we break the continuity of nature into blocks of time that we treat as though they were uniform. As he puts it,

The uninitiated say that, mathematical knowledge of the heavenly bodies being difficult to be sure of, only correlations between the Five Phases and time periods are reliable, but this is also untrue. The uninitiated who discuss the cyclic alternations (*xiaozhang* 消長) of the Five Phases consider only the year. Thus [they know that] after the winter solstice the sun's motion is in the phase of Expansion [i.e., the equation of center is negative] and thus yin, and at the equinoxes corresponds to the mean. They do not realize that in the course of a month there is also an alternation. Before opposition the moon's motion is in the phase of Expansion and thus yang, after opposition it is in the phase of Contraction and thus yin, and at the quadratures corresponds to the mean.

As for the associations of spring with Wood, summer with Fire, autumn with Metal, and winter with Water, these are also true of the month—not only of the month but of the day. The Inner Canon of the Yellow Lord ([*Huangdi nei jing*] *su wen* 素問) says 'when the disorder is in the hepatic system, the onset [of an attack] is between 3 and 7 A.M., and the most serious time is between 3 and 7 P.M. When it is in the cardiac system, the onset is between 9 A.M. and 1 P.M., and the most serious time is between 9 P.M. and 1 A.M.'' Thus a single day has four seasons of its own. How do we know that there are not four seasons in each hour—or in each mark [*ke* 刻, 0.01 day, approximately fifteen minutes], each minute, each instant? And how do we know that there are not a greater four seasons in each decade, century, Era cycle, Coincidence cycle, and Epoch cycle? As for the association of spring with Wood, within a period of ninety days there must be one [completed] cycle of alternation within another. It is impossible that the last hour of the 30th of the third month should belong to Wood, and the first hour of the next day abruptly belong to Fire. Matters of this sort are not to be settled by the methods abroad in the world.

Shen is writing in this second part of his short essay about techniques of foreknowledge that depend, not upon observations of celestial events, but on associating in rotation the Five Phases with periods of time (for instance, the year, month, day, and hour of birth) in order to yield interpretations of the latter. This simple repetitive approach may have begun with astrology, but has been completely abstracted from what happens in the sky. Such methods cannot be reliable, Shen argues, because they imply regular and abrupt transitions from one block of time with its corresponding phase and the next. But such "quantum" transitions belie the continuous variation in motion of the celestial bodies from which the validity of the methods ultimately derives. This underlying continuity of variation, ignore it though we may, pervades time at every level from the fleetest instant to the long cycles of calendrical reckoning (the Epoch Cycle of the Han was 4,560 years).

Anyone familiar with the great British philosopher of physics Alfred North Whitehead (1861–1947) will find this line of reasoning familiar. Shen, like Whitehead nine centuries later, was saying that a central problem for science is the gap that seems to separate our unconnected experiences from the unitary causal world that lies veiled in back of them.[14]

Scientific knowledge is necessarily an act of abstraction. Near the beginning of his proposal of 1074 for a new armillary sphere, Shen argues this point with great clarity—for the first time in history, I believe:

> Degrees [on the equator and ecliptic] are invisible; what is visible are stars. [The paths] followed by the sun, moon, and planets are occupied by stars. Twenty-eight stars are located [exactly] on a degree division; they are called "mansions (*she* 舍)." It is mansions that make it possible to measure degrees, and degrees that make it possible to create numerical regularities. Degrees are things that exist in the sky. When we make an armillary sphere [to measure intervals between real bodies], the degrees exist in the instrument. Once the degrees are in the instrument, then the sun, moon, and planets can be isolated (*tuan* 摶) in the instrument, and the sky no longer is involved. It is because the sky is no longer involved that what is in the sky is not difficult to know.[15]

Shen implies that one can know either about the organismic universe as a whole ("the sky") *or* about particular phenomena in it. Observational, empirical science can yield only knowledge of the second kind (a point about which Whitehead would disagree). In doing so it rules out perceptions of the first kind. They can be reached only by other kinds of knowledge—intuition, illumination, and so on, in which Shen is equally interested.

Cai Yuanding, another polymath, did away with one of the basic confusions of the Han astronomers. Cai wrote at least one book on mathematical astronomy. This detailed study of Ixing's astronomical system is lost, but certain important arguments are preserved in the conversations of Cai's mentor and friend Zhu Xi with Zhu's disciples. It is clear from Zhu's paraphrases that Cai believed inaccuracies of prediction do not imply indeterminacy. Beneath an irregularity may lie a more complicated regularity waiting to be discovered:

> When an astronomical system is first being designed, the discrepant measures of the celestial rotations are combined and included in the computations. So many years later there will be discrepancies of so many fractions of a degree, and after so many additional years, of so many degrees. If from these discrepant quantities correct quantities are computed, and this process is repeated to the limit [i.e., until the magnitude of the correction becomes negligible, *jintou* 盡頭], the astronomical system can be made essentially correct and free of discrepancies.
>
> People today, never having reached a comprehensive and correct understanding (? *da tong zheng* 大統正), simply claim that the discrepancies are inherent in the celestial rotations. They make systems of computation seeking accord with the celestial phenomena, but their ephemerides become increasingly discrepant. The point is this: they do not understand that if the sky is able to manifest a certain discrepancy, it is precisely because the celestial rotation *must* be of that kind (*tian zhi yunxing he dang ruci* 天之運行合當如此).

A discrepancy does not, as Cai's contemporaries think, reflect an anomaly in nature, but rather a more complicated regularity than originally assumed. *Ad hoc* technical adjustments simply obscure the discrepancies. In doing so they also obscure the underlying complex pattern that will keep generating discrepancies until it is understood.

This is an important perception about method. When we remember the gradual discovery in Europe of the various inequalities that complicate the moon's motion, we are reminded that the failure of Hipparchus's (fl. ca. 130–150 B.C.) first inequality to give perfect predictions suggested to Ptolemy (ca. A.D. 100–ca. 165) the evection, the second inequality. The discrepancies for which the evection could not account suggested to Tycho Brahe (1546–1601) the third and fourth inequalities.

Similar processes of discovery can be traced in the history of Chinese astronomy, but Cai was the first (at least the first reflected in the surviving record) to make the point explicit. His own attitude toward the determinate character of the phenomena was decidedly nuanced, even though he did not accept his contemporaries' reasoning about what implies indeterminacy. Zhu quotes him elsewhere to the effect that "there is no constancy in the celestial rotations; the sun, moon, and planets are accumulations of *qi*; they are all moving things (*dong wu* 動物). Their angular motions may be faster or slower, beyond the mean or short of it; they naturally are not uniform."

We have already seen that Cai considers these motions predictable. As Zhu remarks, "Cai was not saying that there is nothing determinate in the rotation of the sky, but that the angular motions of the luminaries are as they are." [16]

The last quotation from Cai is best understood in the light of similar beliefs held by such occidental luminaries as Plato and Ptolemy, for whom the planets are divine and self-propelled. This view was an alternative to the idea that the planets are passively driven in their rounds by some ccommon source of motion that determines the speed of each. A philosopher who finds no evidence for mechanical linkages powering the celestial luminaries is likely to find more plausible the idea that each planet is the source of its own motion. Its velocity is thus internally determined, and arbitrary with respect to those of other planets. The "erratic" retrogradations of the planets are thus accounted for; they could not be explained by those who considered the planets passive. In Athens and Alexandria a source that determines its own motion would be divine; in China it was animallike. To say that it is divine or "a moving thing" does not imply that its motion must necessarily be irregular or unknowable. The astronomer simply attempts to impose order upon whatever irregularities his observations reveal. What matters about Cai's attitude is that he faced the issue of indeterminacy instead of making assumptions that render it all the more problematic. He could thus imply that even when taken seriously it need not impede astronomy.

Zhu Xi, like Cai Yuanding, did not believe that there were inherent limits to the astronomer's power to predict. His attitude emerges in several discussions of a chapter from the *Mencius* (4B.26) which, in explicating the innate moral nature of man (*xing* 性), refers to the work of the astronomer. As Zhu explicates the relevant passage, it would mean: "Consider the sky so high, and its markpoints so distant; if we seek the traces of actual events (*gu* 故), without leaving our seats we can bring before us the solstices of a thousand years."

There is no basis for reading into Mencius's casual statement a pronouncement on the limits of empirical knowledge in astronomy. But Zhu Xi, in one of several conversations about the chapter, relates this passage to that question: "Mathematical astronomers computing backward from the present day are able to proceed without error even to the moment when the physical cosmos was formed. This is possible only because they follow traces of actual events (*i ran zhi ji* 已然之跡). There are sometimes irregularities in the true motions of the sky and of the sun, moon, and planets, but as time passes these recur spontaneously to the norm." Here Zhu Xi understands "*gu*" as traces of what exists or has existed; in other conversations, referring to other occurrences in the same chapter, he explains the word as "why something is so" (*suoyi ran* 所以然) and "what something does" (*suowei* 所爲). He is using Mencius's undefined "*gu*," relating it to Shen-Kuo's undefined "traces" (*ji*), to refer to phenomenological patterns. In a society never touched by Plato's opposition of phenomenon and reality, this is a more original step than it might appear.[17]

In the discussion of astronomical prediction that provided the long paraphrase from Cai

Yuanding quoted above, Zhu Xi begins more or less at the point where Cai had stopped, but moves off in a significant new direction:

> Someone asked why calendrical systems are repeatedly inaccurate. "How can it be that in ancient and modern times no one has studied this matter thoroughly?" Zhu Xi replied "It is precisely because no one has studied this matter thoroughly enough to rule out further change that there are repeated discrepancies. If it were studied with enough precision to yield a definitive method of computation, there would be no further discrepancies. . . .
>
> "The astronomical techniques of the Ancients were imprecise (*shukuo* 疏闊, lit., 'loose') but there were few discrepancies. The more precise (*mi* 密, lit., 'tight') the systems of today are, the more discrepancies appear!"
>
> At this point he measured off one side of his desk with his hands, saying "For instance, if we divide this width into four sections, each is limited in width by its borders with the others. If a discrepancy [between the widths] appears, it will be restricted to one of the sections. Large though it may be, even so extreme that it involved a second or third section, it would still be restricted to the four sections. So it would be easily computed, and any discrepancy easily could be seen. The astronomical systems of today [in effect] divide these four sections into eight, and the eight into sixteen. As the limits [of the sections] become more precise, the frequency of discrepancies becomes greater. Why is this? Because as the limits become more precise they are increasingly overstepped. The discrepancy may be identical, but the precision of ancient and modern systems differs.[18]

Zhu Xi is saying, if I understand him correctly, that increases of precision have led to greater expectations of accuracy, and that it is against these expectations that recent systems were failing; early systems satisfied lower standards. But that is not my point. This is the first clear explanation in Chinese, I believe, of the difference between accuracy and precision. This is not a small contribution to the methodology of the exact sciences.

These concerns with method and with theory of knowledge, although they have been ignored by modern historians, were carried on by the leading scholars of the Qing period. In a recent book, John Henderson traces the growing importance in Ming and Qing philosophy of arguments from mathematical astronomy. He shows that these concepts of quantitative origin largely replaced earlier conceptions such as yin-yang and the Five Phases. For example, scholars between the mid-seventeenth and late eighteenth century became aware through Western astronomical writings, which they studied eagerly, of such secular changes as the slow decrease in the obliquity of the ecliptic. They came to believe, as did many Europeans in the later part of the same period, that these were not entirely predictable, but could only be corrected through observation. "A number of Ch'ing scholars of varying scholastic affiliations thus identified several of the astronomical anomalies and deviations known to them as basically indeterminate, frequently drawing the conclusion that the patterns of the cosmos in general shifted in an irregular and even capricious fashion. They even regarded anomalies not so much as departures from a predictable order as themselves constitutive of the fundamental order, or disorder, of the cosmos."[19]

Limits of Inquiry in the Qualitative Sciences

It is not surprising that the issue of indeterminacy should have arisen mainly in astronomy, the one science that was both quantitative and concerned with prediction. The idea that empirical knowledge and understanding may be inherently limited does turn up in areas of inquiry that are not computational. Sometimes it is brought up by polymaths who are aware of the issue within astronomy. Shen Kuo, for instance, discusses a case in which lightning, striking a house, left its wooden structure unharmed but melted metal objects inside it. "People insist that fire will burn things of vegetable origin before it melts things made from metals or minerals, but in this instance, the latter all fused while not one of the former was destroyed by fire. This is not a matter that human capacities can fathom. A Buddhist treatise says 'Water makes the Naga fire blaze up, but puts out the human fire.' How true that is! People only know about matters in the realm of mankind. Outside that realm what limit can matters have? We may aspire, by our insignificant worldly wisdom and common sense, to get to the bottom of ultimate truths, but that is hardly possible." [20] I have already quoted one of Shen's references to medical theory.

We also find Fang Yizhi 方以智, in his Little Notes on the Principles of Things (completed 1643/1650), using what he had learned from Jesuit missionaries about optics to argue that the tendency of light rays to diverge, and of shadows and images to converge, makes certain optical phenomena unexplainable. He describes an experiment in which a piece of paper with four or five small holes yields multiple images of the sun, but as the paper is moved upward, away from the surface on which they are projected, the multiple images blend in a way that puzzles him to form a single image of the sun. "Sound and light," he argues, "are always more subtle than the 'number' of things." By "number" Fang means amenability to exact quantitative description, as "by acute angles and straight lines," i.e., geometric constructions.[21]

In medicine the idea that one can only hope to understand so much about the vital processes of the human body is natural enough. Medicine ever since the Tang period has been strongly influenced by Buddhist ethics. Since its beginnings, physicians and medical scholars have drawn on numerology, yin-yang, and Five Phases cosmology, and even on astronomy, in order to investigate the links between the internal order of the body and the order of nature that surrounds it. An obvious example is Zhang Jiebin's 張介賓 statement in his Comprehensive Treatise *Jingyue quanshu* 景岳全書 (preface dated 1593) about what is needed to comprehend vital processes: "anyone who does not possess transcendent wisdom is not prepared to master their subtleties (*wei-miao*); anyone who does not possess clarity of moral judgment is not prepared to make fine distinctions concerning what is correct." Empirical observation, in other words, must be supplemented by self-cultivation.

In some such statements Buddhist influence is plain to see. Yin Zhiyi's 殷志伊 preface to his father Yin Zhong chun's 仲春 little handbook of diagnosis and therapy entitled Mental Dharmas of Eruptive Disorders (probably shortly before 1621) is typical: "'Medicine' (*yi* 醫) means 'meaning' (*yi* 意). [The inner meanings of medicine, the patterns of vital processes] may be apprehended by the mind, but cannot be transmitted in words. Because these inherent patterns attain such arcane subtlety (*weiao* 微奧), even though the mind may achieve great constancy [in contemplating them], in [therapeutic] doctrine there can be no fixed rules. The interaction of hot and moist as governed by yin and yang, the relations of mutual production and overcoming among the Five Phases, change from one moment to the next. . . . " Yin begins with a familiar punning definition of medicine, and moves immediately to the Chan Buddhist notion of wordless teaching. Yin's word for therapeutic doctrine or method (*fa* 法) is the same as the term for Dharma in the title of his father's book (in which "mental dharmas" means at one level "doctrines or truths to be grasped by the mind").

Such instances from therapeutic manuals could readily be multiplied. In astronomy, as we have seen, the limits of observation was a live issue with a substantial developmental history. In medicine, however, what we find is reiteration of a familiar theme—a formula, more or less—that is seldom critically examined. My preliminary conclusion, pending deeper study and reflection, is that indeterminacy in medical writings is less significant for the history of medical thought than for epistemology in general.[22]

Conclusion

I have suggested that ideas of astronomical indeterminacy first arose as an explanation for what would now be considered the failure of crude predictive techniques, and that these ideas gradually became established to account for what historians would now explain by the failure of crude assumptions about the character of the celestial motions. As these assumptions were given up, and the crisis subsided, ideas of indeterminacy for a while were apparently used more as a weapon to beat back innovation than as a means to reexamine past failures. These ideas played a productive role again from the Song on, when they were used for diverse purposes, among them to direct critical attention to issues of epistemology and method. Some who used them, including Cai Yuanding and Zhu Xi, did not accept the idea that empirical knowledge was necessarily limited.

Why should an idea that looks so obscurantist, so opposed to the idea of progress, have played such an enduring collection of roles in the history of science? I suggest that the idea of indeterminacy was the one proposition that consistently challenged astronomers to come to grips with the difference between two issues: First, what is involved in predicting future observational data from past observational data? And second, what is involved in making intelligible the nature from which we draw observational data?

This is the difference between astronomy as a collection of data and techniques, and astronomy as a science. Despite the crisis in astronomy that began in the Later Han, the urge to make astronomy a science again never entirely subsided. It became a strong motivation from the eleventh century on, as impulses from philosophy stimulated astronomers, and vice versa. I think it will be possible to show ultimately that discussions of the limitations of inquiry in the Ming and early Qing encouraged the prompt and positive response of leading Chinese astronomers to Western astronomy and its concern for causes and explanations in the seventeenth century.

The issue that I have outlined does not seem to have been important in Western science after Heraclitus and Parmenides. For Plato, observation of phenomena cannot lead to knowledge of reality. It can yield only a thirdhand reflection of the ideas that real knowledge is about. The study of mathematics takes us toward them, but direct apprehension of the ideas is a contemplative, not an empirical, process. Aristotle believed that the reality of things was within them, and could be known directly from them, but "the advances made by the arts and sciences in each civilization were the fulfilment of the potentialities of their natural form beyond which they could not go."[23] The Skeptics denied that one could know with certainty; but their discussions of this point served to suspend judgment on all matters. This was not a doctrine that could greatly influence natural science.

The Stoics were, of course, the school closest in intellectual temper to Chinese cosmology, and they were influential in science, especially medicine. The empiricists among them opposed skepticism and thus indeterminacy. They were much concerned with the possibilities of knowledge, and considered all truth built up from what is delivered through the senses, judged by what they called "right reason."

In the European Middle Ages the analogous issue—a weak analogue—was the relationship of faith and reason. In the mid-thirteenth century we find St. Thomas Aquinas quoting with approval the words that St. Hilary of Poitiers set down nine hundred years earlier: "For he who devoutly follows in pursuit of the infinite, though he never come up with it, will always advance by setting forth. Yet pry not into that secret, and meddle not in the mystery of the birth of the infinite, nor presume to grasp that which is the summit of understanding: but understand that there are things thou canst not grasp."[24] The faith in unlimited knowledge, in untrammeled understanding, is not a characteristically Western faith; it is a modern faith.

In seeking valid Western analogies to the role of indeterminacy in Chinese intellectual history, I would take an entirely different direction. I would prefer to ask whether we can find ideas that appear irrelevant or "unscientific" from a vulgar positivist point of view, but that nevertheless played enduring roles in encouraging discussions of scientific issues. It is not hard, in fact, to think of examples. One is Zeno's paradoxes. It is well known that every important discussion of the continuity of points on a line, an important mathematical problem, from the Greeks to the end of the nineteenth century (Georg Cantor, 1845–1918) focused on those paradoxes.[25]

Let me return finally to the very beginning of this essay.

J. T. Fraser once wrote that limits of inquiry divide the world into phenomena that are predictable and those that are not. The dividing line between these phenomena constitutes a statement of belief, one of those irrationalities on which rationality must always rest. That demarcation usually amounts to a claim about the nature of time.[26] As we consider the many Chinese statements through history that we have reviewed, the issue is indeed in one sense the domain of prediction. It is even more fundamentally what the activity of prediction rules out. What it rules out is an uninterrupted response, at once intuitive and rational, to the concreteness and endless variety of phenomena in nature. That response is what theory in the traditional qualitative sciences, such as medicine, alchemy, and siting, seems always to have striven for.

Theory is necessarily abstract, based on rigorously defined concepts. Chinese scientists looked for a balance of concept and phenomenon, for accounts of nature that did justice to its richness. That, not Occam's razor, nor the necessity of geometric demonstration, was their aesthetic criterion.

No one familiar with the sources would argue that their stance was irrational. I would hesitate to say that it was less rational than that of European positivists of half a century ago, whose faith led them to draw an ultimately indefensible line between positive knowledge and the outcomes of all other mental activity. The Chinese thinkers I have cited were very much concerned with the theoretical ordering of phenomena, and with prediction, in astronomy and medicine. What we find them saying with increasing explicitness is that prediction is a reductive act and thus an inherently limiting one.

I suggested at the outset that cyclical time defined function and order—an abstract order but a comprehensive one, abstracted from immense ranges of the experience that humans can have. Almost every one of the Chinese statements that we have pondered is directly concerned with cyclic time, and many of them with a kind of temporal plenum, in which every moment by the power of correspondence becomes a full cycle, in effect the equivalent of a great year. We have seen coming out of the effort that I have described in a preliminary way a gradually clearer understanding of the ways in which scientists may relate experience and abstraction as they apply their knowledge to problems in the domain of nature.

Notes

1. *Zhou yi*, "Xici da zhuan 周易繫辭大傳," B, 3 (citations to standard Chinese classics are to Harvard-Yenching index versions unless otherwise indicated). Translations in this essay are my own; cf. the less literal translation in Richard Wilhelm, *The I ching or Book of Changes*, trans. Cary F. Baynes, Bollingen Series 19 (New York: Pantheon Books, 1950), 1: 363–64.

2. Marcel Granet, *La pensée chinoise* (Paris: Renaissance, 1934), esp. bk. 2; Joseph Needham, in *The Voices of Time*, ed. J. T. Fraser, 2d ed. (Amherst: University of Massachusetts Press, 1981), pp. 92–135, also published as *Time and Eastern Man*, the Henry Myers Lecture, 1964 (London: Royal Anthropological Institute of Great Britain and Ireland, 1965), reprinted in Needham, *The Grand Titration: Science and Society in East and West* (London: Allen and Unwin, 1969), pp. 218–98; Sivin, "Chinese Conceptions of Time," *Earlham Review* 1 (1966): 82–92; a more detailed and technical discussion can be found in Sivin, *Cosmos and Computation in Early Chinese Mathematical Astronomy* (Leiden: E. J. Brill, 1969). The liturgical foundations of the early Chinese political order are eloquently described by J. G. A. Pocock in *Politics, Language and Time: Essays on Political Thought and History* (New York: Atheneum, 1971), chaps. 2, 7.

3. *Baopuzi nei pian* 抱樸子內篇 (Pingjinguan congshu ed.), 8: 4b–5a; Sivin, "Chinese Alchemy and the Manipulation of Time," *Isis* 67 (1967): 513–27, reprinted in Sivin, ed., *Science and Technology in East Asia*, History of Science. Selections from *Isis* (New York: Neale Watson, 1977), pp. 108–22; fuller discussion in Sivin, "The Theoretical Background of Elixir Alchemy," in Needham et al., *Science and Civilisation in China* (Cambridge: Cambridge University Press, 1980), vol. 5, pt. 4, pp. 210–305, esp. pp. 221–79.

4. *Hou Han shu*, "Lüli zhi 後漢書律曆志," 2: 1492. Astronomical and astrological treatises of the Standard Histories are cited from the series *Lidai tianwen lüli deng zhi huibian* 歷代天文律曆等志彙編, 10 vols. (Beijing, 1975–76).

5. "Ying ri tui ce jı 迎日推策記," pp. 113–18 in *Dai Zhen jı* 戴震集 (Shanghai: Shanghai guji chubanshe 上海古籍出版社, 1980), esp. p. 115. Note that the word *indeterminacy* here and below does not carry any implication of common ground with the oft-misunderstood Heisenberg Uncertainty Principle in modern physics. It merely translates Chinese assertions that there are limitations to observational knowledge.

6. *Zhou yi*, "Xici da zhuan," B, 4–5; Wilhelm, *The I ching*, pp. 367, 370, where *wei* is translated as "that which is hidden" and "first imperceptible beginning." *Laozi*, 21, 1, and 15; cf. the translation of 15 with that of D. C. Lau, *Chinese Classics. Tao Te Ching* (Hong Kong: The Chinese University Press, 1982), p. 21.

7. The famous anecdote about Ding the Cook in chap. 3 of the *Zhuangzi* is about a distantly related conviction, namely that manual skill is not a matter of technical rules but rather of being "in touch through the daemonic in me," as A. C. Graham's translation puts it. A number of similar "knack passages" occur in chapters of the *Zhuangzi* outside the original corpus. In the story of Bian the Wheelwright in chap. 13, for instance, the intuitive skill that comes from long practice is adduced to argue against learning from books—not just orthodox classics, but all books that purport to transmit human experience. For exceptionally perceptive translations see Graham, *Chuang-tzu: The Seven Inner Chapters and Other Writings from the Book* Chuang-tzu (London: George Allen and Unwin, 1981), pp. 63–64, 135–41.

8. *Chungiu fan lu* (Si bubei yao ed.), 3: 10a.

9. The discussion of Han astronomy that follows is documented in Sivin, *Cosmos and Computation*. See also the insights of Yabuuti Kiyosi (Yabuuchi Kiyoshi 藪內清) in "The Calendar Reforms in the Han Dynasty and Ideas in their Background," *Archives internationales d'histoire des sciences*, 24 (1974): 51–65 and the monograph by Yabuuchi and Nōda Chūryō 能田忠亮, *Kansho ritsurekishi no kenkyū* 漢書律曆志の研究 (Kyoto: Zenkoku shobō, 1947).

10. *Hou Han shu*, "Lüli zhi," 2: 1482.

11. Ibid., p. 1496, fuller translation in Sivin, *Cosmos and Computation*, pp. 61–62. The last line contains an allusion to the Confucian Analects, 20. 1.

12. *Sung shu* 宋書, *13*: 1768–69 *et passim*.

13. *Xin Tang shu* 新唐書, 27*A*: 2177. Ixing's computational system was in fact attacked in 733, four years after it was adopted and six years after the astronomer died. The charges were not concerned with technical inadequacy—perhaps because Ixing had anticipated criticisms on that count—but with plagiarism from Indian sources. The best account is in Christopher Cullen, "An Eighth Century Chinese Table of Tangents," *Chinese Science* 5 (1982): 1–33, esp. 30–32. On the numerological cosmology of the Great Expansion system see the section of Ixing's treatise on "Rationale of the Basis of the Ephemerides" in *Xin Tangshu*, 27*A*: 2169–73, translated in Ang Tian Se, "I-hsing (683–727 A.D.): His Life and Scientific Work," Ph.D. diss. University of Malaya, 1979, pp. 419–45.

14. *Mengqi bitan* 夢溪筆談, item 123 (*Mengqi bitan jiaozheng* 校證, 3d ed., [Beijing, 1956], 1: 292). Of the two quotations in the first part, one quotes "Xici da Zhuan," A.9 and the other alludes to it (see Wilhelm, trans., 1: 339). The *Huang ti nei ching su wen* citation is to 7 (22): 125 in the Shanghai, 1954 edition. On the Era and other long cycles see Sivin, *Cosmos and Computation*, pp. 12–21. For a very satisfactory discussion of Whitehead, see *Dictionary of Scientific Biography*, s.v.

15. The *Hun yi yi* 渾儀議 is preserved in *Song shi*, "Tianwen zhi 宋史天文志," *48*: 800–808; I cite the critical text in *Mengqi bitan jiaozheng*, item 127, n. 6 (1: 297), and accept the emendation of *zhou* 書 to *hua* 畫. Shen is using "*tuan*" in a technical sense that draws on several of its early meanings, "to shape into a ball with the hands," "to gather," "to tie in a bundle," "exclusive." For further reflections on the complementarity of scientific and other modes of knowledge in Shen's thought see Sivin, "Shen Kua," *Dictionary of Scientific Biography*, s.v.

16. *Zhuzi yu lei* (*Zhuzi yu lei da quan* 朱子語類大全 [Kyoto, 1668, reprint by Zhongwen chubanshe 中文出版社, Kyoto, 1973]), *86*: 12a, *2*: 14b–15a. There is an interesting discussion of these and other passages in Zhu Xi's writings in Yamada Keiji 山田慶児, *Shushi no shizengaku* 朱子の自然学, Zhu Xi's studies of nature (Tokyo: Iwanami Shoten, 1978), pp. 279–301. Cai Yuanding's astronomical monograph was entitled *Dayan xiang shuo* 大衍詳說. See his biography by Rulan Chao Pian, pp. 1037–39 in Herbert Franke, ed., *Sung Biographies*, 3 vols., Münchener ostasiatische Studien, 16 (Wiesbaden, 1976).

17. These conversations are recorded in *Zhuzi yu lei*, *57*: 14a–17a. James Legge, who in his 1861 translation of the *Mencius* often relied on Zhu Xi rather than on more philologically rigorous later commentators, translates "*gu*" as *phenomena* (*The Chinese Classics* [Hong Kong, 1861], 2: 206–7). For an especially penetrating discussion of the passage from *Mencius* see Patrick E. Moran, "Key Psychological and Cosmological Terms in Chinese Philosophy: Their History from the Beginning to Chu Hsi (1130–1200)," Ph.D. diss., University of Pennsylvania, 1983, pp. 68–71.

18. *Zhuzi yu lei*, *86*: 11b–12a. "Definitive method of computation" is a tentative translation for *dingshu* 定數, which may mean nothing more elaborate than "definitive constants." I translate *cha* 差 as *discrepancies* rather than *anomalies*, since the example concerns error in measurement rather than inequality of motion. A pertinent essay is Hashimoto Keizō 橋本敬造, "Seido no shishō to dentō Chūgoku no temmongaku 精度の思想と伝統中国の天文学" (Ideas of precision and traditional Chinese astronomy), *Kansai Daigaku Shakaigakubu kiyō* 關西大學社會學部紀要, 1979, *11*. 1: 93–114.

19. *The Development and Decline of Chinese Cosmology* (New York: Columbia University Press, 1984), p. 249. I am grateful to Prof. Henderson for his comments on an early draft of this essay. His doctoral dissertation, from which the book is extensively revised, was in part responsible for inspiring me to take up this topic, and provided useful references.

20. *Mengqi bitan jiaozheng*, p. 656, item 347. Mark Elvin has remarked on the implications of this passage for "the probable limitations of human understanding" in *The Pattern of the Chinese Past* (Stanford: Stanford University Press, 1973), p. 233 n.

21. *Wuli xiao zhi* 物理小識 (1st ed. of 1664), *1*: 34a–b. The whole passage is translated (with some misunderstandings) by Willard J. Peterson in "Fang I-chih: Western Learning and the 'Investigation of Things,'" pp. 369–409 in Wm. Theodore De Bary et al., *The Unfolding of Neo-Confucianism* (New York: Columbia University Press, 1975), esp. p. 391.

22. Zhang, *Jingyue guanshu* (photolithographic reprint of 1624 ed., Taipei, 1972), 3: 75b, mistranslated in Paul U. Unschuld, *Medical Ethics in Imperial China: A Study in Historical Anthropology* (Berkeley: University of California Press, 1979), p. 82; Yin, *Zhenzi xin fa* 疹子心法 or *Shazhen xin fa*

痧疹心法, printed with Yin Dachun's *Yizang shumu* 醫藏書目 (Shanghai, 1955), pp. 107–8. The title of the latter work, meaning "Bibliography of the Medical Tripitaka," equally draws on Buddhist imagery.

23. A. C. Crombie, "Some Attitudes to Scientific Progress: Ancient, Medieval and Early Modern," *History of Science* 13 (1975): 213–30. See also on this topic, which must be distinguished from the one discussed in the present essay, E. R. Dodds, *The Ancient Concept of Progress and Other Essays* (Oxford: Oxford University Press, 1973).

24. St. Hilary, *De Trinitatis*, 2. 10, 11, cited in *The Summa Contra Gentiles of Saint Thomas Aquinas Literally Translated by the English Dominican Fathers from the Latest Leonine Edition* (London: Oates, 1924), 1.8 (1: 16).

25. No adequately detailed monograph on the role of Zeno's paradoxes has been published, but see G. E. L. Owen, "Zeno and the Mathematicians," *Proceedings of the Aristotelian Society*, n.s., 58 (1957–58): 199–222.

26. Personal communication, 14 October 1982.

The Evolution of Chinese Science and Technology

Jin Guantao, Fan Dainian, Fan Hongye, and Liu Qingfeng

To know others is wisdom;
to know oneself is sagacity.
LAO-TZU

During the last four centuries, science has become the most important tool in the cognition and transformation of the human world, but the study of the scientific enterprise itself, using the methods of science, is of only very recent origin. The history of science demonstrates that the rate of scientific development varies broadly among different cultures. This paper is an attempt to quantify in very broad terms the development of science and technology in China, compare it with the scientific and technological progress of the West, and explore some of the reasons that appear to account for the difference.

1. Two Sets of Curves

This paper attempts to grasp the differences in the development of science and technology in China and the West, and to show the differences of China's scientific-technological development in various historical periods.

First, we have computed nearly 2,000 scientific-technological achievements in the 2,500 years from the sixth century B.C. to the end of the nineteenth century and have divided them into the categories of scientific theory, scientific experiment, and technology. According to the importance of various achievements in the respective disciplines and the extent of their social impact, we set different scoring scales and drew curves of the progressive rise of science and technology in China and the West.[1]

Second, we have computed the net increase in Chinese scientific and technological achievements in different historical periods. We would like to discuss in the following, through a detailed analysis of these curves, the structure of science and technology in ancient China and the reasons for the scientific-technological backwardness in modern China.

In Figures 1 and 2, the uppermost curves represent the general trend of development of science and technology in China and the West. We can compare these two curves in four stages.

The first stage is around the fourth century B.C. (the period of Greek civilization in the West and the period of Warring States in China) when the levels of development in China and the West are, by and large, the same. The second stage is from the fourth to the eleventh century A.D. when the curve of China shows a gentle upturn and the curve of the

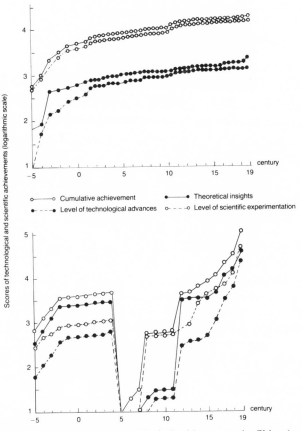

Figures 1 and 2. Levels of scientific and technological achievements in China (top) and the West (bottom). Scale arbitrary, see n. 1.

West has a sharp fall. The third stage is from the twelfth to the fifteenth century when the curve of China continues with its gentle upward movement while the curve of the West, though still lower than that of China, witnesses a marked upturn. At this stage, a revolutionary storm was brewing in the West in the field of science and technology. The fourth stage is from the sixteenth to the nineteenth century when the curve of China continues gently upward, but the curve of the West surpasses the curve of China and turns up sharply. The development of science and technology in China appears as a process of continuous, steady augmentation, whereas in the West there is a period of accelerated development after the fifteenth and sixteenth century.

When we compare figures 1 and 2 further, we immediately notice another even more obvious feature. The relationships among scientific theory, experiment, and technology in China are very different from those in the West. In figure 1, China's three curves are clearly separated from each other. From the total score of Chinese science and technology, technology accounts for about 80 percent, theory for 13, experiment for only 7. These numbers reflect the well-known fact that early Chinese science was mostly the domain of the craft tradition.

To elucidate what these curves show, we will first turn to the history of science in ancient China.

2. *The Universal Technology of Ancient China*

It is well known that paper making, the compass, gunpowder, and type-case printing are Chinese inventions and that they changed the course of human history. We wish to emphasize that these technological treasures not only demonstrate the wisdom of the Chinese nation and of its ancient science and technology, but also reveal the major characteristics of the social structure of ancient China.

These four inventions are fruits of a long cultivation of the technological system of ancient China, reflecting the characteristic continuity of that civilization. That they are technological creations shows that such achievements held a central position in China's ancient science and technology. The technological development of a society is determined by the social need for technology. What social needs did the four great inventions meet? Obviously different from those inventions in agriculture and handicraft that met the immediate needs for food, clothing, and housing, these inventions emerged to satisfy the social need to impose a strong and unified state institution on the vast land. Paper, compass, and printing are used for social communication (transportation). Though the making of gunpowder originated from alchemy, it became a technique after the Tang Dynasty mainly because of the need for a single unified state. It is clearly recorded that gunpowder was first applied to weapons in the Song Dynasty. In the early years of the Northern Song Dynasty, firearms were used to suppress the peasant uprisings led by Li Shun and Wang Xiaobo. The four great inventions demonstrate well that the advanced state of technology in ancient China was closely related to the existence of China's feudal society in the form of a unified single institution. As we know, in the Middle Ages, Europe was greatly fragmented. Its small divisions were relatively independent economic-cultural units with very weak inter-relations. In sharp contrast to this, ever since the first emperor of the Qin Dynasty conquered six other states and assumed absolute authority, the form of a unified and centralized feudal universal state had always predominated in the social structure of China. Powerful and unified administrative control, frequent exchanges in the fields of domestic economy, commerce, and trade and a unified culture and belief, all called for, among other things, developed techniques for communication and transportation, for cultural ex-changes and dissemination, for powerful military forces, for the type of calendar that "tells people the time," for land-measuring and cartography, and for building palaces that would demonstrate the majesty of imperial power. We term all these the unifying technology.

We assessed the technological achievements of ancient China under four categories—agriculture, unifying technology, handicraft, and medicine—by using the earlier scoring method. This gave us the percentage of each category of technology in the whole body of technology (see table 1).[2]

The figures in table 1 show that the percentages of most technological achievements related to the universal social structure are above 30 percent, while during periods when the country was divided, the percentages dropped below 13 percent.

Now, let us look at the handicraft industry. The state of development of handicraft in a society is determined by the development of its commodity economy. Because of the peculiar structure of China's feudal society, the socioeconomic structure differed from

Table 1. Proportion of Various Categories of Technology (percentage)

Dynasties	Spring and Autumn	Warring States	Qin	Western Han	Eastern Han	Wei and Western Jin	Southern and Northern Dynasties	Sui	Tang	Northern Song	Southern Song	Yuan	Ming	Qing
Agriculture	16	26	1	5	4	12	13	1	4	2	7	12	6	2
Unifying technology	13	12	59	24	41	12	13	58	32	53	43	28	34	40
Handicraft	40	43	40	63	47	35	45	27	47	43	39	37	45	46
Medicine	20	18	0	8	8	41	10	14	16	2	10	3	13	12
Others	11	1	0	0	0	0	19	0	1	0	1	20	2	0

those in western Europe. The feudal landlord economy in China had much greater capacity for commodity economy than did the feudal-lord economy of the West. China's commodity economy inevitably stimulated the development of handicraft industry, leading to a handicraft level much higher than that in the West. Table 1 shows that in various dynasties, the handicraft portion always made up 30 to 50 percent of the total technological scores. This being the case, during periods when the country was unified, the sum scores of handicraft plus unifying technology accounted for 70 to 80 percent of the total scores of technology, thus determining the technological level of the society. Therefore, the developed technology in ancient China was entirely a function of the universal social formation and its corresponding landlord economy.

The content of table 1, when presented in the form of a plot, demonstrates that the technological development in a dynasty is linked with the extent of centralization of state power and with the state of development of commodity economy. We can also see that the peak was reached in the Northen Song Dynasty. In the Song Dynasty not only did the unified bureaucratic political formation gradually attain maturity, but there existed a very flourishing landlord and commodity economy. The annual state revenue deriving from commercial taxes had once reached 22 million *min* (string of cash), amounting to about one-seventh of the total annual revenue.[3] At that time, there were as many as six cities with a population of 200,000 and Linan was a big commercial city with over 300,000 households and more than 1 million people. According to *Shihuozhi* (食貨志) of Song history, "the silk submitted by various districts for taxes amounted to 3.41 million bolts." Whereas during the period of Wei, Jin, and the Southern and Northern Dynasties when feudal China was divided, there was a decline of the landlord economy and a general depression of the commodity economy. During this period, the level of net augmentation of technology was also at its lowest point. The unity and prosperous commodity economy of the early years of the Tang Dynasty is well known, as is the high net augmentation of technology. However, after the Anshi Uprising (安史之亂), the commodity economy started to decline and the level of net augmentation of technology also declined. The same is true for the Five Dynasties.

We may conclude therefore that the technological advances of ancient China were closely related to the universal social formation of China's feudal society and to the structure of its landlord economy. We may call this the unifying technological structure. It had two marked features. First, being different from the closed, primitive technologies of other ancient civilizations, it allowed for technology transfer and thus achieved fairly rapid development under the stimulus of the needs of the unified feudal society. Second, it was closely linked with the state formation of the unified feudal society. As long as the structure of China's feudal society remained intact, it was impossible for this type of technology to evolve into a kind of modern and open technological system. The too-close linkage between it and the state institutional formation was very disadvantageous for the emergence of modern technology.

3. *Scientific Theory and Experiment in Ancient China*

If the characteristic of ancient Chinese technology was mainly determined by the feudal society's centralized political structure and the landlord economic structure, then the characteristics of ancient Chinese scientific theory and experiment were mainly functions of the cultural environment. As is known, all ancient scientific theories are closely related to philosophical ideas. In China's feudal society, Confucian ideology and orthodoxy, and the Taoist ideas that supplemented them, were formed after the Qin Dynasty. In ancient philosophy, Confucian ideas held the dominant position. Confucian philosophy, with ethics and morality as its core, had a great impact upon China's ancient scientific theories. From a positive point of view, it left no room for a god with an independent personality and a will to establish himself as a law giver. The emergence of a theory was usually connected with people's direct experience, perception, talented imagination, and inference. These tended to make China's ancient scientific theories have an empirico-materialist inclination, which explains why these theories were more advanced than the theological views of nature that dominated western Europe in the Middle Ages. Ancient China produced many world-famous scientists represented by people like Muo Zi, Zhang Heng, Lui Hui, Zu Chongzhi, Yi Xing, Shen Kuo, Guo Shoujing, Li Shizhen, and Song Yingxing. If we compare figures 1 and 2 we will see that, generally speaking, theoretical knowledge in China was at a higher level than in the West for a long period in the Middle Ages.

The Confucian mode of understanding the world is the rational extrapolation of personal experiences. It promoted direct perception and speculation in formulating theories of natural science. The Confucian ethical centralism in particular made scientific theories become conservative and lack clarity. Dong Zhongshu, Zhu Xi, Wang Chong, and Sheng Kuo all based their explanation of natural phenomena on the extrapolation of human behavior and perception. Wang Chong, for instance, explained the tide cycle with the words "respiration, rise and fall with the sun." Thus a peculiar condition appeared: in those sciences where phenomena can be explained by everyday experience and direct perceptive extrapolation, Chinese science offered brilliant expositions—explanations of meteors, aerolites, fossils, and rainbows. In other fields, where phenomena cannot be explained by direct perceptive extrapolation, Chinese science lacked clarity. Take the global shape of the earth, for example. Even until the Ming and Qing Dynasties, there were still quite a number of astronomers who did not accept the modern explanation. For a long time, the Confucian organic view of nature and its ethical centralism prevented scientific theory from maturing. Even Fang Yizhi (方以智), who was already at the threshold of modern science, said in his book, *An Introduction to Physics* (物理小識), that "sound, air, wind, and power actually expresses people's mind, and instructions are received like echoes which are too mysterious to be foreseen." With this way of thinking, it is very difficult for people to treat natural phenomena as objects for scientific study. Arguments concerning the relation between Principle and Pneuma (理氣之爭) were connected with good and evil, and theories regarding heaven, earth, sun, and moon went hand in hand with the explanation of the court hierarchy. The world was considered as a sympathetic whole of all things on earth, and the scholar's task was to establish a theoretical system offering ethical explanations for everything, including natural phenomena.

Another basic characteristic of traditional Chinese science is its technological propensity. A great deal of summarization of technological experience found its way into the scientific theoretical literature. There were two reasons for this. One was the highly developed state of technology; the other was the empirical and directly perceptive characteristic of Confucian theoretical models. The figures in table 2 show that writings that recorded and summarized technological experience made up about 20 percent of the total scores of theoretical achievements in various dynasties. After the technological high tide

Table 2. Proportion of Writings Summarizing Technological Experience in the Total Scores of Theoretical Achievements in Various Dynasties (percentage)

Dynasty	Spring and Autumn	Warring States	Qin	Western Han	Eastern Han	Wei and Western Jin	Southern and Northern	Sui	Tang	Northern Song	Southern Song	Yuan	Ming	Qing
Summarizations of technological experience	29	25	0	25	6	13	20	100	27	17	18	41	35	23
Other theoretical achievements	71	75	0	75	94	87	80	0	73	83	82	59	65	77

in the Song Dynasty, there came a time of comprehensive summarization of ancient technology in China. This started in the Yuan Dynasty and continued to the Ming Dynasty. The best summarization in the fields of medicine, agriculture, and industry were *Bencao Gangmu* (本草綱目, Compendium of Materia Medica), *Nongzheng Quanshu* (農政全書, Encyclopedia of Agronomy), and *Tiangong Kaiwu* (天工開物, Encyclopedia of Handicraft Industry). Even in purely theoretical studies, there was a strong technological propensity.

The Confucians made the understanding of the natural world serve their ethical theories. Also, because they were realists and keen to enjoy the present life, they did not reject categorically those techniques that could serve their practical needs. But they criticized those techniques that did not have much practical applicability, e.g., "skills for slaughtering the dragon." Consequently, astronomy was attached to calendar-making, mathematics stressed the skill of solving mathematical problems and computational techniques, and biology was almost entirely confined to agronomy and medical science.

Calendars were revised when necessary and became increasingly accurate. But the development of astronomical theory was almost at a standstill. In 2,000 years, there was not much change in the theory of Gaitian (蓋天, the theory that earth was covered by an umbrella-shaped heaven), Xuanye (宣夜, the theory that heaven was shapeless and endless with no substance), and Huntian (渾天, the theory that the earth was surrounded by a heavenlike yolk in egg white and was shaped like a completely round ball). The theory of Gaitian was accepted by some as late as the Qing Dynasty.

In mathematics, only computational techniques were increasingly perfected. This does not mean that there was no theoretical component in China's mathematics. It only means that mathematical theory was inseparable from computation techniques and did not develop into a well-organized structural system with concise ways of expression. The same is true for botanical classification, which was confined to the category of Chinese materia medica and served practical purposes. It is obvious that its technological propensity has prevented China's ancient scientific theories from attaining an independent development.

The cultural atmosphere of ancient China, in particular the mode of thinking characterized by direct perceptive extrapolation, brought disastrous consequences to scientific experiments. In those fields in which direct perceptive extrapolation could produce a satisfactory explanation, the word *experiment* was taken as synonymous with *experience*. As a result, though the ancient Chinese scientists attached great importance to practice on the one hand, they neglected experiment on the other, for they could not get anything more out of experiment than experience.

In those areas where direct perceptive extrapolation could not ensure a thorough understanding of a problem, experiments were totally subjected to the mystic concept of "induction between heaven and man." Such experiments were reduced to witchcraft, performed by necromancers, and despised by the orthodox Confucians. This explains why Chinese cultural tradition, though more prone to empiricism and materialism than that of the West in the Middle Ages, was so unfavorable to the establishment of the method of controlled experiments required by modern science. Consequently, experiments not aimed at practical application but at demonstrating scientific theories were regarded as dispensable in ancient China. This was especially true following the emergence of the Confucian school of idealist philosophy in the Song and Ming Dynasties.

An extreme case here would be the "study of bamboo" by an idealist philosopher of the

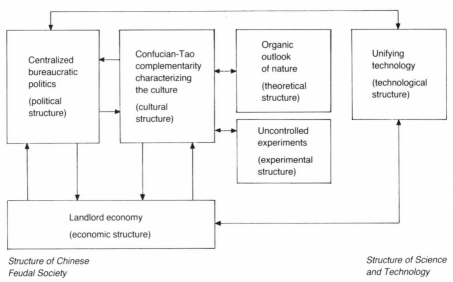

Structure of Chinese
Feudal Society

Structure of Science
and Technology

Figure 3

Ming Dynasty, Wang Yangming (王陽明). During his time, scholars regarded their lives' sole purpose to be the study of objects, the pursuit of ultimate knowledge, and exhaustive inquiry into truths. As the legend goes, after one of his friends named Qian (錢) had sat in a pavilion studying a bamboo for three days and nights and had finally fallen ill, Wang Yangming went to the place himself and observed for seven days, but still could not understand anything about bamboo. He lamented, "How can anything under heaven possibly be studied and understood!" He thereafter tried to persuade others to analyze their innermost being instead, and concluded that "the effort to study objects can be made only with regard to one's inner world." This may sound like a joke, but, in fact, it was a historical tragedy.

Let us recall what changes the world was undergoing when Wang Yangming (1472–1528) was sitting quietly, studying bamboo. Leonardo da Vinci (1452–1519) was painting the mysteriously smiling Mona Lisa, carrying out dissections of human bodies, and designing various types of mechanical appliances. He declared that science would be useless and full of absurdity if it were not conducted through experiments. In fact, this was not his feeling alone but was the sense of other pioneers of the new era of science. At roughly the same time, Ferdinand Magellan completed the world's first round-the-globe voyage; Paracelsus broke the confinement of alchemy and became the founder of medical chemistry; Copernicus and Vesalius were to bring dawn to modern science with *De revolutionibus orbium Coelestium* and *De humani corporis fabrica*.

4. Why Did Modern Science Not Appear First in China?

As the preceding analysis shows, the scientific, technological, and social structures of a society are congruent with one another. Figure 3 indicates the relationship of the structure of the Chinese feudal society vis-à-vis the scientific and technological structure.

The reason that Western science and technology underwent accelerated development after the sixteenth century was that it brought about a condition of mutually promoting, positive feedback effects that connected scientific theory, controlled experiment, and technology.

In contrast, such feedback systems did not exist in ancient Chinese society. Unifying technology could only develop along the track dictated by the needs of the unified feudal state and it was inconceivable that there could be mutually promoting processes between that kind of technology and science. Futhermore, the cultural system of Confucian-Tao complementarity (儒道互補) kept experiment and theory apart. As a result, theory could not guide experiment and could not (or need not) be proved by the latter. It followed that theory, experiment, and technology could each grow but slowly if kept in isolation from one another. Consequently, though ancient Chinese science and technology were more advanced than those of the West in the Middle Ages, their development was confined to the mutually isolating framework even after the founding of modern science in the West. This made it inevitable for them to lag increasingly behind the West.

It is not the purpose of this paper to explain why there emerged mutually promoting, positive feedback connections among scientific theory, experiment, and technology in the West.[4] But we wish to point out that ancient Chinese science and technology meshed so much with China's feudal unifying social formation that the development of the former was totally dependent upon the stability of the latter. The net increase of the scientific and technological knowledge almost completely coincides with the periodic rise and fall of the feudal dynasties. This is quite obvious when it comes to the technological development. Generally speaking, the period during which a unified dynasty achieved a period of peace and prosperity would also be the time when the peak of technological development was observed. Whenever a dynasty collapsed, the net increase of technological level dropped sharply and many successful results became lost in turmoil. Technology was thus seriously constrained by China's feudal society. Inside a closed technolgical system, no matter how advanced a technical invention was, it would meet immense difficulties when it came to transferring it to other economic sectors.

A good example is the story of the textile machines. As early as the Song Dynasty, China had invented animal- or water-powered spinning machines with as many as thirty-two spindles capable of producing thirty to fifty times more than manual spinning wheels did. Historical records show that the spinning machine could "spin a hundred *jin* [50 kilograms] of cotton daily without manual work, reducing the number of women workers two-fold."[5] Though the West did not have similar textile machines until shortly before the Industrial Revolution, the textile technology of the West existed in an open technological system and constituted a link in the chain of technology transfer and development in the Revolution. In contrast, the textile technology flourished as the Song Dynasty attained peace and prosperity but degenerated as the dynasty collapsed and upheaval and destruction set in.

In short, as long as the Chinese feudal social structure remained intact, it was impossible for modern science to emerge in China. In the past two thousand years, that system maintained its ultrastability, despite the periodic falls of dynasties. The long-time stagnation of the Chinese feudal society made it impossible for ancient Chinese science and technology to evolve and mature into their modern forms.

Notes

1. The score of each achievement is determined according to its importance in its discipline and the extent of its social impact. There are four grades: a score of 1 is given for those achievements that are only recorded in the history books of science; grades of 10 are for those that produced a fairly large impact on their disciplines; 100 points are given those having a wide influence in the fields of science and technology; and scores of 1,000 are given to those achievements ranked as having epoch-making significance to the entire scientific-technological revolution or as having great influence on social development. Those achievements that fall between the grades were given 5, 50, or 500 scores as we saw fit. Though such a scoring method is arbitrary and subjective to some extent, we believe it to be useful. The method could be improved with regard to accuracy, but as a way of macroanalysis and first approximation, it does help us reach some conclusions regarding science and technology in history.

Here are some examples of our scoring method: 1,000 to Newton's *Mathematical Principles of Natural Philosophy* (theory), Watt's steam engine (technology), and the invention of type-case printing (technology); 500 to Harvey's discovery of blood circulation (theory and experiment) and to Lavoisier's establishment of new combustion theory (theory); 100 to Linnaeus's *Systema Naturae* (theory) and to voltaic pile (experiment); 50 to Kant's theory of galaxy (theory) and to Zhang Heng's seismograph (experiment); 10 to Gay-Lussac's law of the expansion of gases (theory) and to Humboldt's law of progressive fall of high-layer atmospheric temperature (theory); 5 to the discovery of phosphorus (experiment) and to the establishment of the periodicity of Halley's comet (theory); and 1 to the extraction of white lead (experiment) and to Empedocles' record on the discovery of cochlea (experiment).

2. The scoring of some of the technological achievements was done by dividing the total scores into two equal parts and placing them into two different categories. For instance, the scores of the technique of calendar are divided into two and placed into the categories of agriculture and unifying technology, and the scores of gunpowder are put into unifying technology and handicraft.

3. *History of Song Dynasty* (宋史), vol. 179, *Shihuozhi* (食貨志) (economic records), vol. 13 of Zhong Hua Book Company's edition (中華書局版), p. 4349.

4. On this topic see Jin Guantao, Fan Hongye, Liu Qingfeng, *Evolution of Cultural Background and Science Structure; Scientific Tradition and Culture* (Shaanxi Science and Technology Publishing House, 1983) (金觀濤、樊洪業、劉青鋒:《文化背景與科學技術結構的演變》,《科學傳統與文化 — 中國近代科學落後的原因》, 陝西科學技術出版社, 1983年版)。

5. Wang Zhen, *Volumes on Agriculture* (Agriculture Publishing House, 1963), 22 : 521.

Cultural and Intellectual Attitudes That Prevented the Spontaneous Emergence of Modern Science in China

Qiu Renzong

Summary   The emergence of science was an improbable event in the history of mankind. Only in Europe did all the factors converge to make the birth of natural science possible. The social, cultural, intellectual, and political ambience of ancient and medieval China made the coming about of mathematical-experimental science impossible. Instead, we find two different kinds of knowledge: Confucianism and the study of Confucian classics was one; craft knowledge was the other. Both contain many valuable ideas and some true achievements of the human spirit, but craft knowledge has never been transformed into science. Thus, natural science had to be imported to China, as it had to be imported everywhere else outside the sphere of European culture. If science is to grow in China, it is necessary to create the appropriate intellectual soil for its nurture.

The question of why Chinese science and technology fell behind that of Europe in modern times has been broadly discussed in contemporary Chinese writings (see the list of references at the end of this article). It is easy to see why the question was asked. On the one hand, through the work of Chinese and non-Chinese historians of science (notable among the latter, the work of Joseph Needham), it became evident that in antiquity and through the Middle Ages Chinese science and technology was ahead of Europe in many fields. On the other hand, since the open-door policy began after the Cultural Revolution, it became clear that contemporary Chinese preparedness in science and technology lagged behind that of the West. An answer to the question of how this imparity developed should help in reaching the goal of the program of modernization as far as science and technology go. Understanding the reasons for falling behind will surely assist China in catching up with the scientifically advanced countries.

Detailed formulation of the mode of attack on the problem is not easy. On a first approach, on the surface, "falling behind" and "having been in the lead" speak mainly of quantitative issues: the number of scientific and technological discoveries and the times of their occurrence. But beneath the quantitative issue there is a qualitative one: Did traditional Chinese science have the same quality, or nature, as the science of the West did, in the same developmental stage? Are there specific reasons why the scientific revolution did not, or could not have occurred in China? Why did it have to be imported?

An answer to these questions demands an understanding of the character of modern natural science. Is it a type of knowledge independent of cultural and social contexts?

Could it have been sown and grown in any cultural and social soil? Or, is it a product of a given cultural and social context without which, though imported and transplanted from elsewhere, it cannot take root and eventually bloom. I think the latter is the case.

The emergence of natural science in history was a rather unlikely event; an improbable event. It seems in retrospect that only Europe had provided the conditions that permitted the convergence of all the factors necessary for its coming about. This view does not claim at all that Europe, in some sense, is or was the center of the world, nor does this view underestimate the profound role played by non-European countries in the genesis of the modern world. It simply points to the fortunate confluence in Renaissance Europe of certain peculiarly European traditions. Among them, I want to list: the love of wisdom of the ancient Greek philosophers; Aristotle's logic; the Euclidean system and the idea of deductive systematization; the atomism of Democritus with its underlying mechanism; the subtle association of Christian theology and practice with Aristotelianism; Ptolemy's astronomy and Galen's medicine; the attention paid to inductive thought and experimental testing; the alphabetic system of writing; the founding of the universities; the tradition of democracy; the frequent communication among the many states and countries; the development of commodity economy; the origins of the capitalist mode of production. All these factors, interwoven with the cultural and social practices and traditions, produced modern science.

This kind of background did not exist in traditional China, nor did it exist anywhere else. But let me now turn to China, with which I am moderately familiar.

I want to argue that the intellectual and cultural climate of ancient and medieval China prevented the emergence of the modern natural science we know today, i.e., a particular way of knowing (through mathematical theorems and experiment) embedded in a particular social ambience.

Instead of Greek critical reasoning, what we find in ancient and medieval China are two ways of knowing.

One was Confucianism, promoted through the study of Confucian classics (Jung Xue), held in high esteem as the official philosophy and ideology of Chinese dynasties for two millennia. The socioethical theories of Confucianism were linked with the feudal system of China so profoundly that they became the basic criteria for value for all Chinese intellectuals. But Confucian scholars despised the study of nature, considering it "an insignificant skill." Consistently, instead of observing and experimenting, they advocated introspection as the best and only valid mode of understanding the external world.

Wang Yangming, a Confucian scholar in the Ming Dynasty, was said to have looked at a bamboo for seven days but, not having understood anything about the bamboo through watching it, concluded that the study of objects can only be made by resorting to one's inner world. In general, experimentation was alien, or at least trivial. Liu Xianting, a natural historian of the early Qing Dynasty, wrote that "it was said that a piece of iron could prevent a magnet from attracting another piece of iron and performed experiments to confirm this. It is unnecessary to perform it, because it is only a trivial truth. It was also said that garlic could prevent a magnet from attracting a piece of iron, as well. I have not tested it yet" (Liu Xianting, *Guangyang Zhaji*, vol. 1).

For Confucians, other peoples' experiments were unnecessary, and they themselves were also unwilling to perform even the simplest experiments with their own hands.

Another kind of knowledge, craft knowledge, was also dismissed as insignificant by

Confucian scholars. The body of ancient Chinese science, or what in retrospect may be called that, was essentially craft knowledge. By its very nature, it was pragmatic in its character. Almost all the writings devoted to the recording of craft knowledge were directed toward the solving of practical problems. For example, *Jiuzhan Suanshu* (Arithmetics of Nine Chapters) comprised 264 problems of calculations, together with their solutions. But it paid no attention to logical proofs or mathematical theorems; only to actual calculations. Craft knowledge remained at the empirical level, without any theorizing in the scientific sense.

China did not have an alphabetic system of writing and therefore it was impossible to arrive at symbolic generalizations or to formulate scientific laws with symbols. Such generalizations (of laws and theories about nature) were not there to encourage adequate studies of the rationale of scientific inquiry: deduction, induction, abduction, hypothesis, and so on. The appeal was entirely to intuition and speculation.

The diverse phenomena of the universe were understood in simple speculative schemes such as yin yang and wu xing. For example, electricity was regarded as an interaction between yin and yang; earthquake was explained as having been caused by yang's being inhibited and unable to get out, and by yin's being repressed and unable to evaporate. Specious explanations of this kind offered people vain satisfaction and inhibited further inquiry, in spite of the many inner inconsistencies of the explanations. These inconsistencies were neglected for a long time, or gotten around by ad hoc maneuvers, because of poor logic and lack of the deductive systematization (such as is represented by Euclid's principles of geometry).

Within the framework of yin yang and wu xing, holistic cosmic systems were constructed. Within these, the distinction between natural phenomena and social affairs was blurred. The principle of "Mutual Sympathy between Heaven and Man" assumed that the movement of stars could affect the welfare of humans; also, that human behavior could evoke pleasure or anger from the heavens. This holistic system was informed of astrology and magic, and, being unfalsifiable, resisted changes for thousands of years.

Medieval China had no universities comparable to those of the West. Its particular scheme of education was the imperial examination system. Pupils had to learn the classics of Confucianism. If they passed the tests, they would be appointed government officials according to their marks. The educational system thus served the interests of an autocratic government, rather than the independent inquiries of science.

The study of nature for study's sake was condemned as heretical and was punished accordingly. In one of the classics of Confucianism, "The Book of Rites" (*Li Ji*) we find this: "Anyone who misleads people through exotic technique or odd instrument must be beheaded."

When a Frenchman came to China and reported on the Copernican heliocentric theory and on Kepler's Laws of Planetary Motion to the fourth emperor of the Qing Dynasty, Qian Long, the emperor denounced the theory and the laws as "departing from the classics and rebelling against orthodoxy."

Whatever the dynastic rulers considered necessary in the support of their political interests, e.g., making calendars, was monopolized by the Court. Private calendar makers were beheaded. The astronomers serving the Court at the imperial observatory usually became the victims of political rivalries. If they made erroneous predictions, they would be severely punished for the crime of deceiving the emperor.

Yet, it was not impossible for China to develop knowledge that could become a part of a *future* science. The foregoing shows only the reasons why the lead, originally held by China, was lost. In a very real sense, science could never grow to maturity in the Confucian soil.

References

Chen Yalan. 1983. The effect of Qing Dynasty autocratic monarchy on science and technology. *Journal of Dialectics of Nature* 5, no. 3: 62–68.

Diao Peide. 1983. Notes on the symposium probing the causes of backwardness of science and technology in China in modern times. Ibid. 5, no. 1: 32–34.

He Xin. 1983. Academic disparity between China and the West: A trial research on comparative cultural history. Ibid. 5, no. 2: 38–47.

Jiang Zongju et al. 1983. Why did modern mathematics fail to emerge in China? Ibid. 5, no. 3: 49–61.

Jin Guantao et al. 1982. The structure of science and technology—on the factors delaying the development of science and technology in China in comparison with the West since the 17th Century. Ibid. 4, no. 5: 7–24.

Jin Guantao et al. 1983. Historical change in the structure of science and technology. Ibid. 5, no. 1: 14–24.

Lin Wenzhao. 1983. An analysis of the causes of the failure of science to develop in modern times. Ibid. 5, no. 1: 7–14.

Qiu Lianghui. 1983. On the causes for the lagging behind of China's metallurgical technology in modern times. Ibid. 5, no. 2: 52–57.

Song Zhenghai et al. 1983. Why did Zheng He's voyage fail to lead the Chinese to make the "great geographical discovery"? Ibid. 5, no. 1: 25–31.

Zou Dexiu. 1983. On the causes of backwardness of China's agricultural science and technology in modern times. Ibid. 5, no. 2: 48–51.

Progressive and Regressive Time Cycles in Taoist Ritual

Kristofer Schipper and Wang Hsiu-huei

Summary   Taoist ritual in its social function is called *ke*, a word that basically means "measure," "class." The Chinese word for *science* (*kexue*) is a derivative; it conveys the idea of systematic, classificatory study (*xue*). Taoist ritual can be seen as a metaphorical pursuit of science.

In Chinese thought, the universe is apprehended as an infinity of nesting time cycles that, because of their formal correspondences, may be manipulated as though they were interchangeable, as when the alchemist produces in his laboratory a greatly accelerated model of cosmic process so that he can contemplate the latter as an aspect of the workings of the Tao. Taoist liturgy constructs similar cosmological models as ritual areas in which all beings are classified according to time measures. These models are oblated; Taoism has no other form of sacrifice.

The construction of the visible ritual area enacts the creative process of the universe. The time cycles, which are laid out visibly in a mandalalike structure, belong to a hierarchy of systems of *outer* time, that is, time as it exists in Creation after the opening up of chaos and the diversification of the energies it contained. Time that was before Creation is seen as *inner* time. Inner time is apprehended as a gestational process of ninefold transformation, from an invisible and undifferentiated state to the existence of form. Ritual enacts the simultaneous progression of (accelerated) outer time cycles and the regression of the inner cycle. Both culminate in the final moment of oblation.

In order to enact the passage from outer to inner time, Taoist ritual follows the paradigm of an ancient but hitherto little studied calendar theory with a corresponding divining technique called the Hidden Period (*dunjia*). This theory is based on the idea that the sexagenary time cycle shows a certain irregularity that results in an imbalance, and allows therefore an Irrational Opening (*qimen*). These concepts offered a model of stability in the time perception of this world inasmuch as progressive time was counterbalanced by a hidden regressive cycle.

The present paper discusses these fundamental concepts in relationship to that equally fundamental aspect of Chinese civilization which is Taoist ritual. But many other aspects of Chinese thought and science, such as mythology, theology, medicine, strategy, architecture, and landscape painting, have been influenced by these same theories. Certainly such a characteristic view of time elaborated by this great culture should not go unstudied by scholars of the Western tradition. The Chinese cosmological theories have long inspired Western thought. The concepts of inner and outer time, of the Hidden Period and the Irrational Opening, which have been studied little in modern times, should add a new dimension to our knowledge of these theories. The elaborate treatment given to cosmogony in this respect, the place of placental existence as a bridge between outer and inner time, the attempt to give a precise account of the emergence of order from chaos, all this might well be of interest to scholars in anthropology and comparative religion.

1. *Taoist Ritual*

The relationship between Taoism and Chinese science has been easy to perceive (Needham 1959, 33–164), but difficult to explain (Sivin 1978). One of the questions that arise in this context is the prominent role played by ritual in Taoist traditions. Ritual, as Nathan Sivin has shown, is important in alchemy (1980, 211). It is also persistently present in medicine. And it is altogether predominant in the social function of Taoism. Indeed, in Taoist liturgy there is practically no preaching or discussion, but almost only pure ritual: solemn services and ceremonies often performed in the absence of the very individuals or groups for whose benefit they are done. The manuals for these liturgies occupy more than half of all the texts in the Taoist canon (*Daozang* 道藏), that vast collection of scriptures that constitutes the main body of source materials for the study of Taoism, the sole surviving version of which dates from the beginning of the fifteenth century.[1] Ritual is also of major importance in the living traditions of Taoism. Indeed, in order to become a Taoist master, the disciple is trained almost exclusively in ritual practice, and given relatively little theoretical schooling. What schooling there is concerns, above all, knowledge of cosmological theories and calendrical science and no theology, dogma, or history. But this alone, of course, does not allow us to compare Taoist masters to scientists in a generally accepted way. At the same time, without wishing to extend the debate on the relationship between Taoism and science, we observe that more should be said about the nature of Taoist ritual. To begin with, Taoist liturgy is called *ke* 科, a word that originally meant "measure," "scale," "class," "grade," and "to examine." The Chinese word for science (*kexue* 科學) derives from it; it means "systematic, classificatory study."

This illustration is a modern reproduction of the rubbing of a stone stela, which itself is now lost. The drawing represents the essential parts of the human body (head and torso) outlined in the shape of an embryo. It illustrates a number of themes related to the concept of inner time, discussed in the following paper.

It is nearly impossible to trace the history of the stela, but the description of the Inner Landscape employs the vocabulary of a seventeenth-century Taoist school with an identifiable patriarch, Wu Shou-yang. About the school itself, very little is known.

As with all Chinese landscape painting, this image should be viewed beginning at the bottom.

The Inner Time (of inner life) comprises a cycle of nine transformations (see sect. 4 of the paper) which are shown in the illustration.

1. At the botton of the landscape there is a water gate. It may be associated with the kidneys. Two children, Father and Mother Tao, work a treadmill to reverse the flow of vital energies and to prevent them from streaming downward.

2. Above this, the vital or Original Energies are heated in a caldron. The position suggests the organ of reproduction. The four yin-yang symbols represent the fire phases.

3. The mulberry wood and the Weaver correspond to the Middle Gate (中關), which is shown on the spinal column. The spinning woman is the lover of the young man with the oxen.

4. The fourth stage of the flow of energies is the High Gate (上關), on the occiput.

5. Even higher up along the flow is the divine terrace and the holy mountain, on the top of the head.

6. The next stage is at the Old Man, who is at the end of the regulating tract (*du-mai*) for the energy flow along the spinal column.

7. The seventh stage is the meeting point of the energy with the secondary tract (a tract for the energy flow along the median line, frontally), and is located at the Young Man.

8. Next there is the Lake of Essences, associated with the mouth and the twelve-storied pagoda, identified with the throat.

9. The cycle ends with the production of a new being, the Perfected Immortal (*zhenren*), here shown as a newborn infant in a cinnabar field (丹田). The child is shown playing with a string of cash which follows the pattern of the stars of the Dipper, the Chinese constellation of Destiny. The present picture is meant as a guide for the so-called Inner Alchemy meditation techniques.

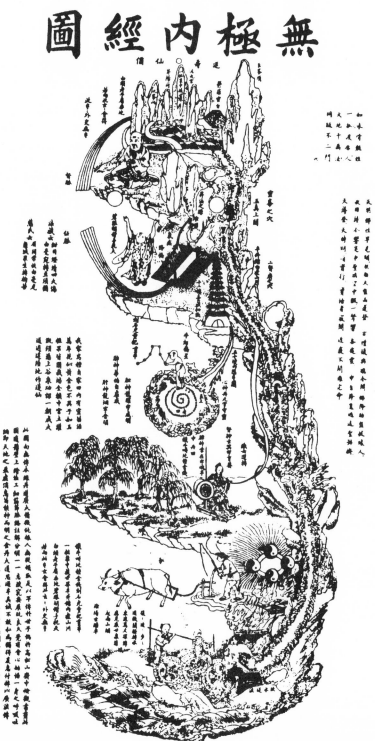

Indeed, Taoist ritual entails the construction of models in which all beings are classified. These models are of a cosmological nature. A service begins with the construction of the model, and ends with its destruction or, in terms of ritual, with its sacrifice or oblation. Let it be noted here that Taoism has no other forms of sacrifice or immolation (see Schipper 1982, 122–25).

We shall turn presently to the description of these models. Let it be said first that they classify beings by time measures, that is, by their relationship to processes such as the cycle of trigrams (*gua* 卦) of the *Book of Changes* (*Yijing* 易經). Arranged in the sequence of the so-called Later Heaven (*houtian* 後天, also called King Wen's arrangement (see Wilhelm 1966, 268–69), this cycle is indeed an important element in the complex cosmological models used in Taoist ritual. But in itself, the circle of Eight Trigrams in this arrangement represents a complete cycle in nature, be it a full day and night, a year, or a complete lifetime. In Chinese thought, such a circular representation illustrated perfectly the virtue of the Tao, that immanent principle of the universe, the workings of which are primarily conceived of in cyclical time. Given the central importance of the concept of Tao since ancient times, speculations about its workings, together with theories of nature cycles to illustrate them, have been elaborated during many centuries, leaving us with a wealth of literature on calendric science, most of which has not yet been studied by modern scholars. These nature cycles, such as the sexagenary cycle of Stems and Branches, the Eight Trigrams and its more elaborate derivative of Sixty-four Hexagrams, formed a theoretical background to which Chinese scholars of the past added direct observations. The history of the interaction between direct observation and theoretical, symbolic systems falls outside the scope of this paper, but it should be said that the symbolic cosmology continued to be conceived of as the model expression of natural processes.

For the Taoists, the theoretical nature cycles illustrated the *ke*, that is the measured, normative, and regulating workings of the Tao. By making cosmological models the very basis of the ritual structure, rituals became the expression of natural processes. For this reason, Taoist ritual, Chinese calendric science, and forms of other Chinese science, such as medicine, share a common set of fundamental representations that form a self-contained epistemological system.

The oblation of this epistemological model of the universe was, in Taoist thought, not only an act of accomplishment inviting renewal by making way for a new cycle (as a recurrence in keeping with cyclical phases) but also a way to compel the universe to conform to this model: a sacrifice to make the world sacred. To oblate the cosmological canon was to make it work, to transform it (*hua* 化) into reality (*zhen* 眞). Nature thus became the replica of the model, and this mirror image was embedded in the structure of the ritual action itself (Schipper 1978).

As a contemporary philosopher has shown, the oblation of an epistemological model can be seen as a fundamental aspect of the pursuit of science (as, for instance, through the publication of a new theory).[2] Seen in this light, Taoist ritual is a kind of metaphorical pursuit of science.

2. The Altar

The construction of the cosmological model in Taoist ritual is linked to the establishment of the altar (*tan* 壇) or sacred area (*daochang* 道場). Taoism does not usually have permanent sacred buildings like temples or sanctuaries. Ritual areas are installed periodically, at nodal points of the spatiotemporal environment (Schipper 1982, 125–35).

Taoism does not render cults to gods or saints of eumeristic origin, but recognizes instead abstract cosmological concepts as agents of the forces of nature and emanations of the workings of the Tao. The cult is centered around the elements that compose nature cycles. The elements are not material but are divisions, or, better, phases of cosmic cycles. These phases are already fairly well known: yin-yang, Five Elements, Eight Trigrams, Sixty-four Hexagrams, Ten Stems, and Twelve Branches and their combinations into the sexagesimal cycle, the Twenty-four Energy Nodes (*jieqi* 節氣), or the Twenty-eight Lunar Mansions. Let us recall what Nathan Sivin says regarding these cycles when discussing the theoretical background of elixir alchemy: "the earliest, and in the long run the most influential kinds of scientific explanation, those so basic that they truly pervaded the ancient Chinese worldview, were in terms of time. They made sense of the momentary event by fitting it into the cyclical rhythms of natural process, for the life cycle of an individual organism—birth, growth, maturity, decay and death—had essentially the same configuration as those more general cycles which went on eternally and in regular order, one fitting inside the other.... All these cycles nested." (Sivin 1980, 222). Sivin discusses masterfully the different cyclical systems and the way they were related and integrated in ever-larger total computation. He then shows how these systems were reproduced in the alchemist's laboratory, enabling the operator to control and accelerate the cyclical forces and thus create with his own hands minerals and elixirs that nature would take thousands of years to produce. This he could do by reproducing the phases of the time cycles, by regulating, for instance, the combustion in the furnace (*huohou* 火候, fire phasing) (266–97). The laboratory, the furnace, and the reaction vessel all corresponded in form and dimensions to cosmological configurations and numbers. Predictably enough, the furnace represented Heaven and Earth, while the reaction vessel corresponded to the original womb, the cosmic egg, the sphere of the chaos from which all was born.

The ritual area for Taoist liturgy is arranged in a similar way: it becomes, through the representation of a combination of symbolic time cycles, a model of the universe. There are different rituals for the installation of the successive components of the model (see fig. 1).

The outer limit of the ritual area is a square called the Outer Altar. The real dimensions of the square may differ, but the symbolic numbers attached to it are always the same: twenty-four pickets, placed at the corners and at equal intervals along the sides, create a demarcation line with twenty-four interspaces. These represent the Twenty-four Energy Nodes; constructed around the equinoxes and solstices, these divided the tropical year of 360 days into twenty-four periods of fifteen days (Needham 1959, 404–5 gives the names of these periods). This cycle is of paramount importance in the Taoist liturgical tradition, as it not only structures the religious year but also provides the fundamental grid for the organization of the community and the geographical network of dioceses (Schipper 1978, 374–81). This year cycle of Twenty-four Energy Nodes constituted a liturgical calender for "all the spirits of Heaven and Earth." These spirits might be actually represented and given a place of worship on the perimeter of the altar. They were not to be represented, however, by images but simply by bamboo or paper slips on which their names were written. These slips were posted upright along the demarcation line of the Outer Altar. Even when identified in this way, the spirits were always considered collectively as a group of 240 (sometimes 120, 360, or 1200) units, and, whatever hierographic tradition might be

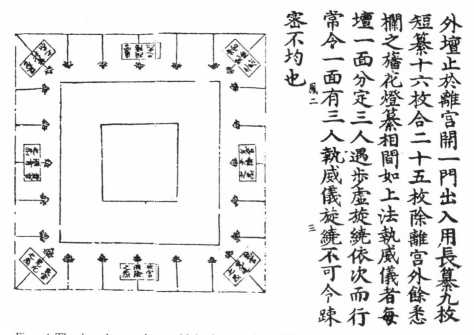

Figure 1. The altar: the sacred area with its three precincts. The Outer Altar has twenty-four spaces between twenty-four pickets. (*Wushang huanglu dazhai licheng yi* 無上黃籙大齋立成儀 2: 3b)

attached to them, they remained abstract and numerological symbols. As expressed in an old liturgical manual: "The numbers of transcendent agents are multiple entities developed in response to the circumstances [of the evolution] of the [Three] Original Energies. They are not deified humans of this world."[3] The commentator of this text, the great scholar Tao Hongjing (456–536) remarks that these divine agents are homologues of the twenty-four body spirits. Hence they are also linked to the Twenty-four Energy Nodes.

A special ritual, called *opening* (*kaiqi ke* 開啓科) is performed at the very beginning of the Taoist service to install and consecrate the divine agents of the Outer Altar. Beyond this demarcation line of the Outer Altar were installed numerous oil lamps, grouped together in patterns representing constellations (fig. 2). These were the twenty-eight mansions (see Needham 1959, 234–37). Another ritual, called the Division of Lamps (*fendeng ke* 分火登科), was used to light and consecrate these lamps. After fabricating new fire, first one, then a second, and finally a third lamp were lit. Only then could there be a general lighting of the other lamps. The ritual reenacted an important phase in the creation of the universe, in keeping with the forty-second chapter of the *Daode jing:* "The Tao created One, One gave birth to Two, Two to Three, and Three to the Myriad Beings" (Schipper 1975).

The next step in the establishment of the altar concerns the middle sphere (*zhongtan* 中壇). It functions essentially as the intermediary stage between the Outer and the Inner Altar. It is here that the rites of passage take place (fig. 3). The middle sphere is usually laid out as a square. At its four corners we find the gates of entrance and exit named Gate of Heaven for the northwest corner, Door of Earth for the southeast corner, Gate of Man for the southwest corner, and finally Road of Ghosts for the northeast corner. These names are traditionally given to the four equidistant points of the cycle of the Twelve Branches

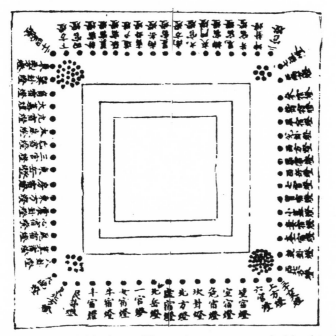

Figure 2. The altar surrounded by lamps. The emplacements are marked by dots. The writing identifies the stars that the lamps represent. (*Wushang huanglu dazhai licheng yi* 無上黃籙大齋立成儀 2: 4b)

Door of the Earth   Gate of Man

Road of Ghosts   Gate of Heaven

Figure 3. Symbolic representation of the middle altar: the Twelve Branches (arranged in a square), the Eight Trigrams, and the four gates (the four corners)

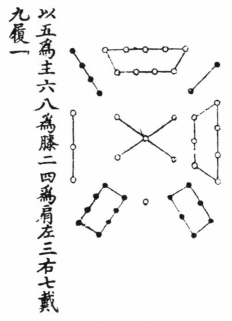

Figure 4. A magic square. The numbers are here rendered as imaginary constellations.

arranged in a square, and with the cycle starting from the sign *zi* 子 in the north. The four corners just mentioned are also connected with four trigrams: *qian* 乾 (northwest), *kun* 坤 (southeast), *xun* 巽 (southwest), and *gen* 艮 (northeast). The other four trigrams of the series are placed between, and the whole sequence of eight follows the arrangement of King Wen. Now the Eight Trigrams in this arrangement are in turn assimilated to a nine-fold structure known as the Nine Palaces (*jiugong* 九宮) (see fig. 4.) This nine-fold structure commands a series of numerological values making it a magic square (Needham 1959, 55–59 on the Nine Halls and the Luoshu diagram).

Those who officiate in the ritual enter the middle sphere through the Door of the Earth. The acolytes remain in this sphere. The different points (Twelve Branches, Eight Trigrams, and Nine Palaces) are established and consecrated during the rites of purification of the altar, after which the highest sphere, the Inner Altar, is closed off. The Middle Altar lies as a kind of tight enclosure around the inner sphere, and this is expressed and implemented by a special rite called "closing the frontiers" (*jiejie* 結界) at the conclusion of the purification ritual. After this, the Master of High Merit, who is the principal officer, will enter the Inner Altar.

This ultimate sphere is oriented differently from the previous ones; the four directions and the center also have different numerical values from those we have seen before. The rites of installation of the Inner Altar are particularly solemn. The ritual begins at midnight and lasts until dawn. The five cardinal points are marked, each by a bushel of (uncooked) white rice grains (symbolizing a measure of life).[4] Inside each of these five measures is placed a sacred writ in the form of a wooden tablet or a sheet of paper inscribed with

Figure 5. An example of a Real Writ: cosmic writing at the moment of the creation of the universe.

mysterious signs, unintelligible for the common human being. These signs are in the so-called real writing and represent the archetypal characters that appeared spontaneously at the moment of the creation of the universe, expressing the fundamental configuration of cosmic energies as they emerged from chaos and coagulated to form all beings (see fig. 5). The text that is recited at the occasion of the rite of placing the five writs in the bushels reads:

> Behold! The Three Energies [the original trinity proceeding from the Tao] suddenly coagulate, creating a point of viridian incipiency on high. The Two Principles [yin and yang] separate, taking for the first time the shape of the Great Ultimate (*taiji* 太極). Pure sound was as yet unheard, the stars were not in their place, when suddenly the energies from the Three Regions gushed forth, producing the Eight Notes of Harmony. [These sound energies] coagulated in the center of the Great Vacuity, as billowing clouds, constantly intermingling, wheeling and turning above the Purple Empyrean. Now floating, now sinking, in accordance with the norm (*ke*), being neither smoke nor dust, neither vapors nor steam, [they] formed characters ten thousand yards square, resounding with the Eight Notes, expressing the essence of the Three Energies, the subtle manifestation of the Five Elements. Oh Great Tao of the Jade Aurora, manifesting itself visibly in the Real Void! The Heavenly Perfected and the Ancestral Beings, paying homage to this revelation, copied it. [These writs] were tortuous and spiralling, clustered and weird. Some called them "Real Writs," others name them: "No resemblance."[5]

These primeval oscillograms resulting from a melodious eight-note Big Bang, transcribed by the first Taoist, are the signs copied on the five tablets that are now installed in the bushels, one at each of the cardinal points. This rite reenacts the very first stage of the creation of the world and the original revelation of the Tao. The five Real Writs are therefore considered to be the basic Taoist text, the first holy book from which all others, including the *Daode jing*, have derived in successive stages of degeneration. Each of the five writs belongs to a cardinal point and has an emblematical number. These numbers are different from those of the magic square, to wit:

nine for the east (placed in the northeast corner);
three for the south (southeast corner);
seven for the west (southwest corner);
five for the north (northwest corner);
one for the center.

These numbers belong to quite another cosmological theory from those that are more generally known. It is called "the Arrangement (of cyclical signs) according to tones" (*nayin* 納音), as it is indeed based on the principle that the cycle of the Twelve Branches and its subsequent development of the sexagenary cycle are subsidiaries of the fundamental Chinese pentatonic scale. This theory has been little studied until now; there are several methods for figuring out the classification of the signs of the sexagenary cycle according to the five tones.[6] A demonstration of these methods would lead us too far from our subject. As we have seen from the text cited a moment ago, according to Taoist cosmology, this arrangement represents the earliest stage, a first phase in the division of species from the central One (more exactly, Three-One). Following the classification of the signs of the sexagenary cycle under the five tones and Five Elements, and their distribution at the five cardinal points, there are a number of well-established theories for arriving at the Nine Palaces and the magic square. The latter are therefore seen as a subsequent stage in comparison to the *nayin* sequence. This sequence stands at the beginning of time in our universe, and the Real Writs that are connected with them stand as the earliest perceptible manifestation of the Tao. Their installation completes the construction of the altar. From this point on, a ninefold ritual of circulation can take place, designated by the general name of "practicing the Tao" (*xingdao* 行道). When this ritual is finished through a nine-fold repetition, the altar will be dispersed (*santan* 散壇), and the Real Writs burned (*hua*; litt.: to transform). This action is considered not so much an act of destruction as one of distribution, publication, and transmission. We shall come back to this point later.

3. *Progress*

The Taoist system of grading (*ke*) was based on the concept of merit (*gong* 功, or *gongfu* 功夫). This concept connotes "accomplishment" or "achievement." To achieve something without failing, to accomplish a full cycle, in giving and taking, in fulfilling a task, by keeping difficult rules, or, more generally, by living one's span of allotted life, all this resulted in *gongfu*. This acquisition of merit resulted in turn in an increase in power (hence the name of *gongfu* for Chinese martial arts), and an upgrading in status, because the Taoist considered that all beings that accomplish cyclical actions of movement accumulate energies that transform and purify these beings. Purification and transformation (*hua*, the term used for the oblation of the Real Writs and the entire altar), implies progress on the universal scale of merit.

"The shining classificatory system (*ke*) of our liturgy is the graded hierarchy of all beings," said a great thirteenth-century Taoist scholar.[7]

The consecrated way of obtaining merit was through the accomplishment of ritual. Indeed, the larger the cycle, the greater the merit and its upgrading power. The creation of the world and its final destruction or "transformation" may be seen as an ultimate cycle. Yet this enormous period could be accomplished metaphorically in one major service. Such a service reenacts the creation of the world through the lighting of the lamps, the closing of the precincts, and the placing of the five Real Writs. It ends with the dispersion of the altar and the combustion of the Real Writs and all other writings (including the name tablets of the divine agents and the holy books recited during the service) in a great holocaust.

In order to evaluate what this ritual process of acceleration of time meant to the adept, we must make a further step in our aquaintance with Taoism. In Taoism, the ladder of merit and spiritual accomplishment is expressed through a hierarchy not only of grades, leading the adept from the earliest stages of initiation in childhood to the highest ranks of mastership and into the realm of the gods and union with the Tao, but also of holy books. Sacred texts, considered to be expansions of the spontaneous Real Writs that we have already encountered, were always kept secret and only transmitted to those who deserved them. This may once have been true for all Chinese literature, but Taoism maintained the tradition. During the early Chinese Middle Ages (the fourth and fifth centuries), the Taoists compiled a large number of "revealed" texts, and these were classified according to their holiness: the holier the book, the rarer it should be. A code (*ke*) was written to lay down the rules for transmission. Some works should be transmitted once every thousand years. If no deserving adept could be found, it might be transmitted after another thousand years to two persons at the same time. Four thousand years was a standard period for important liturgical texts. One code established, in this respect, a grid for nesting time cycles: for those living on this earth, four hundred years of waiting was enough, but divine agents, belonging to a longer time span, transmitted the texts every four thousand years. The greater gods did so every forty thousand years (these divine agents and greater gods of the Taoist pantheon are the abstract hypostases of the forces of nature; see above, section 2). Very holy books could only be obtained every ten thousand years, and so on.[8] To receive such a work after a correct ritual for transmission meant the confirmation of one's grade and implied appointment among the officials of the heavenly bureaucracy. It also meant a life span in keeping with such an appointment and with the period of transmission of the holy book one had received. But what mortal being could hope to obtain such a transmission?

Historical and hagiographical sources dealing with the lives and actions of Taoist patriarchs and saints almost never mention these delays for the transmission of holy books. It seems that they did not apply to the religious practice of this world, or, if so, only indirectly. All Taoist rituals are, in principle, transmission rituals. All confer grades, each one a step higher than the previous one obtained, which allows everybody to advance on the ladder of merit and salvation. All Taoist services comprise a revelation ritual of a fundamental script, a blueprint of chaotic order from which all other scriptures derive, as well as their oblation, that is: destruction, publication, and transmission. Accomplishing in this way a complete cosmic cycle, the time span between one transmission and the next does become, so it would seem, irrelevant as to the period of waiting to be observed *before* obtaining transmission. Thus the time limits for the transferral of holy books appear to have been in the first place a device for grading their salvational power—the longer, the better. But these time limits might eventually be of some influence *after* the transmission, as from the moment of oblation (consumption and transmission) it might be expected that the receiver would enjoy peace and happiness for the next period of, for instance, four thousand years.

Inside the framework of the Taoist liturgical system, the accomplishment of ritual was therefore a factor of progress. Each ritual entailed the transfer of some kind of holy text and the conferring of some kind of rank and title. The system allowed all beings—insects, devils, ghosts, and even stones—to enter into the grid of merit and to climb the ladder of perfection from the bottom of earthly existence up to the very pinnacle of the pantheon and from there up and away into oneness with the Tao. Indeed, as the great liturgist Du Guangting 杜光庭 (850–933) remarked: "Salvation is progress! In order to save myself, I must advance along the grades of the Tao, from vulgarity to perfection." [9]

4. *Inner Time*

The visible altar is constructed as a metaphoric model of the creative process of the universe. The time cycles that are symbolically laid out in its mandalalike structure all belong to a hierarchy of systems of outer time, that is, time as it exists in creation, after the diversification of chaos. But what about time before that moment?

Before the diversification (*fen* 分) of the energies that make up the universe, they existed in an undifferentiated, potential state in chaos, during a period of gestation, evolving from what is called "something chaotically structured" (*Daode jing* 25) to "that which has a name" and is therefore the mother of all beings (*Daode jing* 12). How long was this period, and how should it be measured? These answers could be found by assimilating it to the gestational periods in nature and in particular to human gestation. Indeed, in Taoism, the ten (lunar) months of pregnancy, during which the embryo is considered to pass through a ninefold transformation process, correspond to the time cycle and the process of the shaping of the universe inside chaos. This is eloquently expressed by the sages at the court of the prince of Huai-nan, who elaborated on the famous forty-second chapter of the *Daode jing* in these terms:

> The spirit is that what comes from Heaven, the form is that what comes from the Earth.
>   Therefore it is said:
> "The One brings forth the Two;
> The Two bring forth the Three;
> The Three bring forth the Ten-thousand Beings.
> The Ten-thousand Beings turn their back on Yin and hold unto Yang
> And by the interaction of these [two] energies (*qi* 氣) their union is accomplished" (*Daode jing* 42).
> [Of this it is said]:
> The first month it is an unguent;
> the second month, a tendon,
> the third month, an embryo;
> the fourth month, the flesh;
> the fifth month, the muscles;
> the sixth month, the bones;
> the seventh month, it is accomplished;
> the eighth, it budges;
> the ninth month, it reverses itself;
> the tenth month, it is born, and the body is perfect....
> Thus, the head is round like Heaven, the feet are square like the Earth, Heaven has its Four Seasons, its Five Elements, its Nine Relays, its 366 days. Man, in a similar way, has four limbs, five viscera, nine apertures and 366 joints...." [10]

As is well known, Chinese custom allots to newborn children the age of one year. Thus, the period of ten lunar months that the infant lives in the womb is counted as the equivalent of a full period of twelve months of the lunar-solar year in the outside world. By thus recognizing an existence before birth, the duration of which has no exact equivalence in the time of this world, Chinese custom already acknowledges the difference in nature of inner time versus outer time. Inner time being the same for all human beings, it is seen as an absolute time model. Its absoluteness is only enhanced by the mythical belief that extraordinary people have a longer gestation than common mortals. Divine heroes are born after twelve months, great sages after eighteen months. According to Taoist belief, cosmogenesis is linked to the ontogenesis of Lao Zi 老子, "Body of the Tao." Lao Zi, the "Old Infant," therefore remained in the womb for eighty-one years. This gestation of nine times nine years means a wordly longevity equal to the life span of Heaven and Earth.

The emblematical number of these inner time periods is nine. It governs the transformational phases of the gestation. A hagiographer of the seventh century provides us with the following information:

> Lao Zi is the body of the Tao. His inner existence is different from his outer one, and this difference is the result of the way the body is capable of adapting itself [to phases]. In inner life, [these phases] are named Ultimate One, Real One, Mysterious One, August One, Primordial One, Ancestral One, Most Great One, Natural One, Correct One.... These nine concepts (*yi* 義), although they have different names, have a common origin and correspond to the mysterious workings (*ji* 機); therefore they are all One.[11]

The nine transformations of inner life constitute nine phases of One, while the outside world is governed by the duality of yin-yang and by the cycles that developed from their alternation. The ninefold transformation of one that takes place in the chaos/womb provides us also with the model for the ninefold transmutation of the elixir (*dan* 丹) in the alchemist's vessel. And just as in Taoist ritual, so in alchemy inner time proceeds simultaneously with outer time. The fire-phasing in the furnace reproduces the time cycle of the calendar year while the elixir inside the vessel goes through the nine transformations of the embryo. We also can see that this simultaneous process evolves in opposite directions: the inner process creates form from formlessness, while the outer process goes from form through different stages to annihilation.

However, as we have seen from the traditions surrounding gestation, and as it is expressed in ritual, inner time in principle not only precedes outer time but also determines outer time. Outer time in ritual is telescoped to the extent that creation and destruction, the beginning and the end, take place during the time span of the ritual. In other words, at the moment of the ritual, the duration of ages is reduced to a single *instant*. This instant corresponds to inner time, to the oneness of the ninefold transformation. This moment of absolute time is the instant of chaos, of total communication, one and undifferentiated, yet perceived as an endless multiple. As an old text says of the gestation of Lao Tzu, the body of the Tao:

"Undifferentiated! From it, the heavenly and the earthly are in the process of being [trans]formed! The spirit assumes form in the womb ... changing continuously...."[12]

Inner time does not correspond to the duration experienced in outer time. This is not only shown by the customs surrounding childbirth, but is also the theme of many ancient legends. They tell us how sometimes people lose their way in mountains (a metaphor for the original state, chaos and the womb) and enter fairy realms beyond the world of man. After a few days of blissful sojourn, they return to their village, only to find that aeons have elapsed.

Only very old people vaguely remember that someone named like the protagonist once left the place for the mountains and was never seen again. . . .

The compression of outer time in ritual is obtained through the simultaneous activation of inner time. Outer time is then fused into inner time through the ritual enacting of a return to the womb. Many symbolic elements bear this out, such as the large cape (*pi* 披) that the Taoist master wears during his ritual performance. This vestment represents the clothing of the unborn child, the placenta that is like the shell of the cosmic egg.

Taoist ritual, through the successive stages of the establishment of the altar, passes from the cycles of outer time through a regressive movement into inner time. This return into the womb is enacted at different phases of the ritual, and, for the first time, after the construction of the altar, at the beginning of the ninefold ritual of circulation called "practicing the Tao." When entering, from the Middle Altar into the Inner Altar, the master performs dance steps called "the paces of Yu" (*Yubu* 禹步), and utters the following words in an inaudible way:

> The nine phoenixes, red bird spirits, change into gods of the six *ding* 丁 periods [*ding* is the fourth sign of the Ten Heavenly Stems cycle]. They gather around me as I stand in the center, fire transforms my body. . . .[13]

While purifying the Inner Altar, the master murmurs another invocation, that says:

> Heaven One, Earth One;
> Earth Water [one of the Five Elements; it has the emblematical number one] streams in reverse, entering (the Gate of) the Cell.
> Four level strokes, five upright strokes. The Six *jia* 甲 and the six *ding* periods. . . .[14]

The mention of these particular periods, of the central One, of water that flows backward and the practice of dancing steps, all refers to the same thing: an ancient, famous, but as-yet little understood system of cyclical time calculus called: "the Irrational (or Uneven) Opening (*qimen* 奇門) and the Hidden (or Simultaneous) Period (*dunjia* 遁甲). At the present time, even the correct translation of these terms remains open to discussion. However, we shall present here a short explanation of this sytem that allows the adept to walk backward from outer time into inner time.

5. *The Hidden Period*

In China's vernacular fiction, in its ballads and stories, no magic tricks are more popular than those involving the Hidden Period. Through their knowledge of that calendrical technique, the heroes of the past knew how to confound their enemies, to travel in a flash to distant places, and, best of all, to enter normally inaccessible realms of time and space and thus render themselves invisible to the outside world.

According to tradition, the method was first revealed to the Yellow Emperor—China's greatest culture hero—by the six Jade Maidens, the personification of the six *ding* periods of the sexagesimal cycle (*liuding yunü* 六丁玉女). These calendar maidens stand under the tutelage of a mother, identified as the Mysterious Woman of the Nine Heavens (*Jiutian xuannü* 九天玄女) or as the Mother Queen of the West, Lady of the Ultimate Yin (*Xi wangmu* 西王母, *Taiyin xuanguang yunü* 太陰玄光玉女). The revealed method of the Hidden Period allowed the Yellow Emperor to understand the arcana of nature and to use their transformational power to his own advantage, enabling him to vanquish his enemies.[15]

Later in history, the famous strategist Zhuge Liang 諸葛亮 (181–234), a great protagonist in popular drama, is reputed to have been an expert in the Hidden Period technique. At a strategic point on the border of his territory, Zhuge Liang reordered the landscape to construct a vast area delimited by several circles of landmarks. The latter represented the Twenty-four Energy Nodes, the Eight Trigrams, and so forth. This area thus greatly resembled a giant Taoist altar. When a vast host of enemies arrived in the region, Zhuge Liang led them by ruse into the area, through a particular opening. Once inside the area, this army completely lost its way. Its ten thousand soldiers sought in vain to extricate themselves from the area that had become an unsolvable labyrinth, and they subsequently died.[16] To the present day, the strategic formation of the Eight Trigrams (as Zhuge Liang's labyrinthine area was called) is a set piece for large-scale demonstrations of the martial arts (*gongfu*), with warriors replacing the markers of the different cycles that are used in its make-up.

The Hidden Period thus plays an important part in Chinese military strategy, and its system has therefore been best preserved in handbooks on the art of war.[17] But strategy is only one of the many situations in which the Hidden Period may be used.

In Taoism, the Hidden Period is activated through a rite that combines dance steps with inaudibly uttered formulas and meditation. The dance form itself is called "the Paces of Yu," after Yu the Great, the mythical demiurge who reinvested and reordered the world after the Great Flood. Yu traversed the world, measuring it step by step. He was, however, hemiplegic and advanced with only one leg. This limping gait is imitated by the Taoist master dancing "the Paces of Yu," while taking possession of the Inner Altar.[18] Advancing with measured steps and with one leg—the right one for even (yin) days, the left one for uneven (yang) days—trailing the unused leg behind, he crosses the central area following the sequence of the Nine Palaces according to the numbers of the magic square:

In the subsequent rite for purifying and "entering" the Central Altar, the same grid is used but the dance steps do not follow this sequential numbered order, but a different one that is related to the Hidden Period. We shall come back to this presently.

The Paces of Yu are very old, and one of the earliest documents to mention this dance is a kind of almanac.[19] Here the dance steps are executed in order to determine the place of a given sign in a cycle, together with the direction is space that corresponds to it. It appears therefore that the steps enabled the practitioner to establish directional *angles* in relation to a given axis. If this is correct, we might eventually conceive of the Paces of Yu as having been a kind of primitive practice of geometry.

Returning to Taoist ritual, the Paces of Yu not only served to take possession, as we have seen, of the Inner Altar but also to establish the spot, and the angle, where the Hidden Period was considered to be located. Here the magic square of the Nine Palaces becomes a labyrinth in which the adept might, so to speak, lose himself and disappear to the outside world:

> In order to hide oneself [*yinshen dunxing* 隱身遁形]: take a sword in your left hand, hold your breath, draw a circle with a diameter of six feet around yourself with your right hand.... For the rite of transformation [*bienshen* 變身], take six stalks of one foot two inches long and place them in the order [of the first six numbers in the sequence of the Nine Palaces], beginning with the decade of the Green Dragon [emblem of the East, meaning the first decade of the sexagenary cycle, beginning with *jiazi* 甲子]. These stalks should be placed in an upright way, but coming to the gate of the Jade Maiden [number seven], you take [another] stalk and trace with it a horizontal line on the ground and then place the stalk there, so as to close the gate. Then leave the area by walking backwards, from the Gate of Heaven to the Door of the Earth. When the Gate [of the Jade Maiden] is closed, the body is hidden.[20]

The above is a rather cryptic description activating the Hidden Period; but we can see from it that the adept establishes a closed area in which he sets out the grid of the Nine Palaces. He links the points of the diagram by performing the Paces of Yu. (This can be deduced from another passage left untranslated here; we also did not translate the magic formula that accompanies the dance.) The paces go first, progressively, for the numbers one to six; then, for the remaining three numbers, they go regressively, by walking backward. We shall come back to this presently.

In Taoism, as in Chinese culture in general, the "other world" (*bieyou tiandi* 別有天地), where nature exists in its original, spontaneous state, is related to the image of the mountain and the unspoiled landscape.

The first and most important of holy mountains is the Kunlun 崑崙, the other worldly place where the Mother Queen of the West, Lady of the Ultimate Yin, dwells. She also governs the Jade Maidens of the six *ding* periods. In Chinese, the name Kunlun is etymologically and semantically related to *hundun* 混沌, which means chaos. The holy mountain of the Mother is conceived as being the matrix of the universe. Other holy mountains share this same quality of being chaotic precincts in which life is engendered and regenerated: places for returning to the source, hiding and nurturing. Here the elixirs are to be found, as well as the healing herbs and magic mushrooms. As we have seen already, those who dwell in these mountains belong to a time cycle different from that of the ordinary world.

How can one enter these marvelous places that are described by mystics and by many poets as well, and that have inspired the great landscape painters of China? The first condition is the understanding of the workings of the Hidden Period. Let us listen to the words of the great scholar Ge Hong 葛洪 (283–343) on this subject:

> Those who wish to enter holy mountains should absolutely be versed in the secret arts of the Hidden Period, but the books that are supposed to treat this subject do not explain it clearly. I myself, from my youth on, harboured the desire to enter the mountains, and went about studying works about the Hidden Period. I found more than sixty scrolls, and it is impossible to treat [their contents] in detail. I therefore made abstracts from them, and gathered the essentials in a vade mecum for my own use, but that is not suitable for transmission in writing [here]. I will expose here the bare minimum, trusting that those amateurs who wish to enter mountains will be able to obtain information from specialists of whom there is no lack in our time.... To enter holy mountains, in order to avoid grief, choose the beginning of the [sexagenary] cycle [starting with *jiazi*], the day *dingmao* 丁卯 the first of the six *ding*. This day is called the period of the Virtue of Yin [*yinde* 陰德]. It is also called the Heart of Heaven [*tianxin* 天心]. Then one can disappear, or, as one says: "vanish

in broad daylight." . . . Also, when you enter mountains and forests, take in your left hand a stalk of the Green Dragon, break it in half and plant it under the P'eng star. Then pass through the Hall of Light and enter into the Ultimate Yin. Walk the Paces of Yu. . . . The six *jia* signs are the Green Dragon, the six *yi* 乙 are the Peng 篷 star, the six *bing* 丙 the Hall of Light and the six *ding* the Ultimate Yin.[21]

The description given above of the steps of Yu danced in a pattern that corresponds to the signs of the sexagenary cycle indicates, in spite of its obscure wording, that the adept is in fact performing a mantic dance following the grid of the Nine Palaces, like the one described earlier. Indeed, the description just given uses "holy mountain" or "mountains and forests" (wilderness) metaphorically for the realm of chaotic inner time of the Hidden Period to which the Irrational Opening gives access. The latter is determined and activated by the dance of the Nine Palaces. That this is the case here can be deduced from the many different texts dealing with the *dunjia* system. In spite of their relative obscurity, a few fundamental aspects can be recognized, which we shall explain in the following section.

6. *The Irrational Opening*

As previously noted, the sexagenary cycle is achieved through the combination of two series: the Ten Stems and the Twelve Branches. Both series are evenly numbered, and therefore each sign of the Ten Stems is combined with only six (but always the same six) signs of the Twelve Branches. Thus the stem *jia* 甲 is combined with the branches *zi* 子, *yin* 寅, *chen* 辰, *wu* 午, *shen* 申, and *xu* 戌 and the next stem *yi* 乙 with the remaining six. The term "six *jia*" or "six *ding*" designates these six periodical combinations that begin, in the sexagenary cycle, with the signs *jia* or *ding* (see appendix). In each decade of the sexagenary cycle, there are always two signs of the Twelve Branches that remain unused. For instance, in the first decade starting with *jiazi* 甲子, the branches *xu* 戌 and *hai* 亥 are unemployed. These two signs are termed "orphan" (*gu* 孤). Now when the Twelve Branches are arranged in a cycle, they each correspond to a given direction and hour of the day. Thus *xu* and *hai* correspond to the north-west and to the time of 7 to 11 P.M. In the *jiazi* decade, the fact that *xu* and *hai* are "orphans" influences also their counterparts, that is, the signs situated opposite each other on the compass. In the present case these are *chen* 辰 and *si* 巳 corresponding to the southeast and to 7 to 11 A.M. The latter signs are called "empty" (*xu* 虚).

The orphan-empty axis divides the cycle of the decade into two unequal parts:

1. The empty periods (in the present case, *mouchen* and *jisi*) and the subsequent four periods of the decade; these together are called the Six Rectors (*liuyi*).
2. The periods preceding the empty ones, in this case *jiazi, yichou, bingyin,* and *dingmao.* Of these four, *jiazi* is considered apart as king of the decade. The remaining three periods are termed the Three Irrational Powers (*san chiling* 三奇靈). Of these three, the first (*yichou*) is assimilated to the sun, the second (*bingyin*) to the moon, the third (*dingmao*) to the stars. The last one is the most important and the most powerful.

Because of the influence of the orphan-empty axis, the two categories of the Six Rectors and the Three Irrational Powers have opposite dynamics. The Six Rectors are progressing, the Three Irrational Powers are regressing. This means that when the two categories are set out to match with the Nine Palaces, the Six Rectors occupy progressively the positions numbered one to six, while the Three Irrational Powers occupy regressively the positions

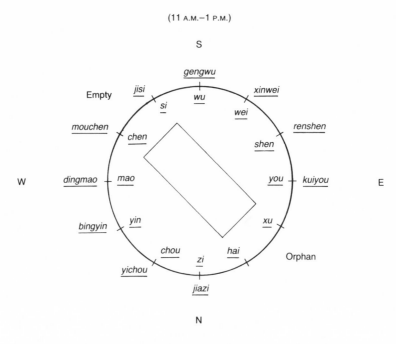

Figure 6. The "orphan" and "empty" signs in the *jiazi* decade. Inside the circle are the Twelve Branches; outside the circle are the ten periods of the first decade.

nine, eight, and seven. Danced with the Paces of Yu on the Nine Palaces' magic square, this gives:

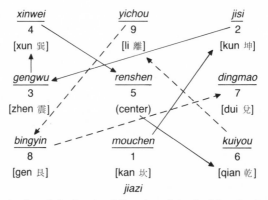

Figure 7. The determination of the Irrational Opening of the *jiazi* decade: the Six Rectors and the Three Irrational Powers on their positions (between brackets the Eight Trigrams).

The powerful Irrational *dingmao* is situated at number seven, with the trigram *dui*, located in the west; this corresponds to the Irrational Opening (*qimen*)[22], also called the Gate of the Jade Maiden or the Gate that is kept by the Jade Maiden (*yunü shoumen* 玉女守門).[23] It opens toward the direction in which one can "vanish in broad daylight." This gate is found by walking backward through the stations of the Three Irrational Powers, the final stage establishing a given angle from the line of the starting point (number one) where the *jiazi* sign, the king of the decade, is located. The six *jia* signs that stand at the beginning of each decade of the sexagenary cycle occupy respectively the positions from one to six on the magic square, in a similar and homologous way with the Six Rectors. Therefore, the position of the kings of each decade differ and consequently the angle in which the king of a given decade stands to the Irrational Opening of that decade differs too. The different angles appear to correspond to the angles existing, during the year, between the Year star (*Suixing* 歲星) on the one hand and the Great Year star (*Taisui* 太歲 or *Taiyin* 太陰) on the other. The latter is the invisible, regressive "anti-Jupiter," also named the "Green Dragon" in the passage of the astronomical chapter of the *Huainan zi* 淮南子 on which these deductions are based.[24]

The six *ding* periods are all yin spirits. A text on *dunjia* tells us:

> The six Yin are the six negative [energies] of the sexagenary cycle. The negative [energy] of the *jiazi* decade is *dingmao*, of the *jiaxu* 甲戌 decade it is *dingchou* 丁丑, of the *jiashen* 甲申 decade it is *dinghai* 丁亥, of the *jiawu* 甲午 decade it is *dingyou* 丁酉, of the *jiachen* 甲辰 decade it is *dingwei* 丁未, of the *jiayin* 甲寅 decade it is *dingsi* 丁巳. These six *ding* are the six Yin. The six *jia* are Yang powers. One should use the six *ding* and not use the six Yang, because Yin is void (*wu* 無), and void means transformation, passing from nonexistence to existence, from life to death, from hidden to manifest.[25]

We have not succeeded in finding a text that explains clearly the reason for adopting the *ding* sign at the seventh place in the magic square as the Irrational Opening. At present, we cannot think of any explanation other than the special situation of the number seven in its association with the west. Indeed, in the two different systems that attribute numbers to the five cardinal points, the *nayin* system (see above sect. 2) and the one corresponding to the magic square, the value of the west is seven, while those of all the other directions differ from one system to another. In the west therefore, there is a state of simultaneousness of the earlier, embryonic stage of the *nayin* cycle and the latter, outer-time stage of the Nine Palaces. This is of course a mere hypothesis. However, Taoist mythology concerning the Mother Queen of the West, goddess of the Ultimate Yin and leader of the Jade Maidens of the six *ding*, gives some support to it.

All this will certainly be clarified by further research on old Chinese calendar systems. What seems well established here is that Chinese religion conceived of two kinds of time, inner and outer, and that it devised theories of the calendar that tried to establish how one could enter from the one into the other. These theories, although highly abstruse, enjoyed great popularity in religion and folklore. They offered a model of stability in the time perception of this world, inasmuch as progressive time observed and present was seen as counterbalanced by hidden regressive cycles.

All these complex representations are perfectly illustrated by that simple time-measuring instrument which is shown on the cover of *The Voices of Time* (Amherst: University of Massachusetts Press, 1981): the Chinese incense clock. In the intricate patterns of the fine traces of incense powder, we can readily recognize a form of script similar to that of the Real Writs that are burned in Taoist ritual. Such a script is called "cloud seal" writing. In the incense clock, the writing is also consumed through the slow burning of the incense powder. The time span of the combustion is intended to be a measure for a period of meditation: a regression toward the inner world, a return to the deepest sources of our being, a moment of oblivion of the outer world and of regeneration of our vital energies.

Appendix

The Ten Celestial Stems:

jia 甲, *yi* 乙, *bing* 丙, *ding* 丁, *mou* 戊, *ji* 己, *geng* 庚, *xin* 辛, *ren* 壬, *kui* 癸.
The Twelve Earthly Branches:
zi 子, *chou* 丑, *yin* 寅, *mao* 卯, *chen* 辰, *si* 巳, *wu* 午, *wei* 未, *shen* 申, *you* 酉, *xu* 戌, *hai* 亥.

The sexagenary cycle (in six decades):

jiazi 甲子	*jiaxu* 甲戌	*jiashen* 甲申	*jiawu* 甲午	*jiachen* 甲辰	*jiayin* 甲寅
yichou 乙丑	*yihai* 乙亥	*yiyou* 乙酉	*yiwei* 乙未	*yisi* 乙巳	*yimao* 乙卯
bingyin 丙寅	*bingzi* 丙子	*bingxu* 丙戌	*bingshen* 丙申	*bingwu* 丙午	*bingchen* 丙辰
dingmao 丁卯	*dingchou* 丁丑	*dinghai* 丁亥	*dingyou* 丁酉	*dingwei* 丁未	*dingsi* 丁巳
mouchen 戊辰	*mouyin* 戊寅	*mouzi* 戊子	*mouxu* 戊戌	*moushen* 戊申	*mouwu* 戊午
jisi 己巳	*jimao* 己卯	*jichou* 己丑	*jihai* 己亥	*jiyou* 己酉	*jiwei* 己未
gengwu 庚午	*gengchen* 庚辰	*gengyin* 庚寅	*gengzi* 庚子	*gengxu* 庚戌	*gengshen* 庚申
xinwei 辛未	*xinsi* 辛巳	*xinmao* 辛卯	*xinchou* 辛丑	*xinhai* 辛亥	*xinyou* 辛酉
renshen 壬申	*renwu* 壬午	*renchen* 壬辰	*renyin* 壬寅	*renzi* 壬子	*renxu* 壬戌
kuiyou 癸酉	*kuiwei* 癸未	*kuisi* 癸巳	*kuimao* 癸卯	*kuichou* 癸丑	*kuihai* 癸亥

Notes

As a general introduction to the theme of this paper, see K. Schipper, 1978.

1. A research program is under way, at the present time, under the auspices of the European Science Foundation, for the analysis and description of all the works (almost 1,500) contained in this canon.

2. Manuel de Diegez, "Science et philosophie," in *Encyclopaedia Universalis* (Paris, 1968), 14: 758–66.

3. *Dengzhen yinjue* 登眞隱訣 (*Daozang*, 421): 3. 22b–23a

4. The five bushels of rice used for the construction of the altar are related to the adept's offering of the early Taoist church, and the movement of the Heavenly Masters has been nicknamed "the Way of the Five Pecks of Rice."

5. Ritual for the Vesperal Communication, *Suqi xuantan ke* 宿啓玄壇科. Nineteenth-century liturgical manuscript (author's coll.).

6. Essentially, this system classifies the periods of the sexagenary cycle according to the series of the Twelve Branches (see appendix), which gives five columns of twelve periods. There are five periods with the sign *zi* as second part of the binome: *jiazi, bingzi, mouzi, gengzi, renzi*. By giving the number one to *genzi*, one obtains, by counting backward, that *mou* (-*zi*) is three places removed from *geng*, *bing* (-*zi*) five, *jia* (-*zi*) seven and *ren* (-*zi*) nine. The numbers are then matched with the five tones, and also with the corresponding directions in space.

7. Jin Yunzhong 金允中 (fl. 1225), *Shangqing lingbao dafa* 上清靈寶大法: 16.18a.

8. These data are based on the *Taishang xuandu siji mingke* 太上玄都四極明科 (*Taozang*, 184).

9. *Shangqing lingbao dafa*: 22, 13a–b.

10. *Huainan zi* 淮南子 7, "Jingshen xun" 精神訓 (Zhuzi jicheng ed. pp. 99–100)

11. Yin Wencao 尹文操 (died 688), cited in *Hunyuan shengji* 混元聖紀 (*Daozang*, 770) 2.37a–b.

12. *Laozi bianhua jing* 老子變化經. See A. Seidel, *La Divinisation de Lao-tseu dans le taoïsme des Han* (Paris: E.F.E.O. 1969), p. 61.

13. *Xuanke bijue* 玄科祕訣 (Secret Formulas for the Liturgy of the Mystery). Taoist manuscript dated around 1880 (author's collection).

14. Ibid.

15. Wang Quan 王瓘, *Guang Xuanyuan benji* 廣軒轅本紀 (dated 881), ap. *Yunji qiqian* 100. 16b–17a.

On the mother as chief of the six Jade Maidens, see *Laozi zhongjing* 老子中經, ap. *Yunji qiqian* 雲笈七籤 18. 6a–b, 21a.

16. Luo Guanzhong 羅貫中, *Sanguo zhi yanyi* 三國志演義, 84.

17. This is particularly true of the *Dunjia fuying jing* 遁甲符應經 by Yang Weide 楊維德 and the *Shenji zhidi taibai yinjing* 神機制敵太白陰經 attributed to Li Quan 李筌. For the short description of the principles of the *dunjia* system, we have used Xiao Ji's 簫吉 *Wuxing dayi* 五行大義, the *Dunjia yanyi* 遁甲演義 by Cheng Daosheng 程道生 as well as a number of handbooks used by today's diviners, such as the *Huopan qimen dunjia* 活盤奇門遁甲 (undated reproduction of a lithograph edition, published in Taizhong by Ruicheng 瑞成 shuju), the *Aotou tongshu daquan* 鰲頭通書大全 and the *Qimen dunjia biji quanshu* 奇門遁甲秘笈全書 both published by Zhulin 竹林 in Xinzhu, and finally a *Qimen dunjia yanjiu* 奇門遁甲研究 by Kong Richang 孔日昌 (Tainan, 1975).

18. On this dance, see M, Granet, "Remarques sur le Taoisme ancien," in *Etudes Sociologiques sur la Chine* (Paris: P.U.F., 1953), pp. 245–49.

19. See Rao Zongyi 饒宗頤 and Zeng Xiantong 曾憲通, *Yunmeng Qinjian rishu yanjiu* 雲夢秦簡日書研究 (Hong Kong, 1982), pp. 20–23.

20. *Bicang tongxuan bianhua liuyin dongwei dunjia zhenjing* 祕藏通玄變化六陰洞微遁甲眞經 (*Daozang*, 857) 1: 11a/b.

21. *Baopu zi neipian* 抱朴子內篇 17 (Zhuzi jicheng ed. p. 78).

22. According to the *Yianpo tiaosou qimen fu* (or *jue*) 烟波釣叟奇門賦 (訣) given in *Dunjia yanyi* and in all other manuals, when one of the Three Irrational Powers (*yi, bing, ding*) coincides with certain auspicious hours of the day, this power receives the name of *qimen* (Irrational Opening). The calculation of these hours implicates a series of Eight Gates (*bamen* 八門) on what is deemed to be the Heavenly Compass (*tianpan* 天盤) of the system. This Heavenly Compass determines the hours (*jing* 更) in coordination with the Earthly compass (*dipan* 地盤) that is related to day periods of three times five, i.e., fifteen days. According to this complex system, whose date of origin remains unknown, the Irrational Opening does not necessarily coincide with *ding* but may be linked to the other two powers (*yi, bing*) as well.

23. The way of finding "the Gate that is kept by the Jade Maiden" is explained in detail in the *Dunjia yanyi* 2: 6b/7a. For example, in the *jiazi* decade, the Heavenly Compass starts with the *zi* hour (11 P.M. to 1 A.M.). The next hours follow the numeral sequence of the Nine Palaces and thus the seventh hour (11 A.M. to 1 P.M.) falls on the seventh case (trigram *dui* 兌). When executing the *dunjia* sequence however, this case is occupied by the *dingmao* period (see fig. 7). This means that the Jade Maiden keeps the Gate at this hour (*gengwu*) and that there and then "one can accomplish hidden, private affairs such as uniting (the yin and the yang)".

24. *Huainan zi* 3, "Tianwen xun" 天文訓 (Zhuzi jicheng ed. pp. 48–49 and 52).

25. *Bicang tongxuan bianhua liuyin dongwei dunjia zhenjing*, 2: 2b.

References

Needham, J. 1956. *Science and civilisation in China*. Vol. 2, *History of scientific thought*. Cambridge: Cambridge University Press.

———. 1959. *Science and civilisation in China*. Vol. 3, *Mathematics and the sciences of heaven and earth*. Cambridge: Cambridge University Press.

Schipper, K. 1975. *Le Fen-teng, rituel taoïste*. Paris.

———. 1978. The Taoist body. *History of Religions*, 17: 355–86.

———. 1982. *Le Corps taoïste*. Paris: Fayard.

Sivin, N. 1978. On the word "Taoist" as a source of perplexity, with special reference to the relations of science and religion in traditional China." *History of Religions* 17: 303–30.

———. 1980. The theoretical background of elixir alchemy, in J. Needham, *Science and civilisation in China*, Vol. 5, pt. 4, 210–323. Cambridge: Cambridge University Press.

Wilhelm, Richard. 1966. *The I Ching or book of changes*. Trans. Cary F. Baynes. 3d ed. Princeton: Princeton University Press.

Mohist Views of Time and Space: A Brief Analysis

Zhang Yinzhi

The summary that follows is that of Professor Zhang Yinzhi's complete paper, and not of the shortened version printed in this volume. It was edited by Professor N. Sivin, to whom the editors wish to express their appreciation.

Summary   Views of time and space held by adherents of the Mohist school appear in six chapters of the *Mo Zi* (墨子), known as the "Mohist canons," "Explanations of the canons," "Major illustrations," and "Minor illustrations." They were compiled ca. 300 B.C., which was a time of rapid economic development, when wars of conquest were frequent, and when political power and the relative strength of social classes were changing. As the possibilities of thought were explored by the so-called hundred schools of philosophy, the school led by Mo Zi (fl. ca. 350 B.C.) and named after him was the most systematic in its integration of all knowledge.

In the six late chapters of the *Mo Zi*, time and space are said to be infinite. This infinity is related to both the macrocosm and the microcosm so that finiteness and the infinite are dialectically integrated. This is a materialist view of time and space. The propositions concerning natural science in which it occurs are part of a larger set that integrates them with propositions concerning philosophical utilitarianism and moral and political views (of which the most famous is the Mohists' notion of universal love).

The Mohist arguments were part of contemporary debates in which time and space were at issue; the arguments of others who took part in this discussion will be examined. Mohist views may also be compared with those found in ancient Greece, Mesopotamia, and India. They are pertinent to the foundations of modern science, to experimental method, and to the mathematizaion of empirical observation.*

1. Background to Mohist Philosophy

From about 500 to 300 B.C. China underwent an era of rapid development in the modes of production (such as the extensive use of iron tools) as well as one of violent political change.

---

* Unfortunately, it was impossible to produce a critically acceptable translation of the complete paper within the period available for the preparation of this volume. With the author's permission and the assistance of Hans Ågren, M. D., the paper was therefore boldly reduced, limiting it almost entirely to direct quotes from the Mohist writings.

The Mohist canons present textual problems of great complexity in the matter of their translation and comprehension. For a masterful essay, bringing a part of the material to the light of contemporary understanding, see A. C. Graham and N. Sivin, "A Systematic Approach to Mohist Optics (ca. 300 B.C.)" in *Chinese Sciences: Exploration of an Ancient Tradition*, ed. Shigeru Nakayama and Nathan Sivin (Cambridge: M.I.T. Press, 1973), pp. 105–52.

The reader may also wish to consult the elaboration of Master Mo's doctrine, in "Time in Chinese Philosophy and Natural Philosophy" in Joseph Needham's essay in *The Voices of Time* and follow up his references to Mohist thought in *Science and Civilisation in China*.

For samples of the chapters from the *Mo Zi* book mentioned by Zhang Yinhzi, see, *Basic Writings of Mo Tzu, Hsün Tzu, and Han Fei Tzu*, trans. Burton Watson (New York: Columbia University Press, 1967).

Characteristic of the era were the continuous wars between the established aristocratic class and the emerging landlords. The emperors of the Zhou Dynasty could no longer maintain their power, precipitating what became known as the Warring State period. The struggle has been described as "the attack on the small states by the large ones, disturbances of the small houses by the large ones, oppression of the weak by the strong, misuse of the few by the many, deception of the simple by the cunning, disdain toward the humble by the honoured . . . .[1]

A result of the incessant wars was that there was competition between the scholars of different schools of thought: the Confucians, the Taoists, the Mohists, the Legalists, the Logicians, the Diplomatists, the Yin-yang school, and others. Our concern is with the Mohists, the followers of Mo Zi, who flourished in the fifth century B.C.

Mo Zi and his disciples regarded themselves as representatives of the humble people, knowledgeable in agriculture and handicraft. They entered politics to debate with scholars of other schools; some were active in politics and science, some created theories about society, nature, and man.

The legacy of the school is carried along in a book entitled *Mo Zi*. It is a collection of the opinions and reports of the conduct of Mo Zi himself and of his disciples. The names of the chapters are: "Honoring Talent"; "Agreement with the Superior"; "Universal Love"; "Condemnation of Offensive War"; "Frugality"; "Lavish Funerals"; "The Will of Heaven"; "Obedience to the Ghost"; "Condemnation of Music"; and "Denunciation of Belief in Fate." Other parts cover mathematical concepts, optics, and kinetics.

The Mohists contributed to cultural, social, and scientific progress and may be viewed as offering the earliest ideas of an objective reality. I will address the Mohists' concepts of time and space in relation to theories of motion and matter.

2. The Mohist Views of Time and Space

Certain chapters originating in the Mohist classic deal with early scientific knowledge. Formally, they are divided into Canons and Expositions.[2]

> CANON: Space includes all the different places.
> EXPOSITION: East, west, south, and north are all enclosed in space.

This is a clear definition of space, appropriate to the knowledge of the epoch, with the exposition clarifying the canon. It suggests that the Mohists had acquired the idea of a referential frame in the cosmos, albeit centered in the human space on earth.

> CANON: Outside bounded space no line can be included.
> EXPOSITION: A plane area cannot include every line since it has a limit. But there is no line that could not be included if the area were unbounded.

Here an idea of finiteness and the infinite is introduced and a relation between them is proposed.

> CANON: Finiteness is possible for a limited area within an unbounded area of space.
> EXPOSITION: Finiteness signifies that the motion of the body is restricted to a limited area of space.

Here Mohist thought ties ideas of finiteness and the infinite to space and motion.

> CANON: The boundaries of space (the spatial universe) are constantly shifting. The reason for this refers to extensionlike concepts, such as length and duration that are measurable.

EXPOSITION: Extension: the body in motion that goes through definite length, occupies a position in the spatial universe (the boundaries of space). Space: length: that the south is opposite the north is equivalent to the opposition between east and west. The motion of any body, in spite of the sun may still be measured in space (length) and time.

Here Mohist thought gave actual meaning to ideas of space and time.

CANON: Spatial positions are names for that which is already past. The reason for this refers to reality.

EXPOSITION: Knowing that "this" is no longer "this," and that "this" is no longer "here," we still call it *north* and *south*. That is, what is already past is regarded as if it were still present. We called it *south* then and therefore we continue calling it *south* now.

CANON: Duration includes all particular (different) times.

EXPOSITION: Former times, the present time, the morning, and the evening are combined together to form duration.

This concept of duration, of past, present, and future reminds one of the Newtonian idea of "absolute, true and mathematical time [which] of itself, and from its own nature flows equably without regard to anything external. . . . "

CANON: Starting is the beginning of time while the body of motion begins to move.

EXPOSITION: Sometimes time can be measured. Sometimes it cannot be measured. It is impossible to measure the body of motion while it begins to move.

CANON: When an object is moving in space, if there were no definite locations (reference points) we could not say whether it is coming nearer or going further away. The reason for this refers to "spreading."

EXPOSITION: Talking about space, one cannot have in mind only some special district. It is merely that the first step (of a spacer) is nearer and his later steps further away. (The idea of space is like that of) duration. (One can select a certain point in time or space as the beginning, and reckon from it within a certain period or region, so that in this sense it) has boundaries (but time and space are alike) without boundaries.

These canons and their expositions resemble greatly the various arguments of Western thought that entered the background of the birth of modern science.

CANON: Infinity is not contradictory to universality. The reason refers to "fullness or not."

EXPOSITION: If the south has a limit, it can be included in toto. We cannot know whether it can all be included or not. Not knowing whether people fill this (infinite) space, we are unable to know whether people can be included in toto. This being so, it is wrong to hold that all people can be included in our love. If people do not fill the world that is unlimited, then people have a limit, and there is no difficulty in including them in our love. If they do fill the world that is unlimited, then what is unlimited is in fact limited, and then again, there is no difficulty in including all people in our love.

Thus, the Mohists have tied the contradiction between finiteness and infinity to the social doctrine of love. In Western philosophy Immanuel Kant perceived in finiteness and infinity a logical antinomy. By contrast, the Mohists saw a dialectical identity, which they employed in both their natural and their social sciences. Thus, the idea of time as a hierarchy of unresolvable conflicts would have been identified, by the Mohists, with the principle, "Time is the devotion to eternal, universal love."

3. *Comparisons between Mohist and Other Contemporary Views of Time and Space*

Confucius, who died at about the time that Mo Zi was born, did not make any systematic statements about time and space. The articles carried in the *Guan Zi* book, which was not written by one single person nor in the contemporary period, did nevertheless suggest the ideology of that period.

"The world is inclusive of everything, the universe is inclusive of the world."

An analysis of the ideograms used shows that "the universe" here indicates time and space. In the *Zhuang Zi* book it is also made clear that "that which possesses reality and exists everywhere without boundaries is space; that which is continuous and exists without beginning and end, is time."

In the same source, we find a conversation between a god of the sea and a god of the Yellow River. It again suggests the belief that the quantity of matter is unlimited, that time is infinite.

Taoism regards time and space as the highest categories of Tao, the Order of Nature. In contrast to Mohism, which is based on materialism, Taoism is based on idealism. The following definition of "the universe" is by Shi Jiao: "The east, the south, the west, and the north, and the sky and the earth are space; the ancient, the past, the present, and the future are time."

The idealistic categories of the Tao were assimilated to the materialist philosophy of Lao-zi and Zhuang-zi, who held that the universe "is so great that there are no bounds and so small that its core is fathomlessly deep."

Mohists welcomed the idea of limitlessness in cosmology, and spoke about what today we would call atomism.

CANON: That which is not able to be separated into halves cannot be cut further and cannot be separated. The reason may be found in the point.

EXPOSITION: In cutting a straight line into halves, one must select a central point. But if the line is limitless, it will be impossible to find a midpoint. The place where one begins to cut is only a certain point of a limited line. If one takes away what comes ahead and behind the point, then the point remains in the middle. The cutting off must be by halves; unless it is to be halves, there can be no cutting.

This is part of the Mohist teaching on infinite divisibility. Their arguments resemble the well-known issues, associated with the name of Zeno of Elea. It is interesting that there is more than superficial similarity between Mohist thought and the concerns of Zeno. We find it expressed in the following:

CANON: If we said a shadow does not move, it is because the motion of the source of light or the object casting the shadow, interferes with our visual illusion.

EXPOSITION: When light arrives the shadow disappears. But if it were not interfered with, it would appear as it itself and last forever.

These ideas exemplify the Mohist theory of time and space as the unity of continuation and interval.

4. The Historical Significance of Mohist Views of Time and Space

The progress of scientific theories is like waves washing the shore, one urging the other forward. The scientific theories of the Mohists were based on thinking and knowledge at the highest level available during the era when they lived. Their theories of time and space corresponded to an epoch when energy came mainly from draft animals. Thus, in retrospect, the Mohist views appear to be intuitive and primitive. We must keep in mind that they lived over two millennia ago.

Still, they produced ideas that integrated motion and matter with time and space, and related finiteness and infinity not only to time and space but also to the human condition.

Notes

1. Fung Yu-lan, *A History of Chinese Philosophy*, trans. Derek Bodde (Beijing: Henri Vetch, 1937), p. 91.

2. The following text of canons and expositions is based on the *Textual Commentary on the Works of Mo Zi* by Liang Qichao (Shanghai: Commercial Press, Ltd., 1924), in Chinese, and on Joseph Needham's discussion of the *Mo Zi* book in "Time and Knowledge in China and the West," in *Voices of Time*, ed. J. T. Fraser, 2d ed. (Amherst: University of Massachusetts Press, 1981), pp. 93–97.

Chinese Traditional Medicine: Temporal Order and Synchronous Events

Hans Ågren

Summary   Time has been of central concern in Chinese traditional medicine, and the use of temporal schedules can be studied in two originally different medical and intellectual traditions. One is the tradition embodied in the Inner Canon of the Yellow Lord (*Huangdi neijing*), from the first century B.C., where resonance ideas of symbolic correspondence between macrocosm and microcosm prevail. Another tradition not involved in resonance theorizing but using time sequences in analyzing the progress of acute diseases is named after its principal ancient text, the Treatise on Cold Damage Disorders (*Shanghan lun*) from the second century A.D. These medical frameworks were never fully integrated with each other, and developments in Qing China and Tokugawa Japan from the seventeenth century on can be analyzed in terms of a continuing conflict between basically irreconcilable ideas.

In Western countries, the study of East Asian medical traditions from the vantage point of the history of science has only recently begun. Eastern traditional medicine has attracted Western followers and exegetes given to uncritical praise, who depend on anecdotal evidence in support of criticism, directed primarily against modern scientific medicine. The field has been dominated by individuals biased against Western medicine. This situation contrasts with that of the other East Asian traditional fields of scientific knowledge such as botany, physics, and astronomy, which have been more carefully studied.

The dominance of nonacademic and pseudoacademic writing on Chinese medicine has had several undesirable consequences. One is the perpetuation of the idea of a monolithic medical tradition based on the philosophic theories of the *Huangdi neijing* 黃帝內經 (Inner Canon of the Yellow Lord) that had been compiled by the first century A.D. Another is a misconception that considers acupuncture to be a universally accepted Chinese treatment modality, consistently endorsed for more than two millennia. An error is also made supposing that all practitioners used similar methods of diagnosis and treatment.

This paper will attempt to delineate two streams of medical ideas in ancient China, for the most part presenting internal evidence to prove that they are more independent than has been generally surmised by Western scholars. One traditional cluster of concepts is that around the *Huangdi neijing* (hereafter abbreviated *Neijing*), largely characterized by correlative thinking (that has also been called "symbolic syncretism"), numerology, and resonance ideas. The *Neijing* represents a vast body of writings on natural philosophy, exerting an enormous influence on Chinese scientific history. The basic concepts are those that were widespread in the Han period (206 B.C. to A.D. 220), in which ideas of Confucian and Taoist origin are integrated, no longer the property of distinct schools.

The other medical tradition is the set of ideas embodied in the *Shanghan lun* 傷寒論 (Treatise on Cold Damage Disorders), which can be attributed to a historical person—Zhang Zhongjing, governor of Hunan Province in the second century A.D. In this work a more descriptive author uses other paradigms in analyzing the progress of disease.

Resonance ideas, pervasive in Chinese natural philosophy, deal with the understanding of events that appear to occur simultaneously or in synchronicity. Resonance (*ying* 應) is a key concept in that it does not support causal logical analyses but rather emphasizes recognition of analogous patterns in different settings. In archaic, pre-Han texts, *Ying* already carried the meaning of "answer," "correspond," "agree."[1] The concept of synchronicity abounds in the *Neijing* texts, but stands in contrast to the sequential analysis of stages in the progress of medical disorders described in the *Shanghan lun*, which presents a more historical way of analyzing events.

Using the different understandings of time as a scalpel in dissecting these lines of thought will produce evidence of two Chinese medical frameworks that are dissimilar but share parts of their vocabulary.

Basic Thought Patterns

Some numerological ideas attained axiomatic status and are found ubiquitously in Chinese ancient thought.[2] Concepts occur in sets of two, three, five, six, and twelve, to state the most obvious examples. "Things are produced in twos, in threes, in fives—in pairs. Hence in the heavens there are the five *zhen* [time-markers 辰: sun, moon, and stars], in earth there are the five elementary substances [*wu xing*, the Five Phases]; the body has the left [side] and the right, and everyone has his mate or double...."[3]

The things thus grouped are thought of as harmonious entities, the dynamism of which is governed by diffuse organizing principles. Various traditions have their own favorite numbers. The most basic analytical tool is the yin-yang dichotomy, into which any phenomenon naturally divisible into two parts was grouped. Almost as common has been a subgrouping of three phases each of yin and yang, which has been a convenient arrangement for divisions in threes and sixes. All events in the universe—physical or psychical—were in the synchronicity tradition interrelated, or "in phase." The reins governing the phase keeping (the "phasers" or "oscillating time waves" to borrow terms of N. Sivin)[4] were objective, nonreligious links between macrocosm and microcosm. Events out of phase with each other were held to bring calamity or disorder and might necessitate human intervention to restore harmony. Five natural substances (fire, earth, metal, water, and wood) gave their names to a system of five phase givers (*wu xing* 五行). They were often called the "Five Elements." "Five Evolutive Phases" or just "Five Phases" is, however, a more satisfactory rendering. Anything conveniently divisible in fives could be analyzed by this thought device, and a given phase in one fivefold cyclical phenomenon corresponded to or resonated with the same phase in all other fivefold phenomena if order was not disturbed.

> There is no happening that does not depend for its beginning upon something prior, to which it responds because [it belongs to the same] category, and so moves.... When the note *gong* is struck from the lute, other *gong* strings [near by] reverberate of themselves in complementary [resonance]; a case of comparable things being affected according to the classes to which they belong.[5]

The Five Phases concept forms a major part of *Neijing* theorizing, but, as will be shown later, it is conspicuously absent from other medical traditions, notably the *Shanghan lun*. Other numerological patterns in primarily nonmedical use were the Eight Diagrams (*ba gua* 八卦) used in divination, and the Ten Celestial Stems (*dian gan* 天干) and the Twelve Terrestrial Branches (*di zhi* 地支) used for cyclic calendar reckoning.

Correlative thinking is not at all unique to Chinese societies: it is extant in all premodern civilizations. What appear to be different are the symbols for connecting different frameworks of observations and speculations. The constituents of later unified theories were traced early by the Chinese themselves. In the *Neijing*, for example, a tradition is found for different geographical origins of medical subspecialties. Moxibustion is connected with the cold and dry nomad North, herbal decoction techniques with the western grassy highlands, thin needle acupuncture with the moist and rheuma-afflicted South, incisions with stone knives (coarse needle acupuncture) with the coastal West, and massage with the central plains.[6] The neatness of the analogies makes its true historical value questionable, but since the medical specialties to some extent carry different philosophical superstructures it can at least be stated that the ancient Chinese were aware of different geographical origins of their medical traditions.

In modern times, this geographical argument has been vigorously adopted by a well-known Japanese scholar and practitioner of Chinese-style medicine, Ōtsuka Keisetsu. Ōtsuka attempts to prove a Yangzi River origin for the *Shanghan lun* tradition as distinct from an origin in the northern Chinese nuclear areas along the Yellow River for the *Neijing* tradition. His main arguments are *Shanghan lun's* association with plants common in the southern areas, the fact that its compiler Zhang Zhongjing was a governor of a province south of the Yangzi, and the absence of certain theories embodied in the *Neijing*, such as the Five Phases.[7] Demarking the two medical traditions appears to be heuristically productive, in the sense that it makes the dissonances due to their forced unification understandable.

The Neijing *Tradition*

Yamada Keiji has suggested that we can find in the *Neijing* traces of three major Early Han schools of medicine that later coalesced into one *Huangdi* school which produced the *Neijing*.[8] The *Huangdi neijing* as we know it is composed of three sections—the *Su wen* 素問 (Basic Questions), the *Ling shu* 靈樞 (Divine Pivot), and the *Wu-yun liu-qi* 五運六氣 chapters (Phase Energetics; Needham's rendering is the "Cyclical Motions of the Five Elements/Phases and the Six Chhi [*qi*]"). The first section was edited by Wang Bing, a Tang scholar of the eighth century A.D., who collected the old texts, rearranged their order, rewrote sentences, and added material in a publication of 762. The formation of the second section has also been ascribed to Wang Bing. The section on Phase Energetics is the most evident later addition, and represents pure medical synchronicity theorizing as it crystallized during late Tang and Song (Sung), ca. A.D. 800–1200. Chinese excavations of graves in 1973 at Mawangtui revealed six medical texts written on silk and buried with their owner in 168 B.C. The texts represent the theoretical state-of-the-art in medicine from late third and early second centuries B.C. Yamada and Akahori argue that they are direct ancestors to certain chapters in the *Su wen*.

These texts deal with conceptions later unmistakably associated with the *Neijing* tradition: stimulation of the skin with moxibustion and acupuncture, pneuma-transmitting channels within the body, (pneuma is *qi* or *ch'i* 氣) are called *mai* 脈 or *jingluo* 經絡 (circulation tracts or meridians) and link acupuncture loci with the inner body, and a comparatively slight interest in drug treatment. Ideas of connections between a tract and one specified internal organ that later became prevalent can be seen in embryonic forms in these manuscripts, but the symmetry characterizing the later developments of pneumatic physiology was not yet reached. Tracts were often called by the part of the body close to them, for example the "shoulder" or the "tooth" tract. In adopting these tracts to the yin-yang terminology the later *Neijing* refers to them by such labels as the "Spleen Foot Greater Yin tract" and the "Small Intestines Hand Greater Yang tract", respectively. Use was now made of a double sixfold yin-yang system in naming the twelve main tracts: an upper and a lower set ("hand" and "foot" sets) of Greater yang (*tai-yang* 太陽), Smaller yang (*shao-yang* 少陽), Yang Brightness (*yang-ming* 陽明), Greater yin (*tai-yin* 太陰), Smaller yin (*shao-yin* 少陰), and Extreme yin (*que-yin* 厥陰). The full use of this sixfold system in the most intact version of the *Neijing*, the *Tai su* 太素 (Grand Basis), edited by Yang Shangshan in the early seventh century, suggests it was firmly established at some point between the Han and the Sui periods, most probably rather early.

The Five Phases concept is found everywhere in the *Neijing*-associated texts. The number five was used, for example, in tagging the main inner organs with their associated phases so that their interrelations could be understood (the liver belongs to wood, the heart to fire, the spleen to earth, the lungs to metal, and the kidneys to water). Another example of their use is that by associating five acupuncture loci distal to the knees and elbows on each of the twelve main tracts with the Five Phases, a linkage between these loci and the corresponding inner organ could be established. An important principle in classical acupuncture is the selection both of the tract connected to the disordered inner organ (the target of therapy) and of the locus on that tract linked to the same organ or the organ preceding or following it in the Five Phases cycle. However, this fivefold system did not mix well with the sixfold circulation tract system of the *Neijing* tradition, and ad hoc modifications are evident. In tract theory, one inner organ is linked with each of the twelve main tracts. The Six Entrails (i.e., secondary inner organs—small intestines, large intestines, urinary bladder, gall bladder, and the "three *jiao*") plus the five primary inner organs equal only eleven. So, the heart was in principle split into heart proper (*xin* 心) and the "heart envelope" (*xinbao* 心包; often anachronistically interpreted as "pericardium"). Fire was similarly split into Sovereign Fire and Minister Fire to make six analytical phases.

The major accretion of speculative metaphysics took place from the late Tang period on. The Phase Energetics section of the *Neijing* is largely preoccupied with a more detailed correlative system employing the Ten Heavenly Stems and the Twelve Terrestrial Branches to produce sixty phases (each denoted by a combination of two characters) used to build elaborate symmetric structures connecting the temporalities of body processes with the shifting temporalities of the body's environment. This group of ideas was one part of the "correlational studies" or "investigation of things and extension of knowledge" (*ge wu zhi zhi* 格物致知) in Song neo-Confucian philosophy, as exemplified by the influential philosopher Zhu Xi (Chu Hsi, 1131–1200).

The *Neijing* texts assert that information from each of the twelve inner organs can be gained by feeling pulses, most typically the radial pulses at both wrists. Pulse lore is found in other Chinese traditions as well, but only *Neijing* develops a system where the pulse impression is not merely a general sign of the disordered body, but is also a signal of the exact pneumatic condition of one specific organ because of an exact localization of its feel at the wrist (three fingers along the radial artery feel the pulse at two depths each: 3 fingers × 2 depths × 2 wrists = 12 possible readings). This pulse theory is perhaps the most transparent example of a resonance idea in Chinese medicine. Modern apologists often use the metaphor "resonating cords" when defending the idea.

A consequence of the preoccupation with correlations was an emphasis on the rhythmical, diurnal flow of *qi* in the tracts and its ties with other rhythmical events in the universe—the time of the day, season of the year, year cycle, and so on. Climate and weather were also knit into medical diagnosis, because no human disorder could possibly be imagined as devoid of extrapersonal components.

The Shanghan Lun *Tradition*

A phenomenalistic approach to medical disorders without major physiological speculations is evident in the *Shanghan lun*[9]. No use is made of any tract system in the recognition of signs and symptoms. The *Shanghan lun* merely knits together *status presens* with an appropriate drug combination. Symptomatological change is followed day by day during the course of a disease. The book's subject was infectious disorders with easily recognizable stages. Rather than being synchronically analyzed, the phenomena of disorder were followed longitudinally in time, and their successive manifestations made the targets for drug interventions.

Chinese medicine does not ordinarily treat a disease (*zheng* 症 or *bing* 病), but treats its type of manifestations (*zheng* 証).[10] The *Neijing* and the *Shanghan lun* share the *zheng* concept of manifestation types but the *Shanghan lun* tradition gives it a more ostentatious function. Different medical problems may have the same type of manifestation in a standard examination and thus get the same treatment. In *Shanghan lun*, the manifestation type is typically called by the very drug combination (*fang* 方) that was thought to affect it. The other typical way of identifying a manifestation type was to use four pairs of opposites, the Eight Rubrics (*ba gang* 八綱)—Outer/Inner (*biao/li* 表裏), Repletion/Depletion (*shi/xu* 實虛), Hotness/Coldness (*re/han* 熱寒), and yang/yin. Combinations of these pairs could produce at least sixteen labels. Facts that were not easily fitted into the standard frame of reference were cause for concern, as evidenced by the term *huai-bing* 壊病 or "ruined disease," an atypical presentation of symptoms arising under the surmised influence of an incorrect earlier therapy.

Theories of pathogenesis were straightforward. External pathogenic tendencies (*xie* 邪, in archaic texts denoting evil influences; Porkert's term is *heteropathy*) penetrate the body and elicit typical patterns of defense along their path to the vital inner organs. This penetration is analyzed in a highly characteristic fashion by dividing it into six stages named the Six Warps (*liu jing* 六經). *Jing* carries an original meaning of "warp threads in weaving" and the corresponding word for "weft" is *wei* 緯. *Warp* is the word used in a technical sense for *tract* in the *Nei-jing* texts (where it parallels an older word, *mai* or *mo* 脈, *channel*). In the *Shanghan lun*, however, *jing* carries no connotation of either tracts or acupuncture, a fact that has often confused unwary medical historians. The Six Warps were named by the sixfold yin-yang terminology. Thus, the march toward exhaustion and death is marked by the Greater yang stage, the Smaller yang stage, the Yang Brightness stage, the Greater yin stage, the Smaller yin stage, and finally the Extreme yin stage where death is imminent. These stages all have their characteristic presentation of signs and symptoms, and their successive analysis by a standard diagnostical procedure determines the correct therapeutic attack. The number of days elapsed since the disease's onset was sometimes used to make an even finer temporal scale. A typical passage in the *Shanghan lun* reads:

> If, in the Greater yang disease stage reaching the eighth and ninth days, the patient develops intermittent fevers and chills with much hot sensation and little chills, and if he does not vomit, is still able to void clear urine two or three times daily, is unable to perspire more than a little, and his body itches, [the manifestation type is such that] a decoction of Cinnamomum cassia twigs (*gui-zhi* 桂枝) and Ephedra herbs (*mahuang* 麻黄) in equal parts, is suitable.[11]

Moxibustion and acupuncture are not unknown in the *Shanghan lun*, but they are wholly devoid of the *Neijing*-type superstructure of pneumatic theories. These techniques are mentioned sparsely, and, at most, only the name of the locus aimed at for piercing or heating is given. Compared with the *Neijing*, the knowledge of anatomy and physiology in *Shanghan lun* is rudimentary. A corollary of this negative statement would be that the level of theoretical speculation is comparatively low. What organ is ill was a question never raised by *Shanghan lun* practitioners.

Mixing of the Frameworks

By the fourth century A.D., attempts had already been made to reconcile the two medical traditions. Wang Shuhe produced a much expanded version of the *Shanghan lun*. As a syncretist he interpreted *Shanghan lun* statements in a *Neijing* framework, furnished with both tracts and Five Phases. The incorporation proceeded in the Song period, and Phase Energetics was applied in an annotated version of the *Shanghan lun* by Cheng Wuji in 1144 (*Zhujie shanghan lun* 註解傷寒論). The different meanings of the word *jing* were disregarded. Pathological tendencies now were understood to enter the body and reach their destinations via the tracts.

This process can be looked at as bringing physiological theories into an empirically deduced clinical lore. The unification attempt was not confined to *Shanghan lun*. The materia medica (*bencao* 本草) were also metaphysically interpreted. From the Han on, the qualities of the plant, animal, and mineral drugs in common use had been increasingly analyzed in a way more or less compatible with *Neijing* physiology. This mingling of frameworks, especially in the Song period, has been discussed with regard to the materia medica by Unschuld.[12] Among classically educated and literate doctors, those pharmacologically inclined would consult the *Shanghan lun* as a therapeutic vade mecum, in the same way that acupuncturists would study the *Neijing* and associated texts.

There was, however, no lasting synthesis of the synchronicity and the phenomenological schools. In fact, in the late Ming and early Qing (Ch'ing) periods, the split became ever more visible as a result of a critical research attitude toward all classics, both Confucian and medical. In China, a major attempt to free the *Shanghan lun* from its *Neijing* garb was made by Yu Jiayan (early seventeenth century), a "traditionalist" arguing for a return to the original, pure texts. Yu worked in the spirit of the School of Evidential Research (*Kaozhengxue* 考証學), which mainly dealt with textual criticism of the Confucian classics. He wrote the *Shang lun pian* 尚論篇 (In Praise of the *Shanghan lun*) in two parts, a work that was to influence seventeenth-century Japan as a catalyst for a Japanese neo-Confucian antimysti-cist movement in medicine. The empiricist critique of correlative thought and numerolog-ical correspondences was far advanced in seventeenth-century China, as has been demon-strated by J. B. Henderson.[13]

In Tokugawa, Japan, the School of Ancient Learning (*kogakuha* 古學派) arose as a politically aware nativist intellectual endeavor, to oppose the Zhu Xi (Chu Hsi) brand of synchretistic Confucianism that was the state philosophy during the Tokugawa shogunate. In Japanese medicine, the results of this new trend was nothing short of an anti-*Neijing* iconoclasm. A series of physicians known as the *koihō* 古醫方 or *kohōka* 古方家 (Old Prescription School) displayed an increasingly intense rejection of the correlational sys-tems. Two major physicians strongly in favor of *Shanghan lun* as a basis for medical learning were Yamawaki Tōyō (1705–62) and Yoshimasu Tōdō (1702–73). They rejected Chinese metaphysics to such a degree that tracts, the Five Phases, and, in the end, even systematic ideas of the *Shanghan lun* such as yin and yang were discarded. Tōyō was one of the first Japanese to dissect a human corpse. He had had access to Dutch books on anatomy, and he wrote an anatomical picture book in 1759. Tōdō advocated a simplistic version of a unitary external and internal pathogenic influence (*doku* 毒, "poison") that affected the body much like the Chinese *xie* 邪. The task of the physician was confined to searching for the right mixtures of materia medica that could be demonstrated to benefit the patient. The *kohōka* severely lacked new heuristic theories to replace the older ones. The vacuum thus created was a factor in the rapid and active assimilation of Western medicine that gained momentum in the late eighteenth century.[14]

The parting of the two traditions in Japan over 200 years ago is still visible today. There is a competition between *kampō* practitioners (dealing with drugs; the successors of the *kohōka*), and the acupuncture and moxibustion specialists still devoted to the old *Neijing* tradition.[15]

Conclusion

An analysis of attitudes toward time within different Chinese medical traditions yields a convenient way of discriminating between the *Neijing* tradition based on correlational studies of synchronous events and the *Shanghan lun* tradition, where disease processes are observed and analyzed in a purely diachronic fashion, focusing on the dynamic change in the manifestation types of the disorder. The former school has been largely identified by Western historians as that of standard traditional Chinese medicine. Its structure can be looked at through the few general scholarly works we have in the Western languages, for example those by M. Porkert and Lu and Needham.[16] The *Shanghan lun* school has been insufficiently studied by Western historians; in contrast, in Japan, the *Shanghan lun* has long held a prestigious place, and studies of its historical role abound.[17]

Notes

1. B. Karlgren, *Grammata serica recensa*, character 890d (Stockholm University, 1964)

2. The correlational systems have been described by Joseph Needham and Wang Ling, *Science and Civilisation in China*, vol. 2, *History of Scientific Thought* (Cambridge: Cambridge University Press, 1962). See also my early paper, H. Ågren, "Empiricism and Speculation in Traditional East Asian Medicine," *Nihon i-shigaku zasshi* (*J. Japan Soc. Med. Hist.*) 23 (1977): 300–317.

3. *Zuo Chuan, Duke Zhao year* 32, *translated* in James Legge, *The Chinese Classics*, vol. 5, pt 2, p. 739.

4. Nested time cycles have been described by N. Sivin in a section on Chinese alchemical theory in Joseph Needham, Ho Ping-Yü, Lu Gwei-Djen, and Nathan Sivin *Science and civilisation in China*, vol. 5, p. 4 (1980), pp. 221–23.

5. Dong Zhong shu, *Chunqiu Fanlu* (135 B.C.), The "String of Pearls in the Spring and Autumn Annals" as translated by E. R. Hughes and excerpted in Needham, *Science and Civilisation*, 2: 282–83. The passage forms part of a chapter called "Similar Kinds Move Together."

6. In chapter 12 of *Su wen, Yi fa fang yi lun* 異法方宜論 "On Different Methods and Suitable Prescriptions." *Si bu bei yao* edition, *juan* 4, pp. 2–3.

7. The hypothesis is described in a historical background section in Ōtsuka Keisetsu, *Shōkanron kaisetsu (Explanation of the Shanghan lun)* (1974), where an early manuscript of the treatise without much trace of *Neijing*-influenced commentary is commented upon and translated (the *Kōhei shōkanron*). The idea is well put, but Ōtsuka may be involved in some foreign domestic politics: the independence of the *Shanghan lun* from other more metaphysical works plays perhaps a little too well into the hands of the Japanese *koihō* (Old Prescription School) which stresses the pristine qualities of the treatise.

8. Yamada Keiji, "The Formation of the *Huang-ti Neiching*," *Acta Asiatica* (published by The Tōhō Gakkai, Kyoto) 36 (1979): 67–89.

9. See note 7 above.

10. The concept of manifestation types is elaborated upon in H. Ågren, "A New Approach to Chinese Traditional Medicine," *Am. J. Chin. Med.* 3 (1975): 207–12, and in Ågren, "Empiricism and Speculation in Traditional East Asian Medicine." An excellent Japanese overview of the meaning of *zheng* is given by Fujihira Ken in *Tōyō igaku o saguru (In Search of Oriental Medicine)*, ed. Ōtsuka Yasuo (Tokyo: Nihon Hyōronsha, 1973), pp. 105–21.

11. From *Shanghan lun*, p. 165; text given in Ōtsuka's commentary cited in note 7.

12. P. U. Unschuld, *Pen-Ts'ao: 2000 Jahre traditionelle pharmaceutische Literatur Chinas* (Munich: Heinz Moos Verlag, 1973), p. 75 ff.

13. J. B. Henderson, *The Ordering of the Heavens and the Earth in Early Ch'ing Thought* (Ann Arbor, Mich.: University Microfilms International, 1977).

14. For a study of the advent of Western science in Japan, see G. K. Goodman, *The Dutch Impact on Japan* (1640–1853). Monographes du *T'oung Pao*, vol. 5. (Leiden: E. J. Brill, 1967).

15. The scene has been depicted in M. M. Lock, *East Asian Medicine in Urban Japan* (Berkeley: University of California Press, 1980).

16. M. Porkert, *The Theoretical Foundations of Chinese Medicine*, East Asian Science Series, ed. N. Sivin (Cambridge: M. I. T., 1974). The German version is M. Porkert, *Die theoretische Grundlagen der chinesischen Medizin*, Münchener ostasiatische Studien, vol. 5 (Wiesbaden: Franz Steiner Verlag, 1973). See also Lu Gwei-Djen and Joseph Needham, *Celestial Lancets: A History and Rationale of Acupuncture and Moxa* (Cambridge: Cambridge University Press, 1980). A review of this work is found in H. Ågren *Brit. J. Hist. Sci.* 16 (1983): 82–84.

17. A remarkable introduction and textbook of *Shanghan lun* and other pharmacological theory is offered by Chō Meichō (Zhang Mingcheng), *Chūgoku kampō igaku taikei (Outline of Chinese Traditional Medicine)* (Tokyo: Yōbunsha, 1974).

For further background on the theme of this paper, see Nathan Sivin, *Traditional Medicine in Contemporary China: A Partial Translation of* Revised Outline of Chinese Medicine, *with an Introductory Study on Change in Contemporary and Early Medicine*, Science, Medicine and Technology in East Asia Series, no. 2 (Ann Arbor: Center for Chinese Studies, 1986).

Zi Wu Flow Theory and Time

Lo Huisheng

Introduction To interpret observations and to coordinate knowledge, the Chinese employed numerological methods of classification.* Since very early times, certain numerals have been used to distinguish among concepts. The most commonly used numbers were two (yin-yang, originally the shadowy and sunny side of a hill); five (for the Five Elements or Phases: fire, earth, metal, water, wood); ten (for the Ten Heavenly Stems) and twelve (for the Twelve Earthly Branches). A combination of the last two constituted the basis of classification in the *Zi Wu* theory.

These modes of classifying and coordinating data also served to unite in resonance otherwise distinct systems, such as a macroscopic and a microscopic variable.

All things in nature, including man and morality, were held to follow identical resonant behavior, provided they were in phase. Events out of phase were judged pathological and in need of therapeutic intervention.

Summary The *Zi Wu* Flow Theory is a basic theory in Chinese traditional medicine, stating that many physiological and pathological processes and medical diagnosis and treatments depend on the periodical time change of the seasons and of the day. The variables in focus are periodical functions of time. *Zi Wu* Flow Theory was profoundly influenced by ancient Chinese natural philosophy. This paper deals mainly with the close relationships between time change and all these philosophical bases.

Zi Wu Flow Theory (*zi wu liu zhu* 子午流注) is a fundamental theory in Chinese traditional medicine. It gradually developed into a strict theoretical system and was based on long medical practice. The theory originated in the medical classic *Huangdi neijing* 黃帝內經 (Inner Canon of the Yellow Lord) and was further developed in other classical works, especially in the *Nan jing* 難經 (Canon of [Medical] Problems), the *Shanghan lun* 傷寒論 (Treatise on Cold Damage Disorders), the *Lei jing* 類經 (The Classified Canon), and the *Zhenjiu jiayi jing* 針灸甲乙經 (The ABC Classic of Acupuncture and Moxibustion).

The *Zi Wu* Flow Theory is part of Chinese classical natural philosophy and is flashed with dialectical light. Thus, it is not only of great medical value, but has also a far-reaching philosophical implication. In this paper, I will deal with the close relations between time change and the Flow Theory from a philosophical view point and pay special attention to the relations between time change and the ontological, epistemological, methodological, and technological bases of this theory.

* The author and the editors wish to express their appreciation to Hans Ågren, M. D. for editing this paper.

Time Change and the Ontological Basis of Zi Wu *Flow Theory*

What is this Flow Theory? An English translation of *zi wu* might be rendered "midnight-noon ebb-flow." *Zi* means midnight, *wu* is midday; *zi wu* is the whole cycle of the day. In an extended sense, *zi wu* means the different kinds of cycles or periodicities in various natural phenomena. The theory teaches that many biological functions in health and disease, medical diagnosis and treatments often depend on the time changes of the seasons, the day, and other periodical natural phenomena. The variables focused upon are periodical functions of time.

Flow (*liu zhu*) means that Qi-Blood (氣, the *qi* "pneuma," and the accompanying blood "pneuma") flows periodically through the Five Parenchymatous Organs/Viscera (*wu zang* 五臟), the Six Hollow Organs/Viscera (*liu fu* 六腑), the channels, tracts, or meridians, and the acupuncture points (*shuxue* 俞穴, or just *xue* 穴).

The Flow Theory was deeply influenced by ancient Chinese natural philosophy, especially by such philosophical doctrines as the Essences and Vital Energy Theory, yin-yang theory, and the Five Phases Theory. The first of these theories deals with the Essences and Vital Energy (*jing qi* 精氣), i.e., the "essential materials and functions of life." Qi is the original source of all things, divided in three parts, Heaven Qi, Earth Qi and *jing* Qi; the last is the "essence of all Qi" 精也者, 氣之精者也.

Essence Qi theory teaches that *jing Qi* was the origin and source of the human body and its physiological functions. "Man was born with Heaven Qi and Earth Qi" (passage from the *Neijing*). Qi and blood pneuma always flow together through the body and the pair is referred to as one unit, "Qi-Blood." However, "Qi is the commander of blood". Qi-Blood performs functions of nourishing and adjusting, and it waxes and wanes in conjunction with the time change.

Yin-yang theory is a basic principle of Chinese natural philosophy. It was used to explain medical phenomena and served as a general program controlling all physiological and pathological processes and directing medical diagnosis and treatment. All things have a yin aspect and a yang aspect, contradicting each other and uniting with each other. There are some basic features shared by yin and yang: the interdependence between them, their growth and decline, and their transformation into each other: from yin to yang and from yang to yin. All things exert a basic periodical change that may further develop into many complex periodical changes.

Yin-yang theory may represent not only many things at the same level, but also at different levels. For example, day as yang and night as yin form a yin-yang system at the first level. But, there is a "yin component within yang." A day time may thus be divided into two parts: A.M. is yang and P.M. is yin.

The Five Phases Theory (*wu xing* 五行) deals mainly with the dialectical relations of "intergeneration" (*xiang sheng* 相生) and "interrestriction" (*xiang ke* 相克) between two systems, in contrast to the yin-yang theory, which deals with the unity of opposites in one system. Originally, the Five Phases had referred to metal, wood, water, fire, and earth in nature. Later, they came to catch broad meanings of five kinds of matters and functions, analogous in certain aspects with the original Five Phases. For instance, the seasons may be distinguished by the Five Phases: spring, summer, long-summer, autumn, and winter.

The Five Phases concept has been applied in the classification of structures and functions in the human body. Liver, heart, spleen, lungs, and kidneys constitute one central set of Five Phases; there are other sets of Five Phases around it, for example, eyes/tongue/ mouth/nose/ears, anger/happiness/thoughtfulness/worriedness/terror. All these bodily sets are analogous to the original Five Phases in their basic features. The basic features of water are coldness, downward motion, moistness, contraction; that of fire are heat, dryness, upward motion, meltability, and so on. Thus, in Chinese medicine, winter, cold, north, kidneys, and the bladder belong to water, and summer, heat, south, and the heart belong to fire.

The Five Phases theory deals with the general expression of unity of opposites between two systems in terms of intergeneration, interrestriction, interinvasion, and interinsult.

INTERGENERATION RELATIONS   This is a pattern of relations promoting each other in a fixed sequence: wood generates fire, fire generates earth, earth generates metal, metal generates water, water generates wood, all to form a cycle. By analogy, liver generates heart, which generates spleen, which generates lungs, which generates kidneys, which generates liver to form a periodical time change in biological processes in health and disease. Each phase in this sequence has a passive and active form: "generate me" (*sheng wo* 生我) and "I generate" (*wo sheng* 我生).

INTERRESTRICTION RELATIONS   Parts of the human body restrain and limit each other, in order to maintain or restore physiological equilibrium. Once this dynamic balance is disturbed or destroyed, the individual might fall ill. Also this relation has a fixed sequence: metal restricts wood, wood restricts earth, earth restricts water, water restricts fire, and fire restricts metal. They form a periodical time change of causal relations. By analogy, the lungs restrict the liver, which restricts the spleen, which restricts the kidneys, which restricts the heart, which restricts the lungs.

Intergeneration and interrestriction are different systems, interacting with and overlapping each other. Wood restricts earth, earth generates metal, metal restricts wood. This overlap is named "coordination of restriction and generation" (*zhi hua* 制化).

INTERINVASION AND INTERINSULT RELATIONS   While the above relations refer to the normal states of the human body, these refer to abnormal states. Interinvasion means that one phase excessively inhibits other phases beyond its normal extent, thus becoming a disturbance of the normal harmony. Interinsult means the reversal of interrestriction: on (*fan ke* 反克). In the normal situation, water restricts fire, but in an abnormal condition fire may, reversely, restrict water.

Time Change and the Epistemological Basis of Zi Wu *Flow Theory*

From an epistemological view, *Zi Wu* Flow Theory pays special attention to philosophical analogy and speculation. It stresses rational analyses aided by this theory. At the same time, Flow Theory emphasizes medical practice and empirical confirmation. It can be said that Flow Theory is usually based on a combination of rationality and perception. This combination is expressed mainly in the Heaven-Man Correspondence Theory (*tian ren hsiang ying* 天人相應).

The Ancients had observed that things change periodically. The yearly, monthly, and daily changes entail periodical time changes of light, temperature, and climate. In order to

fit these environmental time changes together, man gradually formed concepts of periodical changes in the spheres of physiology, pathology, diagnosis, and treatment in coordination with nature. This is the meaning of the Correspondence Theory. "Heaven" means
"nature."

By analogy with the yearly changes in climate, the Qi-Blood flows with different
strengths during different months. The peak of this flow is transferred into different inner
organs during different months. "In January and February, man's Qi is in the Liver. In
March and April, Man's Qi is in the Spleen" (*Neijing, Su wen* section).

In response to seasonal climate changes, Qi-Blood flows outward to the muscles and
shows as sweat in the summer; it flows inward to the organs in the winter. The depth varies.

During the day-night cycle, the strength of Qi-Blood rises and falls, along with the
periodical change of temperature and light. "Man's Qi is born in the morning, it is
strongest at midday, then it weakens at sunset" (*Neijing, Su wen* section).

The Heaven-Man Correspondence Theory has an epistemological basis. It has been
embodied in another theory, "The Five Phases Motions and Six Kinds of Atmospheric
Influences" (*Wu-yun liu-qi* 五運六氣; also rendered as Phase Energetics). The motion of
the Five Phases implies the periodically changing function of various organ systems
following the Five Phases sequence. The six kinds of atmospheric influences denote wind,
cold, summer-heat, wetness, dryness, and fire. The theory concretely emphasizes the
causal relations between the changes in climate and the functioning of the human body.

Time Change and the Methodological Basis of Zi Wu *Flow Theory*

In matters of methodology, *Zi Wu* Flow Theory stresses the deductive method, especially
deduction from ancient natural philosophy about the structures and functions of the
human body. This brings philosophical color into Chinese traditional medicine. But Flow
Theory also pays attention to the inductive method and stresses the importance of summing up medical experience. Furthermore, the theory manages to use a method of metaphors and combines it with both deductive and inductive methods. This methodological
combination shows itself mainly in the analytical methods of the flow model.

Zi Wu Flow Theory teaches that the rise and fall of Qi-Blood in the human body is
analogous to the flow of water and offers a flow model called "*Jing* (well), *ying* (spring), *shu*
(stream), *jing* (river), and *he* (sea) 井、滎、俞、經、合." Qi-Blood flows from weak to strong
just like water flows. *Jing* means that Qi-Blood begins to flow as if from a headwater of a
river. *Ying* stands for a continuation of Qi-Blood flowing slowly like the springs at the
upper part of a river. *Shu* is the convening of many springs into a stream. *Jing* signifies the
more rapid flow of Qi-Blood when, like a large river, it flows swiftly. *He* means that Qi-
Blood flows strongly as when many rivers flow together and enter the sea. Qi-Blood then
flows from the strong to the weak, thus accomplishing a whole cycle.

This ebb and flow of Qi-Blood occurs throughout the human body at different strengths
depending on the season. "Spring Qi lies in *jing mai* 經脉 [channels, tracts], Summer Qi lies
in *sun luo* 孫絡 [capillary channels], Long-Summer Qi lies in muscles, Autumn Qi lies in
skin, and Winter Qi lies in the bones" (*Neijing, Su wen* section).

Qi-Blood flows throughout the body in a cycle of twelve double hours. Qi-Blood flow
reaches its peak strength at various double hours depending on the channel-tract.

According to these periodical time changes it is possible to judge whether Qi-Blood flows normally or abnormally at a certain time. If the flow is abnormal, it is possible either to deduce that inner organs are disordered by some illness and determine when and where acupuncture points should be selected or to determine when the patient should take drugs orally. The diagnosis and treatment of Diarrhea Before Dawn (*wu geng xie* 五更瀉) is one typical example.

It should be noted that *Zi Wu* Flow Theory applied primitive versions of systems theory, cybernetics, and message theory. It emphasizes the important functions of periodical time changes in the process of systems relations, dynamic equilibrium, and message transformations. Flow Theory holds that we should study the human body as a whole, in the view of holism (zhengtilun 整體論), which is analogous to systems theory. *Zi Wu* Flow Theory considered the human body as a large system, and, for example, the Five Parenchymatous Organs/Viscera, the Six Hollow Organs/Viscera, the Five Senses and Twelve Channels (*jingluo* 經絡 —the tracts) are all subsystems subjected to the control and adjustment of the larger system. Different subsystems relate closely to each other by the ideas of intergeneration and interrestriction. Generally, the former is a pattern of negative feedback. There are various periodical relations, either between the human body and systems in the environment, or among different subsystems.

Flow Theory, also, applied a primitive version of cybernetics in stressing a dynamic equilibrium. Once this state is destroyed one could become afflicted with diseases. Medical treatment must then eliminate unbalanced elements in order to restore equilibrium. Flow Theory used a primitive "black box" method of analysis. It held that we should investigate, adjust, and improve the interparts of the human body mainly by a comparative study of the input messages (such as climate changes) and output messages (such as facial color, pulse manifestations) without destroying the body as a whole.

The theory also managed to use a comprehensive analytical method of messages. In the Four Means of Diagnosis (inspection, auscultation, interrogation, and pulse palpation) the theory refuses to make any diagnosis based on only a few isolated messages, but instead collects all the relevant messages, especially periodical messages of time changes and physiological and pathological changes in order to arrive at a correct conclusion.

Time Change and the Technological Basis of Zi Wu *Flow Theory*

In a narrow sense, Flow Theory provides a technological basis for acupuncture treatment. It tells about when and where to select acupuncture points for a given disease.

This technological basis resides in the Sixty-Six (Special) Points (sixty-six *shuxue* or *xue*). Why sixty-six? Each of the Five Parenchymatous Organs/Viscera and each of the Six Hollow Organs/Viscera has distinctive *xue*, totaling sixty-six. These *xue* are points along the channels (tracts) with a special sensitivity to physiological and pathological changes in certain parts of the body. Among the *xue*, periodical relations of intergeneration and interrestriction prevail.

These dialectical structures and periodical functions have important meanings in acupuncture treatment and diagnosis. First, Qi-Blood flows through the sixty-six *xue* rising and falling in strength, peaking in different organs at different times. When the strength of Qi-Blood flow is about to peak in a given *xue* this point can be stimulated by using a needle at that very moment, ensuring a positive clinical effect.

Second, each *xue* has a specific relation with given organs. Pain at a certain *xue* means that the organ related to this point is ill; one should then ascertain whether the Qi-Blood flow is at a peak or a trough at that moment. After deciding whether the disease of the organ in question is hot or cold (*rezheng* 熱症 or *hanzheng* 寒症), an appropriate treatment is selected.

Flow Theory also provides a technological basis for drug treatment. According to the periodicities of the inner organs and the channels, some drugs should be taken orally in fixed time schedules to achieve a positive effect. Some drugs must be taken shortly after the first manifestation of the disease in order to prevent its further progress. For example, acute heart failure due to high blood pressure often develops at midnight. If the patient takes a suitable drug (especially a drug that dilates blood vessels) just before midnight, then this illness can often be prevented. Those stricken by wind (*zhongfeng* 中風,—stroke or apoplexy) due to high blood pressure often fall ill between the end of August and the beginning of winter. If the patient takes some drug directed at tonifying Yin (*yang yin yao* 養陰藥) during this period, then this affliction also can be prevented with a high rate of success.

Flow Theory and Modern Time Medicine

The Flow Theory was based on primitive dialectical thought, paying special attention to the temporal element in medical phenomena. It has a degree of heuristic significance for Western medicine, which itself has been deeply influenced by metaphysical views. But Flow Theory lacks the elements of scientific experiment and strict logical reasoning and possesses some fallacies and errors. Western medicine may contribute greatly in proving many points and in disproving or falsifying some other views of this theory.

Time in Archaeological Thought: China and the West

Synnøve Vinsrygg

Summary   This comparative study questions some of the basic ideas and values that were present at archaeology's birth, and examines some of the social conditions under which it could sprout. Archaeology developed independently in two parts of the world, in China and in northern Europe. In spite of an impressive and propitious head start, Chinese archaeology proved rather stagnant till the new impetus through confluence with European traditions came after 1920. The main focus of the paper is archaeology in Sung China as compared to its European counterpart in the eighteenth and nineteenth centuries. The discussion is centered on the following ideas, considered crucial in relation to the concept of time: the three-age system, evolutionism, time depth, the experimental method, and archaeology and society.

The similarities between Chinese and European archaeology are actually more striking than the differences. The Chinese were well aware that human affairs could follow a linear, irreversible pattern, but the reliable predictability intrinsic to change, perceived as cyclic, proved equally important for making sense of archaeological data. In Europe the importance given to the linear, progressive time concept, combined with the theory of causality, created a reductionist approach that prepared the way for Western experimental method, so decisive for advances in modern archaeology. Archaeology also profited from its close links with geology, zoology, and other sciences.

Different uses of the concept of time may account for the Chinese readiness to bridge the time gap between people of different epochs, whereas the Europeans concentrated on exposing the same time gap to the gaze of research.

Introduction

As far back as we can see in the evolving story of human communities, people have formulated ideas of the past to explain how they became what they considered themselves to be, thus finding justification for their present and their future. This, I believe, is the worldwide beginning of archaeology, as it is of history. These ideas came to be structured in different manners, constituting important elements in myth and religion, following long and winding paths, before entering what we today call modern history and archaeology.

Archaeology developed independently in two parts of the world, in China and in northern Europe. An examination of the series of events that led to the creation of archaeology in China ought to be relevant to Western interests, not only because such study offers historical information from a remarkable country, but also because it involves a topic of the broadest intellectual concern when it comes to questioning the basic ideas and values that presided at the discipline's birth. What we find puts our methods of dealing with the

European past under criticism. It creates perspectives of a new kind, and serves as a background against which to judge and seek a deeper understanding of the European achievements themselves.

No single idea will explain the creation of a discipline like archaeology. However, some concepts present themselves as useful polarizers for the sifting and sorting of a broad spectrum of evidence. The idea of differing views about the nature of time will serve as my polarizer for examining the development and use of archaeology in China and the West, before the two traditions intermingled. No one will deny time's ubiquitous position within this historical discipline. A perception of time, of the past and the present, as well as the relation between them, lies at the root of archaeological knowledge.

The twentieth century saw the confluence of foreign and traditional theories, methods, and techniques in China. Archaeology appears to have been a popular subject in China, developing at a comparatively steady rate, little influenced by changes on the political scene. The achievements within this field have been enormous, especially after 1949, and are well known in the West. Traditional Chinese archaeology is, on the other hand, less known in the West. The most widely employed histories of the discipline pay little or no attention to the indigenous development of archaeology in China. As far as I can ascertain, comprehensive comparative analyses of Chinese and Western archaeological thought at their formative stages do not exist. It must be made clear at the outset that I do not read Chinese, an unfortunate fact that influences and limits my choice of evidence.

As a background for the discussion, I will present short sketches of the state of archaeology in China and in Europe. Important stages of development suitable for comparative studies are chosen regardless of chronological time. For the sake of limiting the discussion, attention throughout will mainly concentrate on archaeology in Sung China (960–1276) and on the eighteenth and nineteenth centuries' development in northern Europe. These periods seem for several reasons most suitable for comparing and contrasting. It could be argued that juxtaposing European archaeological development from the Renaissance to 1850 with Chinese archaeology during the Sung Dynasty, might also reveal interesting similarities in a number of aspects. In my opinion, however, this would conceal some important points concerning the understanding of time in East and West. Through the presentation of my paper I hope to justify this claim. Sung archaeology appears to represent a stage of development that was not surpassed till the Western influence made itself felt.

The discussion will mainly focus on the following ideas judged crucial for the discipline's development: the three-age system, evolutionism, time depth, the experimental method, and archaeology and society.

Archaeology in Sung China

Culturally and scientifically, the eleventh and twelfth centuries belong to one of the most active periods China has ever experienced. Archaeological advancement was just one of a long series of scientific achievements. Its state during the Sung period has been described by Colin Ronan and Joseph Needham as a subject that, at the time, "had risen to a thoroughly scientific level" (1978, 214). We shall inquire into the background of this claim.

The eleventh century witnessed the work of the polymath Shen Kua (1031–95), described by Needham as "one of the greatest scientific minds in Chinese history" (1969, 27). In his Meng ch'i pi t'an, or "Brush Talks from the Dream Brook" (from around 1090), Shen Kua presents his ideas on archaeology, a work to be considered as a supplementary outcome of his wide and erudite achievements. Shen Kua's opinions on archaeology have reached me only in summary form, as interpreted by Xia Nai (1979, 139–41). Their texture and scope, however, are so impressive that they may well serve as a good example of the state of archaeological knowledge before its confluence with European practice.

According to Xia Nai, Shen Kua saw social and moral potential in his ideas about archaeology. Their content may be ordered in five major themes.

First, the social function of archaeology was to serve the progressive political line of the time. In this way it might promote production and influence development of armaments. Shen Kua did not approve of using archaeology for providing concrete data for the restoration of ancient rituals (as advocated by some neo-Confucians at the time), or for satisfying the curiosity of the leisured gentry of the feudal ruling class.

Second, archaeology actualized the tension between materialism and idealism. Material evidence had to be fundamental to archaeological knowledge. Ancient relics only could be reliable. Shen Kua criticized the erroneous reconstructions of ancient ritual objects based on sheer imagination, and emphasized that empirical evidence alone could give safe knowledge.

The third point is somewhat related to the first. Shen Kua found much to admire in things produced in the past, and he objected to attributing them to the ancient "sages" or the ruling classes. Rather, they should be judged as honoring their actual creators, the working people.

The fourth theme concerned the use of archaeological relics and their interpretation. He accused the Confucian archaeologists of the Sung Dynasty of concentrating mainly on superficial descriptions of antiques, being content with naming the objects on the basis of Confucian classics, with a view to restoring ancient rituals. Shen Kua, in contrast, had a functionalist approach. He considered archaeological material as objects of daily use, and was concerned mainly with questions of their manufacture and function. This kind of interpretive study could only be carried out on the basis of empirical specimens. While holding the post as Director of Astronomy, Shen Kua rebuilt an armillary sphere, having made detailed studies of ancient ones, on the basis of extant specimens as well as on documentary evidence. He also studied ancient weaponry. He described the method of using the scaled sights of ancient cross-bow mechanisms, and praised the strength of old swords that had composite blades (formed by a strong midrib of wrought iron and low-carbon steel) and two sharp edges of high-carbon steel. He also experimented with old bronze mirrors. He sought to explain the relation between the curvature of the reflecting faces of mirrors and the size of the image, by optical principles. An outstanding musician himself, Shen Kua also suggested a likely method of hanging an ancient bell with hollowed handle.

His fifth point reflects his insight into a broad field of scientific knowledge. He advocated the use of an interdisciplinary approach to archaeology and practiced such an approach himself through his work in metallurgy, optics, and geometry in the study of ancient measures. Even more remarkable, he embarked upon paleogeomorphological and paleoclimatological studies.

His views of archaeology were those of an outstanding Sung scientist, who based his views on studies of material objects as well as books (Sivin 1975, 383). To a Westerner, they appear strikingly modern.

We shall next turn to the questions: how did archaeology function in the society, how was it organized, and what can we deduce from this situation concerning its "usefulness"?

A collection of antique objects existed in the imperial treasury at the beginning of the Sung period. The fashion of collecting antiques, however, was much older, and was begun by private individuals. The decades preceding Shen Kua had already witnessed an emerging growth of archaeological activity (ibid., 382). With the accession of Huizong (at the beginning of the twelfth century), the imperial collection was enlarged and developed in a systematic manner (Wang Kuo-Wei 1927, 223). Huizong looked toward the past for guidance in handling the problems of his reign. This may be one of the reasons why he gave orders that old objects and illustrations should be collected, stored, and studied. The result was the establishment of an archaeological museum, probably the first of its kind in the world.

The objects treasured the most were things considered to be from great antiquity. It was preferred that they be older than the Qin Dynasty (i.e., c. 220 B.C.). When younger objects were included, a value other than their age had to be demonstrated.

Gathering information about the antiques was another important task for Sung scholars. They achieved such skill at this that much of their typology is still valid. The theoretical basis for their typology is, however, difficult to trace. Treatises on special types of antiques in museums were produced. Although few of the antiques collected in the Sung museums remain extant, contemporary records of the material enable us to picture and form an opinion of the original collections.

During the eleventh and twelfth centuries, branches considered as support disciplines for archaeology were budding. They included the study of inscriptions (epigraphy) and the study of family names (a book on the topic appeared in 1134), along with numismatic studies. In this latter field Emperor Huizong himself produced a book called *Quan Zhi* (Treatise on Coinage) (Ronan and Needham 1978, 214).

The purpose of establishing a museum must have been manyfold. The paramount idea that the past should serve the present and hence guide the plans for the future reflects the fundamental Chinese view of knowledge of the past. Material objects from the past were, in other words, a repository of experience. Although the study of material remains gave evidence of a general search for knowledge, the aesthetic purpose, the value of appreciation, should not be underestimated.

In accordance with these views, the antiques were taken to be of wide public interest. Part of the museum's purpose was to produce practical knowledge, the results of which would be made available among contemporaries and be transmitted to posterity. The most important means for reaching these ends turned out to be rubbings, copies, and descriptions, and techniques for making them were meticulously developed. The chief ministers, for instance, would get those rubbings that were considered important in their decision making. Objects of special interest could be deposited outside the museum. In the eleventh century it was decreed that some archaic bells and tripods of the Three Dynasties, kept in Bi Ke and Tai Chang Halls, must be turned over to the Bureau of Music for study, comparison, measurement, and weighing (Wang Kuo-Wei 1927, 226). When new sacrificial vessels for important temples were needed, antiques in the museums were used as models.

Rubbings and copies of important objects were circulated throughout the country, a fact proving the high esteem such objects were held in. The procedure of collecting data was to a certain degree part of a marketing system. The imperial court employed experts to visit markets, curio dealers, and farmers, in order to secure the best specimens. Bi Liangshi became a favorite of the Court because he was skilled in buying and selling examples of calligraphy, paintings, and other antiques (ibid., 225).

Archaeological remains in the physical environment, such as graves, seem to have been judged worthy of preservation at an early date. In the law codex, T'ang-lu-Shu-i, from the T'ang Dynasty, grave robbery is frequently mentioned, and the penalty for disturbing old graves was quite severe. More than likely these decrees can be ascribed to religious feelings rather than to modern ideas of preservation. In this codex, rules also exist for the right of property of antiques discovered by chance. The rules show that even in those days antiques were regarded as potential state property (Franke 1982, 75–76). However, I have no information as to what extent these laws were enforced under the Sung emperors.

The attitudes toward the past that dominated the Sung period created an intellectual climate under which archaeology could thrive. Sung scholars generally shared the view of Sima Qian who held that the study of any single dynasty failed to promote a full understanding of the past. The ideal history was a comprehensive one from the earliest times (Meskill 1965, viii). Zeng Qiao (1108–66) was a historian who, in *Tong Zhi*, his history of the entire past of China, sees the past as a continuous stream of "meeting and joining" and agrees that the single dynasty view is a hindrance to the sense of that continuity (Wright 1965, 5). It is worth noting that there was no such term as *prehistory* in ancient Chinese literature. The Jinshixue (the study of ancient bronzes and stones) was more or less parallel to history and legendary history (Chêng Tê-K'un 1959, xvi). However, the currently used term for archaeology, *K'ao ku*, "investigation of the past," is recorded as early as the tenth century (Franke 1982, 69).

The Dawn of European Archaeology

In Europe there is not a similar early stage of archaeological reasoning and practice. The beginnings of European archaeology can be seen in an interest in material remains found in the Mediterranean areas as a part of rediscovering antiquity. But this study did not concentrate on objects found in the earth or on their chronology and cultural setting at large. It can therefore hardly be regarded as decisive for the development of modern archaeology.

Private collections had long traditions in this part of the world as well, and served as important forerunners for the archaeological museums. Among the most avid collectors were several clergymen. Antiquarian routines developed gradually in northern Europe during the seventeenth and eighteenth centuries, to a large degree due to private initiative. But the main impulse and growth of archaeology came as a corollary of the scientific inquiry and national feeling emerging in modern Europe.

The actual birth of the discipline in the West did not take place till the second half of the nineteenth century, according to commonly held views. Until 1840 a group of intellectuals in Scandinavia represented an isolated avant-garde. After that time, the development of archaeology was remarkably rapid in many countries in Europe (Daniel 1975). During the nineteenth century archaeology developed along two lines mutually influencing each other.

The first was early Stone Age research. Later designated as Paleolithic study, it was concerned with the oldest remains from man's past. From its beginning it was aligned with the natural sciences, and advances in geology were crucial. This research began primarily in England and France. The archaeologists faced great challenges when trying to convince scientists from other disciplines, the clergy, and the public at large that the remains found in geological strata were products of early human activities. The results of their work were not fully accepted by scientific circles until 1850–60. Due to its association with geology, it followed the forward flow of time that was documented by the fossil record.

The second archaeological line directed its interest to the more recent past, keeping in close contact with history. Particular, known civilizations or events were traced for their antecedents, origins, and development. It aimed, with a humanistic approach, at pushing back the frontiers of history, and found in the newly developed archaeological methods valuable means for this end. The ways of attacking problems were often from historic times backward.

The interplay between the two lines stimulated discussions, and promoted advances in methods as well as in theories. Other crucial factors for formulating and elaborating ideas of cultural evolution were the worldwide accounts from travelers, missionaries, traders, and, eventually, anthropologists and ethnologists. They showed Europe that man's way of living in the contemporary world revealed aspects exceeding the bounds described and recorded by history. Antiquarian routines for structuring and arranging archaeological data were revised in accord with this improved cultural understanding. The collections of empirical data, accumulated in museums, formed the background against which consciously planned fieldwork was then carried out.

In the West the use of fieldwork came to mark archaeology so strongly that the future of its character was said to have laid with the spade. Man's early tools were recognized as the creations of mankind, as remains of human society. The way material objects were combined in the same geological layer was judged a valuable source for interpreting the early history of man, among other things, by proving man's contemporaneity with extinct animals. The new geology gave stratigraphy and relative chronology great importance as an axis around which data were arranged and explained in relation to the theory of cause and effect. Man's remote past was acknowledged and the technological three-age system became an organizing tool that soon resulted in further subdivisions. The biblical chronology was defeated. Nature, not the Bible, offered the clues for studying man's past. Man and his work were brought firmly within the scope of the natural order.

In Sung China, as mentioned previously, antiques were put to a wide variety of uses in the contemporary society. Copies and rubbings made possible a wide distribution to different individuals and institutions. In Europe the direct value of archaeology was not easily recognized in a similar manner. Within academic circles, however, archaeology made an important contribution to strengthening the evolutionary ideas, about to form a new worldview. For geology, as for zoology, archaeology proved a cooperator, supplying support for Darwinian evolutionism. One of the important contributors to early archaeology in Scandinavia was in fact a professor of zoology, Sven Nilsson.

The half century from 1850 to 1900 saw the beginning of systematic archaeological techniques of excavation and protection (Daniel 1975, 152). This necessarily led archaeology into broad contact with numerous related disciplines, promoting its interdisciplinary character.

In Scandinavia, archaeology's democratic bent became obvious at an early date. Antiques had, for a long time, been kept in several wide-ranging collections. In 1807 a state museum for antiques was established in Denmark, after the Danish government had set up a Royal Committee for Preservation and Collection of National Antiques. This committee was charged to "form a National Museum of antiques, to see to the preservation of ancient and historical monuments, and to make known to the general public the importance and value of the antiques" (ibid., 39). An important reason for this idea of diffusion of knowledge to the public was that archaeological monuments were dependent, in part upon the attitude of the farmers who owned the land where they were situated. In Scandinavia, few remains from known civilizations existed. The Romans, for instance, never invaded these northern shores. The discovery of a hitherto unknown past was, accordingly, valuable for securing a national identity, an important task in the political climate of the time. Decrees securing the purchasing rights of the state were proclaimed early in Scandinavia (Klindt-Jensen 1975, 48–49).

The British Museum opened to the public in 1759, but not until years later did the Department of Antiques and Art come into existence. At the beginning this department contained mainly antiques from abroad. Visiting the collections was no easy task in those early days. The person wanting to pay a visit would have to apply for permission. If accepted, a limited visit was allowed, weeks later. An assistant at this department, someone named Vaux, published a handbook in 1851 to provide "some instructions with an hour's passing amusement among numerous and valuable collections of the British Museum" (Daniel 1975, 82). This amusement, however, obviously kindled people's interest. Sir John Lubbock published his *Pre-Historic Times*, based on the three-age system, in 1865. It became very popular and went into seven editions before 1913.

Comparison of the Two Archaeologies

The similarities to be found between the archaeologies of China and the West are more striking than the differences, considering that, more than likely, they developed independently. Some of the topics in which the idea of time seems deeply embedded shall be commented upon.

All preoccupation with archaeological remains is built upon the crucial idea that the link and the relationship between material and nonmaterial parts of a culture is systematic rather than coincidental. Both China and the West accepted this as an axiomatic starting point, and by no means an unimportant one. The "laws" of this relationship are still unsolved but without them, archaeology could not claim that its aim was to reveal human culture in the past.

The Three-Age System

What archaeologists call the three-age system involves the technological stages—the stone age, the bronze age, and the iron age—developing as consecutive stages. One of Europe's authorities on the history of archaeology, Glyn Daniel, expresses his opinion on this idea as follows: "the formulation of the three-age system . . . was without doubt mainly responsible for the nineteenth-century development of prehistory" (1975, 54). On these grounds, it is well worth inquiring about its character in Europe, and then trying to trace its counterpart in China.

The theory of the three technological stages from which archaeology in Europe sprouted is usually attributed to a Dane, C. J. Thomsen. It came about as a result of his organizing of the collections and exhibitions in the Danish National Museum. The principle was established already in 1818, and afterward used for practical purposes in arranging the antiques. It became available in writing through a guidebook in 1836 (with its original title, *Ledetraad til Nordisk Oldkyndighed* [Guideline for understanding the distant Norse past]). Before 1850 it was translated into German and English.

The three-age system was by no means an original idea. It was a very old one and had many close relatives. Very different cultural groups and individuals had developed similar thoughts. Hesiod wrote of the idea of successive ages during the eighth century B.C., but to him the Golden Age lay in the past, and the forward movement of history was regression rather than progress. Lucretius's *De Rerum Natura*, part 5, dating from the first century B.C., is a commonly quoted source on the stone-, bronze-, and iron-age sequence. In Norse literature, also from the Middle Ages, the past is characterized through ages. These may have been prompted by observation of archaeological remains, for they are named after differing burial forms.

Characteristic of the idea of ages in later European history is its gradual combination with the idea of progress, an idea that has been described as based on an *act of faith* (Bury 1920, 5). The notion of progress—where the present is better than the past, and the future is potentially better than the present—is built upon a belief in the perfectability of man and society. It seems to have its origin in Christian tradition. Gradually it gained ground in northern Europe in the seventeenth, eighteenth, and nineteenth centuries. Acquaintance with very different cultures all over the world during this time made the question of cultural stages and progress a hotly debated topic.

The theory of the three ages also existed in China at an early date. Here, as in Europe, it depended upon an idea of linear time. Writings attributed to Yuan Kang, a scholar of the late Han Dynasty, give a clear and well-reasoned account of the technological stages through which man had passed. This source was finished around the year 52.

> The prince of Ch'u asked: How is it I wonder, that iron swords can have the wonderful powers of the famous swords of old? Fang Hu Tzŭ replied: Well, every age has had its special ways of making things. In the times of Hsien Yüan, Shên Nung, and Ho Hsu, weapons were made of stone, and stone was buried with the dead. Such were the directions of the sages. Coming down to the time of Huang Ti, weapons were made of jade, and it was used also for other purposes such as digging the earth, and also buried with the dead. Such were the directions of the ancient sage kings. Then when Yü the Great was digging dykes and managing the waters, weapons were made of bronze; with tools of bronze the Ch'üeh defile was cut open and the Lung-mên gate pierced through. The Yangtze was lead and the yellow river guided, until it poured into the Eastern Sea. Thus, there was a communication everywhere and the whole Empire was at peace. Bronze tools were also used for building houses and palaces. Surely all this was a most sagely accomplishment. Now in our time iron is used for weapons, so that each of the three armies had to submit, and indeed throughout the world there was none who dared to withhold allegiance from the High King of the Chou. How great is the power of the iron arms! Thus you too, my prince, possess a sagely virtue. The prince of Chou answered: I see, thus it must have been. (Cited in Needham 1981, 113–14).

Apart from the jade period here mentioned, the European sequence of stone, bronze, and iron is clearly stated. It must be remembered that jade artifacts were made and used more widely in China than in any other country (Chêng Tê-K'un 1959, xvii). Yuan Kang could draw upon views of philosophers of the Warring State period from the fifth century B.C. onward. The Chinese had been concerned about ancient history and social evolution for a long time. According to Needham (1981, 114) the culture stage sequences were made with conscious reference to the customs of primitive peoples prevalent in China. The food-gathering stage, the agricultural stage, and the development of the art of writing were all mentioned as sequences through which modern man had emerged. The T'ang histori-ographer, Liu Zhiji (661–721), suggested a periodization consisting of high antiquity, middle antiquity, recent antiquity, besides his own modern age. This also indicated a view of history proceeding, "descending" linearly in some sense (Meskill 1965, viii). A dif-ference worth noting is that in China the technological stages were supposed to have taken place fairly recently, thus presenting the whole sequence as part of history or legendary history.

Such presentations of an age system, like the technological age system, obviously do not leave us with a satisfactory explanation of its role in the development of differing archae-ologies. We must try to penetrate below the surface of the age system, in search of its dynamics. I believe there are at least three different ways of looking at the age system: a theological way, a natural organic way, and a positive scientific way. Each of these will promote different uses.

In the theological interpretation, the system is understood to be operated by some deity or religious force that is responsible for its content and direction. The natural organic way considers the system as belonging to some intrinsic pattern in the universe. To make sense of it, the universe has to be related to a larger unity of some kind, of which the observer himself is also a part. Finally, in the positive scientific way, its explanations can be sought within the system itself, the changing ages being constituted and directed by some inher-ent, progressive drive, related to "natural law," necessarily promoting the next stage on certain given conditions, the before-after relations and the cause and effect forming it into a primarily mechanical pattern.

What we are facing in the nineteenth-century European technological age system is the third variant, which had freed itself recently from the theological view. The principles of Descartes may serve as a link preparing the emancipation of science from theology. For Descartes, God became the First Cause, who created the material and the laws for the formation of the world, while the actual construction of the present world was left to the operation of secondary causes—natural laws (Haber 1966, 65).

Within this modern framework, the three-age system in Europe could thrive and develop. Important elements constituting the scientific revolution in the West lent them-selves readily to the new discipline of archaeology. Archaeological items could be mea-sured, weighed, and analyzed in terms of their primary and secondary qualities. Linear, mathematical, progressive time as an independent variable offered itself as an axis around which evidence could be arranged. The experimental method was the very tool needed to employ the inherent dynamics of before-after or cause-effect relationships. The archae-ological data that had been systematically accumulated in the museums were employed for testing new theories and methods; publishing results became commonplace.

The method of typology, very influential for archaeology at the end of the nineteenth century, was formulated by two Swedes, Hildebrand and Montelius, around 1870. Accord-ing to Montelius, typology was a question of tracing the inner relationship between the types of archaeological objects, in order to show how one developed from the other (Montelius 1885, 1). This is a good example of how the linear concept of time combined with the belief in an intrinsic driving force that promoted change, established itself as a powerful idea. Anyone who has frequented old archaeological museums in Europe will have noticed the seemingly unending rows of similar objects arranged to show development through time. Unfortunately the "law" of this typological method is yet to be discovered. Montelius seems to have associated it with natural law. He wrote, for instance: "when creating new forms [of objects], man must always follow laws of development, for these laws are universal throughout nature" (Montelius 1899, 267; my translation).

The sources quoted from the Sung Dynasty in China indicate a somewhat different pattern for making sense of antique objects. Unfortunately, I have no information concerning the role of the age system in arranging the imperial archaeological collections. Perhaps the lack of available information indicates that it was not considered very important. As far as I can ascertain, the primary pattern sought was not a before-after relationship with one growing out of the other. One reason for this might have been that most of their ancient objects were associated with historical facts and legendary history and were thus hardly regarded as a background for cultural history exclusively on their own. The way the relics were used in a contemporary situation, and Shen Kua's inclination to "experimental archaeology," indicate that they were perceived as part of a greater pattern, which pertained directly to the living society. Therefore the linear idea of time for arranging material did not exist in isolation, but was mixed with an idea of past and present, contemplated together. The antiques existed within the "field of force" of which contemporary society was also an integral part. They were products of some dynamics of permanent character, to be found in the cyclical idea of time.

The Idea of Evolution

The idea of evolution is related to the age system, and may be regarded as a further development of it. In both cases, a pronounced or presumed explanation of its motive power was decisive for what could be deduced from the theories.

The Chinese did not believe in the fixity of the species, nor in the idea that the whole world had been created at one particular point in time. Transformation was seen as a fundamental process informing all nature. Thus, evolutionary ideas concerning society as well as nature have a long history in China. In many respects the ideas were related to the thoughts of the old Greeks. The figures serving as founders for the two great Chinese philosophical schools, Taoism and Confucianism, both expressed opinions in this field. Lao-tzu maintained that change is a continuous process of gradual development from small and simple to complex and great (Hu Shih 1922, 31–32). But simple and small remained his ideal. Confucius, who was always socially oriented, conceived of human history as a continuous process of gradual development from crude ways of living to complete forms of civilization, from cave dwelling, hunting, and fishing to advanced stages of agriculture and commerce, from knotted cords to written records (ibid., 33). Both Lao-tzu and Confucius considered their society to be the outcome of this continuous change.

During the first half of the third century B.C., a theory of organic evolution had come into existence. The general tenor of the theory recognized that all organisms come from the same elementary germ common to all species (ibid., 121). In the following centuries, questions concerning the process of evolution were frequently posed. The crucial question was, how does a primary something become all the complexities in the universe? Answers like self-causation and self-activity were offered by way of explanations. Views coming very close to the ideas of natural selection appear (ibid., 133). Close relationships between animals and man were also acknowledged.

Accordingly, the Sung scholars were part of a long tradition that was clearly formulating an idea of evolutionary naturalism. The idea was also applied to geology, where Shen Kua and Zu Xi (1131–1200) presented thoughts of mountainbuilding and erosion (Needham 1981, 111). But the Sung scholars accepted that the universe had passed through many alternating cycles of construction and catastrophe, or as Needham puts it: "they envisaged whole successions of these polygenetic unfoldings rather than one single evolutionary series" (ibid., 110). Yet the Chinese theories remained, at the best, bold hypotheses, because they could not be sustained by evidence obtained through experimental methods that came to exist in modern archaeology and geology.

Charles Darwin's great contribution to the Western world was not the idea of evolution, but the fact that he offered natural selection as a convincing hypothesis for evolution. Within the contemporary historical setting and supported by the availability of the experimental method, the effects were electrifying. The impact of the three-age system in archaeology most likely would have appeared less important had it not been nourished in the wake of evolutionism.

Time Depth

The idea of great time depth in history was not alien to the Sung scholars. Rather, it appears as an elaborated idea, possibly to be regarded as a contribution from Buddhist thought. The Buddhist conviction of the infinity of space and time may have promoted the Chinese interest in the remote past. The idea that the universe had passed through alternating cycles of construction and dissolution was, as mentioned, commonplace among neo-Confucians of the Sung period (Ronan and Needham 1978, 242). The lengths of these periods were expressed in solar years. A gigantic scheme was set forth by Shao Yung (1011–77) and his successors. It covers not only mankind, but also the history of the universe. The cosmic period was supposed to last 129,600 years, divided into twelve cycles of 10,800 years each (Reischauer 1965, 39).

In the Western world we find similar ideas of world cycles widely current among the old Greeks, as in Plato's philosophy of history. The world was not immortal, the period of its duration was 72,000 solar years. Degradation came, and everything in the world started anew (Bury 1920, 9).

European intellectuals working with archaeology had to prove that their times scale and theories of man's development were right, in order to establish respect for their discipline. They had to fight the views promoted by influential representatives from the church that the earth was created in 4004 B.C. Biblical chronology and evolutionary ideas could not be reconciled. Accordingly, they had to penetrate what Thomas Huxley (1896) calls "the thorny barrier with its comminatory notice-board: No thoroughfare. By order, Moses." The immensely long time span of man's past became one of the keystones for the discipline. The task in Europe was to transplant the idea of progress into a secularized sphere with a more comprehensive time scale, one that if combined with evolution, made sense. The only way that seemed opportune for archaeologists to prove their case was by testing their hypotheses against empirical data in the field. From this point of view, the opposition from the church may be said to have promoted archaeological development. Hard evidence was needed. Geology helped archaeologists justify their claims. Archaeology as a link between geology and history is peculiar to Europe. An instigator, approximating the role of the church in Europe did not exist in China. Opposition between religion and science was nonexistent on this level. There was no obvious need to prove the longevity of mankind. Its hypothetical basis was not really disturbing in that part of the world.

The Experimental Method

The experimental method as applied to archaeology requires some explanation. It can be used in two ways. The methods that developed in nineteenth-century Europe may be called experimental from the point of view that they aimed at building, testing, and revising hypotheses about the human past, through fieldwork. This use differs in some ways from the concept of experiment as used in pure science. Its use, however, may be justified for describing the differences of archaeological methods in East and West.

During the last decades, a branch of archaeology called "experimental archaeology" has developed rapidly in the West. Reconstructed iron-age houses have been burnt down, left for some time, and then excavated. Pottery and stone artifacts have been produced and used under close examination, all in order to acquire a better understanding of early man and his activities. This type of experimental method was not common during the beginning stage of European archaeology. In China, however, a related experimental method may be recognized as early as the Sung period.

In Europe it became an important task to search for all "missing links" in the remote past, to construct a continuous chain of before-after relations, strong enough to repudiate biblical chronology. Fieldwork was considered a prerequisite for advancement. The potentials of European archaeology were dependent upon the spade. Stratigraphy in the field helped establish relative chronology. In the museums, typology and comparative methods proved indispensable.

Chinese archaeology did not find it necessary to justify itself in a similar manner. Scholars working with archaeology seem to have contented themselves with whatever data could be obtained from curio dealers or farmers, bought in the market places, or acquired in other ways that Westerners would regard as coincidental or insufficient. No fieldwork was carried out by Chinese scholars.

An example of the differences in attitudes may be shown in the example of the city of An-yang, the capital of the Shang Dynasty. The city had been founded around 1400 B.C. Its location had been recorded by Sima Qian as early as the second century B.C. (Chêng Tê-K'un 1959, xvi), but this information seems to have been overlooked in the following centuries. In 1899 the knowledge was revived by antiquarians, after some curio dealers brought inscribed bones from the site to Beijing. Earlier, bones so found had been used for powdered medicine. In Beijing the finds attracted the interest of the statesman Wang Yiyong. He died shortly afterward, but his successor, Liu Tieyun, made rubbings from the objects and published them in book form. Periodical bone rushes among curio dealers followed and further works and discussions resulted. Serious studies were made by Lo Zhenyu and Wang Kuo Wei who deciphered about half these newly discovered characters, contributing significantly to paleography. But the interpretations encountered opposition from some who considered the material to be forgeries.

The site from which the finds stemmed was known to have been the Shang capital. It was also known that other objects were found together with the inscribed bones. For almost thirty years, no one prevented the site from reckless plundering by curio dealers. The site was even visited by Lo Zhenyu. But "all the time it never occurred to anybody that examinations might be fruitful" (Li 1931, 190).

New ideas of field archaeology were introduced in China by Europeans, (e.g., Teilhard de Chardin and J. G. Andersson), from 1920 onward, yielding immediate and rewarding results. In 1928 the Institute of History and Philology was organized, and from its very beginning archaeological excavations were undertaken as regular works (ibid.) An-yang was chosen as the first big enterprise. For the most part it was run by Chinese scholars (Treistman 1972, 2). Within a few years the results brought attention from all over the world. Within a very short time, the institute in An-yang had developed thoroughly modern planning and routines, though it never rejected the important work of former antiquarians.

I wonder if a parallel situation can be traced within other scientific fields. The habit of walking out into the field, tracing culture layers in stratigraphical sequences for interpreting cultural history, seems to have been undertaken by the Chinese with great quickness and ease, despite the fact that it was a completely new idea. The subject appeared to have been ready for this kind of thought. It brought in its wake readjustment of numerous viewpoints, and presented problems of hitherto unknown kinds. Prehistory as such came into existence for the first time in China, a situation that did not seem to create serious discord in relation to honored traditions.

The kind of experimental method practiced in China during the Sung period may be exemplified by Shen Kua's work. As already mentioned, he did experiments with arms, mirrors, and music. These were undertakings aiming for a better understanding of how things were fabricated, and how they functioned within the older societies, in the hope that such an understanding could serve the contemporary community. In other words, these experiments centered on the past-present relationship, the "they-we ties," the two times contemplated together as an entity, in order to discover common elements. This contrasts clearly with the European treatment of the remote past in the nineteenth century. There "chain relationships" were the focus. Any event or object was, according to this system of thought, to be made sense of primarily when compared to its before-and-after companions. Accordingly, much weight was placed upon tracing the origin, the prototypes, the first of everything in Europe, whereas similar questions were less prominent in China. The European experimental method tended to place the observer outside the experiment, whereas the Chinese way of attacking it included the observer's position in a more direct manner.

Archaeology and Society

Archaeology always mirrors the society of its creators. Our opinion of the past also reflects our contemporary ideas, values, hopes, and fears. It is worth noting that neither China nor northern Europe had impressive monumental architecture from a distant and glorious past comparable to the pyramids of the Mayas or the Egyptians, like Angkor Wat or the conspicuous remains in the Mediterranean areas. In China nonpermanent material had been used for various forms of architecture, with the exception of the Great Wall and a few Buddhist buildings and sculptural monuments like the Cave Temple in Yün-Kang. Grave monuments, however, represented important physical remains in both areas exposed to examination. It is often said that it was no accident that modern archaeology grew up on the continent that gave birth to the nation-state. There can be no doubt that archaeology was used to strengthen national identity in Europe.

China, on the other hand, had long traditions as a state, but the need to reinforce its state image remained alive. History and archaeology supplied means for this end, and may have been of special importance after the Northern Sung had reconstructed the universal state from the short-lived and competing kingdoms of its predecessors.

It was within a Europe strongly influenced by the Industrial Revolution that modern archaeology first found nourishment. Attitudes toward time in such societies differ from those in traditional agricultural communities, a fact that has been amply demonstrated. The invention of the cultural idea of time as something independent, utilitarian, and beneficial for creating progress was at the time of archaeology's birth in Europe deeply rooted among influential groups. Modern archaeology with its concentration on development, progress, and change could serve as a justification in a rapidly altering society, showing that the present trend was just a speeding up of old and ever present tendencies. Man in an unstable and changing Western society may have felt the need for something that helped him transcend the briefness of his own life.

China was a predominantly agricultural society during the period when archaeology took form. The silent and steady advances in that country, though substantial during the Sung period, were less conspicuous than those in Europe, in the seventeenth to nineteenth centuries. China had never experienced any Dark Ages against which to contrast their times of progress. Agricultural societies are necessarily future orientated, but in a way different from industrial ones. Their perceptions of time are modeled on previous experience, which makes them face the future and the past simultaneously. In other words, their orientation to the future and the past are closely related, and accordingly of a general character (Nowotny 1975, 327).

The political and social situation in China at this particular time reveals several interesting aspects that could explain why archaeology got a chance to develop. Nathan Sivin (1975, 370) has stressed that during the Northern Sung Dynasty (960–1126), an expansiveness and openness to talents may have favored the conviction that change could be a useful tool, to an extent and in a way uncommon in Chinese traditions. The important center of activity moved toward the fertile Southeast where economical and social organizations proved propitious and gave vent to some new ideas and activities. Both mercantile undertakings and industry gained ground. The new printing possibilities brought about an auspicious situation for education. Opening up for small gentry to ascend to elite positions may have also proved an impetus for scientific activity in general. As the government showed greater interest in sponsoring various fields of learning, a climate that was also favorable for the development of archaeology seems to have been at hand. The social and political conditions in China and Europe at the time when archaeology developed were accordingly related to a certain extent. But the Chinese experiment turned out to be ephemeral compared to what happened in Europe.

Conclusion

Many of the ideas considered necessary to archaeology's birth in the West were also identifiable in China. Differences existed, however, in their time schedule (with China ahead for a long time), the intellectual climate within which they existed, in the domination they came to claim, and in the way they were combined to make sense and be "useful" in society.

It may be maintained that reductionism of basic ideas, such as the time concept and the theory of causality, were fundamental for European development of archaeological science. The linear, irreversible, mathematical time concept around which archaeological remains could be arranged in cause-effect relationship carried in it rich potentials for modern archaeology as it was built upon the use of the previously mentioned experimental method. That the linear, irreversible time concept was very real to the Chinese mind, also during the Sung period, has been demonstrated throughout this paper. But it was not the only concept that held sway. Another aspect of time, often rather imprecisely referred to as cyclical, was equally influential.

On the surface the historical cycle has its analogy in a life cycle, nature itself encouraging this point of view. The dynastic cycle implies for a Westerner, at first, a sequence of similar political events, an interpretation that appears inadequate. The content of the cyclical time concept in China seems difficult for Westerners to grasp. Our scientific history, our mechanical worldviews present obstacles.

Ideas related to the Chinese cyclical views can be traced in earlier European history, to the Middle Ages. Here we find the opinion that time passes, but not in all spheres of existence. Truth is not something linked to passing time (Gurevich 1976, 235). Dante, in his *Divine Comedy* expressed his contemporary time concept in this way: the history of mankind appears synchronically. Everything is in the present. The system of thought is based on the contrast between "eternity" and "earthly time" (ibid. 238). These ideas lost their significance in Europe after the Renaissance and gained little attention during the formative period of archaeology. No single "monolithic" time reigned absolutely, but the linear, independent time concept dominated and proved very influential for archaeological scientific thought.

The predictability and regularity intrinsic to the concept of cyclical time tends to recommend holism as an ideal. Any observer should be absorbed into a permanent moral dynamics that would influence his self-image. Present and past are linked together. In this way the cyclical perception of time transforms knowledge of the past into ideas promoting actions. But these actions are not innovative, rather they are moulded on experience from the past. History in China was considered the story of the growth of self-conscious reason (Meskill 1965, ix) and could not therefore be easily reduced to purely linear, mathematical metaphors.

The theory of yin and yang and that of the Five Phases, both so influential in Chinese philosophy, belong to the idea of the cyclical time complex, with all its moral connotations. The corpus of traditional principles was the background against which the instances of the history of man could be tested. The repetitive elements existed because the moral law persisted. But this does not imply that the Chinese past could be reduced to one great treadmill. Perhaps one is justified in saying that the Chinese were eager to bridge the time gap among people, whereas the Europeans were eager to expose the same time gap to the gaze of research.

References

Bury, J. B. 1920. *The idea of progress: An inquiry into its origin and growth*. London.

Chêng Tê-K'un. 1959. *Archaeology in China*. Vol. 1, *Prehistoric China*. Toronto: University of Toronto Press.

Daniel, G. 1975. *150 years of archaeology*. London: Duckworth.

Franke, H. 1982. Archälogie und geschichtsbewusstsein in China. In *Kolloquien zur Allgemeine und Vergleichenden Archäologie*, 3: 69–83. München: Verlag C. H. Beck.

Gurevich, A. J. 1976. Time as a problem of cultural history. In *Cultures and time*, 229–45. Paris: Unesco Press.

Haber, F. 1966. *The age of the world: Moses to Darwin*. Baltimore: Johns Hopkins University Press.

Hu Shih. 1922. *The development of the logical method in ancient China*. Shanghai.

Huxley, T. H. 1896. *Science and Christian tradition*. New York.

Klindt-Jensen, O. A. (1975. *A history of Scandinavian archaeology*. London: Thames and Hudson.

Li, C. 1931. Archaeology. In *Symposium on Chinese archaeology*, ed. S. H. C. Zen, 184–93.

Meskill, J., ed. 1965. *The pattern of Chinese history: Cycles, development, or stagnation?* Westport, Conn.: Greenwood.

Montelius, O. 1885 *Om Tidsbestämning inom bronsåldern med särskild hänsyn till Skandinavien*. Kungl. Vitterhets Historie och Antiquitets Akademiens Handlingar 30, ny føljd. 10. Stockholm.

———. 1899. Typologien eller utvecklingsläran tillempad på det menskliga arbetet, *Svenska Fornminneföreningens Tidsskrift* (Stockholm) 10, no. 3: 237–68.

Needham, J. 1969. *The grand titration: Science and society in East and West*. London: George Allen and Unwin.

———. 1981. Science in traditional China: A comparative perspective. Hong Kong.

Nowotny, H. 1975. Time structuring and time measurement: On the interrelation between timekeepers and social time." In *Study of time II*, ed. J. T. Fraser, N. Lawrence, New York: Springer-Verlag. 325–43.

Reischauer, E. O. 1965. The dynastic cycle. In *The pattern of Chinese history*. *See* Meskill 1965.

Ronan, C. A., and J. Needham. 1978. *Science and civilisation in China*. Vol. 1. Cambridge: Cambridge University Press.

Sivin, N. 1975. Shen Kua (1031–1095). In *Dictionary of scientific biography*. 12: 369–93. New York: Charles Scribner's Sons.

Treistman, J. M. 1972 *The prehistory of China: An archaeological exploration*. Newton Abbot: David and Charles.

Wang Kuo-Wei. 1927. Archaeology in the Sung Dynasty. *Chinese Journal* (Shanghai) 6, no. 5: 222–31.

Wright, A. F. 1965. Comments on early Chinese views. In *The pattern of Chinese history*. *See* Meskill 1965.

Xia Nai. 1979. Shen Kua and archaeology. In *Essays on archaeology of science and technology in China*, ed. Xia Nai, 139–41. Institute of Archaeology, Chinese Academy of Social Sciences. Beijing: Science Press.

Space and Time in Chinese Verse

Frederick Turner

Summary Recent studies have begun to clarify the general neural strategy of poetry as opposed to prose as modes of information.

In the cultures studied, the poetic line is about three seconds long and is synchronized to a three-second information processing pulse, deriving from the anatomy of the auditory cortex. Verse uses this cycle as a carrier wave for an additional channel of information, beyond the simply linguistic. Metered poetry brings information to us in a "stereo" mode, using both the right and the left sides of the brain, and inviting a creative integration of them analogous to depth perception in vision.

Using this explanation of metered verse we can examine the differences between Chinese and Western (and other) verse forms. There are two main differences: one is that Chinese verse has a line of four, five or seven syllables (as opposed to the roughly ten-syllable line of most other languages). The other is that Chinese poetry has a much stronger visual component: Chinese script is ideographic, permitting the kind of play on a visual level that Western and other verse can manage on only an auditory level.

The number of syllables in the Chinese verse line presents a problem. The Chinese line would last only one to two seconds if recited at Western rates of recitation, much shorter than the two to four seconds of other poetries. I have solved this problem experimentally by recording and measuring Chinese verse recited by a native speaker, at about two to three and one-half seconds long, agreeing with that of other languages.

The ideographic element in Chinese verse makes possible a kind of visual meaning quite as powerful as that of linguistic sequence. Chinese poetry adds a pictorial, right-brain element to poetry, on top of the existing right-brain elements of poetic meter; this may be related to the spatialized conception of time in the themes of Chinese poetry.

One of the most remarkable, and most strangely ignored, discoveries in the human sciences in the last few decades has been the cultural universality of poetry. It has been known for centuries that the "high" civilizations of Europe, the Middle East, India, China, and Japan possessed poetic traditions of great richness and antiquity. But the resemblance between these traditions could always have been explained as a single peculiar invention propagated by cultural diffusion or as a by-product of a certain stage of economic progress: either as a cultural homology or as a technological analogy.

Now, however, anthropologists have recorded poetry of dozens of societies from all over the world.[1] These societies are often so isolated from one another that cultural diffusion could only be invoked as an explanation if the diffusion occurred at some inconceivably ancient stage of human evolution, when all our ancestors lived close enough to exchange ideas—a stage at which cultural and biological evolution cannot be clearly distinguished, in any case. Moreover, the model of poetry as an epiphenomenon of a particular stage of technological evolution is discredited by the fact that poetry is a feature of societies at every imaginable level of organization and economic development.

It is not simply poetry that possesses this universality, but a very specific set of techniques of versification. Ethologists have remarked on the universality of such relatively simple behaviors as the eyebrow flash; far more astonishing is the presence in totally unconnected human cultures of exactly the same highly complex and at the same time not obviously useful system of making verse.

Recent measurements made by me and Ernst Pöppel show specific quantifiable resemblances between the poetic meters of cultures all over the world. The most remarkable is the existence and length of the poetic *line*. Every poetic tradition, oral and literate, uses the line as a fundamental unit of verse; and wherever it occurs, it takes the same length of time (i.e., about three seconds) to recite. The shortest line is about two seconds long, and the longest is about four, and there is a strong peak in distribution around three.[2]

If cultural diffusion and technological necessity are ruled out as explanations for this phenomenon, the only one that remains is biological inheritance. Something in our physical and neurological organization, evidently, has provided a foundation, even an inducement, for the independent development of verse, metered in three-second lines, throughout the world. Indeed, the evidence is of the same type—such as the universality of eating and sexual activities—as that that has led human ethologists to postulate the existence of *drives* that are expressed and satisfied by given behaviors.

Studies by Ernst Pöppel and others of the human hearing system perhaps provide a partial explanation. The auditory cortex is a marvelously sensitive instrument for distinguishing between different temporal periodicities. Distinctions between very short periodicities are perceived as differences of musical tone and timbre, and distinctions between longer periods are perceived as differences of rhythm and tempo. A hierarchy of thresholds separates classes of auditory experience: very small intervals (less than 0.003 sec.) are not perceived, or rather are perceived as simultaneous; slightly longer intervals (0.003–0.03 sec.) allow the ear to perceive separation between seconds but not their sequence; still longer intervals (0.03–0.3 sec.) permit sequence to be recognized, but allow no time for response; longer intervals (0.3–3.0 secs.) allow for a full range of analysis and response within the subjective present of the hearer.

This "subjective present" is about three seconds long. That is, acoustic information is processed in three-second packages; to use a cybernetic metaphor, we possess a "buffer" which can accumulate three seconds' worth of sound information and then pass all that information along together to the higher processing systems of the brain. A speaker will pause for a few milliseconds every three seconds, while making decisions about the exact syntax and vocabulary of the next three seconds of speech; and a hearer will retain the same amount of information in short-term auditory memory, before editing it and storing the remnants in long-term memory.

Evidently, then, poetic meter imitates the three-second information processing pulse of the auditory cortex. If this is so, one might ask why.

One answer is suggested by the very provocative book *The Spectrum of Ritual: A Biogenetic Structural Analysis*.[3] In that book Barbara Lex summarizes and integrates much research that has been done on ritual and meditative trance states. Most provocative is her discussion of rhythmic "driving" techniques, whereby through regularly repeated photic or auditory stimuli tuned to endogenous brain rhythms, altered states of consciousness can be evoked. It is well known, for instance, that a strobe light can produce epilepticlike seizures in some individuals; and that rhythmic repeated sounds can have calming or stimulating effects depending on their frequency and volume, and on the nervous and somatic systems that are being measured. Essentially, an endogenous brain rhythm, necessary for the regulation of neural functions, is "driven" or amplified by an external rhythm tuned to the same periodicity, causing changes in brain state.

These changes in brain state have been only superficially investigated, but already they appear to involve very interesting processes. Among other effects that have been observed are an overstimulation of either the ergotropic (alertness) or the trophotropic (rest) systems in the midbrain, leading to a compensatory elevation of the activity of the other system; and changes in brain chemistry, including elevated levels of those neurohumors—endorphins and catecholamines—associated with the brain's endogenous reward system.[4] The subjective results of these changes include a feeling of relaxation together with powerful insight, an emotion of social solidarity, a heightened sense of the contents of one's memory and experience as a meaningful whole, and a sense of eternity or transcendence of time. These effects closely correspond to descriptions of the poetic experience given by poets, critics, and readers of poetry.

If the brain possesses its own reward system, what is that system *for*? Or to put it another way—we know that the very powerful pleasures associated with eating and sexual activity evolved to encourage behavior that is essential to the survival of the individual and the species. Why, on the other hand, should those pleasures—equally powerful in their own way—of beauty, of satisfied curiosity, and so on, have been selected for? Surely the only answer must be that our "specialty" as human beings, like the bird's to fly and the mole's to dig, is to construct ordered, harmonious, parsimonious, and predictively powerful hypotheses or imagined worlds, and to test them continuously against perceptual experience—while at the same time using them to calibrate and selectively sensitize the neural mechanisms of perception.

Poetry, then, like the other arts, is a device to awaken and orient the brain's reward system: to put it simply, it sets in motion a feedback process designed to make us more intelligent, better able to cooperate, and more able to predict what will happen next and thus deal with it. The mythic and prophetic elements of poetry act as templates for the future; its symbolism provides a powerful means of organizing information in a hierarchy of importance; and its meter helps to get the essential brain chemicals flowing.

But any poet or reader of poetry will rightly protest that poetic meter does not work like the beat of a hammer or a drum. Variation—especially a deliberate counterpoint between the natural syntactical rhythm of speech and the underlying rhythm of the meter—is the heart of verse.

Thus, although the three-second information processing pulse is evoked and driven by the poetic line, it is a very subtle process, with much room for free play and variation. In fact, poetic meter, like music, is itself a carrier of meaning; to use the terminology of information theory, a wave medium orderly and regular enough to be distinguished from mere noise is systematically distorted in order to carry a significant message. However, like the information conveyed by music—or, indeed, by visual representations—that significant message is not the same as linguistic information. We perceive the richness of meaning in a poetic cadence not as we perceive tha meaning of a sentence, but more as we perceive the meaning of a tune or a picture. We know linguistic information is processed in the left temporal lobe of the human brain, whereas pictorial and melodic information is processed in the right. Thus metered poetry aids the linguistic left-brain understanding with the musical and spatial abilities of the right: poetry comes to us in a "stereo" mode, rather than in the "mono" mode of ordinary prose.

Some experts on the functional bilateral asymmetry of the brain, notably Jerre Levy, believe that the experience of full understanding and the capacity for the creative use of information result from the transfer of information back and forth between the left and right sides of the brain. As the information passes across, it is translated from the temporal ordering mode of the left brain into the spatial ordering mode of the right, and vice versa.[5] Nonexperts listening to music, for instance, show much greater nervous activity on the right side than on the left; whereas expert musicians show the activity more equally distributed on both sides of the brain.[6] The implication is that the experienced musician's deeper understanding of music partly consists in a *translation* of the musical information from the right-brain mode into the left. It seems very likely that poetic meter is a way of facilitating this process of bilateral cooperation.

Most poetry combines the temporal elements of plot or argument with the spatial elements of meter and stanza form and imagery. In this combination lies much of the memorability of verse. Mnemonic systems usually have a prescribed way of associating a sequence of pieces of information with a spatial pattern, like the interior of a house, that can be visualized as a gestalt and thus easily remembered, since, unlike the sequence, the gestalt does not overflow the three-second short-term memory buffer. These memory systems, by combining the left-brain talent for temporal sequence with the right-brain talent for spatial pattern, have anciently been associated with poetry. The blind Homer, who had to memorize his epic poems, used such techniques, and indeed claimed that the muses—the forces of artistic inspiration—were the daughters of Mnemosyne, the goddess of memory.[7] Frances Yates makes a convincing case that the architecture of Shakespeare's Globe Theatre was based on the contemporary mnemonic system known as the Memory Theatre.[8]

Let me summarize the new discoveries about metered verse. First, it is culturally universal. Second, its most salient universal feature is the three-second line. Third, the three-second period matches the three-second information-processing pulse of the auditory cortex, our subjective present. Fourth, verse thus acts as an auditory driving technique, to reinforce an endogenous brain rhythm and thus induce changes in the brain state controlled by the ergotrophic and trophotrophic systems of the midbrain; the human endogenous reward system is activated. Fifth, the variations in metrical rhythm carry information, but do so in a right-brain mode; thus poetry combines left-brain linguistic information with right-brain melodic or pictorial information, thereby putting a much greater proportion of the brain at the disposal of effective communication, and enabling the brain to store information efficiently in its gestalt mode rather than in its easily over-loaded sequential mode.

The case of Chinese verse presents a difficult challenge and suggests a fascinating amplification for the theory of metered poetry I have described. The challenge involves certain technical elements of versification, which I shall briefly discuss.[9]

Poetic meter uses not only the line as a fundamental unit, but also the syllable. Interestingly enough, the length of a syllable—about a quarter second—corresponds closely to another threshold in the brain's information-processing system: it takes about one-third second to respond and react to an acoustic stimulus. Thus the syllable is as "fast" as it could be and still give us time to react, either as speaker or hearer, before the next one comes along. The pause at the end of the three-second line is generally felt by versifiers all over the world not to be a strong enough indicator of the isochrony of the three-second pulse:[10] therefore all forms of verse employ repeated patterns of syllables, similar from line to line, to emphasize the similarity and thus the isochrony of the lines. In Hungarian folk verse, to take a simple example, there is the same number of syllables to each line, combined with a grammatical and semantic unity within each line. Many traditions—most European poetries, and several others—use "feet," which are small groups of syllables, usually two or three, containing a repeated pattern of stress or syllable length. Each line of a poem generally has the same number of feet. The iambic foot in English consists of a lightly stressed syllable followed by a heavily stressed syllable ($\cup$/). The trochaic foot in Latin and Greek poetry has a long syllable followed by two short ones (—$\cup\cup$). Often the unity of the line is further emphasized by assonance, alliteration, regular cadence, or internal rhymes; and the parallelism between the line is emphasized by rhymes between the lines, by regular stanzas, and by conventional patterns of other kinds.

The system that Chinese verse employs is peculiarly fascinating. The Chinese language uses tone not only as we do for emphasis and to indicate certain grammatical qualities in a sentence (e.g., whether it is a statement, a command, or a question), but also as a lexical component: that is, the same syllables with different stress constitute a different word and meaning altogether (see Appendix A) There are four tones in Chinese, two unchanging and two changing. The Chinese verse line is made of a fixed pattern of changing and unchanging syllables.

The challenge and problem for the theory of poetic meter described here are that the Chinese classical line contains four, five, or seven syllables, and thus, given a syllable one-quarter second long, would take between one and one and three quarter seconds—considerably and significantly shorter than the three-second line found elsewhere (see Appendix B).

However, the problem was solved experimentally by recording classical Chinese poetry recited by a native speaker, and measuring the length of the line. It turns out that the syllable when recited in the Chinese tradition of poetry recitation is twice the length of a syllable in nontonal languages. The actual measurements for the four-, five-, and seven-syllable lines were 2.0, 3.0, and 3.8 seconds respectively. Thus the validity of the general theory is confirmed.

The amplification of the theory suggested by Chinese verse is considerably more wide-ranging in its theoretical implications. The pictorial or spatial element in Chinese verse has long been remarked on: written Chinese takes the form of ideograms, descended originally from pictographs. Chinese landscape painting has a stronger linguistic element than Western painting precisely because its forms allude subtly to the forms of Chinese characters. Correspondingly, Chinese verse is enriched by complex references to the pictorial associations that still cling to the ideograms, real or fanciful; the references are the more telling, the more erudite the reader, for an ideogram can often mean a whole history of visual etymology and literary variation to a scholar.

The attention of the Western literary world was first brought to the uniqueness of

Chinese verse by the Oriental scholar Ernest Fenollosa. His essay, "The Chinese Written Character as a Medium for Poetry," was edited by Ezra Pound and first published under their joint authorship in the *Little Review* in 1919.[11]

Their argument has much relevance for my subject. The question their essay proposes is: "In what sense can verse, written in terms of visible hieroglyphics, be reckoned true poetry?" They amplify this question: "It might seem that poetry, which like music is a *time art*, weaving its unities out of successive impressions of sound, could with difficulty assimilate a verbal medium consisting largely of semipictorial appeals to the eye."

Pound and Fenollosa, intent on justifying the new free-verse movement, deliberately or inadvertently ignore Chinese meter and continue as if the only requirement of poetic form is, as they put it, "a regular and flexible sequence, as plastic as thought itself."[12] Upon this error a large body of contemporary Western poetic theory and practice is ultimately founded: for instance, the vast majority of contemporary translations into English of foreign language poetry are in free verse, even when the originals are in meter. This practice greatly falsifies their tone, and tends to suggest interpretations of the poetry that confirm Western modernist prejudices.

Pound and Fenollosa go on to suggest a rather naive theory of perception, based ultimately on a Lockean or Humean model of the mind as a passive tabula rasa containing mimeses or imitations of external realities: "Perhaps we do not always sufficiently consider that thought is successsive, not through some accident or weakness of our subjective operations but because the operations of nature are successive. The transferences of force from agent to agent, which constitute natural phenomena, occupy time. Therefore, a reproduction of them in imagination requires the same temporal order." Pound and Fenollosa assert that the syntactical order of subject-verb-object, which is the normal sequence in Chinese, is founded on the reality of the operations of nature, and, as an example, give a simple sentence: "Man sees horse." "We saw, first, the man before he acted; second, while he acted; third, the object toward which his action was directed." The fallacy of this is clear, for with some scientific justification one could argue for an opposite word order. This event of vision actually takes place in the opposite direction: incident light on the horse is reflected *from* the horse *to* the man; and there is no reason why this order should not be as intuitively compelling to a member of a scientific culture as its opposite might be to one of a nonscientific culture. Pound and Fenollosa were still in the grip of the Enlightenment/Romantic habit of mind, which gave nature the status of a fundamental reality. They thus ignored the extent to which nature is merely a plausible construction of the nervous systems of the higher animals, especially homo sapiens.

But these criticisms do not detract from the real strength of their essay, which is that it recognizes the value of combining the spatial and temporal modes of perception.

"One superiority of verbal poetry as an art rests in its getting back to the fundamental reality of *time*. Chinese poetry has the unique advantage of combining both elements. It speaks at once with the vividness of painting, and with the mobility of sounds." It must have taken some courage to write these words at a time when aesthetic theory was still dominated by the ideas of Lessing, who had insisted that each art form must seek purity by eliminating any element belonging to a sensory mode other than its own—that painting should not tell stories, music should not describe visual scenes, and so on. Pound and Fenollosa are close to our own conception of art as speaking to a single gigantic sense organ, the brain itself as a whole. What they say here suggests that wonderful cooperation between left-brain temporal sequential ordering and right-brain spatial pattern recognition that we have already discussed.

However, the matter is more complex and more interesting than Pound and Fenollosa could have guessed. They characteristically refer to time as a "fundamental reality" and to time and space as simple dimensions; and they assert without qualms that music and poetry are "arts of time" while painting and sculpture are "arts of space." The human experience of time, we know now, is a highly evolved and complex hierarchy of temporalities including, at its most rudimentary levels, spacelike characteristics. At its more advanced levels, where it involves such concepts as past, present, and future, time is more like an immensely powerful organizing fiction that the brain uses to make information practically usable than like an objective characteristic of the physical universe.[13] As to classification of the arts as being of space or time, again, the issue is more complex. The right brain seems, indeed, to process pictorial information, as such, more efficiently than the left: but oddly enough it is also the right brain that, in persons not musically expert, handles melody and musical harmony. Both activities require a gestalt capacity for pattern recognition. The right brain has only a rudimentary sense of time, however;[14] it subjectively exists in a sort of *nunc stans* or eternal present in which entities are related by juxtaposition rather than sequence. On the other hand, the left brain, which has a keen sense of past, present, and future, and of the irreversible passage of time, deals with linguistic and logical information, which requires the capacity to organize material into a meaningful sequence. But the unique qualities of the musical, pictorial, and poetic *arts* seem specifically designed to *overcome* their confinement to one side of the brain or the other. The representational bias of the visual arts all over the world and throughout history—pure abstraction is in panhuman terms a grotesque anomaly—brings to the spatial craft of pattern creation the temporal capacity to tell a story and make an argument. In music, too, when it attains the character of an art rather than a craft or game, the tendency is to supplement the pleasing pattern of sound by mapping it onto a program, a sequence of musical movements, or, of course, the words of a song lyric, chant, hymn, or aria. We have already seen that poetry, the *art* of language, brings to the aid of the merely temporal linguistic understanding, which is rather limited in terms of information capacity, the spatial pattern-recognition talents of the right brain that are evoked by poetic meter.[15]

Thus the ideographic element of Chinese poetry is not a simple matter of adding a spatial right-brain component to a temporal art, but rather one of providing an *additional* right-brain spatial element to an art that is already both left-brain, temporal, and linguistic, *and* right-brain, spatial, and patterned.

In a sense, then, Chinese poetry is only once an "art of time," but twice an "art of space." If we examine the content of Chinese classical poetry, we find a fascinating corroboration of the formal tendencies we have described. Indeed, considering the content, it would be more accurate to say that instead of adding another spatial element to the standard poetic space-time combination, Chinese poetry spatializes the very concept of time itself.

In Robert Payne's eloquent introduction to his collection of Chinese poetry in translation, *The White Pony*, he stresses the curious combination of transience and permanence to be found in Chinese verse:

> Though there is sorrow continually in their poems, it is not the final sorrow of the Vergilian West, which looked forward to the end of the world in some catastrophe or resurrection outside time. There is, in Chinese poetry, a sense of the permanence of the world so great that we remember it

even when the poet breaks out in lamentation, even when he sees the bleached bones on the frontiers.

The peach blossom follows the moving water, the white birds fade into the faint emerald of the hills, nothing is lasting, all disappears, and yet—the poet seems to be saying—how delightful to watch the progress of the world.[16]

This sense of the brevity of human life within a world that is infinite in both space and time, and in which the transient beauty of every moment is eternal, can be found in the earliest poetry—this one, for instance, perhaps four thousand years old:

> *Song of the White Clouds*
> There are white clouds in the heaven,
> Great cliffs are lifted upward,
> Interminable are the roads of earth,
> Mountain and rivers bar the way:
> I pray you not to die.
> Please try to come again.
> (From *The Fountain of Old Poems*)

The poet Tu Fu (712–770) would compose his poetry, fold it into little paper boats, and float it down a stream. This is one of his poems, written about 750:

> *The Village and the River*
> My home is surrounded by a clear stream,
> In the long summer days there is all the silence of a hermitage
> Save where the swallow flit among the beams
> Or where the wild sea gull plays fearless on a stream.
> My wife rules the squares for a game of chess,
> My young son hammers a fishhook out of wire.
> I, who am ill so often, want only to plant flowers—
> My humble body desires nothing more.

His friend Li Po (700?–762) wrote these two poems:

> *Conversation in the Mountains*
> If you were to ask me why I dwell among green mountains,
> I should laugh silently; my soul is serene.
> The peach blossom follows the moving water;
> There is another heaven and earth beyond the world of men.

> *Song of the Blue Water*
> The shining moon burns the blue water.
> On the south lake he is gathering white lilies.
> These lotuses are whispering tenderly.
> Sorrowfully the boatman sighs.

The reference to Chinese landscape painting, which often incorporates verses into its composition, is quite characteristic. So too, the sense that time is not a process of historical development and progress, but an infinite landscape, of which present moments are the details. Li Ho (791–817) here catches a moment:

> *Seventh Moon*
> The Stars near the Milky Way grow cold.
> The bubbles of dew on the dew plate are round.
> Pretty flowers shoot from the ends of twigs,
> Fading grasses grieve in the empty garden.

> The night sky is paved with jade.
> The leaves in the lotus pond are like green coins.
>
> She only regrets because her dancing skirt is too thin.
> She feels faintly cold on her bamboo mat woven with flowers.
> How swiftly the morning wind sweeps away!
> The Great Bear glitters and curves down the sky.

The wind and the stars—the most transient and the most eternal—continually meet in Chinese poetry. It is as if the contemplation of the ideograms, which contain their meaning all at once and have no past and future, reminds poet and reader that the sequential temporal logic of language is only an arbitrary order we impose upon the world, the reckoning up of the ten thousand things that are in reality the single enduring mountain. Information—even when it is full of the grief of war or parting or bereavement—passes from the urgent temporal mode of the left brain into the *nunc stans*, the eternal present, of the right, by means of its patterning into meter; and it is held there and fixed by its further transformation into a visual form, a shape that makes a picture in the mind.

Appendix A

An example of how tone in Chinese can signify lexical differences.

媽 mā	first tone	mother
麻 má	second tone	hemp: flax
馬 mǎ	third tone	horse
罵 mà	fourth tone	scold

Similarly, *jū* (high tone) means "pig"; *jú* (rising tone) means "bamboo"; *jǔ* (low tone) means "god"; and *jù* (falling tone) means "to remember."

I am indebted to Dr. Diane Obenchain of Kenyon College for the first example.

Appendix B

The following are three Chinese poems, in the four-syllable, five-syllable, and seven-syllable classical meters, together with translations, reproduced, with permission, from *A Golden Treasury of Chinese Poetry*, trans. John A. Turner, Center for Translation Projects (Hong Kong: Chinese University of Hong Kong, 1976).

ANONYMOUS
often attributed to Confucius
551–479 B.C., Age of Spring and Autumn

Disappointment

無名氏

猗蘭操

Through the mild breeze,	
In cloud and rain,	習習谷風，以陰以雨。
Across the weald	
I ride again:	之子于歸，遠送於野。
(O mightly Heav'n!)	
To roam unblest	何彼蒼天，不得其所。
The Regions Nine	
And find no rest.	逍遙九州，無所定處。
Benighted souls	
Ignore the Sage;	時人闇蔽，不知賢者。
While the long years	
Bring on old age.	年紀逝邁，一身將老。

TU FU

Gazing at The Great Mount

To what shall I compare
The Sacred Mount that stands,
A balk of green that hath no end,
    Betwixt two lands!
Nature did fuse and blend
All mystic beauty there,
    Where Dark and Light
Do dusk and dawn unite.

Gazing, soul-cleansed, at Thee
From clouds upsprung, one may
Mark with wide eyes the homing flight
    Of birds. Some day
Must I thy topmost height
Mount, at one glance to see
    Hills numberless
Dwindle to nothingness.

杜甫

望嶽

岱宗夫如何，

齊魯青未了。

造化鍾神秀，

陰陽割昏曉。

盪胸生層雲，

決眥入歸鳥。

會當凌絕頂，

一覽眾山小。

LI PO

Cascade

—gazing at the cascade on Lu Shan

Where crowns a purple haze
    Ashimmer in sunlight rays
The hill called Incense-Burner Peak, from far
    To see, hung o'er the torrent's wall,
      That waterfall
Vault sheer three thousand feet, you'd say
      The Milky Way
Was tumbling from the high heavens, star on star.

李白

望廬山瀑布

日照香爐生紫煙，

遙看瀑布掛長川。

飛流直下三千尺，

疑是銀河落九天。

Notes

1. See, e.g., J. Rothenburg, *Technicians of the Sacred* (Garden City, N.Y.: Doubleday Anchor, 1968).

2. See F. Turner and E. Pöppel, "The Neural Lyre," *Poetry*, July 1983.

3. E. G. D'Aquili, C. D. Laughlin, and J. McManus, eds., *The Spectrum of Ritual: A Biogenetic Structural Analysis* (New York: Columbia University Press, 1979).

4. On reward systems, see D. E. Berlyne and K. B. Madsen, eds., *Pleasure, Reward, Preferences: Their Nature, Determinants, and Role in Behavior* (New York: Academic Press, 1973); A. Routenberg, ed., *Biology of Reinforcement: Facets of Brain Stimulation Reward* (New York: Academic Press, 1980); J. Olds, *Drives and Reinforcements: Behavioral Studies of Hypothalamic Functions* (New York: Raven Press, 1977); M. Konner, *The Tangled Wing: Biological Constraints on the Human Spirit* (New York: Holt, Rinehart, 1982); and C. B. Nemeroff and A. J. Dunn, eds., *Peptides, Hormones, and Behavior* (Englewood Cliffs, N. J.: Spectrum Publications, 1984).

5. Jerre Levy, "Interhemispheric Collaboration: Single-Mindedness in the Asymmetric Brain," in *Developmental Neuropsychology and Education*, C. T. Best, ed. (New York: Academic Press, forthcom. See Also "Cerebral Asymmetry and Aesthetic Experience," paper given at the Werner Reimers Stiftung conference on the biological foundations of aesthetics, January 1982, to be published in *Biological Aspects of Esthetics*. But see also J. Levy, "Psychological Implications of Bilateral Asymmetry," in *Hemisphere Function in the Human Brain*, ed. S. Dimond and J. G. Beaumont (London: Paul

Elek, Ltd., 1974); and R. W. Sperry: "Forebrain Commissurotomy and Conscious Awareness," in *Neuropsychology after Lashley*, ed. J. Ohrbach (Hillsdale, N.J.: Lawrence Erlbaum, 1982).

6. T. G. Bever and R. J. Chiarello: "Cerebral Dominance in Musicians and Nonmusicians," *Science* 185 (1974).

7. A. B. Lord, *The Singer of Tales* (Cambridge, Mass.: Harvard University Press, 1964).

8. F. Yates, *The Theatre of the World* (Chicago: Chicago University Press, 1969).

9. See also W. K. Wimsatt, ed., *Versification: Major Language Types* (New York: New York University Press, 1972).

10. John Lotz, "Elements of Versification," in ibid., pp. 6–15.

11. Ernest Fenollosa and Ezra Pound, "The Chinese Written Character as a Medium for Poetry," *Little Review* 6 (Sept.–Dec. 1919).

12. Ibid., p. 64; see also Wai-Lim Yip, *Ezra Pound's Cathay* (Princeton: Princeton University Press, 1969).

13. See J. T. Fraser, *Of Time, Passion, and Knowledge* (New York: Braziller, 1975) and, by the same author, "Out of Plato's Cave: The Natural History of Time," *Kenyon Review*, n.s., 2 (1980): 143–62.

14. Jerre Levy, "Cerebral Asymmetry and Aesthetic Experience," paper given at the Werner Reimers Stiftung conference on the biological foundations of aesthetic, January 1982, p. 8.

15. See Sally P. Springer and Georg Deutsch, *Left Brain, Right Brain* (San Francisco: W. H. Freeman, 1981); M. P. Bryden, *Laterality: Functional Asymmetry in the Intact Brain* (New York: Academic Press, 1982); J. Levy, "Lateral Specialization in the Human Brain; Behavioral Manifestations and Possible Evolutionary Basis," in *The Biology of Behavior*, ed. J. A. Kiger (Corvallis: Oregon State University Press, 1972).

16. Robert Payne, ed., *The White Pony* (New York: Mentor, 1949). The translations that follow are from this volume.

Envoi

The earliest mature forms of modern natural science are usually thought to have been born in the seventeenth century, that is, some two millennia after its time-related foundations were laid in ancient Greek thought. This new way of looking at the world came into being when an amalgam of Greek wisdom and Arab science entered European consciousness, which was ready, with its mixture of ideas and social values, to create and develop quantitative, experimental knowledge.

Future historians may hardly notice that it took another three centuries before the scientific method was naturalized in China. What they might judge important, however, would be the success of the modernization programs of China and the humanization of Western science and technology.

Returning from the future to the past, a question that was often asked in this book—Why was natural science born in Europe?—may be rephrased: Why was it born in Italy?

Science arose in the cities: Padua, Venice, Florence, Rome, Bologna. I do not think that Castello di Gargonza, the location of our conference, had a large role in the scientific revolution, although by rights it should have: the Tuscan countryside around it is beautiful, the summer weather is balmy, and the wine is always good.

Perhaps the credit for bringing about early modern science should not go primarily to a geographic location or even to a particular society. It should go, instead, to the remarkable capacity of the human mind to refuse to take the world as it is and, by mixing the memories of the past with images of the future, to create new realities.

J. T. F.

Biographical Notes on the Contributors

Hans Ågren was born in 1945 and received his B.A. in Oriental languages from Uppsala University, where he later also earned his M.D. and Ph.D. He is now on the Faculty of Medicine at Uppsala as a clinical assistant professor of psychiatry, doing research in the psychobiology of affective illness. He studied Chinese and Japanese medical history in Kyoto on a Japanese scholarship (1971–73) and later did research using primary sources available in Sweden and England on thought patterns and the history of ideas in traditional medical systems in East Asia.

Anindita Niyogi Balslev has an M.A. in philosophy from Calcutta University and a Ph.D. in philosophy (existentialism and Buddhism) from the University of Paris (1968). She has done teaching and research in India, France, the United States, and Denmark.

Denis Corish is Chairman of the Department of Philosophy, Bowdoin College, Brunswick, Maine. One of his main interests is the history of theories of time. He has published articles on time in *Isis*, *Phronesis*, the *Review of Metaphysics*, and in previous volumes of *The Study of Time*.

Fan Dainian graduated in 1948 from the Physics Department of Zhejiang University, China. He is currently the vice editor-in-chief of the *Journal of Dialectics of Nature* and professor at the Graduate School of the Chinese Academy of Social Sciences. His current research focuses on the history and philosophy of physics and history of science in the United States.

Fan Hongye, an editor of the *Journal of Dialectics of Nature*, graduated in 1965 from the Chemisty Department of Jilin University, China. He has published fourteen papers and a book in the fields of history and sociology of science.

George H. Ford holds a Ph.D. from Yale and is Professor of English at the University of Rochester and a former Chairman of the department. He has published books on the poetry of John Keats and on the novels of Charles Dickens and D. H. Lawrence, and has also written articles on the role of time in works of literature. Important literary texts that he has edited include the Victorian sections of *The Norton Anthology of English Literature*. Ford has been awarded a Guggenheim Fellowship, an ACLS Fellowship, and a Huntington Library Fellowship, and he holds membership in the American Academy of Arts and Sciences. In 1983 he was awarded the Wilbur Cross medal by Yale University, a year in which he completed his four-year term as President of the International Society for the Study of Time.

J. T. Fraser, Founder of the International Society for the Study of Time, is the author of *Of Time, Passion, and Knowledge* (1975), *Time as Conflict* (1978), and *The Genesis and Evolution of Time* (1982). He is editor of *The Voices of Time* (1966 and 1981), senior editor of the five volumes of *The Study of Time* series, and author of numerous papers in professional journals on the idea and experience of time.

Francis C. Haber is Professor of History at the University of Maryland, College Park. In addition to other publications, he has articles in *The Study of Time I* and *The Study of Time II*.

Jin Guantao graduated in 1970 from the Chemistry Department of Beijing University, China. He is an editor of the *Journal of Dialectics of Nature*, Academia Sinica. He has published over thirty papers and three books in the fields of philosophy, physics, chemistry, cybernetics, history, and history of science.

Conrad Dale Johnson holds a doctorate in the history of consciousness from the University of California, Santa Cruz. His philosophical studies began with a long immersion in the work of Martin Heidegger, whose concern with "fundamental ontology" he has pursued primarily in connection with the history of the natural sciences. He presently lives and works in Providence, Rhode Island.

Jonathan D. Kramer is a composer and music theorist. He serves as Professor and Director of Electronic Music at the College-Conservatory of Music of the University of Cincinnati, Program Annotator and New Music Advisor of the Cincinnati Symphony Orchestra, and producer and host of a weekly radio program on Cincinnati's National Public Radio station. His compositions have been performed and broadcast worldwide, and several are published and recorded. He has published a number of articles on musical time in several journals and books, and he is working on a book entitled *Time and the Meanings of Music*.

Nathaniel Lawrence is Massachusetts Professor of Philosophy and Chairman of the Department, at Williams College. He holds degrees in biology, divinity, and philosophy. He has taught at UCLA, Yale, and Harvard universities and, since 1956, at Williams College. He is the author of books on Whitehead, on existential phenomenology, and on philosophical themes in modern education, and is co-editor of *The Study of Time II–V*. He is also the author of many articles in professional journals.

Liu Qingfeng graduated in 1969 from the Chinese Literature Department of Beijing University. She is an editor of the *Journal of Dialectics of Nature*, Academia Sinica.

Lo Huisheng (b. 1925, Canton, China) is Associate Research Scientist (Research Professor) at the Institute of Philosophy, The Chinese Academy of Social Sciences, specializing in the philosophy of science and cinema aesthetics. He is the author of four books: Lǔ Xùn and Xǔ Shôu Shāng (魯迅與許壽裳), Introduction to the History of Modern Philosophy of Science (現代科學哲學史概論), History of the Aesthetic Trends of World Cinema (世界電影美學思潮史), Introduction to Modern Cinema Aesthetics (現代電影美學概論).

Samuel L. Macey has over forty publications, mainly in Restoration and eighteenth-century literature. His books include an edition of *Henry Carey's Dramatic Works* and an edition of *A Learned Dissertation on Dumpling*, as well as *Studies in Robertson Davies' Deptford Trilogy* (with R. G. Lawrence), *Money and the Novel*, and *Clocks and the Cosmos:*

Time in Western Life and Thought. He has a Ph.D. in literature, and is a Fellow of the Institute of Management Services and a Member of the British Horological Institute. He is the General Editor of the English Literary Studies Monograph Series. Dr. Macey is Professor of English and Acting Dean of Graduate Studies at the University of Victoria.

John A. Michon was born in Utrecht, the Netherlands, in 1935. He obtained his first degree in psychology at the University of Utrecht and his Ph.D. at the University of Leyden. He is now Professor of Experimental Psychology and Traffic Science at the University of Groningen. Apart from directing the Institute for Experimental Psychology and the Traffic Research Center of the University he is Dean of the Department of Psychology. He is, among other things, Fellow of the Royal Netherlands Academy of Arts and Sciences, Cochairman of the National Council for Traffic Safety, and President of the International Society for the Study of Time (1983–1986).

Qiu Renzong was born in Soochow, China, in 1932, and graduated from Ching Hua University, Beijing, in 1952. He was Vice-Chief then Chief of the Unit for Philosophy of Science and Medicine, Chinese Medical University, Beijing; Vice-Chief then Chief of the Department for Philosophy of Science, Institute of Philosophy, the Chinese Academy of Social Sciences. He was Lecturer, later Associate Professor in the Philosophy of Science. Since 1980, he has been Associate Editor of *Medicine and Philosophy* (a Chinese journal), and a member of scientific societies at home and abroad. His publication include, "Testing Scientific Theories," "On the Subjective Activity in Medicine," "On the Dialectics in the Onset of Disease," "On the Origins of Medicine and Medical Theory in Magic," "Philosophy of Medicine in China, 1930–1980."

Kristofer Schipper was born in 1934, of Dutch parents. He studied sinology and anthropology in Paris with Max Kaltenmark, Paul Demiéville, and Claude Lévi-Strauss. Docteur de 3e Cycle in 1962, he became a Fellow of the Ecole française d'Extrême-Orient, in which capacity he devoted eight years of uninterrupted fieldwork on Taoist traditions in southern Taiwan. Elected to the chair of Chinese Religions at the Ecole Pratique des Hautes Etudes (Sorbonne, Paris) in 1972, he became Docteur d'Etat in 1983. He currently directs the *Tao-tsang* bibliography project of the European Science Foundation. His main publications include *L'empereur Wou des Han dans la légende taoïste* (Paris, 1965); *Le Fen-teng, rituel taoïste* (Paris, 1975); and *Le corps taoïste, corps physique, corps social* (Paris, 1982).

N. Sivin is Professor of Chinese Culture and of the History of Science at the University of Pennsylvania. He is a Fellow of the American Academy of Arts and Sciences and a Corresponding Member of the International Academy of the History of Science. He edits the "Science, Medicine and Technology in East Asia" monograph series and edits and publishes the journal *Chinese Science*. His most recent book is *Traditional Medicine in Contemporary China* (1985).

Ruth M. Stone is an Associate Professor of Folklore and Ethnomusicology at Indiana University in Bloomington, Indiana. She has conducted field research in Liberia, West Africa, and more recently in the Eastern Province of Saudi Arabia. Her publications include *Let the Inside Be Sweet: The Interpretation of Music Event Among the Kpelle of Liberia* (1982) and *African Music and Oral Data: A Catalog of Field Recordings, 1902–1975* (1976), edited with Frank J. Gillis. She also serves as a member of the executive board of the Society for Ethnomusicology.

Frederick Turner was educated at Oxford University in England and is Founders Professor of Arts and Humanities at the University of Texas, Dallas. He was editor of the *Kenyon Review* from 1978 to 1982. He is the author of numerous books of poetry, including *The New World* (Princeton); literary criticism, including *Shakespeare and the Nature of Time* (Oxford); and fiction, including *A Double Shadow* (Berkeley/Putnam). His essay on poetic meter, "The Neural Lyre," was published in *Poetry* (August 1983) and won the Levinson Prize.

Synnøve Vinsrygg earned her Magister Artium degree (equivalent to the Ph.D.) in archaeology at the University of Bergen in 1973. She has worked as a curator and museum lecturer at the Archaeologogical Museum in Stavanger and at the University of Tromsø, Norway. Presently she is doing fieldwork in southern Sudan.

Wang Hsiu-huei was born in 1952 in Taiwan. She holds a degree in classical Chinese from Taiwan Normal University, and is currently a Ph.D. student at the University of Paris. During 1982–83 she was assistant to Professor Kristofer Schipper.

Zhang Yinzhi was born in 1925 in China. He graduated from the Philosophy Department of Zhongshan University, and was appointed Lecturer on the History of Chinese Philosophy which he taught there for many years. In his early years he had acquired an intense love for the Chinese classics and has been engaged in research on the ancient Chinese language ever since. He has written a series of articles, such as "The Study of Ancient Chinese Concrete Words," "On the Teaching of Ancient Chinese Language," and "The Practice and Achievements of the Mohist School." Some of them have been published in academic journals in China. Of his three-volume *Ancient Chinese Language*, he has finished two volumes, printed by Zhongshan University.

Constitution and By-Laws of the International Society for the Study of Time

(Adopted at Williamstown, Massachusetts, 1 September 1974, amended at Alpbach, Austria, 9 July 1979, and at Castello di Gargonza, Italy, 9 July 1983).

PREAMBLE

The International Society for the Study of Time originated in a proposal by J. T. Fraser that was discussed at a conference on "Interdisciplinary Perspectives of Time" held by the New York Academy of Sciences in January 1966. It was unanimously agreed that an international society should be formed on an interdisciplinary basis with the object of stimulating interest in all problems concerning time and that this object could best be obtained by means of conferences held at regular intervals. G. J. Whitrow was elected President, J. T. Fraser Secretary, and M. S. Watanabe Treasurer. It was agreed that the organization of the First Conference of the newly formed Society be left to a committee of these three officers, on the understanding that they would invite authorities on the role of time in the various special sciences and humanities to form an Advisory Board to assist them.

CONSTITUTION

Article I—Name

The name of the Society shall be the "International Society for the Study of Time."

Article II—Object

The object of the Society shall be to encourage the interdisciplinary study of time in all its aspects. This object is to be achieved through the dissemination of information, especially by (a) the organization of conferences, (b) publication of selected papers from those conferences, and (c) any other means that further the goals of the Society.

Article III—Membership

All those who have been invited and have prepared papers to deliver to the Society at one of its conferences (even if circumstances have prevented the address from being delivered) will be invited to become Members of the Society.

Article IV—Corresponding Members

Those who wish to join the Society but have not qualified for Membership under Article III of the Constitution may be Corresponding Members on approval by the Council.

Article V—The Council

The Council shall be the legal authority of the Society and this capacity shall have and hold all its property and funds. It shall be responsible for its budget, shall form the Society's general policies, and shall assist the Officers in arranging for meetings, publications, financial support, and other similar activities. It is to be consulted by the Conference Committee on the general organization of conferences, and no formal invitations to address the Society shall be issued without its approval. The Council shall consist of the Officers of the Society as specified in Article VI, together with six Members of the Society directly elected as provided in Article VII, together with the Editor or Editors of the Proceedings of the Conference during which the other members of the Council took office. Its decisions shall be by simple majority. The President, or in his absence the Secretary, shall preside at its meetings and shall not vote except when there is no majority.

Article VI—Officers

1. The Officers of the Society shall be a President, a Secretary, and a Treasurer, to be elected as provided in Article VII. The duties of the Officers shall be as provided in the By-laws.

2. In recognition of the work of J. T. Fraser in founding and sustaining the Society, he shall be an honorary and perpetual Member of the Society and will be designated as the Society's Founder in its correspondence and publications, and the title of Founder shall be reserved for J. T. Fraser exclusively.

Article VII—Election and Tenure of Councillors and Officers

1. Nominations for the Council and the Society's offices shall issue from the Nominating Committee at each conference. Names may also be placed in nomination from the floor of a business meeting by a majority of those present and voting. If there is more than one candidate for any office, the election shall be by secret ballot.

2. The elected members of the Council shall be chosen at the business meeting of each conference by a majority of those present and voting. They shall serve until the next business meeting.

3. The President shall be a Member of the Society elected at a business meeting at the end of every conference of the Society by a majority of the Members present, and shall serve until the end of the next business meeting, or for five years if there is no conference in that time. The President's tenure can be terminated by a majority vote of the Council, the President not voting. If the office of President becomes vacant between business meetings, it shall be filled by action of the Council.

4. The Secretary shall be a Member and the Treasurer either a Member or a Corresponding Member. Both shall serve at the Council's pleasure.

Article VIII—Obligations of membership

Every Member and Corresponding Member of the Society shall be ready to assist the Officers, Council, and the various committees in discharging their duties to the Society.

Article IX—Committees

1. *Conference Committee.* This committee shall consist of the President and Secretary, together with others, not necessarily Members of the Society, appointed by the President to serve until the next conference. The committee shall choose its own officers, except that the Secretary of the Society shall serve as secretary. Its function shall be to prepare for future conferences of the Society; specifically, it will be responsible for the selection of a place, the choice of speakers, the preparation of a program, and the local arrangements. In order to expedite its work the committee may augment its membership at any time as it chooses, but when this is done the Secretary shall so notify the members of the Council. It shall, through the Secretary, keep the Council informed of its actions.

2. *Nominating Committee.* This shall function during a conference of the Society. It shall consist of the immediate past President, the President, the Secretary, and two other Members of the Society appointed by the President. The names of its members shall be announced as soon as it is formed. It shall nominate Members of the Society for election as Officers, as members of the Council, and as members of the Evaluation Committee, announcing its nominations two days before the business meeting.

3. *Evaluation Committee.* This shall consist of five participants in a conference, not necessarily Members or Corresponding Members of the Society, elected at the business meeting on nomination by the Nominating Committee or from the floor of the meeting. It shall choose its own officers. It shall poll those present at the meeting within three months after its close and present to the Council within six months after the conference an evaluation of the conference based on the poll and its own

considerations, after which it shall cease to exist. On the formation of the next Conference Committee the Secretary shall transmit this report to it for its guidance.

Article X—Amendments

1. No part of this Constitution or the By-laws which follow shall be amended or annulled except as herein provided.

2. The Council may propose amendments to either the Constitution or the By-laws at any conference of the Society; if approved by a two-thirds majority of those present and voting an amendment is adopted. The Council may make such amendments to the Constitution or By-laws or both as may be necessary to qualify the Society under the laws of the United States of America as a tax-exempt organization, gifts to which are deductible or excludable for income, gift, and estate tax purposes, provided that such amendments do not alter the Society's purpose, structure, or modes of procedure as set forth in the Constitution and By-laws. The preceding sentence includes the authorization to change the form of the organization by converting it to a trust or a corporation, as may best suit the stated tax purposes.

3. Amendments may originate also from other Members of the Society. At any business meeting, a vote of five of the Members present shall be sufficient to bring the proposed amendment to the floor. If it is approved by a majority, it is submitted to the Council for approval. If the Council approves, the amendment is adopted. If not, the proposers may instruct the Secretary to poll all Members of the Society, and if the amendment gains a two-thirds majority it is adopted.

BY-LAWS

Article I—Dues

The Council shall be empowered to fix annual dues for Members. Dues for Corresponding Members will be four-fifths of those for Members. No assessment, however, shall apply so as to exclude from Membership or Corresponding Membership anyone who has satisfied the Council as to his* inability to pay. If the dues of any Members or Corresponding Member not exempted by the Council remain unpaid beyond the next business meeting, the Secretary, after due notice, shall remove his name from the list.

Article II—Conferences

Conferences for the presentation and discussion of papers on various aspects of time shall be held at intervals of a few years at the discretion of the Council. In preparing conference programs, the Conference Committee shall respect the Society's interdisciplinary character, and there shall be no conference of the Society devoted to discussions within a single intellectual discipline. Attendance at conferences shall be open to all Members and Corresponding Members of the Society.

Article III—Business Meetings

A business meeting shall be held on the next to last day of each conference to hear the Treasurer's report, to hold elections, and to transact any other business that shall be brought to the attention of the presiding officer. It shall be open to all who have attended the conference, but only those who are currently Members or Corresponding Members of the Society shall be eligible to vote.

Article IV—Duties of the Officers

1. The President shall preside at meetings of the Council and at conferences and their business meeting that come within his term of office if it is possible for him to be present. He shall appoint the Conference Committee and two members of the Nominating Committee and shall preside at meetings of the Nominating Committee. He shall perform such other functions as are provided in this Constitution and By-laws.

2. The Secretary shall preside at conferences and meetings of the Council in the President's

---

* The masculine pronoun is employed in accordance with normal English usage. No reference to the gender of the person so designated is intended.

absence. He shall maintain the membership lists of the Society and serve as secretary to the committees of which he is a member, preparing their agenda and keeping their minutes. He shall be responsible for organizing the Society's meetings and conferences, for correspondence with the Advisory Board, and for notifying the members of the times and places of all conferences. He shall cause a list of the Society's Members and Corresponding Members to be published in each volume of the Proceedings and supply such list, together with addresses, to any Member or Corresponding Member on request.

3. The Treasurer shall be responsible for the Society's finances. He shall prepare and submit to the Council annually and to the Society at every business meeting a report on the financial conditions of the Society and perform such other duties as are usual to the office. He shall receive and disburse the Society's money, maintaining an account for the purpose in a bank or trust company approved by the Council.

Article V—Perpetuation of the Society

If no conference is called during a period of six years, a new Council may be elected by letter ballot by majority vote of the Members of the Society. Such ballots shall contain eight names, be signed by five members of the Society, and shall be sent to every Member. A Council so elected shall select Officers and shall fill the committees of the Society to serve until the next business meeting.